Philosophical Chaucer

Mark Miller's innovative study argues that Chaucer's *Canterbury Tales* represent an extended meditation on agency, autonomy, and practical reason. This philosophical aspect of Chaucer's interests can help us understand what is both sophisticated and disturbing about his explorations of love, sex, and gender. Partly through fresh readings of the *Consolation of Philosophy* and the *Romance of the Rose*, Miller charts Chaucer's relation to the association in the Christian West between problems of autonomy and problems of sexuality, and reconstructs how medieval philosophers and poets approached psychological phenomena often thought of as the exclusive province of psychoanalysis. The literary experiments of the *Canterbury Tales* represent a distinctive philosophical achievement that remains vital to our own attempts to understand agency, desire, and their histories.

MARK MILLER is Associate Professor of English at the University of Chicago. He has published on medieval literature and culture in *Speculum* and *ELH*.

CAMBRIDGE STUDIES IN MEDIEVAL LITERATURE

General editor
Alastair Minnis, *Ohio State University*

Editorial board
Zygmunt G. Barański, *University of Cambridge*
Christopher C. Baswell, *University of California, Los Angeles*
John Burrow, *University of Bristol*
Mary Carruthers, *New York University*
Rita Copeland, *University of Pennsylvania*
Simon Gaunt, *King's College, London*
Steven Kruger, *City University of New York*
Nigel Palmer, *University of Oxford*
Winthrop Wetherbee, *Cornell University*
Jocelyn Wogan-Browne, *Fordham University*

This series of critical books seeks to cover the whole area of literature written in the major medieval languages – the main European vernaculars, and medieval Latin and Greek – during the period *c.* 1100–1500. Its chief aim is to publish and stimulate fresh scholarship and criticism on medieval literature, special emphasis being placed on understanding major works of poetry, prose, and drama in relation to the contemporary culture and learning which fostered them.

Recent titles in the series
D. H. Green *The Beginnings of Medieval Romance: Fact and Fiction, 1150–1220*
J. A. Burrow *Gestures and Looks in Medieval Narrative*
Ardis Butterfield *Poetry and Music in Medieval France: From Jean Renart to Guillaume de Machaut*
Emily Steiner *Documentary Culture and the Making of Medieval English Literature*
William E. Burgwinkle *Sodomy, Masculinity, and Law in Medieval Literature*
Nick Havely *Dante and the Franciscans: Poverty and the Papacy in the Commedia*
Siegfried Wenzel *Latin Sermon Collections from Later Medieval England*
Ananya Jahanara Kabir and Deanne Williams, eds. *Postcolonial Approaches to the European Middle Ages: Translating Cultures*

A complete list of titles in the series can be found at the end of the volume.

Philosophical Chaucer

Love, Sex, and Agency in the *Canterbury Tales*

Mark Miller

University of Chicago

CAMBRIDGE
UNIVERSITY PRESS

PUBLISHED BY THE PRESS SYNDICATE OF THE UNIVERSITY OF CAMBRIDGE
The Pitt Building, Trumpington Street, Cambridge CB2 1RP, United Kingdom

CAMBRIDGE UNIVERSITY PRESS
The Edinburgh Building, Cambridge, CB2 2RU, UK
40 West 20th Street, New York, NY 10011–4211, USA
477 Williamstown Road, Port Melbourne, VIC 3207, Australia
Ruiz de Alarcón 13, 28014 Madrid, Spain
Dock House, The Waterfront, Cape Town 8001, South Africa

http://www.cambridge.org

© Mark Miller 2004

First published 2004

Printed in the United Kingdom at the University Press, Cambridge

Typeset in 11.5/14pt Adobe Garamond   [PND]

A catalogue record for this book is available from the British Library

Library of Congress Cataloguing in Publication data

Miller, Mark, 1964–
Philosophical Chaucer: love, sex, and agency in the *Canterbury Tales* / Mark Miller.
p.   cm. (Cambridge studies in medieval literature, 55)
Includes bibliographical references and index.
ISBN 0 521 84236 0 (alk. paper)
1. Chaucer, Geoffrey, d. 1400. *Canterbury Tales.*   2. Christian pilgrims and pilgrimages in
literature.   3. Chaucer, Geoffrey, d. 1400 – Philosophy.   4. Tales, Medieval – History and
criticism.   5. Philosophy, Medieval, in literature.   6. Agent (Philosophy) in literature.   7. Love in
literature.   8. Sex in literature.   I. Title.   II. Series.
PR1875.P5.M55 2004
821'.1 – dc22   2004056823

ISBN 0 521 84236 0 hardback

Contents

Acknowledgments   *Page*   ix

Introduction: Chaucer and the problem of normativity   1
    Eros and normativity   4
    Normativity, ideology, ethics   12
    Sexuality and moral alterity in the Christian tradition   21
    Philosophical Chaucer and the plan of the book   26

1 Naturalism and its discontents in the *Miller's Tale*   36
    On normative naturalism   40
    The perverse remainder   50
    Agency, gender, and the constitution of the perverse   56
    Imagining intimacy   69

2 Normative longing in the *Knight's Tale*   82
    Ethical and erotic formalism: picturing Emily   84
    Thesean autonomy   91
    Eros and autonomy   101

3 Agency and dialectic in the *Consolation of Philosophy*   111
    The happiness argument and Boethian psychology   114
    Boethian *aporia* and dialectical form   124
    An antinomy at the heart of agency   130
    Boethius, Chaucer, and normative nostalgia   144

4 Sadomasochism and utopia in the *Roman de la Rose*   152
    Erotic pathology and the scene of fantasy   156
    The claim of reason and the deadlock of utopian desire   169
    Being normal   178

Contents

5 Suffering love in the *Wife of Bath's Prologue* and *Tale*   191
   Blood and money   192
   The myth of the subject   197
   The erotics of ambivalence   204
   The resurrection of the dead   210

6 Love's promise: the *Clerk's Tale* and the scandal of the
  unconditional   216
   The politics of narcissism   220
   Grisildan unconditionality   229
   Love's antinomy   239

Notes   249
Bibliography   272
Index   281

Acknowledgments

This book has emerged from conversations with many friends and colleagues, without whose help it could never have come to fruition. The project began as a dissertation written under the direction of Jay Schleusener, whose teaching was its constant reference point and the source of many of its best ideas; as the dissertation evolved into a very different book, Jay has remained a brilliant and treasured interlocutor. From an early stage, Eva Fernàndez helped me think through the issues and pushed the book in new directions, and Janel Mueller and Christina von Nolcken repeatedly forced me to think harder and more clearly. Anne Middleton and Lee Patterson helped me understand far better than I otherwise could have how this book's philosophical and theoretical concerns intersect with a historical understanding of medieval culture. Lauren Berlant and Candace Vogler kept teaching me new ways of thinking about the pressures sex and theory put on each other. The Working Group on Sexuality, Normativity, and Ethics at the University of Chicago's Center for Gender Studies provided a needed forum for working through some of the ideas in the Introduction. Many others have shaped this book through reading drafts and otherwise exchanging ideas, including Bill Brown, Jim Chandler, Bradin Cormack, Elizabeth Fowler, Jackie Goldsby, Elaine Hadley, Laura King, Sandra Macpherson, Carla Mazzio, Michael Murrin, Debbie Nelson, Josh Scodel, Eric Slauter, Richard Strier, Blakey Vermeule, and Nicholas Watson. Beth Helsinger has been a remarkably supportive Chair, and the book is much the better as a result of her interventions. At Cambridge University Press, Linda Bree has been a wise and patient editor and Alastair Minnis offered crucial support and valuable suggestions for revision; the two anonymous readers for the Press also offered very helpful suggestions for the final round of revisions. Support in the form of time to write came from a Morse Fellowship at Yale University and a Faculty Fellowship at the University of Chicago's Franke Institute for the Humanities. The Humanities Division at the University of Chicago also supported the publication of the book through a subvention. Finally, the most important support has come from my family. My wife Dolores, daughter Isabella, and son Paul bring joy to every day; my parents John and Ann were my first and best teachers; and my *suocera* Anna is like another mother. My gratitude beyond words belongs to them all.

An earlier version of chapter one appeared as "Naturalism and its Discontents in the *Miller's Tale*," in *ELH* 67 (spring 2000), 1–44. Several paragraphs from the introduction and chapters two and five appear in somewhat different form in "Subjectivity and Ideology in the *Canterbury Tales*," in Peter Brown, ed., *A Companion to Medieval English Literature and Culture, c. 1350–1500* (Oxford: Blackwell, expected 2005); that material appears here by permission of Blackwell Publishing. The cover illustration is from an MS of Boccaccio's *Teseida*, Bildarchiv d.ÖNB, Wien, Cod. 2617, fol. 53; it appears here courtesy of the Austrian National Library in Vienna.

Introduction

Chaucer and the problem of normativity

This book refines and redirects two views of Chaucer that have dominated the reception of his writing since his lifetime: that he was a philosophical poet and that he was a poet of love.[1] I argue that the *Canterbury Tales* represents an extended meditation on agency, autonomy, and practical reason, and that this philosophical aspect of Chaucer's interests can help us understand what is both sophisticated and disturbing about his explorations of love, sex, and gender.[2] In pursuing this argument about Chaucer, the book opens onto a broader discussion of the long-standing association in the Christian West between problems of autonomy and problems of sexuality, and the premodern intellectual and literary resources for understanding psychological phenomena often associated with psychoanalysis, such as repression, fetishism, narcissism, sadism, and masochism. And in discussing both Chaucer's literary experiments and the philosophical methods and psychological concepts informing them, *Philosophical Chaucer* develops a still broader theoretical argument concerning normativity and its relations to ideology and practical reason. This introduction will sketch the landscape of these arguments to indicate why they belong together in a single book.

The idea of Chaucer as a philosophical love poet has traditionally centered on his career as a courtly writer steeped in the Latin, French, and Italian traditions of psychological and philosophical allegory and erotic lyricism, a career that mostly predates the *Canterbury Tales* and whose crowning achievement was *Troilus and Criseyde*. Such an emphasis brings into relief the moments in Chaucer's poetry when philosophy and erotic life are most obviously conjoined, moments when longing, abjection, and loss open within the erotic subject an urge to speculation that often takes explicitly philosophical form; it also allows for the drawing of close connections between Chaucer's work and that of many of the writers who meant the most to him, such as Alain de Lille, Guillaume de Lorris, Jean de Meun, Guillaume de Machaut, Dante, and Petrarch. I turn to the *Canterbury Tales*, however, because for all the value of the traditional focus, it encourages a restricted notion of what makes Chaucer's poetry philosophical and of what he finds philosophically provocative in erotic life. I argue that Chaucer's project in the *Tales* is philosophical not only in tales like those of the Knight and the Clerk, where such interests are explicit, but also in ones that have been seen as tangential to any philosophical interest or even as antiphilosophical, like those of the Miller and the Wife of Bath. The picture of Chaucer that emerges in these pages is that of a poet as deeply committed to philosophical thinking – and indeed, as deeply committed to dialectic – as Jean de Meun or Langland or the *Pearl*-poet, but one who became interested in pursuing that commitment independently of dialogue form, or for that matter independently of any explicit representation of philosophical topics or themes. What makes Chaucer's mature poetry philosophical is its engagement with the often repressed dialectical structures imbedded not only in abstract reflection but also in every expressive act, even the most routinized, seemingly unreflective ones. The philosophical richness of the *Canterbury Tales* lies in its way of using forms of literary representation, including narrative, genre, character, and tropological language, to investigate the dialectical structure of thought and desire.

Such imbedded dialectical structures, and the conception of philosophical poetry that attends them, are also central to my account of Chaucer's interest in love. As I have already indicated, for me, as for many recent Chaucerians, thinking of Chaucer as a poet of love means attending to his interests in gender and sexuality. Like some such critics, I will be concerned with what Carolyn Dinshaw has called a "touch of the queer" in Chaucer's representations of erotic life – or, as I would put it, with the ways erotic energies trouble and cross presumptive borders between the normal and the perverse, even as in many ways they depend on the constitution of such borders.[3] This book also shares with psychoanalysis interests in the phantasmatic constitution of desire and its objects, the intersubjective structuring of desire and will, and the misrecognitions on which attachment and a stable sense of self depend.[4] But if queer theory and psychoanalysis provide two of this book's most proximate others, one of my central projects here will be to understand how Chaucer and his main intellectual interlocutors might have conceptualized an interest in these topics; or, to put it another way, to see how far we can get in an analysis of such topics without invoking a specifically psychoanalytic account of them. Such a project can be helpful both historically and theoretically, by refining our sense of the continuities and differences between ourselves and the past, and by defining more clearly, for both proponents and opponents of psychoanalysis, the point at which a genuinely psychoanalytic account might be taken up.

In examining the analytical structure of Chaucer's interests in gender difference, sexual desire, and love, I will locate him in relation to a number of ancient and medieval currents of thought in which, by the late Middle Ages, questions of sexuality and questions of agency and autonomy had come to intersect. Perhaps the most important of these currents is the tradition of Christian thinking about morality and sociality that Peter Brown has so brilliantly traced from Paul to Augustine, a tradition that turned time and again to the conceptual and metaphorical links between problems of sexuality and problems of autonomy.[5] Other such currents include an Augustinian and Boethian tradition of thinking about desire and its frustrations, an Aristotelian tradition in philosophical psychology, and an analysis of utopian intimacy developed in Aristotelian and Ciceronian discourses of friendship, all of which were adapted to erotic contexts by, among others, Jean de Meun. In discussing these traditions my interest will once again be both historical and theoretical. On the one hand, they will help us reconstruct an intellectual idiom important to Chaucer and in key respects different from our own. On the other, pursuing such a reconstruction will lead us to theoretical arguments concerning the ways agency and identity are constituted around incompatible demands of practical reason, and the ways an account of those demands can help us to read intersubjective and intrasubjective dramas of misrecognition. Those theoretical arguments in turn will help us to understand a historical phenomenon of interest throughout this book, namely a crisis of

3

intelligibility in the emergent paradigm of western sexuality and romantic love which, I will argue, is conditioned by the problematic structure of practical reason. This crisis of intelligibility in sexuality and love cannot fully be understood either through the analysis of the cultural construction of discourses, practices, subjects, and texts which currently dominates historicist modes of inquiry, or through a psychoanalytic paradigm that seeks its causes in Oedipal structures or traumatic narrative. This is not to say that I take my argument to obviate historicist and psychoanalytic accounts. It is just to say that accounts of the historical and psychological causes of such a crisis need supplementing by an account of the structures of practical reason that inform it.

Reading with an ear for the resonances between problems of sexuality and problems of agency will help us see sexuality less as a sphere of desire and behavior that provided Chaucer with the underlying causes of human behavior than as a highly charged and tropologically rich site on which he explored the drive to autonomy and the grief that attends it. This in turn will help us understand Chaucer's moral seriousness as something other than the moralizing it has often been taken to be – indeed as something in many ways disturbing to conventional moral sensibilities rather than confirming of them, and so as something we need not pass by in embarrassment on the way to supposedly more exciting topics.[6] The effort to recover that moral seriousness, the powerful speculative impulse that attended it, and the poetic resources through which Chaucer pursued it, requires rethinking the relationship between philosophy and the rhetorical forms of philosophical dialogue, allegory, and Canterbury narrative; and that rethinking requires a substantive investigation of the philosophical problems engaged by Chaucer and the traditions to which he belonged. In the course of this effort of recovery, sexuality will emerge both as a provocation to speculate on the structure of agency and the drive to autonomy, and as a place where the abstract work of philosophical analysis meets flesh and bone.

EROS AND NORMATIVITY

Of the philosophical and theoretical terms on which my argument will depend, "normativity" is both the most important and, I take it, the most obscure. I think this obscurity is both a result of the current

4

condition of our intellectual culture and a feature of the concept itself. A good portion of this introduction, and for that matter of this book, will therefore be devoted to giving an account of what normativity is, and why it might be worth fuller critical and theoretical attention. But before turning to an initial unpacking of this term, I want to provide a Chaucerian anchor for what will be some fairly abstract considerations. Let me then point to a scene from the *Knight's Tale* which will receive extended attention in chapter two and which suggests something of the form in which eros and normativity intersect in Chaucer's philosophical-poetic project.

The scene is that of Emily in her garden, performing her springtime maidenly duties under the watchful and desiring eyes of Palamon and Arcite. This scene condenses some key features of a normative picture of gender difference and sexuality which will be of concern throughout this book. In establishing a voyeuristic relationship between desiring men and a desired but utterly oblivious woman, the scene figures the masculine as the site of erotic subjectivity and agency, and the feminine as the site of erotic passivity and objectification, an association that continues throughout the tale as Emily's fate remains entirely hostage to the conflicts among the men whose desires seem to be the only ones that effectively count. While the Knight, here and elsewhere in the tale, adopts a stance of critical distance on what he sees as the pathological desire of the Theban cousins, the portrait of Emily with which he introduces the scene participates in this normative picture and helps to specify its further contours. Emily

> fairer was to scne
> Than is the lylie upon his stalke grene,
> And fressher than the May with floures newe –
> For with the rose colour stroof hir hewe,
> I noot which was the fyner of hem two.
> (I.1035–39)[7]

Through the location of Emily in the garden and the more pointed identification of her attractiveness with that of the floral beauty that surrounds her, the Knight associates the feminine with the natural, the ornamental, and the cultivated. And through the desire this scene kindles in Palamon and Arcite, and even more through his own admiring description, the Knight associates the masculine both with the subjectivity that appreciates all this beauty and with the agency that cultivates the aesthetic object – that is, the poem – in which, like the garden, or for that matter Emily's lovely body, such beauty is both produced and contained.

In these respects, this scene is of course utterly conventional. The aestheticizing voyeurism of masculine desire here seems flat and clichéd, so familiar in the Middle Ages and today that it is hardly even recognizable. That is why I have begun with it, and I think it is also why Chaucer places it so early in the *Canterbury Tales*. I will be arguing throughout this book that one of Chaucer's most characteristic philosophical and poetic interests lies in the unpacking of cliché, the analysis of attitudes that, because of their familiarity and the way they can pass for somebody's version of plain (if objectionable) common sense, tend to fly beneath our intellectual radar. Such cases are always in Chaucer's poetry more complex than they initially appear; and part of what interests Chaucer in such cases is the way their apparent flatness and easy recognizability function to keep their radical incoherence out of sight, and so to enable their psychic and social functionality. What we really ought to say about such moments, I think, is not that they are flat, but that we are used to thinking flatly about the attitudes to which they give expression, and that these flattening habits of mind are essential to their reproduction and inhabitation. The aestheticizing voyeurism of masculine desire is only possible in the first place because we think we know all too well what we see there.

As I have already indicated, it has been known for some time that at the center of Chaucer's literary inheritance was a rich tradition of French and Italian poetry – a tradition exemplified in the *Roman de la Rose* and the writings of Guillaume de Machaut, Petrarch, and a host of others – which combined a strong interest in erotic desire with an extremely refined formalist and lyrical aesthetic sensibility.[8] This scene belongs squarely in that tradition, and that is part, although only part, of what makes it seem so familiar. But, like that tradition at its best, this scene asks us to think about what is at stake ontologically and ideologically in a voyeuristic eroticism, and more broadly in the gendered production of beauty as an aesthetic and erotic phenomenon. As I will argue in later chapters, one thing crucially at stake is the production of an unstable ideology of gender difference, according to which the contrast between masculine and feminine gets figured in terms of parallel contrasts between subject and object, activity and passivity, the human and the natural, soul and body, artist and artifact, and so on. This ideology in itself is familiar enough, both in Chaucer and in medieval culture at large. To pick a few examples, some of which will receive extended attention in the present study and others of which are random selections from a nearly limitless archive: think of the central trope for masculine erotic satisfaction in the *Roman de la Rose*, that of plucking the feminine rosebud, or that text's interest in the Ovidian figures of Narcissus and Pygmalion; or Alisoun's animal sexuality in the *Miller's Tale*, or the Wife of Bath grounding her speaking voice in her "joly body"; or the appropriation of Aristotelian theories of generation, in which the male partner contributes the animating principle and the female partner contributes the matter, in medical-philosophical treatises such as the *De Secretis Mulierum* of Pseudo-Albertus Magnus; or the application in late medieval and early modern English civil law of the principle of "coverture" to the traditional conception of the married couple as a single person, such that "the very being or legal existence of the woman is suspended during the marriage, or at least incorporated and consolidated into that of the husband."[9] As these examples suggest, the widespread dissemination of this ideology in so many sites of cultural authority – literature, art, theology, preaching, popular religion, confession, law, medicine, and beyond – established an identificatory norm with powerful effects on the ways medieval people came to recognize themselves and each other as men and women.[10] And, as the scene of Emily in her garden and many of the above examples suggest, this gender ideology was closely related to an ideology of sexuality. Forms of gender identification necessarily affect and are affected by the ways people imagine themselves and each other as subjects and objects of desire; and this scene from the *Knight's Tale* captures the outlines of an erotic norm, again quite widespread in the culture and of central interest to the French and Italian traditions of lyrical eroticism, which figures masculine desire as inherently voyeuristic and objectifying, and feminine desire – which Chaucer does not directly represent here, but which he does in a host of other places – as a desire for voyeuristic objectification, a desire for being loved as the kind of aestheticized, passive figure Emily is.

This description of the scene, and of the ideology of gender and sexuality it figures, is necessarily simplified, and I do not intend it as a characterization of medieval representations of gender and sexuality as a whole. Much that is far from marginal in late medieval culture runs directly counter to this picture of gender difference: for instance, the feminization of Christ through an increasing emphasis on both his sufferings and his maternal nurturing, or the identification with the sorrows of the Virgin Mary cultivated in the affective spirituality of both men and women. But, while the above package of contrasts by no means presents a totalized or even internally coherent ideological edifice, we should not underestimate the force of the simplifications it expresses, either in the conceptual habits of medieval culture or in the lives of those for whom these habits had practical consequences. This is something Chaucer means to take the measure of in scenes such as the one above. He does so in part by making such scenes problematize the overly neat conceptual packages they instantiate; in this way, Chaucer explores the quite porous structures of identification and desire that swirl around ideological schematisms of this kind. This is somewhat different from the project of accounting for tendencies in medieval thought that run counter to this ideology; it is more a matter of attending to the inner workings of the ideology itself, of tracking its representational logics to see ways in which they both are driven by and lead to beliefs and desires they cannot accommodate.[11] One way Chaucer typically engages in such an exploration is by representing the paradoxically shifting valuations this ideology assigns to the feminine in order to imagine it as contrasting with a masculinity that stands in for the fully human subject and agent. So in Emily the feminine is at once associated with the natural and with a group of terms we would now take as referring to the cultural – the cultivated, the ornamental, and the aesthetic. This raises problems both for what the feminine is supposed to be and for what the desiring masculine subject is supposed to take as its object, problems which it is a principal task of ideology to try to mask, but which nevertheless must have effects on the identificatory and libidinal investments of ideology's subjects. In chapter four I will argue that Chaucer learned a basic literary and conceptual vocabulary for pursuing such problems from the *Roman de la Rose*. But while I think that the standard scene of an objectifying masculine voyeurism is more mysterious than it is usually taken to be, the issues it raises cannot be fully explored if we restrict our scope to "courtly" lyric eroticism. This is one reason why I have focused on the *Canterbury Tales* and left both *Troilus and Criseyde* and a broader survey of the French and Italian traditions aside: for in the movement out of courtly eroticism in the *Tales,* Chaucer opens the text to scenes of desire and conceptual pressures he otherwise could not have taken into account.

I have focused so far on the aspect of normativity most familiar in the study of gender and sexuality, including studies that focus on the Middle Ages and Chaucer. One thing that sets the present project apart from such work is an argument that we cannot fully understand the function of normative ideologies of gender and sexuality, in Chaucer's work or elsewhere, without attending to normative considerations of quite a different kind than those I discuss above. To return to the scene in question: Palamon and Arcite viewing Emily from their prison has long been understood to have Boethian resonances, and these resonances establish a normative trajectory which problematizes the scene's ideology of gender and sexuality in surprising ways.[12] In Boethian terms, Palamon and Arcite's imprisonment reads not just as an unfortunate political abrogation of their freedom but as a trope for a much deeper loss of autonomy, the kind that occurs when a person becomes incapable of ordering his dispositions into a coherent and functional will, and so suffers compulsion by whatever passions happen to arise in him. More specifically, as I will argue later, the kind of compulsion at issue here is not one in which the person's will is elided or erased, but one in which the person is *invested,* and so something that characterizes his will. That is, it is not the case that Palamon and Arcite cannot order their dispositions because something external to their will intervenes to block them from doing so – a massive brain hemorrhage, say, or as in some theories the degrading influence of desire or the body. Their problem is rather that they are devoted to their compulsion; they suffer from what Augustine calls "the perversion of the will."[13] The psychic and social disintegration so much in evidence in the Thebans' fratricidal conflict is in this respect the sign of their imprisonment in their own perverse wills, their self-imposed exile from any possibility of an authentic identity.

Given the history of Chaucer criticism since the middle of this century, it is far too easy to think that we know what it might mean for Chaucer to be interested in such a condition – far too easy, that is, to think that the only form such an interest could take is that of moralizing Christian diagnosis.[14] The result is that critics without much interest in moralizing diagnosis have had little interest in what was, for Chaucer as well as for Boethius and Augustine, the immense and haunting problem of the human creature's psychic and moral alterity to itself, a problem from which the comforts of moralism offer no refuge. But we should remember that the French and Italian poetry of erotic subjectivity, like Chaucer's, was steeped in Boethian and Augustinian thinking; it did not seem like a yoking together of incommensurable thought worlds to Jean de Meun or Dante or Guillaume de Machaut to inflect an investigation of erotic longing with philosophical arguments, and more importantly, with the forms of philosophical dialectic. We can thus perhaps begin to find the philosophical and moral problem of the will's alterity to itself compelling again if we return it to the erotic location this poetic tradition gives it.

In the scene I have been using as a touchstone, the Boethian valence of Palamon and Arcite's overwhelming desire for Emily has two apparently contradictory functions, each of which deeply problematizes the ideology of gender and sexuality the scene nevertheless serves to instantiate. On the one hand, the Thebans' erotic compulsion represents their perversion, that is, their inability to take command of themselves as men properly should – in quite pointed contrast to Theseus, who does manage a masculine self-command, and who later in the tale announces with pride that he is devoted to Diana rather than to Venus. If this scene figures erotic desire as normatively masculine, then, it also figures such desire as a threat to the very masculinity it defines, a disturbance of the norms by which that masculinity regulates itself. But the identification of eros with perversion is itself problematized by another normative function of Emily's desirability that also tracks a concern with autonomy. For, as I will argue in chapter two, when Palamon and Arcite longingly observe Emily's garden activities from behind the bars of their prison, part of what they see there is a figure of a beautifully stylized freedom, the freedom of a subject and agent perfectly ordered with respect to herself – a figure, that is, for the very autonomy they lack. Palamon's contrast between Emily's divinity and his own sorrowful, wretched creatureliness, and Arcite's sense of being slain by Emily's beauty, are not in this context just erotic clichés. For these common tropes suggest that an essential feature of the longing the Thebans feel for Emily is the way she bodies forth for them the perfected form of their own being, a perfection which, in making its normative claims on their fractured humanity, seems to turn away from them, imprisoning them in their privation and self-estrangement, and marking them as unworthy, wounded, and bound by death.

It should now be apparent that this scene is hardly one in which masculine agency and feminine passivity confront each other in a simple binary contrast. Emily – like, I will suggest, such figures as the Miller's Alisoun and the Clerk's Grisilde – functions as an erotic object in a way that seems to require the erasure of her subjectivity and agency, even while she functions as a figure for a normative ideal to which the very men who objectify her, in their abject longing, aspire. Nor do these two aspects of the representation of the feminine finally belong to separate thematic registers, as my initial formulation of the case may have suggested. For Emily's erotic function, far from being opposed to her function as an ideal of autonomy, positively *depends* on it: it is her perfect, stylized freedom that makes her beauty so ravishing. Yet the completeness and seeming divinity of this highly aestheticized perfection in no small way contributes to her objectification, particularly in this context in which subjectivity and personhood as such are imagined as fractured. If the normative picture of gender difference with which I began is deeply problematized in this scene, then, it is hardly the case that the scene serves to explode that picture. Chaucer seems rather to be suggesting that this picture, however incoherent, holds us captive. And perhaps its very incoherence is part of what makes it so captivating.

I do not want to do too much, in what must remain the highly condensed and insufficiently supple form of an introduction, to anticipate my later, more amplified discussion of this scene. I simply want at this early point to suggest the initial contours of Chaucer's complex normative imagination, and something of the conceptual terrain that that imagination inhabits. What is the relationship between a voyeuristic, objectifying eroticism that embodies an ideological norm for masculine sexuality, and an abject, perverse masculinity that locates in the feminine a figure of the autonomy for which it longs? Why is the feminine imagined at once as the locus of passivity and of a perfected agency? Just what is supposed to be "normal" here for identification and desire? How might the normalization of gender and sexuality be understood as both produced and troubled by the normative ethical desire for a coherent will? How might the production of beauty, as both an aesthetic and an erotic category, be involved in these tensions? These are a few of the questions I think Chaucer uses this scene to explore. These too, I will argue, are questions explored by the *Roman de la Rose*, in ways Chaucer found immensely productive even – and perhaps especially – when the *Rose* functioned for him more as an intellectual interlocutor than as a direct literary source.

NORMATIVITY, IDEOLOGY, ETHICS

I indicated at the beginning of the previous section that the term *normativity* needs some unpacking, and that the turn to Emily and her hapless, aggressive admirers was meant as an entry into that discussion. A substantive analysis of normativity, and of its centrality to Chaucer's philosophical-poetic project, will be the business of this book as a whole. In later sections of this introduction I will describe some medieval contexts within which that centrality might be understood. But first I want to locate my interest in the topic and say why I think it is important to current critical and theoretical discussion. Since we can never hope to disentangle the literary-historical and cultural narratives we offer from the conceptual problematics that inform them, this theoretical emphasis is, I think, essential to a historicist project. In turning to theory, then, I do not want to evade questions of historical specificity. I want rather to set the stage for posing them in a new way.

The topic of normativity as it has mostly been understood in recent literary and cultural studies, and in that nebulous discursive formation called "theory," is a branch of the study of ideology concerned with analyzing the social technologies that construct the "normal" – and therefore the abnormal, perverse, and unintelligible – in subjects' desires and identifications. The study of normativity in this sense raises questions about how hegemonies organize populations around cultural norms; how this organizing function produces what comes to count as normal gender and sexuality and their various deviancies; how persons come to recognize themselves as subjects through ideological interpellation; how the constitution of the normal is inflected by the very deviancies or perversions that function as its constitutive outside; and so on.[15] At its best, this mode of analysis, informed by psychoanalysis, feminist and queer theory, Marxism, and Foucauldian historicism, has helped enormously in our attempts to understand the ways ideological normalization produces, organizes, and regulates individuals and social groups, as well as in our attempts to understand the historical and cultural variability of these functions.[16] It has also helped us to think in new and challenging ways about what the interior and agentive life of the human creature is like, given that the creature's subjectivity and agency are formed through its internalization of ideological norms, and given that those norms are always more fragile and porous than ideology must declare them to be. In order to understand what is at issue in that scene of voyeuristic, abject desire in the *Knight's Tale* – not to mention, say, what is at issue in the Wife of Bath's appropriations of antifeminist discourse, or in the circuits of desire running between Walter and Grisilde in the *Clerk's Tale* – we need to think in something like these terms about the operations of normativity.

But as my discussion of Emily has already suggested, in another part of our intellectual landscape there is quite a different account of what normativity is, or at the very least a different use of the same word, which is equally relevant to the various Chaucerian cases I have alluded to. I am thinking of an account very much alive in Chaucer's time, and the one still dominant in contemporary philosophical ethics, in which "normativity" refers to the authority rational and ethical considerations have for agents, and in which an internalization of that authority is understood not in terms of "subjection" but rather as essential to the pursuit of autonomy, or a good life, or happiness.[17] There are significant differences among these three ways of putting the aim of ethical reflection, as there are differences between the theorizations of these aims in the Middle Ages and those current today; and these differences involve important disagreements about what normativity is and where in the life of an agent it comes from. But the crucial points for the purposes of this rather broad contrast are two. First, for the long tradition of philosophical ethics dating back at least to Socrates, the question of what normativity is and where it comes from is addressed in the first instance through attention to the reflective lives of agents, rather than through attention to processes of ideological formation which may or may not be reflectively available to anyone or be part of anyone's aims. The nature of normativity is thus understood in terms of the questions raised by practical reasoning, questions that take such forms as "How should I (or we) live?"; "What should I (we) do?"; "Who should I (we) be?" Second, it is at least a working hypothesis in these philosophical inquiries, and it is often taken as a matter of fundamental intellectual commitment, that the study of normativity seeks to discover necessary features of the structure of the will or of agency as such, and that understanding these features could help us address the questions raised by practical reasoning. The study of normativity in the philosophical sense thus asks what gives an agent reasons to act, believe, and desire in some ways rather than others; what the sources of obligation and justice are; what considerations in the life of an agent compete with obligation and justice, and how to weigh such various claims on an agent's will against each other; what happens to desires and other kinds of motive, and in particular what an agent *does* to or with them, to make them characteristics of her will rather than mere happenings in her psychic life; and so on.

These are questions of quite a different kind from those raised by the study of normative ideologies. The difference between these two traditions of analysis raises the question of whether what I am pointing to is merely a verbal coincidence rather than a problem in conceptualizing a single phenomenon. It is certainly true that each of these traditions has had little to say to the other, and this might suggest that we are dealing with two concepts under the same name. But there is a powerful sense in which these ways of theorizing normativity seem to compete with each other, so that on each side of what is at least a professional and discursive divide it can seem both that the other side is simply getting normativity wrong, and that whatever value its analyses have can be reduced to terms drawn from whichever side one imaginatively occupies. So, from the perspective of ideology critique, talk of autonomy, or of general structures of the agent's relations to herself, can seem to beg questions of the historical conditions within which specific conceptions of autonomy and agency get articulated, and even to reify fantasies of bourgeois subjectivity that have long since been exploded; while accounts of the discursive and political construction of the subject can seem to tell us whatever we might need to know about, say, what distinguishes a person's will from the random flotsam of her psychic life. But from the perspective of philosophical ethics, these very criticisms can seem to beg questions about possible conceptual conditions for any understanding of agency, in favor of a sheer insistence on the possibility of radical historical change which involves its own reified sense of what constitutes, say, bourgeois subjectivity, and what makes it different from other historical forms of consciousness; further, the political and moral motivations of ideology critique seem to require a commitment to the project of saying what autonomy and justice are, even as it at times suggests that such a project is fundamentally misguided.

I am not interested in taking sides in an argument between what looks, in the most polemical instances, like two hostile intellectual camps. The production of polemic here, as so often, is the sign of thought becoming a caricature of itself, stagnated in its attempts to deny the claim of an artificially externalized enemy on its own activity. But the sense of a competition between two perspectives on normativity does suggest that the use of that term in such different ways is neither a verbal coincidence nor a mere difference of emphasis, but rather the sign of a real conceptual problem. This is not a problem that has gone unnoticed in either intellectual tradition: one way of understanding some of the work of Bernard Williams and Judith Butler is that it attempts to make an account of one aspect of normativity responsive to the claims of the other, even as it suggests that there is something fundamentally paradoxical about doing so.[18] It would seem, then, that an account of normativity that does not open itself in both directions of analysis must fail to appreciate something essential about the phenomenon. But it would also seem that to open an account in either direction makes the resources of the other somehow unavailable, or at least deeply compromised.

The present study will not attempt to solve this problem. Indeed I do not know whether it is solvable. It might be possible to develop an account of normativity that could incorporate what is valuable in each line of thinking while explaining why each makes the other seem so problematic. I will make some preliminary suggestions along these lines, but they should be taken as just that, and there is much in the workings of normativity that this book will not be able, or intended, to explain. But I do not know of an account that is adequate in this respect, and I think we should remain alive to the possibility that it may not be possible to give one. In any case, it seems to me that in light of our current understanding of the topic the most intellectually damaging move would be that of prematurely declaring a solution to a problem whose contours we are only just beginning to see. The primary intellectual task of this book will thus be to make the two conceptions of normativity operate in the same discursive space, in order to see better some of the pressures they exert on each other and some of the ways they might illuminate each other.

To say that this problem may not have a solution is not, of course, to abdicate the task of suggesting some parameters for understanding it more fully. In the chapters that follow I will argue that a satisfying account of normativity must rely on the irreducibility of the perspective of agency as both an analytic and a phenomenological category; and I will argue further that the ambition of autonomy is an essential structuring feature of this perspective. My emphasis on the perspective of agency does not depend on some furtive reinstatement of the metaphysics of presence in a subject supposedly possessed of incorrigible self-knowledge. To clarify what it does depend on, it will be helpful to think briefly about a familiar kind of case detached from the textual and historical questions raised by a discussion of Chaucer.

Imagine that I say something to my friend Julia that expresses some form of antifeminism or heterosexism or racism, something that marks her as different from me in a way that aligns me with privilege or power or "normalcy," and marks her as outside such privilege. It need not have been an explosive or flagrant remark; it is best for the purposes of this example to think of it as something relatively minor and thoughtless, such that I would hardly have noticed its implications. Now Julia knows that I am not the sort of person to think that way, so she thinks that in some sense I couldn't have *really* meant it. But she is hurt by it just the same, and she also knows that there is so much in our culture's social and political arrangements and the routinized habits of mind they foster that supports such attitudes, often in ways of which we are scarcely aware, that in another sense *everyone* is the sort of person to think that way; and I did, after all, say it; and so she also thinks that in some sense I *must* have meant it. So Julia asks me why I said it, and in doing so she means both to be pointing to the hurtfulness of what I said – that is, the way it impinges on her and on our friendship – and to be calling me on and reprimanding me for my implication in habits of mind I know to be wrong. Now suppose I respond to her question by saying "I said it because I live in a culture with multiple discourses and institutions and power structures that function to invest this ideology in all of its subjects." My answer would be true, and it would match up with part of what she already thinks about why I said what I did. But hearing such an answer from me now, she is likely to find it evasive of my responsibility for what I said and the concern I ought to have for her and for our friendship. That is because, in answering her question as I did, I was offering a causal historical explanation of my remark; but her question was asking, not for a causal history, but for *my reasons for saying it.* Only *that* kind of answer would own up to what I did to her and to us in saying it, and to the fact that this ideology is not something in the face of which I am merely passive or an unwilling dupe, but is rather something that constitutes part of my will, something I allowed to speak for me and *as* me, and in that sense to be normative for me.[19]

I do not think that we should be willing to say that in finding my answer evasive Julia is simply missing the point of the argument that subjectivity and normativity are culturally constructed. And if that is right, then without denying that everything we do and the norms that inform our actions have a causal history in, among other things, socially determinate ideologies, this kind of case suggests that there is a mode of normative explanation of action that looks *directly* to reasons for acting, no matter what we understand the historical sources of those reasons to be. The above example can also help us to distinguish between explanations that look to the perspective of agency and something quite different with which they are often conflated, the attempt of an agent or collectivity to defend a sense of freedom or the possibility of political efficacy from determinist or constructivist arguments that threaten their dissolution.[20] In my example, the *doer* of the action in question *wants* to adopt the perspective of causal explanation on his own actions, in order to defeat a sense of his responsibility for them; the insistence on the perspective of agency comes not from him, but from the recipient or victim of his act. By separating the question of how a subject or agent wishes to describe himself from the question of how causal and agentive explanations are related to each other, my example suggests that it is a mistake to imagine either that the agentive perspective issues from an agent's relations to himself, or that an invocation of the agentive perspective is fundamentally motivated by an agent's wish to preserve a freedom, illusory or real. We all can and constantly do deploy both causal and agentive explanations with respect both to our own actions and the actions of others. Much of human sociality, including the very possibilities of responsibility, obligation, and the kinds of social bonds in which it matters what someone meant and how they meant it, is structured by our routine dependence on the perspective of agency; and no argument, constructivist or otherwise, can or should change that.[21]

In what follows I will expand on this discussion of the perspective of agency to make three related arguments. First, while the pressures exerted on agents by questions of what to do and how to live always necessarily take ideological form, they cannot be reduced to sheer effects of the cultural formations that produce them, and so cannot be fully understood in terms of the cultural construction of the subject. Second, the perspective of agency is characterized by mobilities and opacities of identification, desire, and self-understanding which also cannot be fully understood through the analysis of ideological and discursive formations. And third, the analysis of ideology and ideological normalization can benefit from attention to such agentive pressures, since these pressures are part of what produces and maintains ideology in the first place.

In taking the project of philosophical ethics seriously in its own terms, then, I am hardly recommending a return to some prelapsarian notion of an unproblematic agency and a normativity redeemed of the abjections and injustices it has seemed always to instantiate. Nor, in discussing autonomy, will I be describing an ambition that could ever be free of ideological blindness, and even, as I will suggest, of a kind of psychosis. My aim is rather to resist an impulse towards redemptive theorizing which operates both in the reactionary defense of normativity and in the progressive critique of it. This redemptive impulse appears, for instance, in the reception of the figure who remains perhaps the most important touchstone for the critical historiography of normativity, Michel Foucault. The difficulty we continue to have in taking the force of Foucault's critique of the repressive hypothesis is, I think, quite closely related to the relative indifference with which his late work on ethics has been met.[22] My claim in this respect would be that as long as normativity seems fundamentally to be a matter of subjection to ideology and to power, and therefore not a matter of anything we might still call ethics, then no matter how much we insist that this subjection involves the very constitution of the subject rather than the repression of something already there in the psyche, no matter how often we say that there is no relation of externality between the subject and power, we will continue to be haunted by the longing for a freedom from normativity, for a self liberated from forces by which it is simply subjected, and in the face of which it is fundamentally passive.

Let me be clear: I do not think we should take the desire for such a freedom lightly, just because it is impossible. On the contrary, my claim is that in conjuring this redemptive ghost, we continue to give voice to a drive towards autonomy which this very conjuring act denies us the resources to understand. The redemptive impulse in the critique of normativity might thus be understood as the expression of normativity's desire to overcome itself. That, at least, would be a Nietzschean way of putting the matter. The problem I am articulating is one that Nietzsche was perhaps the first in modern intellectual culture to appreciate, and the difficulty of understanding it is as symptomatically present in the reception of Nietzsche's work as it is in the reception of Foucault's – unsurprisingly, since when one speaks of Foucault, Nietzsche is often not far in the background.[23] I will conclude this sketch of a theoretical territory by invoking a brief Nietzschean passage that condenses many of the core conceptual concerns of this book.

For Nietzsche, normativity must be conceived in terms of the sublimation of violence and domination into ethical values, mores, and laws, a sublimation that takes place in the production of both social collectivities and individual psyches. But he rejects the proposal that, rather than "submitting abjectly to capricious laws," we should or even could throw off the shackles of normativity:

> Every morality is . . . a bit of tyranny against "nature"; also against "reason"; but this in itself is no objection, as long as we do not have some other morality which permits us to decree that every kind of

tyranny and unreason is impermissible . . . the curious fact is that all
there is or has been on earth of freedom, subtlety, boldness, dance,
and masterly sureness . . . has developed only owing to the "tyranny of
such capricious laws"; and in all seriousness, the probability is by no
means small that precisely this is "nature" and "natural."[24]

It is a natural fact about the human creature that, out of the morass of
conflicting desires, reasons, hopes, fears, beliefs, and other attitudes that
characterize its individual and collective life, it must constitute a functional will for itself. The study of normativity is the study of how the
creature does this: how it makes a will for itself both individually and
collectively by organizing its conflicting attitudes into what Nietzsche
calls "orders of rank," normative hierarchies of value.[25] This activity of
self-ordering through the production of norms, both in and between
individual and collective agency, involves violence and cruelty, tyranny
and unreason, no matter how rationalized or just the norms so produced
may be. This is not a fact that should be apologized away, and Nietzsche
never tires of breaking down the amnesiac defenses with which we hide
this ugliness from ourselves. But neither does this ugliness constitute an
objection against normativity as such – unless, as this passage suggests, we
have been normalized into a redemptive moralism that declares all cruelty
impermissible, and so locates suffering as such an absolute evil that its
avoidance becomes the normative consideration that trumps all others.
This would be misguided for two reasons. First, because it wishfully and
self-deceptively installs a tyranny and unreason of its own, one that
dangerously blinds itself to the suffering it must necessarily install in its
subjects. Second, because normativity is the condition of human functionality, and without it much of what we value – freedom, subtlety, the
beauty and self-mastery exemplified in dance, even beauty and agency
themselves – would be impossible.[26]

I think that Nietzsche, despite his pronounced tendency to imaginative and rhetorical excess, was basically right about normativity. And if
he was right, a critical investigation into normativity must pursue an
account of the ways such phenomena as violence, suffering, injustice,
and unreason are deeply bound up with those of beauty, pleasure, and
autonomy. Such an account is not easy to give: it can seem, for
instance, as though it amounts to a fascistic apology for cruelty and
injustice, or, on the contrary, as though it amounts to an indictment

of the inherent fascism of beauty and morality. The very generation of *both* of these incompatible worries, however, suggests that neither is a necessary conclusion, and that each may participate in the underlying confusion that leads us to think of ideological and ethical analysis as mutually exclusive. But the ease with which these worries get generated is, I take it, one more indication of the difficulty of attending at one and the same time to the two aspects of normativity.

I do not think that this difficulty is local to contemporary US academic culture; I think it is characteristic of the phenomenon itself, and attending to it can help us to see more clearly what that phenomenon involves. But it is a pronounced feature of contemporary intellectual culture that investigations into each aspect of normativity tend to repress the concerns and questions raised by the other. In this book I will pursue extended discussions in the theory of normativity partly out of a desire to address this blind spot in our intellectual culture. But I also have strictly historicist reasons for doing so. I have already suggested through the case of Emily in her garden what I will argue is a characteristic feature of Chaucer's poetry, that he places the two aspects of normativity in the same representational space, and does so in ways that display the workings of both and invite us to think about how they inform each other. And I have also suggested that in doing so he inherits a rich tradition of thinking about these matters, and that what he does with this tradition is part of what makes him important. As long as we proceed from within our own dominant assumptions about normativity, then, this feature of Chaucer's work, and of its imbeddedness in medieval culture, will remain opaque to us. Let me now expand briefly on my sense of the tradition Chaucer inherits, with particular emphasis on its engagements with sexuality, to suggest something of the historical dimensions of this book's conceptual project.

SEXUALITY AND MORAL ALTERITY IN THE CHRISTIAN TRADITION

Because of his dominance as a cultural figure, Augustine provides a convenient place to focus. In a passage from Book 10 of the *Confessions*, Augustine gives voice to one of his most condensed and moving expressions of the longing at the heart of normative Christian subjectivity.

> numquid tunc ego non sum . . . et tamen tantum interest inter me ipsum et me ipsum . . . ut anima mea sequatur me . . . ut non sit rebellis sibi.

> Surely I have not ceased to be my own self . . . and yet there is still a great gap between myself and myself . . . Oh that my soul might follow my own self . . . that it might not be a rebel to itself.[27]

The occasion of Augustine's lament is sexual. Specifically, it is his ongoing susceptibility to sexual imaginings and erotic dreams, accompanied by feelings of great pleasure and sometimes by nocturnal emissions, long after his conversion to Christianity and to a life of chastity. As Peter Brown has argued, this is not to be read as the sign of some peculiarity in Augustine's psyche, but rather as a powerful instance of the way sexuality had come to be seen, during the long development of Christian moral ideology since Paul, as "a privileged ideogram of all that was most irreducible in the human will."[28] One consequence of the figurative power that sexuality came to assume for Christian moral reflection was that the instabilities and opacities of psychic life tended to get associated with sexual desire and sexual fantasy, and sexual renunciation and virginity became central locations for expressing and thinking about the ambition of autonomy. Augustine is the pivotal figure in Brown's story: in Augustine's writings, we find the formulations whereby sexuality was cemented in Christian thought as the paradigmatic locus of the compulsion to normativity, the need the human creature has, in Paul's famous phrase, to "give a law to itself."[29]

Brown's story is particularly salient in the present context because it suggests that, for what was to become for centuries the dominant tradition of thinking about sexuality in the West, erotic life was a site on which the two aspects of normativity were essentially and explicitly related. Augustine, for instance, was deeply invested in reinforcing the cultural hegemony of a sexual norm that had long cast its shadow over the Christian subject, and would long continue to do so. According to this norm, the perfect state of sexual being consisted in the renunciation of all sexual activity and liberation from all sexual desire; meanwhile, the ordinary Christian household became a site of deep moral compromise. As Paul had put it long before in defending the Christian couple from a radical insistence on universal celibacy, "it is better to marry than to burn with desire": a defense this may be, but it is hardly a ringing endorsement of married sexuality.[30] Augustine recognized sexual activity as necessary for the propagation of the body of the faithful, and even thought of sexual desire as, within limits, beneficial to married sociality. But he also thought that sexual activity and desire must be constrained, that they were licit only in the service of their reproductive function, and then only in a loving heterosexual marriage sanctioned by the Church.[31] And even this necessary function remained under the shadow of death: in our fallen state, reproductive activity was little more than the propagation of mortality. This suggests that the reason Augustine thought sexuality had to be disciplined was not, say, that norms of sexual behavior or identity seemed to him to be closely tied to medicalized norms of health, and thus raised questions about the state's interest in managing a productive population.[32] It was rather that the phenomenology of erotic life had such a powerful grip on his moral imagination that, even though he regarded sexual offences as relatively minor on the scale of moral faults, they could stand in for the very possibility of moral fault as such. To return to the passage from the *Confessions*: to discipline sexuality was to do what little the human creature could to bring under control the most telling reminder of the "gap between itself and itself," the profound ache with which it hears the call of "its own self" as one it both must and cannot follow. To say, as Augustine and a long tradition before and after him did, that sexuality was the propagation of death, was thus to do more than repeat the ancient naturalist commonplace, according to which a mortal creature reproduces to attain a kind of second-rate immortality through the serial production of creatures individually doomed to die. It was to locate sexuality as a kind of death in itself, a site on which the creature confronts its willing investment in its deprivation of a divine normative principle, a principle that might order its dispositions perfectly, and so release it from the state of living death in which all of its activities are shadowed by passivities, shadowed that is by its own dull resistance to life.[33]

We should not be surprised that the problematics articulated by such figures as Paul and Augustine maintain a deep cultural sedimentation in later periods. As I have already indicated, this sedimentation will be of continuous interest throughout this book. And if we acknowledge the cultural authority of this sedimentation for the later medieval period, then however that authority is revised, contested, or even deformed, we should expect that the two senses of normativity I outlined earlier – normativity as the drive towards ideological normalization and normativity as the drive towards a will at one with itself – so deeply interpenetrate during the long history of the construction of sexuality in the Christian West that we risk seriously mischaracterizing either if we focus on it to the exclusion of the other. That we are already engaged in telling the story of how these problematics of normativity develop over the course of the Middle Ages is suggested by the fact that some of the best work on medieval gender and sexuality is concerned with writing chapters in the history of western moral psychology – with doing, that is, what Nietzsche called "the natural history of morals."[34] And what has begun to emerge from this work is a sense that the later Middle Ages provides amazingly rich and varied sites on which the two aspects of normativity intersect in eroticized fashion. Some of these sites are religious, such as the inversions and collapses of gender categories involved in associations between Christ's bleeding wounds and lactation, the loving devotion lavished on the naked, suffering body of Christ by men and women alike, and the elaboration of an eroticized mysticism. Some cross between devotional and secular contexts, such as the concern with the moral value of the virginal female body, or the development of an eroticized ethics of friendship in same-sex clerical and monastic settings and in the discourse of marriage. And some belong squarely to the literary culture out of which Chaucer emerged, a culture which, if it did not exactly invent literary subjectivity and western romantic love, as some have claimed, did exhibit a burst of interest in the thrills and abjections of erotic passion, the analysis of erotic objectification, and the glorification of a single-minded devotion to the erotic object, and inflected each of these developments with the increased interest in ethical and psychological theory that came in the wake of the rediscovery of Aristotle.[35] These features of the late medieval cultural landscape suggest that the two aspects of normativity continued to intersect in ever more complicated fashion as erotic desire became in many ways identified with the self's deepest commitments, even while an identification of sexuality with psychic and moral alterity remained deeply lodged in the cultural imagination.

As I hope by now is clear, the present study is in part an attempt to push harder than we have hitherto on the underlying conceptual problematics that informs both this history and our attempts to understand it. But the lines of intellectual productivity and value may run the other way as well. In my sketch of the conceptual shape of the problem of normativity, I suggested the difficulty of attending at one and the same time to its two aspects, its function in processes of ideological normalization and its function as a register of claims on the perspective of agency; and I suggested further that our attempts to understand normativity, sexuality, and their intersection are hampered by what is mostly a failure even to acknowledge that this difficulty exists. Now I want to suggest that, given the insistence with which late medieval representations of sexuality simultaneously embed normative ideology and what is often quite profound thinking about normative claims on agency, renewed attention to these representations with just this set of concerns in mind might enable us, in Foucault's phrase, to "get free of ourselves" in a way we need to do to go on thinking about these matters in productive ways.[36] Further, if Foucault is right that the medieval construction of sexuality provides the crucial prehistory of the more distinctively modern processes by which it came to seem that sex offered a secret truth about one's innermost self – and here, after all, Foucault is developing lessons he learned from Peter Brown – this getting free of ourselves may be somewhat closer to getting to know ourselves than we are inclined to think. The very "middleness" of the Middle Ages its occupation of a middle distance in the historical imagination in which we cannot quite see immediate precursors to ourselves, but in which contemporary western culture remains more directly implicated than it is, say, in ancient Greek "practices of the self" – gives it real heuristic value for our thinking about the ways sexuality and normativity remain entangled today.[37] If such a thought seems worth pursuing, then it suggests the value of a study of normativity that foregrounds its relations to sexuality and focuses historically on medieval culture. That goes some way towards describing the present project, but stops well short of describing a book on the *Canterbury Tales*. One reason this book has the focus it does is that the perspective of agency is hard to keep in view in a discussion that covers a large discursive territory. As I have already suggested and will argue further, an analysis of agency is not the same thing as an analysis of the subject: tracing the cultural and discursive circuits through which the subject is constructed will not tell us what an agent is or what it is like to be one. But, as I have already indicated, the main reason for this book's focus is that Chaucer himself undertakes a powerful and searching exploration of the intersection of normativity and sexuality, and the sustained effort to track the subtlety and energy of Chaucer's writing has much to teach us. More specifically, as I said in discussing Emily in her garden, exploring the joint conceptual and historical problematics of normativity is essential to the most basic literary-critical project of this book, that of understanding Chaucer as a philosophical love poet. I will conclude this introduction with a quick literary and historical sketch of the Chaucer I will be discussing, together with a brief overview of the plan of the book.

PHILOSOPHICAL CHAUCER AND THE PLAN OF THE BOOK

It is easy to understand why *Troilus and Criseyde* and the *Knight's Tale* have been seen as Chaucer's great philosophical-erotic poems. More than anything else he wrote, these two long poems give ample attention to explicitly represented philosophical themes and problems, and both engage erotic desire as a central philosophical preoccupation and a powerful impetus to philosophical reflection. Further, both were probably written around the middle of Chaucer's career, when he may have also been engaged in his translations of the *Consolation of Philosophy* and the *Romance of the Rose*. And both show him to be steeped in French and Italian poetic traditions that combine interests in courtly erotic lyricism and philosophical dialectic. But while I think there is much of interest in the *Troilus*, I will discuss it only in passing; and I will not begin with the *Knight's Tale*. As my paradigmatic text for introducing Chaucer's philosophical poetics and its intersection with erotic life I will rather take the *Miller's Tale*, which has long been regarded as perhaps the most antiphilosophical, not to mention anti-courtly, of Chaucer's poems; and only in the context provided by that tale will I turn to Chaucer's engagements with courtly eroticism in the *Knight's Tale*, and from there to accounts of what he learned from

Boethius and the *Rose*. In making the opening pair of Canterbury narratives rather than the *Troilus* the occasion for identifying Chaucer with a species of philosophical poetry, I will argue that as Chaucer leaves behind a poetry concerned with adapting philosophical sources and directly representing philosophical themes, his writing becomes more genuinely philosophical, that is to say, a more powerful and capacious vehicle for speculative endeavor.

My argument thus provides both a version and an inversion of a familiar narrative of Chaucer's poetic development. That narrative goes something like this: as Chaucer's interests develop in the formative years of the *Canterbury* project, they take him away from the abstract concerns of his dream-visions and of the Boethian literary tradition of Alain de Lille, Guillaume de Lorris, Jean de Meun, and the like, and thus away from the philosophically idealist commitments of courtly eroticism. Instead he moves towards an interest in ordinary talk and daily social life, the richly variegated spaces of conflicting opinions and motives that philosophy has always tried to cleanse of its impurities. These spaces exhibit people's concerns with all sorts of things: love, certainly, but also just plain sex, not to mention money, prestige, power, and so on – and the intellectual purchase of extended reflection, as even a philosopher must admit, comes fairly far down on such a list. According to this story, the *Canterbury Tales* constitutes both a radical break with Chaucer's earlier writings and a development of comic and skeptical tendencies that had always been part of his work. Think for instance of *The House of Fame*, in which the narrator's Dantean agent of visionary instruction is a pedantic windbag of an eagle, and in which the source of the "tidings" on which opinion and fame are based is a whirling wicker cage from which truth and falsehood escape at random, sometimes getting inextricably combined into a single discursive lump as they try to squeeze past each other through the cage's narrow openings.[38] *The House of Fame* is a text with a strong and overt investment in a major philosophical problem, that of the relation between representation and truth; just as *Troilus and Criseyde* and the *Knight's Tale* show a strong investment in major philosophical problems such as the conflict between free will and determinism, and the structure and motives of moral deliberation. But *The House of Fame* also treats its topics skeptically, not just in the quasitechnical sense that it articulates a position according to which we can never definitively sort truth from falsehood in the representations on which all discursive knowledge depends, but also in the colloquial sense that it treats this philosophical problem itself with ironic detachment. *The House of Fame* thus pursues the problem of truth and representation not in the technical mode of epistemological theory nor in the sublime mode of Platonist mythography, but rather through intentionally playful tropes that make it hard to maintain the somber tones of philosophical seriousness.

In the *Canterbury Tales*, so the story goes, Chaucer mostly leaves this sort of overt philosophical thematization behind, and when he bothers to engage it at all, either so greatly ups the ante on its silliness that it cannot be taken seriously – think of the barnyard philosophizing of the *Nun's Priest's Tale* – or exhibits it as a form of psychic and political pathology, as in what is now perhaps the dominant reading of the *Knight's Tale*.[39] But for the most part Chaucer simply goes straight for the world of "tidings." He will no longer anxiously and ironically explore the wish to be Dante, privy to visions which transcend the possibilities of linguistic expression; he will just be one pilgrim among others, and one not terribly deserving of notice at that. Further, unlike in *The House of Fame*, this rejection of the visionary model will now less be expressive of a philosophical position capable of abstract formulation – as in that poem a species of skepticism or anti-idealism – than a device to enable attention to what is really of interest to him, the great comic landscape of human talk.

I think such a story has much to recommend it. But it can also be misleading. For one thing, it seems to suggest for the *Canterbury Tales* some version of what has variously been called the "genial Chaucer," or the "liberal-humanist Chaucer," or the "ironic Chaucer" – under whatever label, a Chaucer who, through slipperiness or wisdom or bad ideology, refuses to adopt a philosophical or political position, imagining himself a subject without an ideology, and preferring the urbane wit of a wry but pleasant-humored detachment from the muddlings of the all too situated pilgrim narrators.[40] Any such view of Chaucer's identity as a poet is, I think, badly mistaken, and the Chaucer I will be conjuring is considerably more tough-minded and disturbing than this one, and considerably less the victim of bourgeois ideology.[41] What the view of

Chaucer as "genial" responds to, besides his sense of humor, is his utter disinclination to preachiness and polemic: as Lee Patterson rightly puts it, "Chaucer's . . . characteristic relation to the world was analytical rather than rhetorical."[42] But that is just to say that the task Chaucer sets himself is not that of urging some philosophical theory or legislating some moral or social program, but rather that of critically examining the space of individual and collective action and motive, the drives to theory and moral and social legislation, and the opacities and disjunctions that appear between the normative theories we spin and the worlds and identities we inhabit. And that is essentially a philosophical project, even if, as was always the case for Chaucer, it is less directed than philosophy usually is towards the goal of saying what is true about the problems it investigates.

Another potential danger of the standard narrative of Chaucer's career is that, for critics still inclined to read the *Canterbury Tales* as a serious intellectual project, Chaucer can seem to have developed an interest in politics and sociality in his later work which is fundamentally opposed to the philosophical impulse; on such accounts, philosophy then becomes associated with a politically and ideologically bankrupt idealism involving a wish for freedom from the vicissitudes of history.[43] No doubt the *Tales* do reflect a stronger and more capacious interest in an analytics of politics and sociality than Chaucer's earlier work. That is part of what makes the *Tales* so well suited to the study of ideological normalization. But we can begin to see why this interest in politics and sociality bears no necessary relation to a rejection of philosophy if we briefly turn to another familiar story about Chaucer, one that attempts to explain his concern with the analysis of political and social formations and of the subject positions of those who inhabit them. This story relates Chaucer's basic habits of mind to some important demographic and economic changes in late medieval England: plague, depopulation, a shortage of labor, the infiltration of a money economy not only into urban mercantile centers but into the furthest reaches of the English countryside, the spread of literacy, and so on.[44] Perhaps the most global effect of these changes was to make England a society without a workable articulate view of its normative social structure and its functional social relations. In Chaucer's lifetime, the prevailing view concerning the structure of English society, and the only one that offered a presumptively comprehensive theory of social structure and social relations was still the three estates model. But while Gower and other contemporaries of Chaucer could still refer to the three estates model with confidence that everyone would assent to its obvious truthfulness, demographic and economic changes were making it increasingly ill-fitted to social reality. While it may have taken a keen and penetrating intelligence to think well about this lack of fit, we can be sure that in some sense it registered with practically everyone. We might say that the three estates model had something of the function for late medieval England that the notion of US social and political arrangements being built on principles of justice has for us: it was necessary for the well-functioning of the social system that almost everyone believe in it, even while it was incoherent in the daily experience of many if not all of its subjects.

As Patterson and others have argued, Chaucer himself was someone who, like his comic self-representation in the *Tales*, never quite belonged anywhere in the society of which he got to see so much; and this displacement helped to make him an acute observer of a rich and varied landscape of social norms, and a keen analyst of the political and psychic functions of those norms. Chaucer's early writerly career had been as a poet of and for the aristocracy, working within recognizably courtly poetic forms. But in writing the *Tales*, he left this career behind in favor of a poetry with a less easily identifiable audience and strong interests in social locations that do not fit well with articulable social structures, and in more wide-ranging disjunctions between persons' identifiable social roles and their inhabitable senses of self. Far from making the *Tales* antiphilosophical, however, this interest in the incoherence and opacity of the norms by which people live is just what I have been saying makes Chaucer's later poetry philosophically rich, even when it is emptied of any obvious philosophical themes.

The large structure of this book – two chapters on the *Canterbury Tales*, followed by two on Chaucer's main philosophical interlocutors, the *Consolation of Philosophy* and the *Romance of the Rose*, followed by two more that return to the *Tales* – is partly shaped by my sense of how, by the time of his main work on the *Tales*, Chaucer came to understand the intersection between his poetic and philosophical interests. As I have suggested, Chaucer is less interested in the abstract articulation of philosophical problems themselves than he is in the ways persons inhabit them, in what we might call the affective and political life of philosophical problems. While I will be arguing that philosophical work can help us clarify Chaucer's interests in affect and politics, it will be truest to those interests to allow the work of philosophy to emerge from the welter of beliefs, desires, and commitments that constitutes the practical attitudes people live by and which Chaucer was so good at capturing. Also, it is essential to my argument that Chaucer was a poet rather than a systematic thinker. Matters of literary form, among them genre, narrative, tone, metaphor, and character, are at the core of my readings and of the ways I understand Chaucer to engage philosophical questions from the situated perspectives of the Canterbury pilgrims. Again, beginning and ending with the poetry – and specifically, beginning with the *Miller's Tale*, a poem whose philosophical engagements emerge from questions of poetic form and narrative investment rather than from explicitly philosophical passages or themes – will allow this feature of Chaucer's interests to emerge most clearly. Finally, and perhaps most importantly, philosophy as I understand it, and as I think Chaucer understood it, is more a matter of probing a difficult and evolving set of problems than it is of laying out doctrines that can be neatly summarized and classified according to schools of thought. In fact, such summaries of philosophical doctrine can be in a sense anti-philosophical, insofar as they make it hard to capture what I am calling the work of philosophy, its dependence on the risk of thought and on the practical and conceptual difficulties that motivate it.[45] Beginning, as it were, *in medias res*, in the midst of a situated subject's engagements with philosophical problems, is thus in my view truer to what philosophy is and why it matters, as well as to how it matters to Chaucer, than beginning by systematically tracing the philosophical positions Chaucer and his main intellectual interlocutors held.

Apart from such considerations, the order of the chapters also allows for a progressively broader and deeper understanding of the central philosophical issues Chaucer's poetry engages. Chapter one begins the book's discussions of normativity by posing the question of why there should be a problem concerning normativity in the first place. More specifically, the chapter addresses what is perhaps the simplest form of an answer to normative questions, an appeal to nature as normativity's ground. The Chaucerian locus of such an appeal is the *Miller's Tale*, which in its polemical critique of the *Knight's Tale* stages an implicit argument that nature determines desire and its objects. The Miller means this argument to provide a basis for action and identity generally speaking, and he also means for it to underwrite a picture of sexual desire and gender difference which has antifeminist and heteronormative implications. I argue, however, that a naturalistic theory cannot answer the questions concerning action, identity, and desire the Miller faces. As a consequence, his belated, nostalgic way of holding to such a theory does as much to undermine his sense of normative gender and sexuality as it does to support it, and in the process reveals queer identifications and desires which the narrative can never effectively keep out of sight. In pursuing this argument, the chapter begins the book's project of locating Chaucer's interests in gender and sexuality within the frame of his philosophical concerns, and specifically of his interest in the structure of practical rationality.

Central to the Miller's naturalism is the idea that practical reason is an unwarranted excess whose exercise only distracts from the ends nature has already provided. Since chapter one argues that this idea is incoherent, chapter two addresses the question of what place practical reason might have in determining the ends of action. The chapter does so by turning to the *Knight's Tale*, which in its idealization of Theseus as the embodiment of practical wisdom is the object of the Miller's critique. The chapter elaborates the Knight's ideal of a Thesean deliberative rationality that could ground right individual conduct and a just polity. While this ideal directly engages the normative questions naturalism evades, I argue that it is finally unable to capture the complexity of the Knight's own sense of the grounds of action and identity. Once again, sexuality provides a central site on which this complexity gets registered. For the deliberative rationality for which Theseus strives is predicated on the renunciation of erotic passion, and as such it cannot accommodate either the Knight's glamorization of Palamon and Arcite's erotic suffering or his identification with a formalist ethical and erotic ideal whose clearest embodiment is Emily. In pursuing this argument, the chapter continues the book's concern with the ambivalences of normative masculinity and its consequences for both sexes, while refining its analysis of the difficulties involved in understanding the basis of practical normativity.

While chapters one and two explore those difficulties in the context of specific and problematic attempts to answer normative questions, neither chapter provides a direct analysis of why normativity resists grounding in a comprehensive theory. Chapter three takes up that task in the context of an extended reading of Boethius's *Consolation of Philosophy*. The chapter does so partly through careful attention to Boethius's dialectical method, which I see as at least as important as Boethius's philosophical views for understanding Chaucer's interest in agentive self-division and misrecognition. Since Philosophy in the *Consolation* is a figure for the Prisoner's own reflective capacities, I read the dialogue as pursuing an interior argument that arises from conflicts in his most basic intuitions concerning action and desire. These conflicts, hardly peculiar to the Prisoner, are paradigmatic for a rational creature, and Chaucer found ways to represent them through a range of poetic means independent of dialogue form. Further, Boethius's dialectical investigations of self-division provide the terms for a philosophical analysis of many of the psychological phenomena central to Chaucer's representations of erotic life, including repression, fetishism, and masochism. Chapter three thus provides the core of the book's argument that we can understand such phenomena in ways independent of psychoanalysis. More specifically, the chapter argues that such phenomena have a source that is not in itself sexual, and that cannot be fully understood through the causal analysis provided by a psychoanalytic history of the subject. That source lies in an antinomy that structures practical rationality, and that insures that an investment in having a coherent agency and identity is necessarily inflected by an investment in self-dissolution and self-punishment. In this sense, agency and identity are constitutively masochistic, even as masochism becomes a name for a condition of agentive and psychic life rather than an avoidable or aberrant psychosexual condition.

While chapter three brackets sexuality to ask how the conditions of practical rationality help to shape psychological phenomena, chapter four asks how this analysis might be brought to bear on erotic life. The chapter does so through a close reading of the *Roman de la Rose*, since that text played a central role in mediating philosophy and poetry for Chaucer, as well as in shaping his sense of sexuality as a site for such mediation. The chapter returns to the ambivalences animating hegemonic masculinity, and argues that they exemplify a crisis of intelligibility in the emergent structures of western romantic love. This crisis is epitomized in the poem's representation of the courtly lover, whose desire depends on the interpenetration of sadomasochistic structures with a longing for utopian sociality. I argue that the analysis of practical rationality developed in chapter three, especially when it is elaborated in terms of its consequences for understanding the late medieval application of classical friendship theory to the erotic scene, provides a set of terms for understanding why sexual desire involves wishes for violence directed towards both the erotic object and the desiring subject. Chapter four thus continues the previous chapter's projects of recovering the deep history of psychological phenomena often thought of as distinctively modern and associated with psycho-analysis, and of offering an analysis of such phenomena derived from the intellectual traditions most important to Chaucer. The chapter also serves as a bridge back to questions of literary representation, through an argument that allegory functions in the *Rose* as a supple vehicle for speculative endeavor and for representing the mobility of fantasy, rather than a static embodiment of abstract concepts. That suppleness, I think, is what drew Chaucer to the *Rose* throughout his career, and what makes the *Rose* closer to Chaucer's project in the *Canterbury Tales* than has been allowed by accounts focused on the question of literary realism.

With the theoretical and contextual work of chapters three and four in hand, chapters five and six return to the *Canterbury Tales* to elaborate the book's discussions of intersubjectivity and the ideal of a utopian intimacy in which "two become one." Chapter five does so by expand-ing the book's scope beyond its earlier focus on the incoherences of normative masculinity, to examine in the *Wife of Bath's Prologue* and *Tale* the contours of a feminine subjectivity more directly trained on such an ideal than are the men. Despite the Wife's commitment to that ideal, I argue that she remains in the grip of fantasies of narcissized self-interest, of instrumentalized relations with others and with her own body, and of subjectivity as a private interior space, all of which were central to the book's discussions of masculine subjectivity as well. By turning to a feminine subjectivity for which utopian intimacy is a central value, the chapter provides a deeper appreciation of how those fantasies are structured by intersubjective desire. The chapter also advances the book's discussion of masochism, moving beyond the earlier chapters' focus on the conceptual structure of courtly desire to develop a fuller account of a masochistic erotics not reducible to courtliness. Such an account is facilitated by the turn to a feminine subjectivity fractured by incompatible but overlapping desires to resist the objectifying desire men have for it, to yield itself up to that desire, and to shatter the very subject position made for it by patriarchal ideology.

My discussion of the Wife of Bath, like all of the book's discussions of sexuality, explores attractions and resistances to an ideal of love that is incompatible with naturalist, instrumentalist, and subjectivist fantasies and the ideologies of gender and desire that circulate around and through them. Chapter six turns to the question of what would be required to constitute oneself and one's desires in relation to such an ideal. The Clerk offers Grisilde as a model of loving self-constitution, but while Grisilde embodies unconditional love and strength of will, her very strength and unconditionality implicate her in violations of maternal duty and in her own subjection to Walter, whose sadistic hunger for knowledge and control of her is both fueled and enabled by her exemplary patience. In keeping with my claim that Chaucer's poetry is most powerful philosophically when it explores the conflicts in our beliefs and values, I argue that he means to produce what has been, since the tale's first reception, a divided response of admiration and repulsion at Grisildan unconditionality. If Grisilde embodies what love would have to be not to be fractured, there is finally no way to avoid such fracturing, not because we are somehow flawed or lacking, but because our divided response to Grisilde is the sign of an irresolvable split in love's conceptual and affective structure. Chapter six thus completes the book's argument that an analysis of practical rationality is essential to the analysis of sexuality and ideology. For love emerges from this discussion not as the redemptive other to the pathological desires and ideologies that inform so much of erotic life in the *Canterbury Tales*, but rather as itself structured around a Boethian antinomy of the will that is a source of such pathologies.

CHAPTER I

Naturalism and its discontents in the *Miller's Tale*

One of the strangest moments in the *Miller's Tale* is the one in which Absolon, who has been waiting in the dark at Alisoun's window for a long-anticipated kiss, finds himself savoring the taste not of her mouth but of the "hole" she has so unceremoniously proffered. This moment will serve as a useful entry into the intersection between Chaucer's representations of erotic life and his philosophical poetics, and specifically into the way he combines an interest in the instability of hegemonic norms of gender and desire with interests in ethics, agency, and practical reason.

> This Absolon gan wype his mouth ful drie.
> Derk was the nyght as pich, or as the cole,
> And at the wyndow out she putte hir hole,
> And Absolon, hym fil no bet ne wers,
> But with his mouth he kiste hir naked ers
> Ful savourly, er he were war of this.
> Abak he stirte, and thoughte it was amys,
> For wel he wiste a womman hath no berd.
> He felte a thyng al rough and long yherd,
> And seyde, "Fy! allas! what have I do?"
> (I.3730–39)

I begin with this moment partly because of its distance from the explicitly philosophical themes that crop up from time to time in Chaucer's poetry: in the place of epistemological subtleties or worries over the freedom of the will, the Miller offers us some dirty sex and a good joke. In fact, insofar as there is any conceptual content to the moment, it lies not in abstract philosophizing but in the way Absolon's ill-fated kiss expresses the deep *anti*philosophical animus of the Miller's naturalism. As many critics have argued, here as elsewhere in the tale the Miller sets out to "quite" the *Knight's Tale* by deflating that tale's romantic and philosophical ambitions, baring the most basic natural facts of animality, bodiliness and desire which the Knight and his characters, and their surrogates in the *Miller's Tale*, seem so intent on sublimating.[1] On such an account Absolon, who throughout the tale has seemed more interested in adopting a theatrical posture of love-longing than in attaining any erotic payoff, is finally brought into intimate and unmistakable contact with "the real nature of what he sought"; and with this unveiling of the real object of human, or at least masculine, desire, the perverse displacements of desire operating in the lyrical complaints and philosophical speeches of the *Knight's Tale* are supposed to become compellingly clear.[2] This polemical function of the moment, and the force with which the tale in other ways sets out to give what Kolve calls "a counter-vision of human experience" to the Knight's, is more or less what prompted Muscatine to call the *Miller's Tale* a case of "fabliau . . . virtually made philosophical."[3] On Muscatine's account, and for critics such as Kolve who share that account's basic commitments, the tale achieves (or "virtually" achieves) philosophical status not because it has any direct philosophical content but because of the deftness and density with which Chaucer marshals poetic resources to capture a distinct view of human purposes and of how we ought to pursue them. Such an account is helpful, then, in foregrounding Chaucer's interest in the ethical and conceptual stakes of literary representation, and in suggesting that that interest is perhaps as important a clue to what makes his poetry philosophical as are the more overtly philosophical moments he sometimes includes.

In recent years, however, a challenge has been mounted to the Muscatinian reading of the tale, which requires a reformulation of those stakes and of how Chaucer engaged them. A number of critics with interests in gender and sexuality have begun to raise questions that disturb a naturalistic account of Absolon's kiss and of the *Miller's Tale* as a whole. What does it mean for Alisoun, who throughout the tale has functioned as a more or less passive object of desire, to present her "hole" to be kissed, and so to become at this fateful moment not merely an object but an agent? Just which hole does she put out the window, the one with lips and hair or the one in the middle of her ass? Why does the Miller conflate these holes, and what does it mean for Absolon momentarily to conflate them with the hole in a bearded face? And how are we to interpret the fact that there are questions and conflations here at all, given the Miller's apparent insistence that there should not *be* any, since what this moment is supposed to reveal is a determinate, compelling, and naturally given object of desire?[4] Under the pressure of such questions, gender identity and erotic desire have begun to look considerably less natural than they have often been taken to be here, and for that matter less natural than the Miller seems to take them to be. I think that the earlier critical discussions of the tale's naturalism capture quite well the Miller's preferred self-understanding. But the more recent critical development points us to the further question of what *other* understandings circulate through the text, and of how Chaucer conceived the Miller's relation to them. In what follows, I will argue that the weird sexiness of Absolon's kiss expresses a mobility of desire and gender identification that is deeply unsettling from a naturalistic perspective, and whose very possibility naturalism must deny. This is part of what I mean in referring to "naturalism and its discontents," and understood properly, I think, it brings with it significant consequences not only for a reading of the *Miller's Tale* but for an understanding of Chaucer's project in the *Canterbury Tales* as a whole.

That kind of argument, however, sounds less like a philosophical one – or at least less like a philosophical one we might attribute to Chaucer – than one dependent on relatively recent developments in feminism, psychoanalysis, and queer theory. It will be a central project of this chapter and this book to argue that what a number of critics have found to be Chaucer's feminist, psychoanalytic, and queer affinities can be understood in a new way, and one more responsive to how Chaucer might have conceived them, by attending to a philosophical analysis of practical rationality familiar to Chaucer from Boethius, and familiar to him in its extension to matters of gender and sexuality from a number of places, most centrally the *Roman de la Rose*. At the same time, attention to the issues raised in feminist, psychoanalytic, and queer criticism throws into relief the ethical and psychological import of Chaucer's philosophical interests. One need not adopt any of the specific technical arguments of psychoanalysis or other modern theories to make out Chaucer's understanding of these matters. Remaining agnostic with respect to such arguments, while pursuing an alternate path through some of the territory they mark out, can help us both to tell richer stories of the self-understanding of the past, and to understand more clearly what is at stake in accepting, modifying, or rejecting the theories through which our own culture seeks to understand itself.

The focus of this chapter will be on articulating more fully than the critical literature has so far the conceptual and affective structure of a naturalistic theory of desire, action, and identity. The Miller's commitment to such a theory, I will argue, serves as both a prop for and a disturbance to the normative masculinity the tale also embodies. But while both philosophical naturalism and the ideology of gender and desire with which it intersects in the tale will emerge in this discussion as sites of self-deception and misrecognition, my project will be less that of exposing ideological error than that of exploring what is compelling about naturalism and understanding what motivates it. In fact, I will argue that the very idea of such an exposure participates in the underlying assumptions that give naturalism its force.[5] What interests Chaucer in the *Miller's Tale*, I think, is the way naturalism expresses a picture of persons' relations to themselves and others that, however problematic, exerts a deep claim, and not only on the Miller. That claim will be of interest throughout this book; another reason I begin with the *Miller's Tale* is that it provides particularly condensed expression to a package of intuitions concerning identity, desire, and action to which Chaucer returns time and again in the *Tales*. And what gives those intuitions their power cannot be understood through an exclusive focus on gender and sexuality. No small part of naturalism's power stems from the way it links a set of normative intuitions concerning gender and desire to a broader theory of normativity as such, that is, a theory of what it means for the human creature, to adapt Paul's famous phrase, to "be a law to itself." Investigating the imaginative power of this broader theory can help us account for the pressures the Miller's conceptions of gender and desire are under, and pursuing an account of those pressures can help us understand how the ideological "regime of the normal" expressed in this tale gets constructed and inhabited. Further, an investigation of a naturalistic theory of normativity will land us squarely in philosophical territory, engaging problems in ethics and the theory of action concerning the relations of desire to its objects, to the actions of those who are moved by them, and to the identities of those whose desires they are. What makes the *Miller's Tale* philosophical, I will argue, is Chaucer's use of poetic resources to explore such problems, not in the abstract form of philosophical theorizing, nor through the representation of a distinct and coherent worldview, but by staging the dialectical play of the Miller's troubled engagement with them, an engagement for which gender and sexuality provide the central scenes. Chaucer's main goal is thus not the clarity of a solution to philosophical problems but rather an appreciation of what makes those problems deep, and what roots them down in our practical lives.

I will begin, then, by returning to the "naturalism of exceptional force and vitality" which, however problematic, seems nevertheless to inform the entire tale.[6] If this at first takes us far away from the spectacular strangeness and complex eroticism of Absolon's ill-fated kiss, I hope that in doing so it will enable us to return to that moment, and others that are perhaps less spectacular but just as interesting, and see in them a strangeness that is both more unsettling and more familiar than we otherwise might imagine.

ON NORMATIVE NATURALISM

As Muscatine, Kolve, and others have argued, various features of the *Miller's Tale*'s mode of representation, including narrative structure, characterization, tone, and the use of descriptive detail, suggests a picture of the human creature as a happy animal inhabiting a world in which it is perfectly at home.[7] Unlike the *Knight's Tale*, which takes place against a barren landscape in which all human projects seem to need elaborate management and are constrained by loss, absence, and ultimately death – so that, as Theseus says at the end of the tale, it seems that our true home must be somewhere else – the *Miller's Tale* represents a world of wonderful plenitude and freedom, alive with sensual experience and youthful energy, a place in which immersion in the pleasures of the here and now is all anyone could want. The central figure in this world is Alisoun, the object of desire that sets the plot and all of the male characters in motion; and, as the portrait of her that introduces her into the tale suggests, she functions as both the single most compelling instance of a desirable natural object and as a synecdoche for the plenitude of pleasures that the rest of nature offers: "She was ful moore blisful on to see / Than is the newe pere-jonette tree, / And softer than the wolle is of a wether" (I.3247–49); "Hir mouth was sweete as bragot or the meeth, / Or hoord of apples leyd in hey or heeth" (I.3261–62). Alisoun's centrality to the plot's and characters' energies, the perfect natural sensuousness of her portrait, and her status as a readily available object of desire, "For any lord to leggen in his bedde, / Or yet for any good yeman to wedde" (I.3269–70), all go to suggest two of the main ways in which the tale represents a world perfectly fitted to its human inhabitants, a world that is, in Marshall Leicester's apt phrase, "the plaything of one's projects."[8] First, this is a place in which everything you could want seems to be ready to hand, present for the immediate gratification of desire. Second, it is one in which what you want is compellingly clear, and is made so just by the natural disposition of the world: unless you are a pervert or a fool, and an even bigger pervert or fool than even Absolon, what you want is Alisoun.

For now I want to pass over the masculine, antifeminist, and heteronormative bias in this picture; the Miller pretty clearly has such a bias, and how and why it matters – and, in particular, what makes it more interesting than a mere occasion for critical exposure – will, I hope, become clear later. What needs clarifying first is just what it means to describe this picture as a species of naturalism. Kolve puts the point well in saying that the tale represents "an animal world in which instinct takes the place that reason holds for man, a world in which instinct and necessity are one."[9] As Kolve's appeals to instinct and necessity suggest, his point is about the practical normativity of "the natural," the way nature is supposed to settle questions of what to do, and so to take the place, at least initially, not of reason as a whole but of practical reason specifically. The tale presents a picture of human life according to which desire and its objects are determined by a set of naturally given facts: the fact that such a creature as Alisoun exists, for instance, is supposed to be enough to settle the matter when it comes to male erotic desire, which is the Miller's central case. That much says, in effect, that nature determines both our ends – the goals towards which action aims – and our disposition towards those ends, the motivational structure by which they appear as goals for us. If instinct takes the place of reason in the tale, then, it does so first of all because according to the Miller's picture there is no role for reason to play either in deciding what our ends are or in giving those ends a normative claim on us, in making them count for us.

The Miller's project of "quiting" the *Knight's Tale* to a large extent depends on the success with which he can make the practical normativity of "the natural" seem both self-evident and adequate to any needs reason might address. The Knight's narrative centers on moments like Palamon and Arcite's paralyzed love for the inaccessible Emily, the destruction of individual and civil concord to which that love drives them, and the transfixion of nearly everyone in the tale by their grief over Arcite's death. These are moments in which the world is anything but the plaything of our projects, moments in which the objects of our desires seem to call to us as though from behind some barrier or from infinitely far away. Such moments of privation and longing seem to the Knight and his characters to demand lyrical complaint or publicly edifying spectacle or efforts at philosophy, in each case as though the failure of desire to reach through to its object awakened a genuine need for several kinds of reflection: practical reasoning about what we really want or what we ought to do, and about how to make our beliefs about what to do effective at motivating us; but also speculative reasoning about who and what we are, about the nature of the world we inhabit, and about what it means that we suffer in the ways we do.[10] But as far as the Miller is concerned there can be no genuine needs here of any kind. If desires and their objects are transparent in just the way he thinks they are, then everything that counts about who we are and the world we live in must be transparent too; the reflective efforts of the Knight and his characters are not, as the Knight would have it, *responses* to privation, but ways of perversely *generating* a sense of privation where there is no genuine lack. The Miller, then, must make both practical and speculative reasoning seem excessive from a practical point of view, willful acts of self-mystification by a creature for whom nature has already provided all that happiness could require. Only then can the impulse to reflection shown in the *Knight's Tale* seem equivalent to its parodic appearances in the *Miller's Tale*: as the love Nicholas shows for his own gratuitous cleverness in deferring sex with Alisoun in order to concoct an elaborate plan to fool John; the ridiculous and self-regarding postures of Absolon as he sings silly love songs and plays Herod on a high scaffold; and John's gullible worries concerning an end of the world that anyone can see is not about to come, a concern that diverts him from the cuckolding taking place nearly under his nose.

To achieve this further defeat of reason the Miller must do more than insist on the natural determination of human ends and their motivational transparency. For a world in which desires and their objects were naturally determined could still leave plenty of room for the frustration of happiness, even a world as rich and alive with desirable things as that of the *Miller's Tale*. We could face conditions in which it was not immediately obvious how to get what we want; then there would still, at the very least, be a practical role for reason to play in determining the means to our ends. Lyrical and philosophical reflection might not immediately be called for, but calculation would, and in the right (or wrong) circumstances the calculation required could be quite elaborate, and could still result in frustration. In the extreme case we could find ourselves with no means at all, and the objects of our desires would then remain tantalizingly out of reach, as Emily in her garden is for the imprisoned Palamon and Arcite. Such a condition would hardly allow for the glad animal spirits of the *Miller's Tale*; a creature determined by instinct in this way might just as well be nature's victim as nature's favored child. And what is worse, such a creature might easily form the *thought* of itself as nature's victim; then the door would be open wide to the complaint and speculation the Miller finds so nonsensical. For the creature that formed this thought would no longer merely suffer its frustrations as it were in animal fashion, just by coming up short in its reach for whatever it happens to want at the moment. It would have a conception of itself as a suffering creature, and this conception would add to its suffering in a myriad of ways, allowing for anticipation and fear of future suffering, despair of relief, and so on; such a creature might even, like Palamon in the *Knight's Tale*, come to envy the animals instead of identifying with them.[11] For the Miller's project to get off the ground, then, he must suggest not only that nature determines our ends and provides for their motivational transparency, but also that nature determines and provides the means to our ends. Then the connection between desire and its objects will look completely seamless, and there will be no gaps left for practical reason to fill and speculative reason to reflect on.

The Miller manages this further suggestion partly through a wealth of descriptive detail that lays the circumstantial groundwork for the most central and the most trivial acts in the tale, so that the question of means can never so much as arise. Absolon may be reduced to courting Alisoun through her window, but the window is conveniently placed at a height that allows a kneeling lover to offer himself for a kiss; when Alisoun wants to chase Absolon off, there is a stone lying about in her bedroom, ready to be thrown; when Absolon wants to play Herod, there's a scaffold handy for his dramatic posturing, and when he wants revenge, there's a nearby blacksmith to lend a hot blade; when John's servant Robin wants to know what is happening behind Nicholas's locked door, he can peek through the hole the cat uses to creep in and out; and so on.[12] This descriptive density has the effect of suggesting a world so full of means to our ends that it is ready made for human action. That is what drives the Miller's polemic against the Knight home, for in a world with the plenitude of utterly compelling pleasures that this one offers, and one so dense with all imaginable means to our ends, instinct can do all the work of mapping out a course of action, and there is no practical function left for reason to play. The proper thing to do in such a world is just to reach out and take what you want, as "hende" Nicholas does early in the tale with Alisoun when "prively he caughte hir by the queynte" (I.3276), and as he seems to forget in concocting his elaborate ruse.[13] And given the extent to which nature has prepared the way for human happiness, fitting the world so perfectly to human desire that there is no space even for the question of means to come up, there is no space either for the sense of privation and suffering that gives rise to speculative reasoning in the *Knight's Tale*. The direct target of the Miller's polemic is practical reason, then, because he thinks that by defeating the need for practical reason in the way he does he will provide all the argument he needs to insure the defeat of speculative reason as well. If there is any role left for reason to play in human life, it would seem to be restricted to the happy contemplation of our good fortune as creatures blessed by nature. This, in effect, is what the Miller means his tale to be: a celebration of the blessed natural state of the human animal, a narrative expression of the particular pleasure we can take, as reflective creatures, in contemplating our inhabitation of a world that gives us everything we could want and ample opportunity to get it, a place in which there could never be a question about who we are or what we should do.[14]

I have meant the above account of the Miller's naturalism to be a way of spelling out the underlying conceptual commitments of his basic understanding of himself and his project in the tale. These commitments have been recognized in some form by many critics, and as I have already suggested, Muscatine and Kolve in particular have been helpful in suggesting that the way these commitments inform the tale's entire mode of representation makes it a case, as Muscatine puts it, of "fabliau . . . virtually made philosophical." I agree with Muscatine and Kolve that, however funny the tale is, Chaucer means it as more than an occasion for laughs, and as more than the expression of a churlish man who simply fails to see what the Knight's concerns are: the *Miller's Tale* engages the normative problems raised in the *Knight's Tale* with complexity and precision, rather than merely evading them with a joke. The further question I now want to pose is how to understand Chaucer's philosophical interest in that complex engagement. Muscatine, in unpacking his notion that Chaucer makes fabliau nearly philosophical, outlines what he takes to be the tale's "assertions" of "the binding, practical sequentiality of all events," of the "ethical imperative" of "physical action," and of "the purest fabliau doctrine, the sovereignty of animal nature."[15] Kolve gives explicit formulation to a view that is, I think, implicit in the critical procedures of Muscatine and many other critics when he says that the tale "presents a contrary view of human experience" to that of the Knight, and so "required of Chaucer the invention of a counter-art: nonhierarchic, nonhieratic, addressing no truth beyond itself."[16] What links Muscatine's and Kolve's claims is the idea that the tale expresses an essentially subjective worldview, a set of self-contained and self-consistent assertions, a pure doctrine that points only to its own truth. If that idea is right, then the way to locate Chaucer's philosophical interest in the tale is by laying out the theory the tale, and through it the Miller, assert; and in specifying the relations of the first two *Canterbury Tales*, we will say what most critics have said, that the Miller's theory opposes the Knight's, and, depending on how one understands those theories, that the Miller subverts the Knight's ideology, or lacks his greater wisdom, or simply sees things differently.

While I agree that the Miller's *theory* opposes the Knight's, I think there is more to be said about what it means to have such a theory, and what interests Chaucer in the Miller's having it, than emerges from attention to that theory considered as a set of propositions about the world given expression in literary form. As I will now argue, what makes Chaucer's project in the tale philosophical is his interest in naturalism as a site of misrecognition. In pursuing this interest, Chaucer stands squarely within the Socratic or Platonic philosophical tradition, with its central concern of tracking the dialectical relationship between what people are prepared to assert about themselves and the world and the competing beliefs they cannot articulate and would even disavow, but which nevertheless the pressure of philosophical reflection shows them to have. This concern is the basis both of Socratic method and Platonic dialogue, and as I will argue in chapter three, it is the basis as well of Boethius's use of dialogue form in the philosophical text with which Chaucer had the most frequent and deepest engagement, the *Consolation of Philosophy*. Let us turn, then, to the question of how the Miller inhabits the naturalistic views his tale expresses, the range of claims those views make on him, and the multiple ways he disposes himself towards those claims.

The character of the Miller's investment in his naturalistic theory begins to look a bit more complex than one of simple belief when we notice a peculiar paradox that attends a project of the kind he pursues. The various features of the tale that support a normative naturalism are targeted against what the Miller takes to be the enemy, a perverse refusal to live in the world like the happy animals he thinks we are. His polemical strategy is to hold the enemy up to a withering public laughter, first at the sheer folly of such a refusal, and second at the satisfying justice of the enemy's appropriate punishment, brought about by a series of narrative coincidences that seem to be less the effects of chance than signs of the natural order of things asserting themselves. What is peculiar about this, however, is that if anything like the Miller's naturalism were right, then there could not be such an enemy in the first place. If desire and its objects were determined by a set of naturally given facts in such a way that instinct alone picked out our ends and made them transparent to us, then there would be no room for the perverse displacements of desire that the Miller is so interested in exposing. Anything anyone did would be neither more nor less than the sign of instinct's operative power; the possibilities for action represented by the Knight, his characters, and their surrogates in the *Miller's Tale* would either simply be impossible, and no one would do anything like them, or they would not be perverse, since if they did exist they would just be another set of ways for naturally determined desire to operate. This, then, is the problem: the point of the Miller's naturalism seems to be its recommendation of an ethos, a way of life suited to the human animal; but a naturalistic view of human action – at least one as thoroughgoing as that expressed in this tale – cannot have the normative force the Miller wants of it. It cannot recommend one way of life over another, since on such a view there can be no such thing as going wrong.[17]

The point is abstract, and it will take some time to suggest its upshot for an understanding of the tale; but it is, I think, the crucial step for understanding the sense in which the tale might best be understood as philosophical, as well as the way Chaucer's interest in the misrecognitions naturalism requires opens out into his interest in the discontents to which my title refers, including those discontents for which gender and sexuality serve as central *topoi*. The initial force of the paradox can perhaps best be seen if we notice a related problem about the motivation for telling a tale such as this. Paradox notwithstanding, the Miller is clearly committed to a naturalistic repudiation of what he takes to be folly; that, on nearly everyone's account of the tale, is his main reason for telling it. His point seems to be that if there is such a thing as perversion, at least it can have no claim on him or those who think like him. But if we grant the thought, strictly unformulable in the Miller's terms, that the errors and perversions he parodies and punishes somehow do exist; and if we accept the supposed normative transparency of the natural, the plain fact as the Miller would have it that desires and their objects are just there to be seen, perspicuous and inherently compelling; then those who suffer from such errors would hardly be enemies to be argued with. They would be more like pathetic madmen, inexplicably blocked from the world that is before their eyes, worthy perhaps of pity or of a quick mocking dismissal, but not of the sustained effort of a polemic. If the Miller's victory can be so easily won, and if what counts about us and the world we inhabit is the joy we can take in our naturally blessed condition, then large portions of his narrative project look like a waste of time. He ought just to have left behind the aspects of his tale that mock the misguided and punish them for their foolishness, and have concentrated instead on straight appreciation of the world's bounty of the kind expressed in Alisoun's portrait. In this respect, then, the Miller's polemical project in the tale, with its dove-tailing plot that functions like an intricate narrative machine to bring his point home, looks disturbingly like Nicholas's plan to cuckold John, an excessively clever construction designed to crush an enemy that needs no defeating, a deferral of animal pleasure by a creature whose rational capacities have interposed themselves where they do not belong. In telling a tale that means to make normative claims of a naturalistic kind, the Miller locates himself both as the kind of creature for whom his own ethos cannot be right, and as the kind of creature who, in the terms of that ethos, is perverse.

The depth of the problem of perversity here begins to emerge if we imagine an alternative version of the tale that, unlike the Miller's, would concentrate on straight naturalistic appreciation.[18] Such a tale could still in a rather restricted sense have normative force: in its pure expression of glad animal spirits it could be taken to recommend itself as a model for human life. But it would not be able to give any expression to the normative problems to which it would be a response, the questions of what to do and how to live to which it would purport to give an answer: any such expression would be strictly ruled out from the beginning, since it would fall like a shadow across the tale's celebratory spirit, giving the lie to the views of action and motivation to which it must everywhere give voice. Such a tale would then be something more like a case of pure ideological posturing than the expression of an ethos, since its possibility would require a wholesale denial of the very problems that bring it into being. The *Miller's Tale* shares with this imagined case something of the quality of ideological posturing, since it too cannot squarely face the questions it purports to answer. But far from engaging in a wholesale denial of normative problems, the tale gives them loud expression in its polemical purpose. The Miller wants to recommend a way of life that the Knight and Absolon and their like are missing, and he wants to do so by exploring and exposing the error that leads them astray from their proper path. That motivation contaminates the Miller's naturalistic project from the ground up, as though in order to bring our condition as happy animals into view the Miller needed to cast it against an unaccountable perversion, an impossible possibility that, despite his apparent self-assurance, still does have a claim on him. What in the imagined case of pure naturalistic appreciation appeared only as a shadow slanting in from outside the narrative's scope appears here already on the inside, at the base of what sets the narrative in motion, at the heart of its deepest concerns. This shadow in the Miller's heart makes the relationship between the official naturalistic story and the inadmissible normative questions that motivate it more complex and unsettled than in the imagined case, and so makes of the *Miller's Tale* something considerably more interesting than a case of pure ideological bad faith.

The relation between the Miller's naturalism and the problems that motivate it might then be put as follows. It is the most evident thing in the world to the Miller that we can go wrong: he thinks that the Knight is wrong, that his whole romantic aristocratic ethos is wrong, that the social order that supports him and would silence the Miller's voice in favor of a more suitable one is wrong. The Miller cares about this; it is what motivates his speech from the beginning. The problem of ethical normativity, then – the problem we face of trying to find a right way, and of wanting to say what such a way might be, what makes it right, and how we can follow it – is the problem he wants to address, just as the Knight does. But the Miller's way of addressing this problem is to wish that it would go away, or more precisely to wish that it could never have arisen, that we were the kind of creatures for whom it could not arise, like animals who really are just moved by instinct's operative power, or perhaps like small children who do not yet have the responsibility of owning up to a course of action and having reasons for it. What the Miller imagines, then, is an "animal" or "childlike" condition in which normative problems would never have arisen, but in which the supposed fact of this condition plays the part precisely of providing an answer to as yet unasked, and indeed unaskable, normative questions. Normative naturalism thus gives voice to a nostalgic longing for a condition that, even from the Miller's own point of view, never was and never could have been.[19]

Chaucer's project in the *Miller's Tale*, as I see it, is one of exploring this paradoxical response to the problem of normativity, of representing its expression in a way that opens up spaces for thought both about what makes such a response compelling and about some potential consequences of the attempt to think this way. And this is essentially a philosophical project, although one for which the explicit representation of philosophical themes matters very little, and one for which issues of literary form and a concern for the conceptual and psychological dynamics of cases are essential. In fact, as I suggested earlier, we can say more precisely that Chaucer's project in the tale – and, I would argue, in the *Canterbury Tales* as a whole – is not only philosophical but, like the projects of Jean de Meun, Langland, and the *Pearl*-poet, dialectical. Philosophical dialectic frequently takes the literalized form of dialogue: in the aforementioned poets, as in Plato's dialogues and Boethius's *Consolation of Philosophy*, a figure given philosophical authority engages with interlocutors who often resist the arguments he or she makes, and in so doing give voice to their resistance to philosophical reflection. But, as I will argue with respect to Boethius in chapter three, philosophical authority itself has its source in beliefs, desires, and other attitudes which the interlocutors already have; the point of Socrates or Lady Philosophy making an argument is to unpack the inner logic of their interlocutors' views, revealing their incoherences and opacities, and thus exerting pressure on them to acknowledge the claim of views they disavow. As I have been arguing, in the *Miller's Tale* Chaucer reveals such incoherences and incapacities, and the dialectical relationship between the views the Miller avows and those he will not acknowledge, in the absence of dialogue form. Here there is no Lady Philosophy to lead the Miller through the tangle of his intuitions towards philosophical clarity; for what interests Chaucer centrally, both here and throughout his poetry, is less the production of clarity than an understanding and exploration of the tangle itself, of the necessarily opaque and incoherent situatedness from which people engage the problems philosophy tries to articulate.

THE PERVERSE REMAINDER

I began this chapter by claiming that the *Miller's Tale* links an ideology of gender and erotic desire, and specifically an ideology of normative masculinity, to a broader theory of practical normativity as such.

Having offered a sketch of that broader theory and the misrecognitions it entails, for the rest of this chapter I will focus on the question of how Chaucer's philosophical interests can help us read his interests in ideology and the psychology of erotic life, and how problems in the representation of gender and desire can help us better understand what is at stake philosophically for Chaucer in the tale.

The moment that perhaps links these concerns most explicitly is that of the Miller's confrontation with the Reeve in the tale's prologue. The Reeve has been angered by the Miller's announcement of a tale about the cuckolding of a carpenter, as though fears of his own wife's infidelity inclined him to take the coming story as a personal attack. The Miller replies by recommending to the Reeve his own attitude about such fears:

> I have a wyf, pardee, as wel as thow;
> Yet nolde I, for the oxen in my plogh,
> Take upon me moore than ynogh,
> As demen of myself that I were oon;
> I wol bileve wel that I am noon.
> An housbonde shal nat been inquisityf
> Of Goddes pryvetee, nor of his wyf.
> So he may fynde Goddes foysoun there,
> Of the remenant nedeth nat enquere.
> (I.3158–66)

The Miller wants this little piece of advice to communicate his sense of himself as a practical-minded purveyor of sound common sense, and up to a point this is just what the passage does. To judge yourself to be a cuckold, especially in the absence of compelling evidence, would reflect a pointless and excessive anxiety; the Reeve, like anyone else, would be much better off just believing that he is not one. This is advice straight from the heart of the naturalism that informs the tale, as becomes clear in the Miller's elaboration of it into the general principle of divine plenitude: as long as we can taste of God's plenty we should be happy, and there should be no need to worry about "the remenant." As in the tale, the world's plenitude is supposed to exempt us from the need to look beyond present satisfaction. Whatever is left over when a husband is satisfied is God's concern, or his wife's, but not his, and any inquiry into it is supposed to be as excessive as a Reevish marital suspiciousness.

To inquire into this "remenant," then, is just another way of erecting a barrier between ourselves and the objects of our desires, which in the absence of such artificial barriers are there for the taking.

As I have meant to suggest in eliding the "us" to whom the Miller means his general ethos to apply with the "husband" whose situation this passage more specifically describes, this advice also shares with the tale as a whole a tendency to universalize the perspective of an antifeminist heteromasculinity. While antifeminism has more virulent strains – the Miller's attitude towards his wife, as towards Alisoun, is after all a species of appreciation – "woman" as an object of appreciation here is fundamentally a means to an egocentric end, little more than a place for a man to find his own pleasure, as is suggested most starkly in the thought that the "there" in which "a husband" finds God's plenty is his wife's "pryvetee," that is her genitals, rather than *her*.[20] That egocentric pleasure-seeking, in turn, is what constitutes his desire for her, as indeed it constitutes desire more broadly speaking throughout the tale. While a respect for his wife's "pryvetee," in the sense of her privacy, may seem to provide a generous-minded alternative to this identification of the masculine with the free activity of pleasure-seeking and the feminine with passive objectification, it is really part of the same attitude, a way of seeming to grant his wife her freedom while allowing himself to ignore *her*. The recommended husbandly attitude towards the sexual availability of a wife here is roughly equivalent to the attitude one might take towards the food in a magic refrigerator that replenished itself whenever anyone ate from it: in such a case, it *would* be selfish, not to mention somewhat crazy, to care whether someone else ate from it, since you could always eat your fill. But in its application to another person, we could only call such an attitude generosity if we thought there were something generous about imagining our relations to erotic others as fundamentally like our relation to food, that is as a relation of consumption.[21] Indeed, as the Miller's comparisons of Alisoun to fruit and Muscatine's reference to her as "delectable" suggest, fantasies of consumption are an important feature of the way the Miller imagines the masculine relation to an erotic object.[22] To bring us back to the terms more directly in play in the passage under discussion, what licenses the recommended carelessness there is the equally ungenerous thought that what this husband cares about in the sexual relation is just "getting his." That is what constitutes his wife's value for him, and that is why what she does in her spare time is supposed to be of no consequence to him.

The attitude this passage expresses is, at least in some respects, a familiar one, and it finds frequent expression in the tale that follows. I think it matters to Chaucer both because it can so easily be recognized as the voice of a brand of patriarchal common sense and because there is a duplicity in the Miller's rejoinder to the Reeve that calls into question just what we think we recognize here. The Miller says that he does not care about his wife beyond her role as a source of his pleasure, and more than that, that husbands need not care about their wives in any other way. This is what licenses his decision to believe that he is not a cuckold: his belief, even if false, is supposed to give nothing away, and adopting it saves him from the perverse self-frustrations of those who, like the Reeve, do not simply follow nature's course. If that is the case, however, why does the Miller need to believe that he is not a cuckold, especially since such belief amounts, as he says it does, to an act of will? According to the logic of his own announced position, as long as his potential cuckoldry does not interfere with his wife's erotic availability to him, and so with her function as the ready-to-hand locus of his satisfactions, it just should not concern him, and he should need no particular beliefs about the matter at all. The Miller should, in effect, be even more careless than he manages to be, and his decision to adopt a belief in this regard suggests that the thought of his potential cuckoldry matters to him in a way he refuses to acknowledge. This is so even if we think of the danger of cuckoldry as being primarily its threat to a purely ego-centric sense of manly mastery and pride rather than to the character of his marital relations. That his wife's "pryvetee," in the absence of any diminished erotic availability of her, could pose such a threat at all already suggests that she is more than just a locus of present satisfactions. And that suggests that no matter how unconcerned he claims to be with his wife's private affairs, he is not content simply to take God's plenty where he finds it and leave the rest for someone else. Even if he were receiving all the "foyson" he could handle, his wife's private activities are something more than a superabundance of plenty that does not concern him.

My point is not that the Miller is "really" afraid he is a cuckold. To locate the causal source of this passage's duplicities in some imagined antecedent psychological fact like a fear of cuckoldry would be to miss the scope of the problem the Miller faces: it is not merely "personal," the sign of a bad marriage or a nervous character, and it is not restricted to the erotic context that provides its occasion. That is partly because these duplicities are ideological, part of larger structurings of gender and desire that do not depend on anyone's particular sexual experiences. But even within the Miller's own engagement with these issues, the ambivalence of his posture of carelessness towards his wife is part of a broader ambivalence in his posture of carelessness towards "the remenant," towards whatever remains of the world's pleasures when he is done with them; and here as well the Miller does not manage to be as careless as his own views require. For it is one thing to say that we *need* not inquire into an innocent remainder, quite another to say, as the Miller also does, that we *should* not be inquisitive. If we ought simply not to care about "the remenant" as long as the world's plenitude is available to us, then a prohibition of inquiry seems as oddly excessive as a decision to believe in the fidelity of one's wife. The "remenant" should just be the sum of pleasures we do not find the occasion to enjoy, something that could never make a claim on us, something we would never need to confront or deny. But apparently God has his secrets too, secrets that, like a wife's, one might not want to know: the entire constitution of the world, or some coming fate, may make of the Miller's recommended carelessness nothing more than a willful blindness, and he knows it. Under the pressure of the Miller's prohibition, then, another "remenant" comes into existence behind or beneath the "remenant" that is just the innocent remainder of untasted pleasures: a shadow remainder that functions as a receptacle for things best kept out of sight.

This shadow remainder haunts the Miller's picture of a world of plenty perfectly fitted to desire in much the same way that the category of the perverse does. In each case, the Miller declares himself to be unimplicated in whatever possibilities shimmer into existence there: they are simply external to him, occupants of the empty spaces beyond the proper life of the human animal. And in each case, the declaration of nonimplication is partly motivated by a claim that these empty spaces continue to exert. Further, in the face of this ongoing claim, the Miller's commitment to drawing a firm line between the natural and the perverse, between the all-encompassing space of God's plenty and the remainder where secrets go to hide, seems to leave him on both sides of the line at once, as a happy creature of nature and a secret pervert. God and his wife may be harboring damaging secrets, but the most damaging secrets seem to be the ones the Miller is harboring from himself, the inner companions to the metaphysical and erotic secrets that may be out in the world waiting for him.

A moment ago I said that my point is not that the Miller is really afraid he is a cuckold, and I want to be clear here that my point is not that he is really, secretly, a pervert. I do not mean to suggest that there just is some secret there, waiting to be exposed, but rather that a worry about secrecy, however muted by the Miller's loud avowals of carelessness, is a structural product of the way he responds to the problem of normativity. According to the Miller's naturalistic theory of action, questions of what to do or how to live are settled by two fundamental relationships we have to the contents of our inner lives. The first is one of observation. Those contents, paradigmatically our desires, are introspectively available; all we need to do to determine what they are is look and see the plain facts of nature in us. The second is one of passivity. Once we have seen what our desires are there is nothing further for us to do to make them effective at moving us; it is just of their essence that they reach through us, commanding us the way a desire for Alisoun or for one of those succulent ripe fruits on the "pere-jonette tree" is supposed to do. These two features together are what yield the motivational transparency of the natural on such a view. One of the problems with this, as I suggested earlier, is that in a sense it leaves no room for being wrong. Anything anyone does becomes the sign of a naturally determined desire's operative power, and if "being natural" is the reason an action counts as right, then any action will be right. But we might also say here that if the Miller wants to hold on to the notion of error and the category of perversity, as he clearly does, then if someone acts in a way the Miller deems to be perverse, then this too must be the sign of a naturally determined desire in operation: on this view it would just be a natural fact that some desires are perverse and the people who have them are perverts.[23] And this thought helps to specify the character of the problem the Miller faces in being the kind of creature who, in terms of his own ethos, is perverse. For if his way of conducting himself in the tale or elsewhere shows signs of motives that his naturalism does not endorse – signs, that is, of the ongoing claim of the perverse and of whatever constitutes that "remenant" no one is supposed to care about – then such motives on the Miller's own account can only be present in him as features of his nature, characteristics of a secret perverse self he never knew he was.

The Miller's posture of carefree animality is supposed to insure that such secrets cannot exist. But the naturalism by means of which he seeks to justify this posture has the effect not of dispelling the possibility of such secrets but of reifying them into mysterious presences that then become the objects of a prohibition, an imperative not to look: what he means to be a way of dispelling any worries about metaphysical and erotic secrecy, the kinds of worries that seem to him to drive the Knight and the Reeve, only reinforces those worries by closeting them. One powerful form that the Miller's longing for a state of carefree animality takes, then, is something like a phenomenology of the closet, a relation-ship to a territory of secrecy which he is committed to saying does not exist and cannot matter, and which has the hold it does on him precisely by virtue of the way he seeks to deny it.[24] This is not to say that there are some naturally given facts in the Miller's closet, waiting to be known. The whole conception of a person's inner life as having a space of secrecy in it, composed of determinate inner objects potentially avail-able to introspection even if clouded by self-deception, and compelling merely by virtue of their interior presence, is part of the self-deception involved in the Miller's naturalism. The phenomenology of the closet at issue here is thus one in which a restless, unlocalizable worry appears not as the opposite of a careless self-gratification but as its hidden other face, the same thought in different form.

AGENCY, GENDER, AND THE CONSTITUTION OF THE PERVERSE

I have argued that the Miller responds to the problem of normativity in part by dispersing its claims into the various perversions represented in the tale, and that in doing so he constructs them as sites of an interior secrecy he does not want to examine. To understand the specific contours of those sites – to understand, that is, Chaucer's project of exploring the psychology of secrecy and disavowal attending normative naturalism and the ideology of gender and desire with which it intersects – we need to look more closely at the perversions and the various fates they meet. The place to start, however, is not with the perversions themselves, but with what very nearly amounts to their opposite, the figure of Alisoun. For while she provides the cornerstone of the normative views by which perversion is judged in the tale and gender and eros are brought within the orbit of the Miller's preferred version of "the natural," this very function produces perverse effects that will help us understand what happens to Nicholas, Absolon, and John.

As the description of Alisoun as synecdoche for nature's plenitude and her function in the tale as the unmoved mover of male desire suggests, the narrative proceeds as though to be human just is to be a man desiring a woman, and to be a woman is little more than to be the thing men desire – that is, as though the contrast between male and female straightforwardly tracked a contrast between activity and passivity, or more precisely between being an agent and being a place, object, or locus of activity; and further, as though a possessive heteromasculine desire were the only form desire could take.[25] What makes each of the male characters perverse from this perspective is the particular way each fails to respond properly to Alisoun, and so fails to participate adequately in the surrounding ideology of gender and desire. But there is an aspect of Alisoun's representation that is fundamental to her function in the tale, but that cannot be accommodated to the set of oppositions on which these views of gender and desire are based. For the Miller means his picture of the human to have quite a general scope, to describe not just how it is for him, or even how it is for men, but how it is for everyone; and if any of his characters manages to exemplify this picture in its ideal form rather than a perversion or deformation of it, it is Alisoun.[26] She alone never acts in such a way as to erect an artificial barrier between herself and her own pleasure; she alone consistently lets instinct settle questions of what to do, or rather lets it prevent those questions from even arising; and as a result she alone remains unpunished by the crushing inevitability of cause and effect at the tale's end. The Miller, then, identifies with Alisoun as the perfect exemplar of the human on his own account, the embodiment of the ethos he lays claim to and recommends, even as she also serves as a purely passive object of desire, the thing outside the all-male world of action that sets that world in motion.

Here as elsewhere, then, an analysis of the ambivalences of gender and desire in the *Miller's Tale* depends on an analysis of the tale's engagements with ethics and the theory of action. For if it is puzzling that Alisoun seems to serve mutually exclusive functions in the tale, as passive object and as perfect exemplar of action, there is a sense in which this is just what we should expect from a figure of fully realized normative naturalism. On a naturalistic account action is, oddly, at its base a species of passivity, a way of being moved by forces to which we make no contribution: the only thing we do with respect to those forces is observe them, like objects in a kind of inner theater. Or alternatively, insofar as this view is supposed to tell us how to act rather than just describing what it is we do when we act, then when we act rightly, we do not make a contribution to these forces; if we make a contribution, it seems, the only kind it could be is the perverse one of turning our desires from their proper path. To say that the Miller identifies with Alisoun, then, is in part to say that she serves as the best figure for these two basic features of his view of action, an under-lying passivity on the one hand, and a spectatorial relationship to desires on the other. That is why she never violates the tale's ethos, and is never violated by the operations of its plot. The fact that this also means that she is excluded from the territory of action into the status of an object, then, can help us bring into further focus the sense in which the Miller suffers from a kind of nostalgic longing. For Alisoun's double function amounts to the recognition, however dim, that his view of action is in fact a wish for escape from the conditions of agency, a wish to be passive with respect to his own motivations, and so to become a pure and perfect object – a wish that is already foregone by the time it finds expression, since it arises, as I have said, precisely in response to the need to find a right way of acting.

This suggests that the problem with Alisoun's representation has an inwardly directed version as well: we might say that, as manly a man as the Miller is, his own preferred version of himself looks like a woman, or at least like what he takes a woman to be. One occupant of the Miller's "remenant," then, is a wish to be, or be like, a woman, and while such a wish must be an embarrassment to the Miller's most prevalent attitudes, a secret shame that can never be acknowledged, it is also quite directly the product of those attitudes. And more: if to be the perfect human is to be, or be like, a woman, we might just as well say what the narrative trajectory of the tale also suggests, that to be a man is to be perverse, and to deserve punishment. And here too we find support from the Miller's naturalistic views, for according to them to be a man – to be the active one, the doer, rather than the site or locus or object of the action – is to make a contribution to the forces that move you, to interpose yourself between desire and its issuance in action: this is what the Miller and all his male characters do in failing to remain transparent to the motive force of natural desire. What emerges from the intersection of the Miller's naturalistic ethos with the gender views that seem so tightly bound to it, then, is a wish for a kind of effeminacy, which takes the form of a desire to castigate whatever in him is masculine. This, in effect, is the gender-inflected form that his broader wish to escape his condition as an agent takes.

While the punishments visited on Nicholas, Absolon, and John are nominally directed towards external enemies, then, they are first of all directed towards the Miller himself, as ways of imagining a self-castigation that need never reveal itself as such. I will begin with Nicholas, for his case is most fully accommodated to the terms generated by the Miller's ethos. As I have already suggested, this "handy" man nearly remains faithful to the vision of a world provided for his own practical use, and his reward is a night "in bisynesse of myrthe and of solas" (I.3654) with Alisoun; and while his plan for cuckolding John exceeds the pure goal of appreciative immersion in the world's plenitude, it does so in much the same way as the Miller's tale does, and the Miller seems to regard it with gleeful enjoyment as much as suspicion. The punishment for Nicholas's tendency to defer animal satisfaction – the punishment the Miller brings on his own masculinity – is the humiliation and pain of being struck "amydde the ers" (I.3810) by Absolon's hot borrowed blade. The initial thought here seems to be that Nicholas, having displaced his erotic impulse into the more intellectual pleasure of a carefully orchestrated trickery, needs to be brought back to the material fact of his body by way of pain. Pain, then, is supposed to do what eros was initially supposed to do but could not, for the Miller any more than for Nicholas: provide a territory of sheer animal sensation incapable of being gotten wrong, incapable of being rerouted or reinterpreted, a sensation that can just be seen for what it is, and that, being seen, presents an agent with a transparent motive, in this case a motive to cry out and seek relief. Part of what counts about Nicholas's pain, then, is that it is overwhelming; it makes him passive with respect to its motive force; in the face of it, we might say, the body takes over. But part of what counts about it is also that it is humiliating, and humiliating precisely because of the way it makes him passive. The clever man who thought he could become a little prime mover in the world is reduced to his animality; his rationality is humiliated, and so is *he* – there is, in this moment, nothing of him that he *could* interpose between affect and action.

But if pain is supposed to provide a site of subjective determinacy and transparency, and so to rescue the key elements of a naturalist theory of action and identity from the trouble gender and eros create for it, that trouble reemerges when we ask exactly what happens to Nicholas. Given the shape of a colter – the thin blade at the front of a plow that makes an initial cut in the soil to prepare the way for the larger plowshare – and given Absolon's intention of taking vengeance on Alisoun and her "hole," one possibility the scene suggests is that of Nicholas receiving Absolon's blade in *his* hole "amydde the ers."[27] The function of anal penetration as the mechanism of humiliation and pain would then be that of extending Nicholas's newly restored passivity to the territories of eros and gender. For what needs humiliating is not just Nicholas's rationality but also his manliness, his existence as the doer of erotic life: he must be broken down, made forcibly into the feminized man that alone can be in possession of an agency with a passivity at its base, and so can live according to naturalistic norms. Since the Miller wants to live according to those norms – since he wants to be the passive agent, and wants this punishment visited on himself as much as he wants it visited on Nicholas – another occupant of the Miller's "remenant" is a desire for the scourging humiliation of anal penetration. This is one paradigmatic form of what he imagines the desire to be passive, to be acted upon rather than to act, to involve. But it is not the only form at issue here. For however powerfully the scene alludes to anal penetration, it stops short of actually depicting it; and the hand's-breadth of skin burned off Nicholas is broad enough to open other possibilities.

In a highly suggestive reading of the tale, Glenn Burger has argued that we are invited to see the moment as a cauterizing rather than a penetrative thrust.[28] If the Miller thinks of Nicholas's imaginative excess as a wound in need of cauterizing, then he figures that excess as a site of leakiness that should be sealed off, and associates it with the feminine through the "wound" of that other leaky "hole" in whose place Nicholas has put his own. Nicholas's anus is thus still in the picture, and still a threat to masculine propriety. On this account, however, the most readily apparent aim of the Miller's self-punishment is that of mortifying the shamefully feminized man, sealing him back up into the hard, self-enclosed body that ought to be his, rather than, as in the anal penetration reading, that of forcibly producing the feminized man the Miller's ideology requires. I do not think we need to choose between these readings, however incompatible they may be; the passage suggests both without giving any definitive depiction of just what Absolon has done, and if Chaucer had wanted to give such a depiction he certainly could have done so. The passage's suggestive openness, its way of simultaneously expressing shame at and desire for feminization in performing its basic function of a humiliating return to passivity, is one of many places in the tale in which Chaucer indicates how indeterminate the contents of the Miller's "remenant" must be, and how tortured the logic by which naturalism gets instantiated.

In the interpenetration of a shameful and desirable effeminacy with a wish for mortification, we begin to touch on the territory opened by the figure of Absolon, in whom the Miller explores effeminacy and its ideologically appropriate punishment with a thoroughness that borders on delectation. Absolon, more than any other character in the tale, suffers from an inability to live the life of a happy animal. He is deeply taken with the postures of love-longing – lyrical and dramatic expressions of passion, vows of servitude, wakeful nights – all of which take such ridiculous forms that they seem designed to keep the possibility of an erotic payoff at bay, and so to prolong the time of a theatrical self-regard as much as possible. Absolon's displacement of the erotic impulse suggests a certain aversion towards what, on the Miller's account, ought to be its proper object; and in the context of his squeamishness about farting, his fastidious speech, and his obsession with fresh breath, this aversion begins to look like it has its source in a more general aversion towards the human body and its orifices, the places where inside and outside meet. As far as the Miller is concerned this is all quite unmanly, as he makes clear through repeated suggestions that Absolon is infantile and effeminate, most notably in the moment when Absolon tries to woo Alisoun through self-infantilization and self-effeminization: "I moorne as dooth a lamb after the tete" (I.3704); "I may nat ete na moore than a mayde" (I.3707). We can unpack Kolve's notion that the hole-kissing brings Absolon into contact with "the real nature of what he sought," then, as follows. Being a man, Absolon wants *this*: a creature with holes and hair, with a body, just like him, a piece of the natural world, a solid chunk of physical reality; and the disgust and humiliation he shows afterwards, as he rubs his lips with sand and straw and chips and weeps like a beaten child, while it shows him cured of the extravagances of love *paramours*, confirms him in the foolish aversion to reality and bodiliness that led to those extravagances in the first place, and so underlines the justice of the moment that exposes and punishes him.

The thought that the Miller's punishment of Absolon is also a self-punishment may seem more counterintuitive than the same thought in the case of Nicholas, for while the fondness in the Miller's representation of Nicholas makes an identification between the two relatively straightforward, the representation of Absolon is all mockery and disdain. But it should not be surprising that an unacknowledged wish for what looks to the Miller like effeminacy should involve disdain for a figure that embodies that wish directly. Further, there is a deeper sense in which Absolon embodies the Miller's ideal, or rather a peculiar kind of literalization of it that reveals its consequences more thoroughly even than Alisoun does. For Absolon seems to have nothing but a spectatorial relationship to desire; he seems to want to do nothing with respect to his desires but observe their display; in Absolon, the reduction of action to observation and passivity has become complete. The figure of Absolon, then, gives expression to the thought that the very views by which the Miller supports his sense of carefree manliness have as their upshot something he finds disgustingly unmanly, an aversion to the body and to the female, which he otherwise wishes to represent as the ultimate object of male desire. This aversion is yet another occupant of the Miller's closet, as is its companion here, the desire to punish himself

for it by way of a humiliating confrontation with the body that simultaneously arouses and disgusts him.

We can further understand this mingling of arousal and disgust
by turning to another feature of the scene that links it to that of
Nicholas's punishment. Just as Chaucer suggests that Nicholas is
both sodomized and cauterized and that the Miller's investment in
the scene depends on both possibilities, so here he conflates Alisoun's
vagina and anus into one "hole" to suggest that the Miller's joke on
Absolon depends on incompatible pictures of what Absolon kisses and
how that matters.[29] On the one hand, the Miller states that Absolon
"kiste hir naked ers," and he must be thought to do so for the moment
to produce the monumental disgust in him that makes his punishment so fitting. On the other hand, for the scene to achieve its purpose
of exposing the "real object" of masculine desire, Alisoun's genitals
must be thought to be at issue when she puts her hole out the window,
as indeed they must when Absolon confronts that long-haired thing
that seems in the dark to be a bearded face, unless Alisoun has an
extraordinarily hairy ass. But doing both jobs at once with Alisoun's
"hole" requires the Miller to gloss over the distinction between what,
on his view, is desirable and what is disgusting – as again he must, and
even more directly, in the punning punch-line that follows the scene,
"his hoote love was coold and al yqueynte" (I.3754) – as though at this
central moment in the Miller's gesture of comic exposure he could no
longer tell the difference between what arouses desire and what
quenches it, or could not make the difference stick. The effect of
this conflation is to keep the self-humiliation the Miller figures in the
scene squarely in the territory of erotic desire, in the form of an erotics
of disgust and self-degradation that inflects both the Miller's imaginative identification with the feminine and his picture of intimate
contact with the female body. But the Miller hardly has a settled,
univalent relationship to such an erotics. The most readily apparent
aim of self-punishment here, as in the cauterizing of Nicholas's anal
"wound," is that of mortifying the passive agent or feminized man.
But the desire to mortify the passive agent is at the same time a desire
for the Miller's core normative ideal to be broken down, and so for
the collapse of a major support for the naturalized masculinity that
authorizes his disdain of a figure like Absolon.

The unsettledness evident in the Miller's diagnostic and punitive impulses becomes even more evident when we turn to John; for John's perversity and punishment, unlike those of Nicholas and Absolon, never even provisionally comes into focus in the terms provided by a normative naturalism. In the Miller's initial portrait of John we hear that "Jalous he was, and heeld [Alisoun] narwe in cage, / For she was wylde and yong, and he was old / And demed hymself been lik a cokewold" (I.3224–26). This description makes John look like a figure for a self-defeating Reevish worry that provokes the very situation it fears: it would seem that John's problem is a refusal of the carelessness the Miller avows, a refusal to be happy with what he can get from Alisoun without asking too many questions. But we never see John as the jealously restrictive husband, despite the opportunities the Miller has to cast him in such a light.[30] Instead John seems completely unpossessive of Alisoun, leaving her unguarded on his many business trips and remaining sublimely unconcerned on an obvious occasion for jealousy, when Absolon awakens him in the night singing love songs to Alisoun at his window. The Miller wants, of course, to cast this as folly in itself, since it leaves John vulnerable to Nicholas's machinations and Alisoun's betrayal. But charging John with an incompatible jealousy and unguardedness hardly helps in diagnosing his error; and worse, the only apparent space afforded in the Miller's view to an unpossessive desire for another of the kind John seems to have for Alisoun is that of the very carelessness the Miller says John violates. In fact, John becomes very nearly a mouthpiece for another feature of the Miller's avowed carelessness, a general commitment not to know secrets, when he echoes the Miller's comment from the tale's prologue: "Men sholde nat knowe of Goddes pryvetee" (I.3454). In this sense John begins, as Nicholas and Absolon do, to become a figure for an aspect of the Miller's naturalism, and the Miller seems to be setting up his own self-deception for punishment. But on closer inspection John cannot even be described in these terms. The first thing we learn about him is that "he lovede [Alisoun] moore than his lyf" (I.3222), and the strength of his love for her is borne out by his immediate reaction to Nicholas's news of the impending flood: " 'Allas, my wyf! / And shal she drenche? Allas, myn Alisoun !' / For sorwe of this he fil almoost adoun, / And seyde, 'Is ther no remedie in this cas?' " (I.3522–25). The fact that John loves Alisoun more than he does his own life, that the end of the world for him means first of all her death, provides the wedge in his psyche that opens him to Nicholas's plot. It also provides the clearest case for his perversity on the Miller's account; for the Miller's carelessness, and his entire view of motivation, is predicated on nothing mattering more than one's own life. More pointedly, no *one* can matter that much. Other people are at most the objects or instruments of self-gratification: in the genesis of motivation, self-interest always comes first.[31] This is something even Nicholas and Absolon, perverse as they are, seem to realize. Their problem is that in seeking self-gratification they transfer their attention from their ends to the means of achieving them, and so displace the properly gratifying object from view; but for all that they are still after self-gratification, and with a little chastising their knowledge that Alisoun is the properly gratifying object can be brought back into focus for them. But this saving knowledge is not available to John; he is too far gone, outside the realm of a fundamental self-interest altogether, into a territory of motivation the Miller has no easy way of imagining, even as its alienness from a naturalistic view is palpable to him.

The extent of that alienness will become clearer if we notice another feature of John's character, a general willingness to be moved by altruistic motives, as shown by his fears for Nicholas's health and life when Nicholas has locked himself in his room as the first step in his trick. John is the only character in the poem for whom altruism is even raised as a possibility. The closest anyone else comes is Gerveys the blacksmith's indifferent willingness to lend Absolon his blade, but unlike Gerveys, John is actively concerned to attend to others' needs, even when doing so serves no apparent self-interest. This is a big mistake according to the Miller's theory, a point he underlines by making John's altruistic inquiry the step by which he enters into Nicholas's plot. Still, John's altruism is easier to accommodate to naturalistic intuitions than is his love for Alisoun; for altruism can be sorted with a thought that motivates and underlies the Miller's view of motive, namely that there is a clean split to be made between a concern for oneself and a concern for others.[32] This split is what allows for the thought that a concern for oneself always comes first, preceding any concern for another; and it can be preserved even when the possibility of altruism is admitted. The thought would then be that there is a clean distinction to be made between altruism and egoism: in a given instance, one is moved by one or the other, and the Miller's point would be that being moved by anything but egoistic concerns is foolish. Love, however, is a harder case, for it cannot be sorted so easily. John's reaction to the thought of a flood is clearly not motivated by a fundamental self-interest of the kind the Miller's other characters display. What moves him is the thought that Alisoun will die, not the thought that he will lose a major source of self-gratification; and further, we would expect an egoistic concern to express itself here in something notably lacking in John's reaction, a fear of his own death. But if love is not the expression of a fundamental egoism, neither is it a form of pure other-directedness. John is not moved by sheer impersonal concern for another, as though, for instance, he recognized an impartial duty to save Alisoun. It never occurs to him to worry about the rest of mankind perishing; and it is hardly the expression of a sense of duty when the sorrowful thought of Alisoun's death almost brings him to the ground, or when, imagining the flood drowning her, he quakes with fear and breaks into uncontrollable weeping and wailing. The disaster he faces is deeply personal; it goes to the heart of him, to what matters most to the particular person he is; only his heart cannot be figured in egoistic terms, or in any other terms that derive their significance from the underlying thought that a concern for oneself can be neatly distinguished from a concern for others.

In a sense, then, it is clear enough what makes John perverse on the Miller's account, and so what the Miller means to castigate in himself by way of John's punishment: John wants to be a lover, and to be loved; he wants intimacy of a kind that makes a concern for the desired other a constitutive feature of his concern for himself, and that makes her something without which he has no life he can recognize as his own. But since the Miller's naturalism offers no way of understanding such desires, all of the terms it provides misdescribe John, and in doing so create the need for further descriptions, even if they are incompatible with the ones that came before. So even as the Miller wants to say that John is a fool for love, he tries to cast this folly as jealousy and possessiveness, as though caring for someone as much as John does could only be a kind of hyper-possessiveness, an instance of the impulse to possession which has lost touch with the carelessness that is supposed to go along with it. But the Miller knows this cannot be right; he knows that John and the Reeve are worlds apart. This is the reason, I think, for the odd formulation by which the Miller tries to cast John's attitude as a version of Reevish suspiciousness, saying that he "demed hymself been lik a cokewold" (I.3226). Nothing John does suggests he thinks himself *likely* to be a cuckold. But from a naturalistic perspective, he is in a certain sense *like* a cuckold, for he has already been "betrayed" in the integrity of his narrow self-interest by the claim on him of another, who is free to return his love or not. Since John obviously does consider himself to be subject to that claim, he can in this sense be said to judge himself to be like what the Miller takes a cuckold to be, someone who lacks a relation of perfect possession to the object of his desire. The fact that he lacks this relation for a reason practically the opposite of the Reeve's – because the trope of perfect possession does not apply to his attitude rather than because it does apply but he fears it has been violated – only serves to underline the Miller's problem in bringing John into clear view. Nicholas and Absolon can at least be provisionally identified from a naturalistic point of view, and thus can be punished with a precision designed to set them back on the right path; but there is no setting John right, for from the point of view from which he appears to be perverse there is no way to say even what he is.[33] Instead the Miller does the only thing he can, bringing John in for as heavy a punishment as possible, having him suffer a broken arm, betrayal by his wife, and a resounding public humiliation in which his folly is made into a huge joke, he is held by everyone to be mad, and any explanation he tries to offer is drowned in the ensuing laughter. If John cannot be set right because he cannot be identified, he will simply be broken, and broken in such a way that everyone sees there is no identifying him: he is outside the space of intelligible discourse altogether, simply insane.

The problem posed by the figure of John, then – the problem the Miller poses for himself through the figure of John – is that of the lover, the one who desires intimacy. This problem is so deep because the Miller knows that intimacy cannot be what his picture says it must be, simply a matter of coming close to some desired object by possessing it. If that is so, then the problem of intimacy cannot be figured in terms of a contrast between masculine and feminine that tracks contrasts between activity and passivity, agent and place; and someone who desires intimacy cannot be figured as having the kind of relations to herself that naturalism imagines, namely, relations of observation and passivity between her and the objects that make up her inner life. I will explore each of these features of the problem at greater length; they are perhaps only implicit in what I have said so far. But first I want to be clear about what I think the bare fact of the Miller's interest in intimacy suggests. With an acknowledgment of the problem of intimacy the Miller's entire naturalistic posture is made more deeply problematic than it is by any of the perverse phenomena we have examined so far, for those phenomena have each in their own way participated in the commanding tropes by which the Miller's picture finds expression. In fact we should expect that something would exceed the representational capacity of these tropes, since, as I have been arguing, naturalistic convictions cannot provide the terms for their own understanding. In the problem of intimacy, then, we find the specification within the Miller's preferred arena of erotic life of the more general problem posed by his views as a whole: just as the only way to understand the Miller's denial of the normative problem is to see that denial as a response to the normative problem, so here the only way to understand the denial of the problem of intimacy is to see that denial as a response to the problem of intimacy.

The problem of intimacy – or, a bit more specifically, the problem of love conceived as a species of intimacy – was one of Chaucer's central interests throughout his poetic career, and it will remain a central interest throughout this book, especially in the final two chapters. Another reason I begin this book with the *Miller's Tale*, then, is that the tangle of naturalistic commitments in the tale and the discontents those commitments produce – a tangle that at first takes root in the ground of an objectifying, possessive erotic desire – leads to an engagement with intimacy that can neither be collapsed into such desire nor cleanly distinguished from it, however clear and distinct our definitions of the two may be. That is to say that Chaucer's interest in love is itself dialectical; or so at least I will argue as this book progresses. For now, let us remain with the version of that interest Chaucer pursues here.

In the Miller's case, an engagement with the problem of intimacy is most immediately evident with John, but pressures similar to those that appear in his representation appear as well in the figures of Alisoun,

Nicholas, and Absolon. The attempt to imagine these characters in the Miller's preferred terms, after all, produces the paradoxical figures of the passive agent and the feminized man, figures that the narrative simultaneously valorizes and repudiates: the conflict of intuitions and impulses here suggests the restlessness that becomes most insistent with John. To explore fully the form taken in the narrative by a desire for intimacy and its denial, then, we need to return to the figures in whom the Miller manages that denial more successfully, to suggest how, in spite of this, the problem of intimacy does arise, as the very motivation for its denial.

IMAGINING INTIMACY

Again it will be helpful to begin with Alisoun; for if intimacy is at issue in the tale, she is the embodiment of what the Miller imagines the presumptively masculine agent wanting to be near, and a desire for that nearness is the Miller's paradigm for what moves an agent to act. As I have argued, the Miller thinks of this nearness as a kind of touching, the kind expressed so gleefully by Nicholas when he teases John with a joke John is in no position to understand: "And after wol I speke in pryvetee / Of certeyn thyng that toucheth me and thee" (I.3493–94). The laugh here comes from the thought that the matter which pertains to Nicholas and John is actually a *thing* that *touches* them, or rather, that they touch; and the Miller allows Nicholas this joke because while John is supposed to think that this thing is just his, in touching John's thing – that is, in touching Alisoun's – Nicholas gets possession of the object of John's desire.[34] I have already suggested that Alisoun's status as an exemplar of action presents a problem for such a reifying account of what she essentially is; but it also presents a problem for such an account of what it would mean to want to be near her. For the Miller knows that in wanting to touch her, one wants to touch not just a thing, but an agent; not just an object, but a subject of desire. Here we should remember the Miller's warnings about inquisitiveness in the tale's prologue: "an housbonde shal nat been inquisityf / Of Goddes pryvetee, nor of his wyf." "Wyf" here is commonly read as an abbreviated possessive parallel to "Goddes," rendering the sense of the warning as "husbands should not be inquisitive of their wives' secrets," or, following the *double entendre*, "husbands should not be inquisitive of their wives' genitals." But the lines also just say that husbands should not be inquisitive about their wives, period. According to the Miller's ideology, this is all supposed to amount to the same thing: wives just *are* their genitals, and it is better not to be inquisitive about any secrets concerning those things, since they may have been busy with someone else. But in the context of the Miller's problems in keeping the notion of "woman" or "wife" clearly determined by that of "thing to be possessed or enjoyed," another thought expressed in this warning against inquiring into wifely "pryvetee" is that in order to keep thinking of your wife as defined by her genitals, and in order to keep thinking of her genitals as just a "thing," you have to try not to know too much about them or her, which requires not knowing too much about what you want in wanting them or her.

The hole-kissing scene provides an example of this problem of knowing too much, for under the pressure of exhibiting the ultimate object of desire the Miller's whole notion of coming near to a desirable object, particularly a gendered object, falls apart. But the problem is not local to any particular moment in the plot. From the very start, Alisoun is represented as having her own life of desire, a "likerous ye" (I.3244) that is essential to her sexiness both in the portrait and afterwards.[35] Her desiring eye, to be sure, is presented as one more object of consumption for the masculine gaze that wanders over her soft woolliness, sweet mouth, and supple, thin body; it is part of what makes her the perfect object of desire, and we are not invited to imagine it as much more than that. But that is already enough to disturb her ideological function; for it means that for her to be the satisfying object of an eroticized masculine look she must be able to look back, to have a desiring gaze of her own. The scopophilic thrill her portrait is supposed to provide could not exist if she were seen simply as an object, or again simply as an animal: there is no such thrill in looking at the pear tree or the sheep to which she is compared.[36] Nor could it exist if she were the kind of human the Miller imagines us to be, or imagines that we ought to be. For the thrill of looking at her would again be dampened if she were merely passive with respect to a desire that, as it were, looked out through her eye; the masculine looker does not want to imagine that her desire is, in effect, helpless, but that it is hers to bestow where she will, and that it might be pointed *here*. The thrill the portrait offers is not even that of a male observer imagining having his way with a woman, reducing her as a practical rather than a theoretical matter to a state of passivity, for then too the desire in her eye would be extinguished, or at least forcefully set to the side. The thrill is more like that of imagining a seamless return of desire, a perfect interaction between two agents who want exactly the same thing in exactly the same way. It is a thrill that depends on the desire for intimacy.

It must be said right away that the passage averts the possibility of intimacy on which it depends. If this scopophilic portrait of a woman with desire in her eye imagines an erotic interaction in which two agents want exactly the same thing in exactly the same way, the most immediate way they can be said to want it is with the desire of the man; Alisoun is, after all, the Miller's creation, and the thrills she provides are the ones he wants her to. In this sense the portrait provides the Miller with a way of imagining a desiring eye, like that of Pygmalion's statue come to life, that cannot help but be trained on him, since that is the way he made it. It is the erotic charge, that is, of a narcissistic wish for the other's desire to be an echo or reflection of one's own, even as it somehow, impossibly, maintains its status as other. In linking Narcissus and Pygmalion in this way, as figures who express a masculine desire for a love object that is simultaneously a perfect object and an agent, I am following Jean de Meun, and suggesting that the *Miller's Tale* is one of many places in which Chaucer takes up and pursues further what he finds interesting and expressive in the *Roman de la Rose*.[37] I will expand on the notion of a scopophilic narcissism in the *Rose* in chapter four. For now I want to note that a return to the dominant gender ideology in the *Miller's Tale* can help us unpack the structure of such narcissism: it involves the desire for a woman, the erotic locus or place, to be like a man, the erotic agent, and not just any man, but the very man who desires her. The narcissism of the Miller's desire thus opens onto a narcissized homoeroticism that is very nearly adjacent to it, and that is part of what it means for the Miller to want to be a "feminized man" and to imagine the self-castigations of anal penetration and of a humiliating confrontation with the disgustingly desirable female body.[38] This narcissized homoeroticism is another occupant of the Miller's "remenant," and suggests a further sense in which his tale pictures a perfect match between desire and the world; in effect, the tale's dominant trope of a desire perfectly matched to its object is here figured as the desire of a man who reaches out to possess his own image.

It is worth pausing for a moment over the topic of the Miller's homoeroticism; for while I have meant it to be implied for some time now, and while it is taken by many to be the first and most obvious consequence of attending to the problems of gender and desire in the tale, the bare fact of a homoerotic desire here tells us very little, and it is easy to make the wrong thing of it. We can take our cue from a line I have already cited from the Miller's description of Alisoun's animal sexiness, that she is "softer than the wolle is of a wether." Leicester reminds us that "a wether is a male sheep that has been castrated before it reaches maturity," and remarks that as a consequence "the thought of touching Alisoun has its scary side."[39] The comment is suggestive but needs unpacking. What exactly would be scary about touching an Alisoun figured in this way? An appeal to "castration anxiety" will tell us little: the question concerns the tropological value of castration rather than the explanatory value of an anatomically anchored anxiety related to some supposedly universal psychic event.[40] The first thing to notice is that Alisoun – not, as Leicester's comment implies, her masculine desirer – is the one being imagined as a castrated male, and a sexy one at that: remember that we are supposed to find the thought of touching her wether-like softness arousing. If Alisoun-as-sexy-male is being figured here as castrated – as lacking power, cut off from mature development, perhaps as passive – then the desire for such a one is what a desire for her is imagined as being. This is what I mean by calling the homoeroticism at issue here narcissized: it imagines the object of a homoerotic desire as figuratively "castrated," and so imagines that the desiring, uncastrated male is the sole locus of power and activity in the erotic scene. But the point needs putting more broadly, since the Miller clearly wants us to think of Alisoun's sexy softness as womanly, and since the narcissistic figuring of the object of desire as passive is hardly restricted to homoeroticism in this text. The trope of Alisoun-as-wether is a kind of gloss on the general impulse in the poem to figure erotic life in terms of a clean split between activity and passivity: it imagines that to be an object of desire is to be castrated, powerless, passive; that one cannot be both desired and active; that to be an object of desire is to be no more than an object, to be objectified. The scary side of the thought of touching Alisoun would then be the thought that she might be aroused by the touching, that she might desire you, so make of you an object, a castrate. This is a way of putting a fairly familiar thought, that part of what is involved in narcissism is an aversion to being desired.[41] But it is crucial to remember that even the thought of being the object of a castrating masculine desire, fearful as it is, is not merely aversive. Like the fantasies expressed in Nicholas's anal penetration and Absolon's kiss, what is being imagined here is an erotics, and one not fundamentally powered by narcissism. For what is being imagined in each of these cases is the *desirability* of the other's agency, the fact that what makes the other appear in the Miller's gender ideology as "masculine" is essential to what constitutes the possibility of their sexiness.

Given the Miller's obvious investment in a heteronormative self-conception, the desirability of what that very self-conception persistently figures as the masculinity of the love object is a high price to pay for keeping the desire for intimacy out of sight. And, as I have suggested, it cannot even do that, since the impossibility of a purely objectifying desire is central to the emergence of a homoerotic desire here; and, to return to Alisoun, the erotics of her portrait is itself already predicated on the centrality of her desiring look. This means that part of what one wants in desiring her is to be desired by her, and so to be close not just to her body or her "thing" or anything else that can be imagined as simply a touchable or possessable object, but to be close to *her*. But to want this is to recognize that she might look back at you, not with desire, but with aversion; or she might not look back at all. This is knowledge that scopophilia, in its imagining of a seamless interaction between agents, wishes to avoid. The scopophilic eroticism of Alisoun's portrait, together with her representation as a touchable thing, means then to guarantee a kind of intimacy, a condition in which a desired nearness could never be lost because the ultimate object of desire is always close by, ready to hand like the rest of God's plenty, and always looking back at you with desire, never averting her gaze. But in representing the object of desire as necessarily close by, the Miller also distances himself from it, banishing the desired other from the scene of intimacy; or at least he tries to do so, substituting a simulacrum of the other, perhaps her body, in any case a projection of her into the erotic scene as an object that can never really satisfy the desire for intimacy whose satisfaction it is supposed to guarantee. This structure of desire is one that first of all sends its object away, so that it then can be brought back in another form: a form consistent with the Miller's naturalistic picture, in which a concern for oneself precedes and underlies any concern for others, and other people are just one kind of thing whose possession is what it means to bask in nature's plenitude; and a form consistent also with the nostalgia of his naturalism, in which he freezes himself in longing for a condition that is necessarily already lost, and lost precisely because of the way he imagines that it has been guaranteed.

A structure of desire in which one pushes the desired object away in order to bring it back in another form: here the Miller is beginning to sound again like Nicholas, who bypasses the opportunity for immediate sex with Alisoun in order to have her in another form, as the sign that his will can fill the scene of an action in which others become little more than his instruments. Even in the figure of Nicholas, however, the Miller cannot imagine this sort of desire through to a moment of completion. There is a moment of completion, of course, to which the Miller refers with a rather vague description of Nicholas's activity with Alisoun in bed: "Ther was the revel and the melodye; / And thus lith Alison and Nicholas, / In bisynesse of myrthe and of solas" (I.3652–54). But after all the queynte-grabbing and talk of touching people's things that has come before, this quadruple euphemism for the tale's sole moment of erotic satisfaction is a bit surprising, and more so since erotic satisfaction is the tale's prime example of the gratification of human desire. It would not take much to say, as the Merchant for one is quite willing to say, just what is involved in this "solas" in a way that would drive home the Miller's point about desire. If, however, the Miller were more specific in just the way he has been specific all along, one thing he would certainly lose would be the thought that Alisoun and Nicholas were doing something *together* there in bed. If Nicholas were not just doing something to Alisoun, the most the Miller could show while remaining consistent with his picture would be them doing something to each other, or more properly to the objects each took the other to be. This could be sexy in its own way, but it is evidently not the kind of sexiness the Miller wants of the moment: it would come too close to what he elsewhere imagines either as mere build-up, a reach and a grab that might produce a startled jerk back as much as a return of desire, or as punishment or victimization, the reception of a violating thrust. The result of this is that the central moment of satisfaction in the tale, what ought to provide the best case for a picture of the world as a place of plenitude, must be left blank, pointed to with multiple euphemisms but not represented. This silence is the sign of another version of what happens there in bed, a version essential to the Miller's sense of the moment as one of the ultimate happiness, the moment towards which all of the more tangible arousals he does represent are aimed, but a moment for which, it seems, he has no words.

If in Nicholas's case the problem that a desire for intimacy poses for the Miller is expressed in a moment in which something is not shown, in the case of Absolon it gets expressed in a far more spectacular moment in which something is shown. I am of course referring to the moment in which Absolon finally does draw near enough to Alisoun to touch her, the moment of that ill-fated kiss, which the Miller imagines with a sensual precision and slow-motion relish unmatched by anything in the tale outside of Alisoun's portrait. Here we are taken inside the phenomenal scene of the perceiving and desiring agent, the scene whose supposed specular passivity plays such a crucial role in the view of action that the Miller offers. Absolon wipes his mouth "ful drie" with antici-pation; he kisses Alisoun's "naked ers" "with his mouth," "ful savourly." During the moment of anticipation what is waiting for Absolon is the face of his beloved, in particular her beautiful, succulent lips crying out to be kissed. What impales Absolon on the Miller's joke is that those lips are still phenomenally there for him in his savoring the kiss of her ass, and their residual image and the savoring associated with it even lingers after Absolon starts to realize that something has gone wrong. What he does first is just to register error and jump back. What is there for him is still a face, only not any longer a woman's, for he knows that a woman does not have a beard. But the face is not exactly a man's either, since the sensation of beardedness only registers strongly enough to call into question the image of a woman. There is even a moment in which the object as it is for Absolon – the object, that is, of his perceptions and affects – loses its facedness entirely, becoming a bare unrecognizable thing with unreadable features. When Absolon feels "a thyng al rough and long yherd," that thing is no longer a bearded face of indeterminate gender, and not yet an ass; and when he cries out "what have I done?" he does so because he does not yet know what he has done, he only knows it was awful.

What makes the phenomenally rich features of this scene problematic for the Miller is that, while he must make them accessible to impale Absolon on the joke, neither the perversity they represent nor the punishment they provide can finally be cast in naturalistic terms. Absolon's problem as he is humiliated by kissing Alisoun's ass is not that he has the wrong object of desire present to his consciousness, leading him astray, as Nicholas might be said to have when he too cleverly presents Absolon with a target for his borrowed blade. Nor does the scene serve to reveal some normatively transparent object of perception and desire, something that, like Nicholas's pain, cannot be gotten wrong. What the scene does instead is to explore how what is phenomenally present can suddenly change faces, and change us with it. The humiliation in the moment for Absolon, and what makes the joke on him so biting, is that by the end of it he has become an ass-kisser: that may not have been his intention, but it is a fact about him, at the moment the only fact that counts. And if the shifting character of the object's identity is humiliating, the course of its transformation is even worse. The change, both in Absolon and in what he encounters, is not a matter of a switch from one determinate identity to another. When the object of his perception and desire becomes a mere "thyng al rough and long yherd," Absolon not only does not know what he has done, he does not know what he has become; the sheer attractiveness of a world of plenty perfectly matched to human desire, and the definitive human identity that goes with it, has been replaced by the sheer aversiveness of a world with nothing in particular in it, a world of disgusting thinginess that leaves him with nothing to want and no one to be.

Compared to this, being an ass-kisser – or being any of the various kinds of creature constructed in the Miller's relationship to his closeted "remenant" – would be a positive relief. Consider one such possibility produced in this scene. The appearance of that bearded face is partly meant as a reprimand to Absolon: it suggests that the passive lover or female man deserves to be confronted with the disgusting manliness of the love object he has in effect been wishing for. This is what the Miller has Nicholas understand to be the force of the joke on Absolon when, in a remarkable act of something like telepathy, he exclaims "A berd! A berd!" (I.3742); so the Miller clearly has a lot invested in enforcing this sense of what is so humiliating here. If we follow through on the thought that in punishing these representatives of a perversion internal to him the Miller is expressing a wish for self-punishment, we can take this as further confirmation of a homoeroticism that the normative masculinity the Miller exemplifies simultaneously disavows and depends on. In the joke on Absolon, that is, we have one more expression of the Miller's disgust towards his own ideal of the female man, where his disgust serves to keep the scene's identification of a homoerotic desire internal to that ideal out of sight, and helps to define some of the contours of that desire's sexiness. This does not mean, however, that a homoerotic desire is what's "really" in there, a secret in the depths of the Miller's soul that drives or at least inflects all of his other desires and identifications. That way of locating such a desire and describing its explanatory force would derive from thoughts that the tale's naturalism is meant to support: that desires are inner objects that define us simply by their presence, and that our relationship to them is fundamentally one of observation, of seeing them for what they are or of covering them up and denying their existence. As I have been arguing all along, this is the crucial step in the Miller's self-deception; if a closeted homoeroticism structures his psychology in this way, or indeed if any of the various occupants of the shadow-remenant do so, they do so to the extent that this self-deception is successful, *not* as some secret fact about him that only we are in a position to see. It would be better, then, to describe this moment as expressive of a longing for the homoerotic, produced by the Miller's more obvious longing for the heteronormative, and in exactly the same naturalizing terms. For what the Miller gains in bringing Nicholas in on this version of the joke – and what would be perpetuated in any critical account that stopped here – is the preservation of a naturalistic account of subjectivity and action, the preservation of the thought that inner life consists of a set of facts that just are what they are, and that, if known, would tell us what to do.

But the scene of Absolon's kiss does not stop here, and in fact it never really started here at all. As I have suggested, the joke on Absolon works because his perceptions and attitudes help to constitute the object that is phenomenally there for him, and that object, in turn, helps to constitute him, in the particular way that we are constituted in and by our relations with objects that are also subjects and agents – that is, other people. The kind of humiliation Absolon suffers, then, is one of a family of reciprocal relations between agents, of which intimacy is another. Part of what binds this family together is that such reciprocal relations are not grounded in some primary relation each agent has to himself; on the contrary, the relations any agent has with himself are in part determined by the reciprocal relations he has with others. This is one reason why there is no set of inner objects in a person that just are what they are first, and that tell him what to do; and therefore why there is not the kind of basis the Miller imagines for generating motive out of an antecedent self-interest. More to the point, *within* the conduct of reciprocal relations who and what each person is, what each person wants, and who and what each takes the other to be depend on any number of things, including what each person does, what they do together, and even just what happens between them and to them. However well Absolon's punishment fits his perversity, he is humiliated by that kiss not because he is a pervert or a fool, but because he is in the condition the Miller knows we all are in: the condition of creatures for whom the normative problem cannot be answered by recourse to some set of determinate interior facts, creatures whose identities outrun anything internal to them but who are bound by those identities nonetheless, partly because they are essentially determined by the fact that they live in a world with others who matter to them not just as objects but as agents.

One powerful motivation for holding to the Miller's picture of the human, then – and a motive that is neither peculiar to him nor dependent on the force of a suspect ideology – is that we are vulnerable, just as Absolon is, to being made and unmade in relation to others who may have nothing more than our humiliation in mind. They may have something much better in mind, of course; but even in the best case of mutual goodwill, there is no way to say beforehand what the endpoint of reciprocal self-constitution will be, or even if there will be an identifiable end. This in itself can be a fearful thing. To the extent that we want to be able just to look and see who we are and what we want, and to look at another and see a determinate thing whose normative claim on us is transparent, it can seem that reciprocal relations require us to act blindly – or worse, to live in a world in which nothing is definitively identifiable at all, including ourselves. A particularly heightened version of this fear – heightened in a way determined by the Miller's conceptual commitments – finds expression in the progression of Absolon's kiss to a point at which his relationship to the world is one of sheer aversion to its thinginess. For given the way Alisoun's desiring eye is essential to her sexiness from the start, given the way she always looks back at her male observer, making a claim of reciprocity on him even from her "nether eye," the closest she comes to being the purely animal, purely bodily object that makes no agentlike claim is in the moment when she becomes that bare unrecognizable "thyng al rough and long yherd," terrifying in its failure to take part in any sense of what Absolon has done to or with it. Here the Miller's picture of the normative power of the erotic object – his picture of the other's body as what is tangibly real, and of this reality as the source of motive – becomes a picture of the other as utterly alien, something you can have no identifiable relation to, something disgusting. This is yet another of the discontents naturalism brings in its wake, in which the fantasy of a seamless connection to the world opens on to an abyss of disgust and the sadness of a radical isolation from everything that is supposed to fill that world with value.

The character whom the Miller has the most trouble imagining as alone in this way, and who therefore figures most directly both the Miller's knowledge that he is not alone in this way and his sense of what this entails, is John. For John's entire way of thinking and acting is predicated on an acknowledgment of the others in his world. More than that, he has one particular other who *is* his world; for him, the loss of her and the end of the world amount to the same thing, which is why Nicholas's gag about a second flood has the power it does over him. And now it should be somewhat clearer what it means for the Miller to punish John in the way he does. Breaking John's arm is the least appropriate of the punishments, for nothing that is at issue in the possibility John represents has to do centrally with the body. A broken arm hurts, but it does not hurt John where he lives; at most it is a kind of rearguard action on the Miller's part, an attempt to pull John's case back within a naturalistic orbit after the fact. The public and mocking denial of John's rationality is more interesting, in part because it just misses its mark. For it is not so much John's rationality that gets denied, despite the crowd's solidarity in declaring his madness; his fate is not that of having no reasons, but that of having no one listen to the reasons he so evidently has: "no man his reson herde" (I.3844). John's punishment, then, is less a denial of the rationality of intimacy than an attempt to destroy the possibility that the desire for intimacy might have reasons for it, born of the fearful fact that the reasons you have might be ones that no one else is willing or able to hear. This is also the reason for John's other, and worst, punishment, his betrayal by Alisoun: as it turns out, even the person he wants intimacy with does not care to hear him, and does not share his reasons. The fact that this fearful isolation is behind both of the latter two punishments suggests that the Miller partly means the tale's final moment to take something of intimate concern and make it the occasion for a public scene, as though to deny its intimate scale, and by sidestepping intimacy to make of John's isolation an instance of the radical isolation the Miller fears, one that can presumably be avoided by participation in the solidarity of the crowd.

But John's isolation, fearful as it is, is quite unlike that entailed by the Miller's picture, for nothing says that John is in principle alone or unhearable; it just turns out that way. This suggests that here as elsewhere the Miller's nightmares are part and parcel of the wishes his naturalism embraces; for both his fantasy of seamless connection to the world and his nightmare of radical isolation participate in the wishful attempt to deny that it can just turn out that way, that who you are and the happiness you seek can rest on such contingencies. And here as elsewhere the Miller reveals his further sense that he cannot fully identify himself with the wishes that power his narrative, in either their idyllic or demonic form. For just as John is an object of greater hostility than either Nicholas or Absolon and so receives the heaviest punishment, there is a pathos in John's situation that goes deeper than that attending the other male characters, and that brings with it a sympathy lacking in their cases.[42] And this pathos is just what the Miller has said it is all along, the intimate pathos of staking your heart on someone only to find somewhere along the way that they have no such stake in you. The Miller depends on this pathos in making John out to be a fool; but once it is admitted, mere carelessness is no longer a viable option, for nothing in the world of God's plenty could replace what has been taken away.

CHAPTER 2

Normative longing in the *Knight's Tale*

In chapter one I characterized the Miller's naturalism as a species of normative nostalgia, a longing for grounds of action and identity which seem perpetually to reside in some fantasized past – in this case the "past" of an "animality" foregone by the Miller's very need to lay claim to it. Normative nostalgia, of course, is hardly local to the *Miller's Tale*. The myths of the Golden Age and the Fall depend on it, and it is a long-standing interest of Chaucer's: as he puts it in his lyric poetry, the "Former Age" of wholeheartedness, simplicity, and peace has been replaced by duplicity, tyranny, undisciplined appetite, and a general "Lak of Stedfastnesse." Chaucer begins the *Canterbury Tales* with a tale in which this interest is wide-ranging and explicit. As the long speech with which Theseus concludes the *Knight's Tale* suggests, for the Knight all of life is in some sense a "fall" into materiality and individuation, a loss of the pure, unified, unimpeded activity of the Prime Mover; and this metaphysical nostalgia mirrors a social and ethical nostalgia for a lost chivalric ideal which the Knight projects on to the tale's classical setting.[1] In this chapter and the two to follow I will continue exploring Chaucer's interest in normative nostalgia. In doing so I will move beyond the trope of nostalgia to try to understand the broader structures of normative longing that inform it. I will argue that for Chaucer and the intellectual tradition to which he belonged, normative nostalgia is so powerful because it captures what they took to be fundamental features of normativity itself, features that make normativity necessarily an object of longing.

My argument thus continues to focus on the way Chaucer's philosophical interests can help us understand the metaphorical and psychological structures that inform his poetry. At the same time, I will argue that the ultimate source of normative nostalgia is nothing peculiar to medieval culture or its Christian and classical inheritances. I think there is something about the way agency depends on the ambition of autonomy that makes such nostalgia, if not inevitable, at the very least deeply compelling. In other words, Chaucer and his main intellectual interlocutors were substantially right about the source of normative nostalgia, even if they understood that source in historically determined metaphysical and theological terms which we may not share. As I will argue most pointedly in chapter three, Chaucer understood this problem concerning agency and autonomy from his reading of Boethius; and as I will argue in chapter four, Chaucer learned from the *Roman de la Rose* an interest in how this problem structures not only ethical normativity but erotic normativity as well. The historical and conceptual dimensions of my argument thus quite directly depend on each other. I think we can learn something philosophically and theoretically from this historical engagement with normative longing; and in order to make out the form of that engagement, we must try to provide our own best account of the sources of such longing.

One purpose of these chapters is thus to elaborate and clarify an argument I began, mostly by way of example, in chapter one, concerning the relation between ethical and erotic normativity in Chaucer's poetry. In chapter one, I argued that in order to understand the nostalgic structures informing the Miller's unstable gender identifications and erotically charged fantasies of self-punishment, we need to see them as instances of a broader normative nostalgia informing his ethics and theory of action. Put broadly, my claim there and in the following chapters is that Chaucer understood his representations of gendered and erotic norms as part of an investigation of the structure of practical rationality, and of what it is about autonomy that resists grounding in a comprehensive theory. In pursuing this thought, for large stretches of the coming discussion I will more or less bracket gender and sexuality, and lay out some problems of ethical normativity on their own ground. That analytical move, as much as the many thematic and rhetorical links between the *Knight's Tale* and the *Miller's Tale*, provides the rationale for turning now to the Knight. For the Knight himself, while centrally concerned with the intersection of ethics, gender, and erotic life, and with the longing that informs each, seeks for large stretches of his tale to bracket the erotic in favor of a focus on the ethical by itself. In doing so, the Knight develops a theory of action and autonomy that is about as good as Chaucer thought it was possible to produce, one that avoids many of the defects of naturalist theory. But for all the Knight's philosophical intelligence, he remains ideologically imbedded, and that imbeddedness finds expression, among other ways, in his attempt to bracket an erotics he finds deeply disturbing. In making the *Knight's Tale* the center of this chapter, then, I mean to make the bracketing of the erotic an object of analysis rather than simply to take it as an unquestioned rhetorical move. In doing so, I will try to remain true to Chaucer's sense of how sexuality provides both an impetus and an impediment to reflection.

ETHICAL AND EROTIC FORMALISM: PICTURING EMILY

I will begin with Emily, for as I suggested in the introduction to this book, her erotic function in the tale is deeply bound up with the philosophical work Chaucer means her representation to do. I claimed in the introduction that the apparent flatness and obviousness of the aestheticizing voyeurism in the scene of Emily in her garden needs further scrutiny: we may not know as well as we think we do what we recognize there, or what drives that all too familiar attitude.[2] The notion of Emily's aestheticization is partly meant to capture the way the wound of desire she generates in her male admirers is tied to the production of lyrical eroticism, as in Arcite's theatrical declaration that "the fresshe beautee sleeth me sodeynly / Of hire that rometh in the yonder place" (I.1118–19). More broadly, Palamon and Arcite's consuming obsession with Emily – their sense of being penetrated and overwhelmed by her, figured most obviously, but not solely, in the conventional courtly language of being stung unto the heart – suggests another feature of the aesthetic, its lavish excessiveness. Emily absorbs Palamon and Arcite not only in desire but in contemplation as well, and in so doing she exceeds the possibility of putting her to the merely instrumental function of providing them with erotic gratification. The point becomes clearer if we turn from Palamon and Arcite to the Knight himself. For an aestheticized and lyrical eroticism is central to the way the Knight imagines Emily's attractiveness from the moment he first introduces her, as he describes the seamless integration of her floral beauty into the walled-off garden she inhabits. Emily

> fairer was to sene
> Than is the lylie upon his stalke grene,
> And fressher than the May with floures newe —
> For with the rose colour stroof hir hewe,
> I noot which was the fyner of hem two.
> (I.1035–39)

While Alisoun's portrait in the *Miller's Tale* depends on appeals to the pleasures of taste and touch, and does so in a way that directs our attention to a world of pleasures beyond her, Emily's portrait depends almost exclusively on the visual, and her visuality directs us only to the garden that encloses her. More precisely, such visuality directs us to a group of nested formal structures, including the garden itself, its patterns of rose-red and lily white, and the mirroring of those patterns in Emily's appearance. Emily is not so much contained in this structure as figuratively constituted by it; her beauty seems inseparable from the idea of a representational self-enclosure. Given the constitutive nature of this self-enclosure, the one element of strife in her portrait – the sense of competition between Emily's beauty and that of the flowers – only adds to the formal stasis of the scene. Here, in these antagonistic elements whose reflection of each other provides for their common participation in a beautiful aesthetic structure, we have the picture of woman as perfect formal object nearly at its purest.

The formalist visuality of Emily's portrait emphasizes her availability to the pleasures of looking, and so defines the desire for her, like that for Alisoun, as a species of scopophilia. But the scopophilia at issue here is purer than that in the *Miller's Tale*. For Emily's portrait, unlike Alisoun's, emphasizes her distance from her male desirers, her unavailability, and her unconsumability; there is no question here of anyone's touching or tasting her. The visual pleasure Emily provides is not that of an object that makes itself available as an instrument of pleasure, as Alisoun with her "likerous ye" might be said to do; it is rather that of a beauty indifferent to any desires that may be directed its way. Emily's unavailability thus links her beauty to the idea of the aesthetic object's autonomy; for her attractiveness depends on her uselessness, on the impossibility of putting her to an instrumental function. The Knight figures this feature of Emily's aestheticization, among other ways, in the helpless longing she generates in Palamon and Arcite, who gaze at her through prison bars that ensure both their visual access to her and the impossibility of acting on their desires.[3] But it is already a feature of the Knight's appreciation of her, and that to which he invites his audience. To be sure, in the Knight's distanced, commanding, and relaxedly admiring production of Emily's portrait, her beauty seems to be simply that of the aestheticized feminine object perpetually available to the contemplative mastery of an overseeing masculine subject. But, as I will argue, the very possibility of a feminine beauty preserved in its unassimilable otherness depends on a fracture within the masculine subject that denies it the very mastery it seems already to have achieved.

One of the ways the Knight – and later, Palamon – imagines the otherness he wants to preserve is by hyperbolizing it: "as an aungel hevenysshly she soong" (I.1055), as though her expressive capacities were a marker of a special proximity to the divine. This suggests that Emily does not, in the manner of a work of art like Pygmalion's statue, simply exhibit in her perfection the signs of another's creative power; rather she gives voice to her condition in a way that enacts and enhances it. This tendency to imagine Emily as enacting rather than simply exhibiting her perfection appears in other features of the portrait as well. The Knight, for instance, represents her as a participant in the production of her formal completeness, as she literally fashions it while moving about the garden: "She gadereth floures, party white and red, / To make a subtil gerland for her hede" (I.1053–54), adorning herself in the very play of colors that marks her aestheticization. More than just a fantasy of a perfect object, then, Emily also represents a fantasy of a perfect subject and a perfect agent. The Knight's portrait of Emily, like the Miller's representation of Alisoun, is in part an attempt to imagine a normative ideal for the human, a perfectly ordered interiority that functions as an object of ethical as well as erotic desire. And, as in the *Miller's Tale*, the relations among these aspects of feminine perfection can help us see how the *Knight's Tale* engages two sets of intersecting normative problems: those concerning the normalization of gender and desire, and how that normalization is related to the production of the abnormal or perverse; and those concerning the construction and functioning of an ethos, a normative ideal to which an agent grants authority. I want now to sketch rather quickly the way the intersection of these two aspects of Emily's normative function radiates out into the rest of the tale.

One of the problems Alisoun posed for the Miller was that normative hyperbole led to a confused inability to locate the space of her agency: since her agency was grounded in a perfect responsiveness to her "natural" desires, it was paradoxically an agency with a passivity at its heart. Something similar happens with Emily. In a peculiar passage in the middle of Emily's description, the Knight sets aside his emphasis on her artifactuality to describe the stirrings of desire in her heart:

> Er it were day, as was hir wone to do,
> She was arisen and al redy dight,
> For May wole have no slogardie anyght.
> The sesoun priketh every gentil herte,
> And maketh it out of his slep to sterte,
> And seith "Arys, and do thyn observaunce."
> This maked Emelye have remembraunce
> To doon honour to May, and for to ryse.
> (I.1040–47)

The Knight offers this utterly conventional scene to explain why Emily got up to engage in her usual springtime activities. One thing he wants is to explain how her doing so issues from her life as an agent: not only from her desires, but from her habits, what she was "wont to do," and from the way her desires and habits are inflected by her attentiveness to what she perceives as her duty, her "observaunce." And in associating her actions with the compulsory force of seasonal stirrings in the noble heart, he seems further to want to generalize this explanation to the status of a normative ideal, and to figure that ideal as natural. But this association has the effect of eliding his agent-centered explanation of what Emily does with another, quite different, one in which her desires are considered merely as phenomena in a causal sequence. From the perspective of this other explanation, there seems to be no space for considering Emily's actions as distinctively hers, or even as actions. Her "observaunce" appears less as something *she* can be said to *do* than as an instance of what happens to all noble hearts when seasonal prickings set them in motion: "this *maked* Emelye have remembraunce / To doon honour to May, and for to ryse."

As I argued in the introduction, action is necessarily available to both agent-centered and causal explanation, and there is no reason why one cannot be caused to do something of which one is nevertheless fully the agent. But these kinds of explanation can cut across each other in confusing ways. Perhaps the most familiar form of this confusion occurs when the perspective of causal explanation seems to exhaust the explanatory possibilities, making the language of agency seem like an obscure metaphysical redundancy we cannot justify, even if we may also feel we cannot do without it. The broadest exemplification of this crossing of perspectives in the *Knight's Tale* occurs in the way scattered comments on fate, together with the overall architecture of the plot, with its obsessive parallel narrative structures and its obscure divine conspiracies, serve to make Theseus's pretensions to the status of a little Prime Mover in human affairs look naïve. As readers of the tale we, it seems, are in the position to see that the deck is always already rigged, that the idea of effective historical agency is a sham, a failed gesture of protection from the fact that we are helpless before impersonal forces that determine our every move; and it seems that the Knight suspects or fears that this is the case as well.

This paranoia is a problem for the Knight, given his deep identification with Theseus as a redemptive political and ethical authority. But in Emily's case the Knight is in a somewhat odder bind. For with Emily he seems to think that the language of causal explanation, rather than exposing the language of agency as a sham, might inform it, as though Emily's passivity in being caused were what it meant for her to act as she does. The little allegory of May saying "arys, and do thyn observaunce" functions to personify May as an agentive figure that embodies the voice of normative authority; it is something like the voice of Emily's conscience, and so in effect represents the authority of the reasons Emily has for getting up and attending to her duties. Here then, as in the *Miller's Tale*, we have in the representation of the feminine an expression of the appeal of normative naturalism. For this is an image of action with a passivity at its base, and this passivity is supposed to figure a condition of pleasing naturalness, an unbroken continuity between natural processes and our actions. But while May's normative authority is supposed to effect this continuity by providing a figure for Emily's reasons, the causal explanation the May allegory provides effaces the very territory of acting for reasons which it was supposed to ground.

In keeping with the characterization of Emily's objectification as aesthetically formalist, we might describe the problem in locating Emily's agency by saying that she functions as a formalist ethical ideal. She figures, that is, an ideal of ethical action as grounded in the agent's responsiveness to a perfect formal structure: Emily's appreciation of that structure is supposed to be what supplies her with her reasons for acting. Such a characterization would capture what I suggested earlier, that Emily's status as an ethical ideal is bodied forth in the aesthetic activity of her self-fashioning. It would also give weight to Kolve's notion that in looking at Emily from behind the bars of their prison Palamon and Arcite are seeing a figure of a beautifully stylized freedom – a figure, that is, for the very autonomy they lack, and lack not simply because of their practical circumstances, as the Boethian valence of that prison suggests. The longing the Thebans feel for Emily is in part the longing for an autonomy that calls to them as the perfected form of their humanity, which Emily, despite her self-fashioning activity, seems always already to have achieved; and which, in making its normative claims on their imperfect and fractured humanity, seems to turn away from them, making itself useless to them, imprisoning them in their privation and self-estrangement. This is the structure of the normative longing the Knight captures in Palamon's contrast between Emily's divinity and his own sorrowful, wretched creatureliness, and in Arcite's sense of being slain by Emily's beauty.

While Palamon and Arcite provide the initial occasion for the Knight to figure such a relation to a normative ideal – and while, as many critics have noted, they are supposed to stand in figurative opposition to the possibility of mastery Theseus represents – the Theban cousins are hardly alone in such longing. For on a Boethian account privation and self-estrangement are the routine conditions of human life. We are meant to see ourselves as implicated in the longing Palamon and Arcite feel for Emily, a longing for a perfection that simultaneously calls to us and turns away from us, or, as both Augustine and Boethius would put it, from which we willingly turn away. And this longing radiates out from Palamon and Arcite to the rest of the tale, for instance into the "Prime Mover" speech that is supposed to provide the tale with narrative and conceptual closure. For both Theseus, in his failed attempt at the end of the tale to articulate a basis for action by imagining a place for human life within the formal order of the cosmos, and the Knight, in his identification with that attempt, long for precisely the kind of agency Emily represents: an agency imagined as gaining its structure and its motive energy – and finally, as that speech suggests, its freedom from death – from its seamless participation in a beautiful formal structure.

To emphasize Emily's function as a figure of autonomy is not, then, sentimentally to evade her objectification. It is rather to locate the desire for her in two mutually reinforcing structures of abjection. One is that of longing for erotic contact with an object constituted as desirable by its unassimilability to any use you might want to make of it. The linked divinizing and aestheticizing of the erotic object is the form taken by recognizing and desiring its autonomy, in the context of a scopophilia that tries to imagine a contemplative distance and insulation from the claim the other makes on you. That claim in effect reappears here as an unbridgeable distance between you and an erotic object useless to you and indifferent towards you, and that reveals you to yourself as base and unworthy. The other structure of abjection is that of a longing for a normative ideal that seems at once to found the possibility of a coherent agency and to close itself off from you, sealing itself as both the Prime Mover and Emily do into an idealized space of formal stasis, and sealing you into a world of change, decay, and death, a barren world in which the untouchable feminine is the one thing that gives your life value. Here the ideological work of Emily's representation appears as an attempt to deny the pressing reality of this death by imagining a masculine position of contemplative mastery from which the pleasures of an aestheticized feminine would be perpetually available. But the pleasures of that representation are not finally separable from the abjections it instantiates, from the glamor of insatiable longing for a perfection that, in its unbridgeable distance from you, leaves you wretched, at a loss, impotent. The desire for Emily, however objectifying and bound up in a fantasy of mastery, is also then the desire for such an impotence. Mastery and impotence here are not two opposed postures but two aspects of the same attitude.

Such a claim needs a good deal of unpacking, which this chapter and the two that follow it will provide, partly by way of an account of how an interest in such structures of the will comes to Chaucer from the *Consolation of Philosophy* and the *Roman de la Rose*. But the first place to turn is to the figure of Theseus in the tale itself. For in the representation of Theseus as a normative ideal, something to which the Knight is even more explicitly and thoroughly committed than he is to the normative function of Emily, the Knight gives expression to the depth and intelligence of his *resistance* to formalist desire and the abjections it instantiates. If a Thesean ideal finally collapses into such a desire, then, we had better have a good account of what that ideal is, or our account of the collapse will be too hasty, and as a result we will miss the depth of the problems at issue here.[4]

THESEAN AUTONOMY

Let us begin with Theseus by returning briefly to one of the most obvious differences between the ethical imaginations of the first two *Canterbury Tales*. While the Miller's ethos turns on the conviction that a man should always act on his appetites, the Knight's turns on the conviction that a man should only act on proper reflection, that he should be prudent and judicious. What mainly annoys the Miller about the *Knight's Tale* – what gets that polemical burr stuck in his side – is what he sees as the perpetual refusal of the tale's male characters to stand up and be men, to stop turning their desires into objects of elaborate practical reasoning and theoretical speculation. The Knight's men seem to the Miller to be incapable of just acting and being done with it, and for this reason they seem to have no self-possession. For the Knight, however, reflection is essential to self-possession. As the Knight exhibits in the early characterizations of Palamon and Arcite, to act unreflectively on one's appetites – to act, that is, as the Miller will recommend – is to leave oneself open to individual and civic fragmentation. The impossibility of unreflective self-possession is evident not only in Palamon and Arcite, but in the Knight's ethical model Theseus. Theseus shows a habitual anger when he unexpectedly confronts perceived infringements on his honor, as when he accuses the obviously grieving Theban widows of enviously disturbing his triumphal homecoming (I.905–8), or when, confronting Palamon and Arcite battling in the grove, he announces the "short conclusioun" (I.1743) of their death sentence.

Theseus's embarrassing egocentrism in these moments of sudden surprise – his initial tendency to misperceive them as personal affronts – contributes to the Knight's attempt to imagine the goal of self-possession as that of reflective self-command, of the work of constituting a will whose coherence is never finally secured, since there will always be more surprises waiting, more lapses to be endured and overcome. Understanding the work of reflective self-command is the central goal that informs the Knight's representation of Theseus; he is, in effect, a figure for an antinaturalistic theory of autonomy.

While there is broad critical agreement on something like the above characterization of the Knight's Thesean ethos, there is also a widely shared view that this ethos entails an invidious form of rationalism.[5] I think there is something to this charge, but it needs to be put carefully, partly because the Knight's ethos is quite pointedly *resistant* to ethical rationalism. For one thing, however committed to prudential and judicious reflection the Knight may be, he consistently makes clear distinctions between the time for reflection and the time for action; and when the time for reflection is past, the Knight values above all else the aggressive pursuit of policy. Once Theseus brings himself to understand the motives and plight of the grieving widows, for instance, he heads for Thebes without delay and assaults the city until it can offer no resistance. By contrast, part of what makes Palamon and Arcite seem comical is their tendency to wallow in poorly directed reflection, as in the symmetrical speeches at the end of part one, in which each considers the hopelessness of his current situation at length while imagining the possibilities for action available to the other. The Thesean ethos of the tale, then, is properly understood as an ethos of decisive action rather than as one that privileges reflection for its own sake. Reflection is a value to the extent that it enables decisiveness, and it is a necessary value because without a notion of proper reflection one would be left, as in the Miller's theory, with no workable notion of decisiveness at all. For the Knight, significantly, proper reflection in a given instance can mean no reflection at all, as when Theseus simply "slough [Creon] manly as a knyght / In pleyn bataille" (I.987–88). The just reward for Creon's crimes is supposed to be self-evident, and the Knight thinks there could be no good reason to question it. What counts in defining the decisiveness of a course of action, then, is not that someone goes through any particular process of thought before deciding to pursue it, but rather that it meets what we might call the condition of reflective endorsability.[6] According to such a condition, *if* the course of action in question were to be brought under reflective scrutiny, it would stand up as the right one. When you resist the urge to scream obscenities at an overly aggressive driver, for instance, your restraint would presumably meet such a condition. But that example suggests that part of what is involved in understanding the application of such a condition is knowing the difference between cases when you need to engage in reflective scrutiny and cases when you do not: if you had to think it through each time you exercised such restraint, that would be less a sign of self-command than an indication of a peculiar character defect.[7] The Knight is sensitive to such distinctions, and part of the point of Theseus's military adventures is to bring them out.

Theseus, then, does not march under the banner of Mars for nothing: he is less a figure of philosophical authority than one of martial virtue, the courageous and purposeful exercise of military and political power in the service of justice and civil order. This is the meaning of the schematic contrast between Thesean polity and the Theban civil war associated with Creon.[8] And Theseus does not serve justice in this way simply because he considers it rational to do so, nor does the Knight think he should. Some of Theseus's motivation simply stems from his Martian disposition: he relishes the display and exercise of violent military power, he is moved by anger and the love of battle. The Knight does not think there is anything wrong with this; he does not want to extirpate such passions so much as he wants to dominate them with a powerful will, and so to be able to give free rein to them where it is appropriate to do so. Nor does he think there is anything wrong with another aspect of Thesean motivation, his self-regarding love of honor. Theseus wants to be known as the man who took vengeance on Creon, the man to whom gratitude for a just political order is due: as he assures the Theban widows, "al the peple of Grece sholde speke / How Creon was of Theseus yserved / As he that hadde his deeth ful wel deserved" (I.962–64). As far as the Knight is concerned, these are a good ruler's normal attributes, without which he would not have the motivational structure to conduct himself as he should.[9]

As valuable as these attributes are to the Knight, it remains the case that a self-regarding concern for honor and a disposition to violence leave Theseus vulnerable to displays of egocentrism and misdirected anger, as he shows when first confronting the Theban widows: " 'What folk been ye, that at myn homcomynge / Perturben so my feste with criynge?' / Quod Theseus. 'Have ye so greet envye / Of myn honour, that thus compleyne and crye?' " (I.905–8). Meeting a group of weeping, swooning, black-clad women kneeling two-by-two in the roadside, Theseus initially sees the public posture of grief as a personal affront, an envious resistance to the free display and celebration of his virtue. This embarrassing misperception is compounded by the fact that Theseus, as the just and merciful ruler, ought to understand this scene rightly, as in fact he does immediately afterwards, with seemingly nothing intervening to alter his perceptions: "And telleth me if it may been amended, / And why that ye been clothed thus in blak" (I.910–11). Part of the oddness of the moment for Theseus, then, is that everything he needs to see to know how to act rightly is in plain view before him; and he is the kind of person who can and does act rightly in the face of such things; but he somehow misses this, as though he had forgotten the most obvious truths about the world and about who he is in it. And this oddness is compounded by another. For Theseus's vulnerability to such a moment proceeds *not* from some weakness in his character that competes with the virtues I have been describing – as though this were Theseus's "dark side" coming out – but rather from features of his character which are *essential* to his being the virtuous figure that he is.[10] Since Theseus is driven to such forgetting by features of his character which he has no way of foregoing – and further, the foregoing of which would make him unfit for rule – the Knight must place a high ethical premium on considerations of prudence and judiciousness, which require the development of a reflective distance on one's immediate attitudes and the cultivation of a more objective view of the scene of action than those attitudes afford.

Since an appeal to the normative authority of objectivity is frequently taken to bring with it a great deal of conceptual baggage which it does not in this case have, and since the Knight himself is concerned to detail what the cultivation of an objective view entails, it is worth examining at length the passage where the Knight most directly elaborates on the relation between autonomy and objectivity. At the end of part two Theseus comes upon Palamon and Arcite battling in a grove, ankle-deep in blood. On hearing the Thebans confess that they have violated his commands, Theseus immediately announces his "short conclusioun" (I.1743) that they be put to death, at which point the ladies in his company weep for pity and beg Theseus for mercy: "And on hir bare knees adoun they falle / And wolde have kist his feet ther as he stood; / Til at the laste aslaked was his mood, / For pitee renneth soone in gentil herte" (I.1758–61). By initially locating pity in the scene in the company of ladies surrounding the men, the Knight sets up an emblematic tableau in which Theseus's embodiment of the hard sentence of justice is opposed by a womanly show of feeling, the embodiment of mercy's softness. But with the quick movement of pity natural to Theseus's noble heart, the Knight leaves aside this emblematic mode of representation, and the conflict between mercy and justice takes place within Theseus. The point of this shift in representational mode seems to be to mimic the nature of the problem Theseus faces. At the moment of the scene's high emblematic mode, Theseus is captured by an anger which comes to him with the full force of a natural, even inevitable, response, and which brings with it a posture of judgment which he represents as definitive and final. As long as he imagines his identification with this posture to be total, the ladies' attitude appears as "wommanly pitee," no part of the proper manly (and lordly) response to what has happened. But Theseus responds to that display of feeling with the quick movement of pity that is proper to the noble, not just the womanly, heart – proper, that is, to the heart he both claims as his own and imagines as normative for anyone in his situation. The ladies' pity, then, represents a disposition to right feeling which Theseus already has, and one which is conducive to the judgment he will soon declare to be right: "Fy / Upon a lord that wol have no mercy" (I.1773–74). Theseus's problem is one of recognizing the normative claim this disposition has on him, the way it issues from an identity he recognizes as more deeply his than that of the merciless dispenser of justice. This requires him to see his distinctness from the posture he initially identifies himself with, to take a more objective view of himself and the scene than his subjective absorption in his anger initially allows him.

It should already be clear that the distinction between subjective and objective views here is not the dualist distinction between a view from within some particular person's consciousness and a view from outside subjectivity altogether. Nor does it bring in its wake the related dualism between the irrationality of a mind clouded by passion, accidents of character, and egoistic motivation and a pure rationality unsullied by desire or the "merely personal." The view Theseus comes to, as he says, is appropriate to a certain kind of ruler with a certain kind of ethical character, rather than one belonging to a purely rational appraiser with no particular character at all; and his adoption of this view is quite deeply and personally motivated by his desire to be that kind of ruler, and even by the emotions of the moment such as pity and compassion. Theseus's mercy gets its objective character from two things: that it can stand up under reflective scrutiny, and that it allows Theseus to see his angry judgment as a partial response, driven by features of his subjective state which are both internally inadequate and insufficiently responsive to the scene before him.

Reason does of course have a central role here, as is suggested by the process of reflection that follows on Theseus's initial movement by pity:

> And though he first for ire quook and sterte,
> He hath considered shortly, in a clause,
> The trespas of hem bothe, and eek the cause,
> And although that his ire hir gilt accused,
> Yet in his resoun he hem bothe excused,
> As thus: he thoghte wel that every man
> Wol helpe hymself in love, if that he kan,
> And eek delivere hymself out of prisoun.
> (I.1762–69)

Through the exercise of his rational capacities Theseus moves from being sheerly possessed by the passion of anger to a state in which "his ire hir gilt accused," that is, in which Theseus has driven an initial wedge between himself and the angry accusation of guilt, seeing the accusation as issuing from the passion moving him rather than from himself as a totality. And through the further exercise of his rational capacities Theseus moves past feeling split into parts – moved by an anger and a pity which present him with incompatible pictures of the scene before him and of his own interior dispositions – and is able to pull himself together and see the rightness of a merciful path of action. Theseus's reason enables him thus to move from being controlled by a passion which from the point of view of his own most authoritative identifications he does not want to be moved by, to being moved only by what from that same point of view he wants to be moved by. In a sense, then, the pity that finally moves him is not the same as the pity that initially appeared in conflict with his anger. For the pity that is the upshot of his deliberations is not in the same sense a passion, not something that simply arises in him as an event in his natural history, seizing and compelling him. At the end, the sheer *affect* of pity is not what compels him: if that were the only thing at issue here there would be nothing to get him past the point of a conflict of affects. What gives pity its final motive force is rather the fact that it belongs to a larger practical attitude that gives meaning to the desires, beliefs, reasons, and other psychic states that attend it – the attitude of mercy that has become normative for Theseus. And that attitude has become normative for him because it has stood the test of reflective endorsability. Theseus is moved by mercy because it is proper to the ends he has freely chosen, and so is expressive of his autonomy.[11]

If the Knight is in no way concerned to banish emotion, desire, and character from the scene of action, then, he remains concerned to banish passion in a technical sense. He wants to cast the sheer undergoing of subjective states, the fact that they can arise in us unwanted and move us whether we want them to or not, as the main threat to the achievement of autonomy. The Knight's favorite trope for this undergoing is that of "subjection to the animal": as Theseus says, the merciless lord who fails to exercise discretion is a lion; in effect, such a lord allows himself to be controlled by brute facts of the nature he shares with animals that do not have the capacity to choose their ends. The Knight indicates Theseus's alignment with this banishment from the beginning of the tale by having him march under the pennant of the Minotaur: Theseus is the slayer of the man-beast, restorer of the boundary between the human and the animal. The use of the trope becomes almost obsessive in the descriptions of Palamon and Arcite in the first half of the tale, particularly during their battle in the grove: "thou myghtest wene that this Palamon / In his fightyng were a wood leon, / And as a crueel tigre was Arcite; / As wilde bores gonne they to smyte"

97

(I.1655–58). It is important to note that the impulse to violence here remains to some extent an object of admiration, as it does later in the tournament Theseus organizes. The Knight's point in casting this violence as animalized, then, is to indicate a failure properly to direct a disposition to violence which is not in itself blameworthy, and which humans have in some form simply by virtue of being the kind of animal they are. To put the Knight's view most broadly, such failure to shape the animality that is necessarily part of being human is what constitutes a privation of autonomy, and what distinguishes the Thebans from Theseus.

We can more clearly see the difference between this view and the rationalism often attributed to the Knight if we notice that, while he locates this privation most obviously in what we ordinarily think of as passions – in the overwhelming power of erotic desire and military anger, for instance – he locates it as well in the way Palamon and Arcite undergo their rationality. And rationality, too – that is, the capacity for reflection and representation – is, on a standard classical and medieval definition, something that is necessarily part of being human simply by virtue of the kind of animal a human is. As I have already suggested, it is not as though the Theban cousins simply find themselves perpetually hurtled into rash action by uncontrolled emotion. For long stretches of the poem they become almost exclusively creatures of pointedly defective reflection, bound by imprisonment or exile to nearly hopeless and often incoherent deliberation, to overly florid expressions of their love for Emily which continually stop short of the lyrical expansiveness they aim for, to sententious efforts at consolation, and to contemplative immersion in their suffering. What these moments share with the moments of erotic and military passion is the quality of undergoing: here too Palamon and Arcite find themselves compelled by whatever subjective state happens to arise in them.

This feature of the representation of the Thebans reaches its comic extreme as Arcite multiplies legalistic and mutually exclusive defenses of his claim to Emily. Arcite argues that Emily is really his, because he loved her first "paramour" (I.1155), as a human creature, while Palamon did not love Emily, exactly, but only felt "affeccioun of hoolynesse" (I.1158), a passion for divinity. But, Arcite continues, suppose that Palamon did love Emily first, he should remember the old saw that no one can give a lover any law, for love is a natural law which compels beyond the power of "positif lawe" (I.1167), mere human legislation – that is, Arcite just cannot help himself. And, in case his previous arguments do not hold, neither of them can get her anyway – an argument which serves to defeat Arcite's claim as much as Palamon's. Then, somehow as a logical conclusion, Arcite concludes that "therfore" (I.1181) it is each man for himself; and finally, nonsensically, that they have to endure their life in prison and each take his own chances, as though, considering their acknowledged powerlessness, there were any chances for them to take. While Arcite is unreservedly committed to the thought that one way or another Emily is his, the sententiousness, bogus technicality, and internal contradictions of his speech serve to rob any of its arguments of legitimate conviction, a lack which Arcite clearly feels, since he cannot rest with any of the reasons he trots out in his defense. But despite his own sense of the complete dispensability of any of his reasons, he is never able to engage in the minimal thought necessary to articulate a coherent basis for his claim, much less that required to hold up his underlying motives for appraisal and so potentially take command of himself in the way Theseus does. Instead he remains compelled by each of his reasons serially in the moment it comes up for him, as though his reasons were subjective states he merely undergoes, over which he exercises no authority. This is the sense in which Palamon and Arcite are "subjected to the animal": not that there is some animal nature lurking in them under a thin veneer of civilization, but that even those dispositions which most obviously depend on their distinctively human capacities – such as their capacity to form reasons – function for them solely in what we might describe as their animal aspect, under which they appear not as autonomous activities but as undergoings of the brute facts of human nature.

My point in elaborating the Knight's theory of autonomy at such length has been to suggest that it is a good theory, considerably better than the one usually attributed to him. As I have suggested, what makes an action, reason, or desire autonomous in this theory is its reflective endorsability. A person's rational capacities play a central role in the activity of reflective endorsement, but it is finally the person, not his or her reason, that determines what is endorsable and does the endorsing. The Knight does not imagine that reason constitutes a separate metaphysical or psychological territory from that of desire or the passions: as we have seen, reasons can function in his theory as passions in the technical sense, and there is such a thing for him as a rational desire.[12] The Knight therefore cannot think that our job as agents is to submit one part of ourselves – the body, animality, desire – to another part that knows the truth or the law and administers it to the rest. Further, the notion of reflective endorsability allows for quite a supple sense of a person's agentive relations to the contents of his or her subjectivity. If Theseus were to engage in introspection he would find an opaque, shifting, and contradictory subjectivity; the Knight is quite clear that no reified subjective contents can either determine anyone's psychology or tell them what to do. Even the presence in Theseus of what he comes to recognize as the right disposition does not track out into action independently of a deliberative activity that goes well beyond mere observation. For, as I have shown, Thesean deliberation changes what it means to be moved in a particular way. Even though Theseus was moved by pity at all stages in the deliberative process, the pity that emerges as part of the larger attitude of rightful mercy is not the same thing as the more narrowly "passionate" pity with which Theseus began, precisely because it is now supported by authoritative reasons.

To return to the Knight's ethos of decisiveness: the reflective endorsability of an action is what makes it decisive, for that is what makes it expressive not merely of the reasons or desires of the moment but of the reasons and desires an agent wants to be his, in light of the kind of person he wants to be. These are the kind of deliberative considerations to which Theseus is generally open, and which Palamon and Arcite hardly allow to enter into their minds. The Knight's theory is therefore able to respond to what theories of autonomy often imagine as the "accidents" of character, the particular dispositions of particular persons, without depending on a reified, naturalistic notion of what being some particular person consists in. This is what makes his theory good: it allows him to appeal to something theories of autonomy must appeal to, a normative authority that orders an agent's dispositions, providing him with a basis for identifying with some dispositions rather than others, while preserving the sense in which that authority proceeds from the agent himself, from his own desires and reasons, and so takes the form neither of an imposition or repression, nor of a demand issued from an abstract, impersonal source.

Through the Knight's representation of Theseus, Chaucer took the opportunity, right at the start of the *Canterbury Tales*, to lay out the contours of a theory of autonomy that is about as good as he thought it was possible to produce. It is a theory that, as I have argued, avoids the conceptual problems in naturalism and formalism which remain of such interest to Chaucer elsewhere in his poetry, including elsewhere in this very poem. Even here, however, Chaucer remains less interested in theory itself than in the situatedness out of which theory gets produced and the blindnesses that always attend its insights; he wants to understand what further thoughts about agency this theory cannot accommodate and, more ambitiously, he wants to understand why autonomy resists grounding in any comprehensive theory. For the Knight, these opacities and resistances emerge from the place of the erotic in the poem. As I have suggested, his articulation of a Thesean ideal depends on the bracketing off of an erotics to which the Knight remains quite deeply attracted. I will now turn to the ways erotic desire problematizes a Thesean ideal, linking it to the very formalism the Knight uses it to repudiate, and opening the tale to possibilities of autonomy which a Thesean ideal provides no terms for understanding.

EROS AND AUTONOMY

Much of what I have said so far about the contrast between Theseus and the Thebans depends on a widely shared critical view that the first half of the *Knight's Tale* pursues an essentially comic project, in which Palamon and Arcite are held up for ridicule and Theseus is imagined as embodying a clear alternative to Theban psychic and civil perversion.[13] This project more or less reaches its peak in Theseus's "God of Love" speech concluding the first half of the tale, a speech that diagnoses Theban folly from a supposedly secure position of Athenian wisdom. The second half of the tale, on such an account, exhibits the collapse of this comic project as the Thesean goal of rational self-governance and just polity begins in various ways to look unattainable. It is certainly true that the second half of the tale is full of moments that threaten such a project: examples would include the horrifying description of the temple of Mars, Emily's terrified visit to Diana's temple, the unfolding of a divine conspiracy that supersedes all sublunary plans of action and seems to unmask them as a sham, the brute bodily subjection of Arcite to his mortal injuries, the obsessive *occupatio* of Arcite's funeral, and Theseus's failed attempt to offer a coherent philosophical consolation in the "Prime Mover" speech that concludes the tale. I agree, then, with those accounts of the tale that describe the first half of it as, at the very least, much more carefully managed than the second half. But the problems with Thesean autonomy that most clearly emerge in the second half of the tale are, I think, present even at the peak of the Knight's comic project and in the midst of his articulation of a Thesean ideal, however he may wish to obscure this through a rhetoric that initially keeps Theban perversion at arm's length. To see how, let us return to Theseus's deliberations on confronting Palamon and Arcite in the grove.

The success of Theseus's practical reasoning there depends, as I have said, on his not calling into question his basic understanding of who he is and what he admires. Theseus is a good, magnanimous ruler, a man of *megalopsychia*, proud, sure, and aggressive, prudent and just – in a word, noble. The normative authority of such a self-conception is what grounds his sense of autonomy: a free action, or for that matter a free desire or belief or other attitude, is one that can in principle stand the test of reflective endorsability, and the criterion of an attitude's endorsability is that it be appropriate to the noble person Theseus understands himself to be. But Theseus is also perfectly aware that such self-understandings can be questionable, and that not calling them into question can be disastrous; for that is just what he thinks is the case with Palamon and Arcite, who have been driven into what Theseus thinks is the deepest folly by their unquestioned commitment to a love that determines everything that counts for them. Theseus knows, then, that the danger of being overcome by the passion of the moment – as he himself is overcome when he angrily condemns the Thebans to death – is not the only, or even the main, threat to autonomy. A much greater threat comes from passions that you would identify not as alien to your proper will but as constitutive of it, but which seem nevertheless to take you away from yourself, leaving you devoted to the very loss you suffer. This is the structure of divided identification and normative longing we have already seen in Augustine: "Surely I have not ceased to be my own self . . . and yet there is still a great gap between myself and myself . . . Oh that my soul might follow my own self . . . that it might not be a rebel to itself." And for the Knight, as for Augustine, that structure is associated paradigmatically with erotic desire. Upon concluding his deliberations in the grove, Theseus makes the association between eros and self-division in saying that Palamon and Arcite have become subject to a God of Love that "kan maken, at his owene gyse, / Of everich herte as that hym list divyse" (I.1789–90). It seems to Theseus, in other words, as though Palamon and Arcite are no longer in a position to give themselves a law, but are subject to the law of another; but this heteronomous law is heart making, it constitutes their deepest identifications and desires. This is why, as Theseus mockingly says, "And yet they wenen for to been ful wyse / That serven love, for aught that may bifalle" (I.1804–05). However blindly moved by anger Theseus can be, he knows that he is not being wise in such moments, for he identifies wisdom with his characteristic capacity to rule justly, which such anger disturbs. The problem Palamon and Arcite present, however, is that of a folly that looks exactly like wisdom from the perspective of a person's deepest volitional characteristics, a folly that can only appear as such from outside the commitments that constitute the person's character. Neither love nor anger may constitute such a folly for Theseus, but that does not mean that nothing does; and whatever might constitute Thesean folly, on his own account the very character on which he relies for deliberative success would keep him from knowing it.

The Knight's theory of autonomy establishes an idealized version of Thesean character as the objective anchor for practical reasoning. But on Theseus's account of how folly gets its hold, autonomy depends on a much more ambitious reflective drive, one that does not stop when it reaches an agent's central projects and most characteristic concerns. The Knight does not have a very clear idea of where that drive might lead, and it makes sense that he would not, since, for all his ethical seriousness, both he and his hero Theseus are warriors, and reflection that extends much beyond the kind Theseus pursues in the grove might delay the military pursuit of policy in a way the Knight would find unmanly. But the Knight and Theseus do attempt to formulate a basis for autonomy in this more ambitious reflective drive, precisely when forthright manly action has begun to look impossible, as Theseus, the Athenians, and even the Knight's narrative itself become transfixed by grief after Arcite's death. In this extreme case of motivational evacuation, in which both individuals and the polity need to move on but none of the reasons for doing so can reach through the sense of loss engulfing everyone, Theseus seeks grounds for action by looking not only beyond the perspective of a particular character, but beyond any partial creaturely perspective whatsoever. The core idea of Theseus's consolatory final speech is that if we could just see the universe as the "Prime Mover" does – as a "faire cheyne of love" (I.2988) – then death would appear not as a loss but as the return of materially differentiated finite substances to the perfect and stable whole from which they derive their essences, and from which they had originally descended into this world of corruption. As a number of critics have noted, Theseus is anything but successful at making the identificatory leap to such a perspective.[14] He keeps getting sucked back into the world of phenomenal appearances in which death *is* a terrible loss, and finally his metaphysical ambitions give way to contradictory attempts at pragmatic exhortation. Or rather, Theseus never really leaves that phenomenal world, and even his sweet dream of a fair chain of love is itself motivated by the pressure death continues to exert on his imagination. Far from providing an objective anchor for practical reasoning, the thought of a world ordered by its participation in a loving originary oneness remains unmoored from the space of action it is supposed to inform.

The first problem with the Knight's theory of autonomy, then, is that while he tries to ground it in the normative authority of an ethos he admires, he knows it requires something more ambitious; but he cannot formulate what that something might be in a way that retains meaningful contact with the scene of agency. This problem is one of the main sources of the ethical and erotic formalism I discussed earlier in the chapter. The only way the Knight can imagine a source of normativity immune from the possibilities of psychic and ethical fracture that grip Palamon and Arcite and haunt a Thesean ethos is to think of it as a perfect formal structure, like the chain of love that binds the elements into a cosmos expressive of divine oneness, or like the beautifully cultivated garden that mirrors the beautifully cultivated Emily within it. And the way he tries to imagine an agentive participation in such a structure is through the production of a formally perfect reason, a reason that directly binds the agent's motive to normativity's source. For Theseus, having such a super-reason would involve articulating the principle that grounds autonomous action: if he could just "declaren [his] sentence" (I.3002) as he sets out to do at the beginning of that final speech, then he would be able to act freely in a way that even death could not compromise. For Emily, having a super-reason would involve having the voice of normative authority perpetually there whispering in her ear "arys, and do thyn observaunce." In both cases, having a super-reason – a reason that admits no subjective interference, but tracks straight through to the scene of action – would be like being infallibly caused to do the right thing, and somehow having this causedness function as a fulfillment of agency rather than an effacement of it. The Knight remains quite close here to the Miller's fantasy of an agency with a passivity at its base, not out of a Millerish refusal of the normative authority of reflection, but out of his frustrated attempt to imagine that authority in its most powerful form.

We can see how the ethical formalism that emerges from this attempt opens on to an erotic formalism by attending to the functions of gender and beauty in the Knight's fantasy of a super-reason. For Theseus, the reach for such a reason is full of masculine effort, and as he continues to contemplate a landscape marred by death, this masculinity remains as abject as that of Palamon and Arcite. For Emily, having such a reason is an accomplishment as effortless as knitting the floral garland for her head, and this effortlessness informs the beauty that ravishes that same abject masculinity, not only with the force of an impossible desire for erotic possession, but with the force of an impossible desire for normative completeness. And this dual impossibility adds a beauty of its own, a luster akin to that of a far-off place one contemplates inhabiting, or a garden one longs to enter but from which one is debarred. To revise a relevant Augustinian phrase, Emily might thus be thought of as a postcard from the "land of likeness."

But this function of Emily's beauty is inflected by something quite different, and this further inflection of the erotic gives rise to another and seemingly opposite problem with the Knight's theory. Palamon and Arcite see Emily and are overcome by desire. One thing this means, as I have just said, is that they are overcome by their desire for and admiration of her "likeness" to herself, and so by their responsiveness to the ideal of a formally perfect ordering of the will. At the same time, however, in being overcome by desire Palamon and Arcite become passive, not in the Knight's idealized version of being moved by a super-reason, but in a way he finds damaging to autonomy. So for the Knight the problem of erotic desire and the beauty to which it responds is in large part the problem of what to do with this conflict of intuitions concerning the value of being overcome by love as Palamon and Arcite are.

I argued earlier that a Thesean self-possession is predicated on the banishing of passion in a technical sense. The Knight casts the sheer undergoing of subjective states as something to be avoided, and sees such undergoings as no fit part of an agent's motive, whether or not they are undergoings we would normally describe as "passions." But the Knight himself, as distinct from a critical reconstruction of his ethos at its clearest, mostly means one thing by this: that erotic passion, if not just aversible, is at least extremely suspect. The Knight may not seem to have such a restricted focus. After all, violence and its relations to anger and pride most immediately threaten to carry Theseus away from himself, and they are the focus of some of the Knight's most striking losses of narrative control, such as in the terrifying portraits in the temple of Mars and the obsessive description of Arcite's injuries. But the obviousness of the danger posed by violent passion allows the Knight to imagine its management, even if that management is not always sucessful. Theseus constantly reflects on the dangers inherent in violence, and his most dominant self-representation is that of the just servant of Mars, the one who directs his military impulses towards a rational end. Because Theseus devotes himself to noticing his tendency to excess in this regard, both he and the Knight seem confident that reflective endorsement, at least in principle, can provide a way for the individual agent to manage his violence; and they seem equally confident that forms of social regulation – tournaments, for instance – can do the same thing in the collective case, even if they cannot shield us from terrible accidents of fate.

But things are different with eros. Theseus serves and manages Mars, but he does not in parallel fashion serve and manage Venus. Instead he is devoted to Diana, and in his speech on the powers of the God of Love he banishes eros to the past of a youthful folly from which he declares himself now to be immune. As several critics have recently argued, the Knight seems intent on shielding Theseus from eros in other ways that radiate out into the narrative's gender politics. In comparison to Boccaccio's treatment of the story, the Knight deeroticizes and generally deemphasizes the relationship between Theseus and Hippolyta, and suppresses Theseus's Ovidian history as a betrayer of women, something that quite interests Chaucer elsewhere.[15] Further, in the scene of Theseus in the grove, the shift in representational mode which articulates the Knight's theory of reflective endorsement has a disturbing double effect: it liberates Theseus from his emblematic identification with military anger, but fixes Hippolyta and the other women in the scene in their emblematic identifications with womanly pity. The women thus end up as quasiallegorical representations of one aspect of a universalized masculine subjectivity.[16] The Knight's short line on Palamon and Arcite is that they are fools for love. His short line on Theseus seems to be that he is wise because he is not a lover. Wisdom – and, as I have argued, autonomy itself – seems to the Knight to depend on preventing eros from being a passionate undergoing that might sweep you up and bear you away. And this contrast between Theban folly and Athenian wisdom depends on an impulse to allegorize the feminine and to efface feminine agency, something we have seen not just in the grove but in the initial representation of Emily as well.

This restriction of what is in the abstract quite a capacious understanding of passion suggests that there is something about erotic life which the Knight feels as a deep threat to his ideal of Thesean autonomy and his sense of the stability of gender difference. And the key to understanding this threat, I think, lies in the Knight's ambivalence over the value of Palamon and Arcite's being overcome by Emily's beauty, his way of casting their passion as both pathological and glamorous. The Knight wants to imagine that all decisive action – by which he also means all action expressive of a will that has freely chosen its ends – is, if not the actual upshot of a deliberative process, at least in principle open to reflective endorsement. He seems to imagine that the threat posed to autonomy by pride and military anger is that of being moved in ways that simply run counter to one's authentic ends. The danger here, in effect, is that of being caused to act by passions that, however subject you are to them, can in principle be identified as alien to your own deepest identifications. But erotic compulsion of the kind figured in Palamon and Arcite is different. For it is not as though the desire for Emily simply subjects them to failures of self-command. It certainly does make them act in ways that violate principles of justice and self-interest to which they themselves are committed. It does so, however, *not* because it moves them in ways that run counter to their own deepest identifications, but rather because it generates an over-whelming new territory of identification. Erotic desire creates for Palamon and Arcite an ordering of the will that could never be the product of deliberation, and that might well not stand up to any process of reflective consideration. Loving Emily is not something they would choose prospectively or could argue themselves into, and even once they are committed to it, they might never be able to articulate a set of considerations in light of which it is the right thing to do. Palamon and Arcite are subject to a kind of necessity that violates the Knight's conditions of autonomous action, and that makes these lovers not even *care* whether they would choose the ends they now have. But nevertheless the Knight also makes it clear that such loving opens up a space of exhilarating freedom, a space in which these lovers confront a perfection that calls them out of the identities they had once seen as theirs, a space in which they care about something so deeply that it now serves as an organizing principle for everything in them and in the world they inhabit.[17] And, to return to the ordering of gender, this is not exactly feminization, but neither does it sort very well with anything the Knight is prepared to recognize as masculine, at least insofar as Theseus remains at the center of the Knight's masculine ideal.

The first problem eros presented to the Knight's theory of autonomy was that it revealed that theory's reliance on a more ambitious drive to reflective distance than it was able to accommodate. The second problem eros presents is that it reveals the Knight's ambivalence over relying on reflective distance at all. On the one hand, as the central tropes by which he represents Palamon and Arcite suggest, it looks to him as though erotic compulsion could not be anything but an imprisonment in desire, an exile from one's authentic self. This sense of the matter is backed by the Knight's commitment to a theory of autonomy of the kind outlined above. For Palamon and Arcite cannot be decisive in the way Theseus is; they are not acting in ways that could in principle stand the test of reflective endorsability; and this makes it look as though their passion were a case of fixation in a condition like the one Theseus suffers momentarily when he is moved by anger and pride. The Knight tries to shore up this inadequate association between the passion involved in the cousins' loving and that in Thesean anger. This is the point of their fratricidal impulses, their incoherent self-understanding, and, allegorically, of their Theban genealogy: because they are moved in ways that cannot be accommodated to a Thesean autonomy, the Knight wants to suggest that there is nothing to distinguish them from a Creonlike monstrosity in which all possibilities of social and psychic order are destroyed. But it is also true that, in emerging "neither quick nor dead" from the undifferentiated mass of Theban bodies which is the result of Theseus's supposedly definitive destruction of that city and everything it represents, what they ultimately emerge into is the ongoing life of Thesean polity and of the Knight's narrative. And they emerge, not just as figures for a danger which Theseus and the Knight want, if not to destroy, then at least to contain, but also as figures for both the depth and the attractiveness of the compulsion they exhibit. This is captured in part by the Knight's attraction to the very features of Emily which occasion Palamon and Arcite's abjection, an attraction related to the glamor of the Thebans' suffering. If they are figures for a kind of psychic ill-health, it is an ill-health that involves the utter disregard for mere health because of the sheer weight of something that matters so much that it utterly abolishes the mattering of anything else. This is a possibility of authentic action and identity that the Knight neither can nor wants to do without, however difficult it is to accommodate in theory. And in fact the Knight's Thesean ethos depends on such a possibility in disavowed form; for, as we have seen, that ethos itself is the site of undeliberative commitments which the Knight knows might not stand up to reflection, but about which he cares so deeply that they constitute a locus of autonomy for him.

In the light of these problems, the Knight's Thesean ethos begins to look less like his basic ideal than a rather uneasy compromise solution, dependent on incompatible conceptions of the source of normativity, neither of which can be recognized as such without calling into question the Knight's notion of reflective endorsability. I do not think the

Knight's uneasiness or wish to compromise in this respect is peculiar to him, nor can its ultimate source be found in any of the various suspect ideologies in which he is implicated. In the next chapter, through a reading of Boethius's *Consolation of Philosophy*, I will argue that agency is necessarily structured around such an uneasy compromise. Understanding Boethius's interest in this compromise will thus help us understand better a common thought about the *Knight's Tale*, that Chaucer began the *Canterbury Tales* with it in order to engage head-on what he learned from Boethius. But before turning to Boethius I want to close this chapter with a few final thoughts on Emily.

One way to encapsulate my argument concerning Emily's beauty is that it embodies both of the Knight's radical promptings. On the one hand, the tug of her beauty on her admirers figures the way we can find freedom in the kind of specific passionate attachments that wither away under the drive to reflective distance. This is the thrilling freedom of a commitment to a desire that seizes you, and to which you devote yourself with no question of reflective endorsability entering your mind. You could never endorse it anyway, but what is more, you do not care: even if your love turned out to be a gross violation of prudence, as it does for Palamon and Arcite, you would devote yourself to it anyway. And not just because you cannot get over it; even if you could get over it, you would not want to. It would diminish your sense of a life worth living to get over it, or to turn it into a reflective consideration subject to endorsement or rejection. In this respect, "Emily" holds out the pleasures of a violation of the normative authority of reflective distance, the discovery of a normative ground and a kind of autonomy that does not derive from practical reason. Yet Emily's beauty, imagined as it is as a formal perfection that supplies practical reason with its ultimate guarantee, at the same time figures the attractiveness of the very normative authority whose violation it compels. Emily is at the center of the tale's normative imagination because her attractiveness simultaneously embodies the Knight's conflicted intuitions concerning autonomy and his fantasy of how those conflicts might be resolved.

CHAPTER 3

Agency and dialectic in the *Consolation of Philosophy*

Despite Chaucer's deep engagement with the *Consolation of Philosophy* throughout his poetic career, virtually no major study of the *Canterbury Tales* in the last fifteen years has had much to say about Boethius.[1] The reason for this widespread exhaustion or boredom with Boethius is that the underlying critical terms for understanding Chaucer's relation to the *Consolation* have remained unchanged for quite some time. There are, of course, important disagreements within this broadly shared set of terms. Opinion runs from the view that the *Consolation* is the source for a set of core philosophical doctrines which Chaucer illustrates in his poetry, to the view that Boethius stands for a philosophically and politically dangerous idealism that Chaucer subjects to a searching critique; there is also a moderate position according to which Chaucer is in many ways committed to Boethian ideals, but nonetheless reveals their limitations by placing them against a rich panoply of competing desires, beliefs, and other commitments.[2] Underlying these disagreements, however, is a shared belief that what centrally matters about the *Consolation* is a set of philosophical doctrines or positions that can be independently summarized in clear propositional form, and that can therefore become in a straightforward way the objects of a propositional attitude, whether belief or qualified assent or outright rejection. That is, the fundamental goal of Boethian philosophy is understood to be that of saying the truth about the topics it engages; and one's relationship to such philosophy – Boethius's, or Chaucer's, or for that matter ours – is understood to be fundamentally cognitive or intellectual, one of assent or dissent.

This is a recipe for critical exhaustion for two reasons: first, because we have all known for a long time what Boethius's philosophical positions are, so very quickly there can be nothing new to say on that score; and second, because focusing narrowly on those positions virtually requires us to be insufficiently attentive to the dialectical character of Boethian philosophizing. As I will argue, it is this dialectical character that finally matters most both for an assessment of Boethius's philosophical achievement and for an account of that achievement's importance to Chaucer. Boethian dialectic has not exactly gone undiscussed by Chaucerians, and much of what is best in the critical discussion of Boethius attends to the dialectical character of the *Consolation* in ways that complicate the sketch of critical views I have just offered. I agree with Winthrop Wetherbee, for instance, that both Boethian dialectic and the philosophical and poetic traditions that grow out of the *Consolation* are more interested in exploratory psychology than they are in the abstract articulation of a doctrine.[3] But dialectical form tends to be imagined in even the best discussions of the *Consolation* as something essentially external to the philosophy itself – perhaps, as Seth Lerer has it, as a necessary treatment for the confusions that must be transcended to reach the realm of true philosophical thought, or perhaps, as Wetherbee has it, as a register of the passionate human commitments that philosophy cannot adequately take into account.[4] I will argue, however, that the problem posed by dialectical form in the *Consolation* concerns aporias that arise internally to the very nature of philosophical reflection; the problems that arise concerning the relationship of philosophy to something else, such as prephilosophical confusion, or the emotions, or the limits of linguistic expression, derive from this more basic one. My argument is in some respects similar to ones that have been made about Platonic dialectic.[5] As is the case in such discussions of Plato, an emphasis on aporetic structures is not meant to discount the arguments that occupy so much of the *Consolation,* or the powerful claims that are meant to be the upshot of those arguments. I have no doubt that Boethius, and for that matter Chaucer, is committed to the power of those arguments and the truth of those claims. Attention to the aporetic dialectics of the text suggests instead that no one's fundamental relationship to these claims, or to the work of philosophy that surrounds the articulation of these claims, can finally be one of either assent or dissent, even in the ideal case in which nothing "unphilosophical" intrudes to spoil the day.

Understanding the more complex forms taken by a relationship to the work of philosophy will bring us back to Wetherbee's point about a Boethian interest in exploratory psychology. As I will argue, the *Consolation* provides ways of understanding psychological phenomena – such as repression, disavowal, perversion, fetishism, and masochism – which we have come to associate too narrowly with modern sexual forms and their psychoanalytic theorization. A fuller understanding of Boethian dialectics will thus help as well with this book's project of deriving medieval conceptions of such phenomena by detaching them from the sexual context we have come to think of as their ground, and clearing a path for understanding them in other terms; this will then set the stage for a return to the analysis of sexuality in the next chapter's discussion of the *Roman de la Rose*. More specifically, the complexities of misrecognition, disavowal, and attachment in this analysis will emerge as the psychological upshot of the structure of practical rationality. This is in keeping with a broader medieval and classical tendency to derive accounts of psychology from accounts of agency, a tendency Daniel Westberg and Candace Vogler have illuminated in the work of Aquinas.[6] This tendency is counterintuitive to our dominant modern intellectual traditions, shaped as they are by an empiricist explanatory trajectory that works the other way around – a trajectory, that is, that takes accounts of psychological states as the basis for an understanding of action. Far from arguing that Boethius, the *Rose*, or Chaucer are protomodern, or that it takes psychoanalysis to reveal the underlying truth of their texts, I will be reconstructing a mode of analysis made virtually unrecognizable by the empiricist idiom of high modernity, an idiom in which we remain deeply embedded, however we may protest to the contrary.

Given the depth of our entanglement in these matters and the real philosophical difficulties Boethius engages, such reconstruction will require extended philosophical work in the context of close reading of Boethius's text rather than the kind of capsule summaries on which intellectual history traditionally relies. In order to be clear about how the revisionary reading of Boethius I will ultimately suggest emerges from concerns we have long recognized in the *Consolation*, I want to begin with the familiar, the core argument concerning desire and happiness in Books II and III of the *Consolation*. Understanding what is both powerful and elusive about this argument – quite apart, at first, from any attention to the specific form of the Prisoner's engagement with it – will take us some way towards an account of the psychology that emerges from Boethius's analysis of action and that informs his use of philosophical dialogue.

THE HAPPINESS ARGUMENT AND BOETHIAN PSYCHOLOGY

Philosophy's argument concerning desire and happiness is familiar enough from its classical sources.[7] The argument goes as follows. If we ask what people want, the first thing we might do is produce a list of multiple goods. People want all sorts of things: possessions, money, power, fame, sex, love, honor, and so on. But if we then ask why people want these things, the answer is that they want them because they think that having these things will make them happy. What people really want, then, is happiness, and they want whatever particular goods they say they want because they think that these are the things whose possession will bring happiness. But then a little reflection about the status of these goods raises some troubling questions. Can you *really* get happiness from something that might suddenly disappear from the world? Or from something you just happen to have by luck, something that might disappear from your grasp if your luck changes? Or from something that, however satisfying the possession of it is, leaves other wants unmet, so that desire for things you lack continues to press in on you? The answer to these questions, Philosophy says, is no; our ordinary pictures of happiness are shot through with anxiety and bitterness. And this suggests that what we really want in wanting happiness is something other than possession of any of the goods we ordinarily say we want. For none of the goods we routinely pursue can be said to be fully and truly good; they are all missing something; they all leave desire, even in its apparent fulfillment, haunted by lack. Real happiness can only be achieved through the possession of what is supremely good: something that suffers no lack, something that can never change, something that relieves you of the desire for anything else. And there is only one candidate for the status of a supreme, unchangeable, perfect good that contains within itself all other goods, and that is God. True happiness, then, rests in union with the divine; and since everyone wants happiness, what everyone really wants is union with the divine. What is more, since all action aims at the good, union with the divine is the end towards which all action – even the most vicious, unjust action – aims. It is the intended aim of everything everyone does.

There are a host of problems with this as a philosophical argument. For one thing, its logic involves collapsing two very different claims about the relationship between action and an agent's notion of what is good: on the one hand, that everything an agent pursues is pursued under the aspect of some good – "omne appetitum appetitur sub specie boni," in the scholastic formulation that would become a commonplace by the later Middle Ages – and on the other, the much stronger claim that all action aims at one thing, which is "the good" as such.[8] We might well think, for instance, that people always perceive the ends they pursue as in *some* sense good – morally good in some cases, but more often just pleasant, or useful for some other end we have in mind – without thinking that there is any one final end which is *the* good, and towards which all action of whatever kind aims. What makes the collapse of these distinct claims into one formulation so much as credible is just a plain article of metaphysical and theological faith: that there is such a thing as a "supreme good," something in which a complete and permanent happiness, free from any taint or lack, resides, and something that contains within itself everything that truly deserves the label of a good. The function of this article of faith is important, and I will return to it. But we should not allow ourselves to think that we are somehow beyond this faith just because we have a cultural and historical distance on it, utterly disavow it, and can subject it to critique. Nor should we assume that Boethius is simply some sort of naïve or authoritarian adherent of tradition. The first thing we must do is try to see both what makes this argument powerful and what makes it problematic from Boethius's own point of view.

I take it that one motive for consigning this argument to the scrap heap of history is that, in claiming that desire has only one true object, it seems to rely on a thin and overly prescriptive psychology. There is some sense to this objection, but its sense is more limited than we may be tempted to believe. It might seem, for instance, that the claim that what people "really" want is happiness denies some obvious facts about what people want in pursuing the many goods at which action aims.

Don't people sometimes become so fixated on the pursuit of wealth or power or sex – or, for that matter, obsessive hand-washing – that they just don't care whether or not doing these things makes them happy? And for that matter, don't people sometimes sacrifice themselves and their personal happiness for a greater cause, like Bogart in *Casablanca*? One might think Boethius is advocating a strange kind of Stoicism in which passionate attachments and deep commitments of these kinds are not only prohibited but, insanely, declared to be impossible.[9] This would make it look as though the happiness argument provides too slight a notion of people's attachments and commitments to the actual goods they pursue, as though they took the form of an attachment to the instruments by which one pursues a happiness separately conceived. But anybody who ever wanted sex or clean hands or any of those other goods knows that our attachments to these things is more than merely instrumental. So if it looks like Boethius is denying this, the hinge on which the happiness argument turns will look like simple nonsense.

Part of the work of what follows will be to suggest that this objection is misplaced. It takes something Boethius knows full well and seeks to investigate – and moreover, something he reveals to be quite difficult to understand – and occludes it by pretending that it is common sense he somehow does not know or ignores. The core mistake being made in this objection, I think, involves the assumption that happiness amounts to a desirable psychological state, so that any investment in a state of affairs known by the agent to entail undesirable psychological states – as is certainly the case with an obsession or a self-sacrificing commitment – looks like an investment in something quite different from happiness.[10] But the various terms from Aristotle and Boethius and Aquinas that get translated as "happiness" – *eudaimonia, felicitas, beatitudo*, or for that matter the English word "happiness" itself on a sufficiently supple account of it – are not well understood by an empiricist psychology that takes its start from the description of psychological states. Happiness is not a matter of "feeling good" or of being in any other desirable psychological state; it should rather be understood as something like an agent's fulfillment in pursuing an activity she sees as good. Some such definition would allow us to hold on to what is lost if we think of being happy as like being in a good mood. For the activities in which agents find fulfillment – not just dramatic pursuits of self-sacrifice, but ordinary activities such as jogging or raising children or watching movies – can entail much in the way of undesirable psychological states, without that compromising the happiness agents find in them.

With this objection to the happiness argument set aside, we can now see how surprisingly rich is the account of desire on which that argument relies. In thinking about the psychic life of Boethian dialectic, let us begin by granting something to which Boethius, and for that matter Chaucer, is surely committed, a belief in a perfect divine essence that is the metaphysical ground, source, and telos of all being. What is interesting about the happiness argument is that, given this enabling belief, it is simultaneously easy to assent to the argument and impossible to take its force. The argument says that union with the divine is the one thing everyone actually wants and the one goal everyone's actions actually aim at. In a sense this is prescriptive: it says that you will only reach *felicitas* if you achieve *beatitudo*.[11] But the sense of a prescription here is quite restricted, for this is also a claim about what everyone already wants and already does. This was the source of the objection above, but we should notice an attractive result of this initially unattractive claim. On this account, the ordinary desire for the many things people want, which Philosophy refers to as the desire for the "goods of fortune," and the desire that aims at union with the divine are not to be conceived as naturally reified psychological states that can be cleanly marked off from each other. This account rather suggests that the reification of psychological states is something that people *do*. The desires for fame, money, erotic satisfaction, and so on are desires for "false goods," and so diversions from the desire for *beatitudo*; in this sense, to be sure, we are dealing with two kinds of desire. But the former kind are also expressions and representations of the latter: they are ways that a creature that perpetually "dreams of its origin" gives voice to its desire to return to the state of repletion it knows it lacks. The ordinary desires that occupy human life are more properly understood then not as *opposed* to the desire for union with the divine, but as *deflections* of it. To use an Augustinian term that has already had an important place in my discussions, they are *perversions*, "turnings-away" from the very thing that would fulfill them and towards the substitutions by which we both represent it and fragment it.[12]

As Philosophy puts the point in Book III, "human depravity, then, has broken into fragments that which is by nature one and simple;

men try to grasp part of a thing which has no parts" (III.pr. 9) ("Hoc igitur quod est unum simplexque natura, pravitas humana dispertit et dum rei quae partibus caret partem conatur adipisci").[13] The language of grasping here suggests that an essential feature of perversion is a fantasy of mastery: what all the goods of fortune have in common is a tendency to figure the relation to objects of desire as one of possession, and moreover one in which happiness consists in the perfection of possession, a condition in which nothing could intervene between us and the world to tear the objects of our desires from our grasp. This further suggests that perversion involves the fantasy of a perfected instrumental relation to the world, as though it were the world's manipulability that ideally could render it up to us as a space in which happiness could be attained. But, as Philosophy insists, these fantasies involve a falsifying reification and fragmentation of an object of desire that is metaphysically simple. Perversion, that is, operates according to a logic of fetishism, whereby desire gets cathected on to objects that are imagined as discretely possessable instruments of satisfaction, even as that very imagining depends on the way the fetishized objects point to an object of desire which cannot be broken into parts, and our relationship to which cannot be properly understood in instrumental terms.[14] And, as I suggested above, this structure of fragmentation, reification, and deflection applies not only to objects of desire but also to desires themselves. It is part of what constitutes a desire for any of the goods you ordinarily want that it deflects your desire for happiness by fragmenting and reifying what is already for you a desire for *beatitudo*. Philosophy's argument then is simultaneously an argument about the constitutively perverse construction of the phenomenal world and about the constitutively perverse structure of the psyche.[15]

One of the characteristics of a perversion is that we simultaneously think of it as something that characterizes our will and something by which we are compelled. It is not as though the shoe fetishist, for example, could simply substitute some other object for the one on to which his desire is cathected, and it is not as though he could simply put an end to his attraction to shoes. But then neither is it the case that he is simply passive before the object's power: he devotes himself to the shoe; he invests himself in his fetish. Boethius captures this double structure in the rebuke with which Philosophy counters the Prisoner's initial outburst of grief over having been forced into exile:

> You have not been driven out of your homeland; you have willfully wandered away. Or, if you prefer to think that you have been driven into exile, you yourself have done the driving, since no one else could do it.

> Sed tu quam procul a patria non quidem pulsus es sed aberrasti; ac si te pulsum existimari mavis, te potius ipse pepulisti. Nam id quidem de te numquam cuiquam fas fuisset. (I.pr. 5)

The Prisoner seems to think of his unhappiness as the result of his sheerly passive victimization by forces beyond his control. Philosophy counters that if he is the victim of a lash, it is a lash he wields himself. The argument of books II and III suggests that what Philosophy finally has in mind here is nothing local to the Prisoner, but rather the way we all drive ourselves into exile through our devotion to the goods of fortune, which we routinely think of ourselves as just naturally desiring. In this sense we are all in the Prisoner's situation of imagining ourselves to be passive in the face of what causes our loss of happiness, and we do so in part to hide from ourselves our willing investment in that loss. The trope of the Prisoner driving himself into exile involves the collapse of this distinction between activity and passivity, as well as the redirection of his sense of a homeland from a geographical to a spiritual location. His homeland is the origin and *telos* Philosophy says we perpetually dream of, and from which we have wandered away, like a drunken man who knows he has a home but cannot find his way back to it. If the tropes of dreaming and drunken wandering are helpful in suggesting both that everything we do is a way of trying to get back home and that nothing we do is done in full self-consciousness, the trope of driving oneself into exile suggests that we positively desire the suffering that attends our perverse self-deflections from happiness, as though we wished to punish ourselves, or as though we suspected that punishment were what we really deserve.

One way Boethius has of understanding this psychic structure, in which desires that come with apparently perspicuous labels are simultaneously expressions of the desire for *beatitudo* and veilings of it, and in which we seem to desire both the veiling and the tearing away of the veil, is that it is a structure of repression. "You have forgotten what you are," "quid ipse sis, nosse desisti" (I.pr. 6), Philosophy tells the Prisoner, and she hardly thinks that this could be a matter of mere absent-mindedness. Our commitment to our ordinary pictures of the world and what we want from it, expressed in the daily business of living as much as in anything we are prepared to say, is a purposeful, motivated forgetting of our true identities and our one true desire, which we cannot properly name and whose force we do not understand, but which we simultaneously give voice to and work to keep out of sight in everything we do. The ordinary condition of the human creature, then, is one in which we are compelled by a false picture of happiness, a picture in which happiness consists in the possession of a set of goods we seemingly cannot help desiring. But since we drive ourselves into exile, we are the makers of the picture by which we are compelled. We cling to our false view of happiness in such a way that we reify it, making it real for us; we represent the world and our own desires to ourselves in terms of this picture, and give it power over us in doing so. And because of our investment in imagining the substantial reality of this picture, we repress the many signs of its incoherence, such as the anxiety and lack which always track it even in the best cases.

We are now in a position to see why I claimed earlier that what initially looks like a thin and overly prescriptive psychology has its advantages. One advantage is that it makes available a way of understanding the links among the psychological phenomena I have just catalogued: perversion, fantasies of possession and mastery, the instrumentalization of the world, the reification of psychic life, fetishism, masochism, and repression. These phenomena have been essential to this book from the start, and it is far too easy to think that to discuss them at all is to invoke a specifically modern technical discourse such as psychoanalysis, and so perhaps to invoke a further explanatory trajectory that leads to such concepts as the Oedipus complex or castration anxiety. But Boethian psychological theory allows for a different kind of explanatory trajectory, one more responsive to the ancient and medieval concern with agency and the normative structure of the will, and one that might help us clarify our understanding of the historical specificity attending such psychological phenomena. The rest of this section will suggest the basic form that such an explanatory trajectory might take.

Since on any adequate theory of repression, repression is something people do rather than just something by which they are victimized, one basic question any such theory must try to answer is what *motivates* repression. This is something other than the question of what *causes* repression, and a failure to keep these questions separate can lead to a good deal of confusion. However committed Boethius may be to a metaphysics we would reject, his theory of repression has the advantage of trying to answer the question of motive directly, and of doing so in a purely formal way that does not require an appeal to some specific traumatic content which then must be posited as universal. As we pursue this formal account we will see that, far from an overly thin psychology, what Boethius offers is quite a capacious one that accounts for both the depth and the specificity of our attachments.

On Boethius's account, in order to redirect our actions and desires towards our true *telos* we would have to give up much of what we want and much of what we believe about ourselves and the world. One thing that motivates repression, then, is just the desirability of what we ordinarily desire – the desirability of more money, say – and the believability of what we ordinarily believe – in this case, that having more money will secure some greater quantity of happiness. But the motivation runs deeper than this. Any of the local desires and beliefs we adhere to can be called into question easily enough, and the falsity of each of them routinely registers with us, although often not in ways we could articulate. I get more money, and still I am not happy; in fact, I may be less so, as the ante is continually upped on my perceived need for more. Often what will happen in such a case is that my continued dissatisfaction will ever more desperately lock me into the false belief in money's liberatory power that contributes to my unhappiness. Another thing that can happen, of course, is that I can reject the belief that money will make me happy. But even this hardly amounts to overcoming my repression of my true desire: the most likely outcome here is that I simply add some other possessable good to my picture of what I want, and aim, say, at money and political power together. What keeps repression in place, then, is something much larger and less clearly defined than the desirability of any particular goods or the believability of any candidate answers to the question of where happiness lies. It is something more like the sheer weight of the entire world in which we act, and our nearly inevitable sense of ourselves as having a recognizable and functional identity in that world.[16] This weight takes the form of multiple local and momentary stabilizations of our attitudes – convictions that money or fame is what we are after, that we ought to be properly pious, that our self-interest trumps other considerations, that justice constrains us – stabilizations that jostle each other in ways of which we are usually only vaguely aware, and that are individually dispensable without challenging the structure of repression at all. This weight also takes the form of larger-scale stabilizations that we almost never question or even bring to articulate awareness, such as the conviction that instrumental reasoning is the only thinking in principle required to get what we want. And these larger-scale stabilizations can persist so strongly partly because they can express themselves differentially locally, and so can allow for the substitutability of object-fixed desires. So, if money does not do the trick, then sex will, or power; in any case, when I am in the grip of this larger unarticulated conviction, the only question that occurs to me is that of the means I can find to the ends I am prepared to recognize.

In the grip of these functional dreams of normalcy, the human creature will typically not stop to reflect on its condition enough to disturb its routinized sense of what it wants and how to get it. But, as the *Consolation of Philosophy* and the *Knight's Tale* explore at great length, there are times when this sense of a functional routine gets disturbed. Something happens that you cannot succeed in picturing as merely a practical impediment to being happy. Then, instrumental reasoning utterly fails you, and it begins to seem as though the very nature of things denies you the possibility of happiness. An unbridgeable gulf has opened between you and the object of a desire you cannot forgo: perhaps a love object has come to seem in principle unattainable, like some emanation of the divine that, in its perfection, could never allow itself to be polluted by contact with your wretched creatureliness; perhaps someone who matters to you intimately has died, leaving the entire world scarred by his absence; perhaps your own death, and the death of all the projects to which you have devoted yourself, has become imminent because of some terrible and unjust turn of events. The first thing the creature will typically do in such a case is complain, as though by absorbing itself in its grief – and perhaps even by making that grief the occasion for the production of beautiful self-expression, in little gems of lyrical love poetry or melancholic lament – it could somehow simultaneously fill up the distance between itself and its lost object and impale itself on the impossibility of doing so. This is the territory Freud charted in "Mourning and Melancholia," in which a fixation on the psychic pain of loss allows the grieving subject to imagine the continued interior presence of the lost object in the desire that fixation keeps alive.[17] But again this concern is hardly specific to psychoanalysis; for this is also the territory charted in much of the lyrical eroticism in medieval poetry, including Chaucer's, as well as in the literature of grief and consolation such as *Pearl, Sir Orfeo*, and Chaucer's *Book of the Duchess*.[18] And, as *Pearl* and the *Consolation* and the philosophical valence of Palamon and Arcite's laments suggest, this is also the situation in which the creature both becomes available for philosophical therapy and digs in against its own desire for a cure. In the *Consolation*, it is immediately after the Prisoner "poured out my long sad story" ("continuato dolore delatravi," I.pr. 5), that Philosophy remarks that he has "willfully wandered away" from his true homeland ("non quidem pulsus es sed aberrasti," I.pr. 5). She thus diagnoses his absorption in his misery, like that of the dreamer in *Pearl*, as a way of working to keep himself from moving towards a cure, even as it is also a request for the very therapy it resists. According to the *Consolation* and the traditions of writing that grow out of it, philosophy – conceived as the impulse to extended reflection rather than as a technical discipline – emerges in the psychic life of the human creature as a therapy for a condition of divided identity and desire which the creature masks as normalcy, and to which it positively devotes itself, even in those moments when its suffering of that condition becomes most manifest.

This initial sketch of Boethian psychology begins, I hope, to give a sense of its depth and complexity. I now want to turn more squarely to the dialectical structure of the *Consolation* to think further about how such therapy works and about what impedes it. This in turn will lead us to the aporetic structures to which I referred at the beginning of this discussion, and which, I think, are ultimately the source of the psychological phenomena sketched so far.

BOETHIAN *APORIA* AND DIALECTICAL FORM

In turning to dialectic, it is important to notice that Boethius does not simply dramatize a process of confused resistance to Philosophy's arguments, in which the Prisoner exhibits his carnality, emotionalism, and human partiality, and only gradually transcends these impediments as he gives way to reason's claim.[19] The Prisoner does of course object at times, and often in a confused way. But more commonly, and more strikingly, he engages in repeated gestures of facile assent to Philosophy's claims. In the core middle stretch of the dialogue, for instance, when his contributions go beyond such comments as "that is true," "certainly not," "this is a beautiful and precious idea," and so on, they are usually excited elaborations of Philosophy's points, meant to prove that he is "getting it." And then, at the end of Book III, as Philosophy presents her theodicy in an argument that does no more than draw out the consequences of claims to which the Prisoner has long ago agreed, the discussion takes a striking turn. First, in response to Philosophy's repetition of the familiar claim that God "is the supreme good which rules all things firmly and disposes all sweetly," "est igitur summum . . . bonum quod regit cuncta fortiter suaviterque disponit" (III.pr. 12), the Prisoner replies "I am delighted, not only by your powerful argument and its conclusion, but even more by the words you have used, so that at long last the folly which so tore me to pieces is ashamed" ("Quam . . . me non modo ea quae conclusa est summa rationum, verum multo magis haec ipsa quibus uteris verba delectant, ut tandem aliquando stultitiam magna lacerantem sui pudeat," III.pr. 12, translation mine). But the Prisoner's brave announcement of an end to his self-laceration is perhaps qualified by his continued desire to displace the shamefulness of his condition on to some distinctly locatable cause: as he puts it, it is his folly that is ashamed, not him. Sensing that he is still making things too easy for himself, Philosophy suggests some logical stock-taking in terms that promise both the production of rare beauty and an ominous conflict: "But would you like us to cause our arguments to clash against each other? Perhaps from such a conflict a beautiful spark of truth will fly forth" ("Sed visne rationes ipsas invicem collidamus? Forsitan ex huiusmodi conflictatione pulchra quaedam veritatis scintilla dissiliat," III.pr. 12, translation mine). And such a conflict is just what Philosophy produces:

> "No one can doubt that God can do anything," Philosophy said. "Anyone whose mind is stable," I said, "could not possibly doubt it." "So there is nothing that he, who can do anything, cannot do." "Nothing." "Now God cannot do evil, can he?" "Hardly!" "Evil, therefore, is nothing, since God, who is incapable of nothing, cannot do it." (translation mine)

> "Deum," inquit, "esse omnium potentem nemo dubitaverit." "Qui quidem," inquam, "mente consistat, nullus prorsus ambigat." "Qui vero est," inquit, "omnium potens, nihil est quod ille non possit." "Nihil," inquam. "Num igitur deus facere malum potest?" "Minime," inquam. "Malum igitur," inquit, "nihil est, cum id facere ille non possit, qui nihil non potest." (III.pr. 12)

Now, suddenly, things do not look so easy: "Are you playing with me, weaving a labyrinth of arguments from which there is no exit?" ("'Ludisne,' inquam, 'me inextricabilem labyrinthum rationibus texens?'" III.pr. 12, translation mine). But there is nothing particularly labyrinthine about this argument. Philosophy has introduced nothing new here, and in contrast to other more convoluted passages that provoked no such resistance, but in which substantive claims *have* gotten smuggled in under the guise of sheer logical operations, this stretch is a model of argumentative transparency. That is part of what gives the Prisoner's earlier agreements their facile character: for if he really agreed then, it would seem, he ought to be having no such trouble now. The Prisoner's sudden loss of his bearings makes it seem as though he has never had any real understanding of what he has been agreeing to.

This is more than just the familiar problem of not fully grasping the ramifications of an argument as you are presented with it. That makes it sound too much as though the Prisoner's overly easy agreements were the sign of a merely cognitive limitation on his part, and it gives too slight a sense of his investment in agreeing so readily. As Philosophy prepares to turn her attention from false to true happiness, for instance, the Prisoner interrupts:

> But this is clear even to a blind man ... and you revealed it a little while ago when you tried to explain the causes of false happiness. For,

unless I am mistaken, true and perfect happiness is that which makes a man self-sufficient, powerful, worthy of reverence and renown, and joyful. And, to show that I have understood you, I acknowledge that whatever can truly provide any one of these must be true and perfect happiness, since all are one and the same.

Atqui haec . . . vel caeco perspicua est eamque tu paulo ante monstrasti, dum falsae causas aperire conaris. Nam nisi fallor ea vera est et perfecta felicitas quae sufficientem, potentem, reverendum, celebrem laetumque perficiat. Atque ut me interius animadvertisse cognoscas, quae unum horum, quoniam idem cuncta sunt, veraciter praestare potest hanc esse plenam beatitudinem sine ambiguitate cognosco. (III.pr. 9)

What is wrong with the Prisoner's somewhat overexcited contribution here is not that it fails to include the specification that union with the divine is the only thing capable of meeting these criteria. It is rather that, in his eagerness to declare everything perfectly clear, he is ignoring – or rather, working to keep out of sight – the very thing that provoked the dialogue in the first place, namely his sense that the possibilities for his happiness have been quite deeply affected by what has happened to him. Here we have another form of repression than the one so easily moralizable as the motivated forgetting of one's divine origin. For here what is getting repressed is the ongoing claim of the very appearances that are supposed to be melting away; agreement here serves the function of denying the force of Philosophy's arguments even more effectively than would a digging-in-of-the-heels disagreement. For what the Prisoner proves that he has understood here is nothing more than the definition of an abstract concept. Far from merely presenting difficulties of application, the problem with such an abstract concept in this case is that it blocks a proper appreciation of philosophy by offering the chimera of a theoretical solution to what is finally not a theoretical problem. The Prisoner's goal – the human goal, according to Philosophy – is not to be capable of providing true definitions of happiness, but *to be happy*. The Prisoner's display of understanding is as much of a diversion from this goal, and as much a sign of his resistance to it, as was his earlier wallowing in grief. This is something Philosophy herself suggests with a dry humor that the Prisoner could not appreciate, as she responds to his interruption by addressing him with condescending affection as her "alumnus," a term that has a range of meanings from "scholar" or "pupil" – as though the Prisoner had regressed to thinking that what is at stake here was book-learning – to "nursling" and "foster-child," as though his regression were even more extreme.[20]

In a sense, then, the Prisoner's overt resistance to Philosophy's argument for the insubstantiality of evil is a sign of philosophical *progress*: at least he has finally begun to see how deeply counterintuitive Philosophy's argument is, how it runs against the grain, not only of his perception of his own personal misfortunes, but of much more deeply seated beliefs about the structure of the world. Whatever evil is, surely it is *something*. Is he to believe, not merely that what has happened to him is not so bad because it does not really compromise his ultimate happiness, but that *nothing* has happened to him? What could this even mean? Having been brought to this point, the Prisoner might now be able to hear the terse humor in the remark with which Philosophy greeted his early outpouring of grief: "what you regard as a change has greatly upset you," "Ea tantum animi tui sicuti tu tibi fingis mutata pervertit" (II.pr. 1). What makes that earlier comment read like a rather unsympathetic joke is the extreme bluntness with which it jars against what the Prisoner must take to be his most basic observations of empirical reality. While there may be a question as to how one should regard the change he has undergone, it would seem to be just a fact that there has been a change; this much does not seem to be a matter of how anyone *regards* anything at all. But if the jarring produced by this earlier comment had the feel of a confrontation between a subjective world of phenomenal appearances and a philosophical claim that comes at the human as though from beyond all appearances, by the middle of the dialogue the Prisoner can have no such comfortable misunderstanding of the case available to him. For since then he has been led through a process of thought in which he has granted that Philosophy makes sense of what he *already* believed from the beginning. Philosophy does not proceed by supplying doctrine the Prisoner must accept because of some authority external to him; she rather proceeds by taking the simplest logical steps from the very appearances to which the Prisoner has appealed, and calling on beliefs he already has. And if he now sees how strange her argument is, so that he does not know how to make sense of it and his earlier agreements look facile, we might well ask what he was *supposed* to have done as Philosophy took him through the earlier stages in her argument, stages which at the time seemed clear enough. Should he have manufactured disagreement, or obstinately held out against lines of thinking whose force he certainly felt? The grip of this deadlock on the Prisoner's intuitions will only tighten in the next sections of book IV, as Philosophy extends her argument to claim that evil men are powerless, to which the Prisoner replies that "to doubt that would be to disregard the nature of things and the force of argument" ("Quisquis . . . dubitat, nec rerum naturam nec consequentiam potest considerare rationum," IV.pr. 2). The nature of things and the force of argument may require him not to doubt the point, but it is quite a different thing for him to find the argument convincing or bring himself to give it his wholehearted assent. And what could be more evident than that evil men are often quite powerful? What could be more evident to Boethius as he sits in prison, waiting to have his head stuck in a vise until his skull cracks open and his brains seep out of his ears? But the Prisoner cannot simply rest with this apparent self-evidence, digging in his heels against the power of philosophical reason. The force of argument compels his *assent*, not just his submission; it does not just have power over him, it has authority for him, an authority he must grant whether he wishes to or not. For it gains its authority from nothing more than beliefs he already has, together with the logical pressure of reflection on what those beliefs entail.

In examining the aporetic deadlock to which Philosophy's arguments lead the Prisoner, I have been putting the issue in terms of the Prisoner's intuitions and the claim of Philosophy's arguments on them. But the Prisoner is hardly particularized here, and as I have said, Philosophy is not the voice of an external authority: this *aporia* is supposed to get its grip from nothing more than the rationality common to everyone. And it is clear that we are not supposed to see this rationality as simply muddled or confused. In book V, for instance, it turns out that even such basic categories as space and time are products of our capacities as knowers rather than features of the basic structure of reality. In fact, any knowledge that can be put in propositional form contains an irreducible subjective element that marks its difference from the act of intellection, which alone can know the pure forms of things.[21] This suggests just how deep the problem of the normative authority of reflection goes: reflection might lead towards a more objective view of the objects of thought, but no one could say that a belief in space and time, or a dependence on propositional knowledge, is simply subjectivist folly, for there is no way to imagine a human life without such things. On Boethius's account, then, it is a basic condition of the human that the reflective drive cannot reach an absolute limiting point, a perspective stripped of all subjective contribution. There is no point at which a rational creature, no matter how intent on reflection, can declare itself free of the danger of finding itself compelled once again by the incoherent seemings that masquerade as a firm and fixed reality. Nor is there any way to put a principled stop to the drive towards a more objective perspective, a drive that ultimately takes the creature away from any of the appearances that give it a recognizable footing in the world.

At the beginning of this chapter I claimed that the problem concerning dialectical form in the *Consolation* concerns aporias that arise internally to the nature of philosophical reflection. The point, however, needs putting more strongly. It does not simply concern *philosophical* reflection, or even any distinctive act of reflection at all, but rather the entire agentive and subjective life of a creature with reflective capacities. In the next section I will address agency directly; for now let us turn to the constitution of subjectivity. If the reflective drive does not come at the creature from outside – if it is the product of the internal structure of rationality – then one upshot of this argument is that subjectivity cannot constitute a realm of determinate appearances detached from what they are appearances of.[22] We can say, for instance, that it seems to the Prisoner that the possibility of his happiness has been destroyed by what has happened to him; but the force of Philosophy's argument is not just that this is an incorrect appraisal, but that *it is not the way it really seems to him.*[23] The point is crucial for understanding the way Boethius – and, I think, Chaucer – conceive of psychological phenomena. One way of putting one of the central arguments in chapter one would be to say that, while it seems to the Miller that what he wants sexually is to possess a woman as a pure object, that is not the way it really seems to him: we need some such formulation to account for the phenomenal structure of his desire, in which the wish for a pure erotic objectification is driven by desires and beliefs that wish cannot accommodate and serves to repress, but which become apparent under reflective pressure. In Boethian terms, this suggests that the drive towards reflective distance is already internal to the most "unreflective" action and the most reified, subjectively "present" desire or belief. While the literary form of philosophical dialogue represents dialectic through a conversation between the Prisoner and Philosophy, that representational mode serves to display the dialectical structure of psychic life and all of its contents. The most obvious, transparent things you would say about what you want and what you think can thus never be reports on pure subjective seemings. Desires or beliefs that have the feel of reportable psychological states function instead as internally fractured reifications that always remain dialectically engaged with the reflective drive they serve to refuse.

AN ANTINOMY AT THE HEART OF AGENCY

Let me turn to one more example of the aporetic structures this text works to make manifest, which will return us more squarely to Boethius's concerns with agency and autonomy, as well as to the problem I raised in the book's introduction concerning the two aspects of normativity. As I have already suggested, much of the second half of the *Consolation* is devoted to tracking the consequences of the happiness argument. One such consequence is a Platonist proposal for the reform of the judicial system:

> based on the principle that wickedness by its very nature makes men miserable, we see that an injury done to another causes unhappiness in the doer rather than in the recipient. But at present, lawyers take the opposite tack. They try to arouse sympathy in the judges for those who have suffered grave injury, when those who have harmed them are much more deserving of pity. Such criminals ought to be brought to justice by kind and compassionate accusers, as sick men are taken to the doctor, so that their disease of guilt might be cured by punishment. In this way, defense attorneys could be dispensed with, or, if they wanted to help their clients, they would become accusers.

> Hinc igitur aliis de causis ea radice nitentibus, quod turpitudo suapte natura miseros faciat, apparet inlatam cuilibet iniuriam non accipientis sed inferentis esse miseriam. Atque nunc ... contra faciunt oratores. Pro his enim qui grave quid acerbumque perpessi sunt miserationem iudicum excitare conantur, cum magis admittentibus iustior miseratio

debeatur; quos non ab iratis sed a propitiis potius miserantibusque accusatoribus ad iudicium veluti aegros ad medicum duci oportebat, ut culpae morbos supplicio resecarent. Quo pacto defensorum opera vel tota frigeret, vel si prodesse hominibus mallet, in accusationis habitum verteretur. (IV.pr. 4)

Boethius is not so naïve as to think that this proposal could exactly be put into practice. Even if we tried to imagine a comprehensive judicial reform such that compassionately accusatory defense attorneys made sense, there would be unsolvable problems concerning how the reformed system would work in a world in which people guilty of crimes mostly do not desire to be cured by punishment, and so seek defense of more conventional kinds, and in which the injuries done to victims are considered at least as worthy of concern as the diseased soul of the criminal. Such a judicial system would have to dispense with so much of the network of conceptual, emotional, and social relations binding our notions of guilt, injury, compassion, defense, punishment, and justice that those notions would become unrecognizable. But these conceptual relations, the beliefs and emotions that express them, and the political and social institutions associated with them, all have a normative authority that cannot be dissipated by anything Philosophy says. Someone who is not moved by the injury done to the recipient of a wicked action is not being properly affected; likewise, a defense attorney who tried to help his clients by pleading for their conviction, even if he believed that their conviction and punishment would result in their being cured of moral disease, would not be a good attorney. And of course Boethius knows this. But Philosophy's proposal is not thereby rendered absurd. For as she indicates in the first phrase cited above, the proposal gains its normative authority from that of the argument concerning happiness, to which the Prisoner has already assented. If wickedness by its very nature makes men miserable, then this proposal has a normative authority that cannot simply be dismissed.

This example helps to drive home the point that the aporetic deadlocks into which Philosophy leads the Prisoner cannot be resolved in the way it is so frequently suggested they might be, by transcending all earthly appearances and commitments. It is not even right to say that the text works to keep in view the costs of such a transcendence. The *Consolation* suggests the inadequacy of any such formulation through the epistemological considerations I have already discussed from book V: for how are we to transcend space and time? Still, in the face of that question one might imagine that the text is advocating a complete mystical transformation, even if it suggests that such a thing would be strictly speaking unrepresentable, or impossible for all but the saints. The example of Philosophy's judicial reform, however, suggests that the world of ordinary appearances and social relations and political institutions must necessarily maintain a normative authority for us, or we would simply not be functional in it, and there would be no way to tell whether we were philosophically enlightened or just massively lacking in ethical resources. And even the attainment of a mystical *beatitudo* would not change that. Nothing short of a complete transformation of the entire world could change it, and that will only happen when we *collectively* return to that homeland from which we perpetually wander, and see God "face to face" as full members of the *civitas dei* that will only be realized at the end of time. If philosophy is a therapy for self-estrangement, then, it is not a therapy that can result in a cure; it is more like an exploration of our resistances to understanding that self-estrangement, and a critique of the compromise arrangements in social and psychic life which keep that self-estrangement in place, but without which it would not be possible to do anything.

To see the impact these considerations have on conceptions of agency and autonomy, let us return to the notion, introduced in the previous chapter, of reflective endorsement. In effect, all Philosophy does until quite late in the dialogue is require the Prisoner to ask which of his attitudes can support his conviction under reflective pressure. The centrality of the trope of imprisonment for representing the Prisoner's inhabitation of attitudes that cannot stand up under such pressure, the repeated suggestion that such unendorsable attitudes are marked by pathological compulsion, and the promise of Philosophy to free the soul of its self-imposed chains, all suggest that autonomy is the condition towards which philosophical reflection aims. But the *Consolation* does not stop with this questioning by holding up an admirable character as the ground of endorsability, as the Knight tries to do in his Thesean theory. Instead, Philosophy argues that action and belief and desire necessarily aim at autonomy in the much more ambitious way the Knight tries to keep at bay. For the *Consolation* takes its start from the questionability of all of the attitudes that depend for their authority on one's character; it poses the question of what actions, beliefs, and desires might be said to be *truly* autonomous, with the implication being that nothing can be so if it can turn out, from some future turn of events or some further position of reflective distance, to take on the nature of a compulsion. And this expanded range of the compulsive quite pointedly includes such things as an attachment to glory and honor and political power, which as we have seen are essential to the motivational structure of Thesean agency.

There is real force to the way the *Consolation* makes such character-specific attachments wither away under the force of the reflective drive. For Philosophy's arguments reveal the claim on the Prisoner of an imperative to leave behind any attachments that can be seen as accidents of some parochial fact about the agent who has them: accidents, perhaps, of his particular character, but also accidents of what we would now call the agent's culture and ideology, and even, as Philosophy insists, accidents of the way members of the agent's species are constituted as knowers and perceivers. As each of these categories of accidents in rather different ways suggests, the notion of the accidental here includes things without which agency would be inconceivable. But the imperative to leave such things behind, as we have seen, derives from no more than the intrinsically normative force of the ambition of freely chosen ends, an ambition without which agency would *also* be inconceivable. While we may find Boethius's formulation of the ground and *telos* of this drive in the simplicity of divine Being to be itself parochial, dependent as it is on theology and a metaphysics to which we do not subscribe, this does nothing to diminish the force of the problem concerning agency and autonomy posed by the *Consolation*. For Boethius's metaphysical commitments suggest that ways of understanding the reflective drive can themselves be parochial. No doubt we have our own parochialisms on this score, since we have hardly understood these problems once and for all. Whether or not we share Boethius's sense of where the reflective drive ultimately leads, we are subject to its normative authority, and subject in ways that define our freedom, even as they also make the very territory of that freedom unrecognizable.

My argument in this chapter, then, does not just concern the interpretation of Boethius, or even the question of his relevance to Chaucer.

I have wanted so much from the *Consolation* partly because I think it can help us understand a difficult philosophical problem; and this is worth doing both for its own sake, and because our substantive understandings of the problems texts engage must necessarily inform our interpretive engagements with those texts. The *Consolation* powerfully captures a problem in the theory of autonomy that continues to be of interest in philosophical ethics. In aiming at autonomy, we aim at a position from which we could in principle identify, and fully inhabit, all and only those attitudes worthy of endorsement, attitudes that would not from a position of further reflective distance appear as terribly wrong, nightmares of our personal or cultural or speciate history. As Kant and contemporary philosophers influenced by him have argued, this is something that, as reflective creatures, we must want; there is no way not to want this, there are only ways of repressing the desire for it.[24] Now let us imagine that we could get to such a position. Who would be free, there? Boethius's answer to this question is roughly the same as the one offered by Bernard Williams in *critique* of Kant, although the conclusions they draw from this are quite different. There would in a certain sense not be a "who" there; there would just be "the characterless moral self."[25] As the increasing silence of the Prisoner in the late stages of the *Consolation* suggests, this would be a creature without a voice; or, to the extent it had a voice, it would be merely the utterly impersonal voice of assent to the deliverances of what Thomas Nagel calls "the view from nowhere." Such a creature would be one with no projects, and no particular attachments. According to Boethius, it would lack a sense of time and space in which to pursue projects, and its activity would consist in nothing but a ceaseless and unchanging contemplation of the divine perfection, which is an activity without the kind of temporal and spatial structure, and internal and external impediments to overcome, that projects have. But we do not need to put the point in a Boethian way. A creature of pure autonomy would not preferentially care about some things or people or projects more than others; and such preferential caring is an essential feature of what we mean by a person's "character."

For Williams, this gives us a reason to suspect that something is wrong with the Kantian imperative. What drives Boethius's argument – and Kant's for that matter – is that all such preferential attitudes can look, from a position of reflective distance greater than we usually take towards them, like sources of subjection. So in aiming at autonomy, in a certain indefeasible sense we aim at being creatures without such attitudes. Part of what gives Williams's counterargument its bite is that if you ask almost any of us whether we would want to be such a creature our answer would be no. And this is not just because there is some metaphysical or theological belief we do not share with Boethius or Kant. What was attractive about the Knight's theory of Thesean autonomy was that it took account of the specificities of character and concrete historical relations and particular social and political responsibilities; even if we disagree with some of the specificities in this case, we recognize that there is no such thing as an agent without such commitments, and certainly no such thing as a life we would want. Without such commitments, we would be divorced from most of what we care most about, and it is questionable whether we would be able to care about anything at all.[26]

We should not think Boethius denies this, just because he represents a movement whereby such cares are transcended; instead, the *Consolation* suggests that we inevitably want incompatible things out of our agentive lives. But Boethius does not take the upshot of this to be a tragic story about desire; instead he wants to outline a problem concerning the conditions necessary for a functional agency. On the one hand, in order to persist as an agent with a psychologically and socially functional character, with the particular cares, concerns, and projects an agent necessarily thinks of as characteristically hers, a person must heed the imperative towards a reification of her psyche and of the world of objects in which she operates; she must fetishize the objects of desire these reifications yield up to her; she must embrace her historical imbeddedness in socially sanctioned norms that are necessarily ideological. On the other hand, her very activity of doing so is always inflected by another imperative towards reflective distance, an imperative she necessarily associates with the autonomy that *also* characterizes her actions, desires, and will as hers, but that marks her potential difference from everything particular about her. Autonomy is such a difficult problem, then, because agency is structured around an antinomy, a conflict between irreconcilable imperatives neither of which can be set aside.[27]

My references throughout the preceding paragraphs to ideology, a concept Boethius did not have in any rich sense, are meant to flag a further upshot of this argument for the problem concerning normativity I raised in the book's introduction. If agency is structured around an antinomy between what we might call the law of historical-ideological imbeddedness and the law of reflective distance, and if those laws function in the lives of agents in ways that constantly intermingle, so that our imbeddedness in personal, social, and speciate history is always inflected by the drive to reflective distance on it, while every attempt at reflective distance remains necessarily ideological, then I think we have good reason to say that "normativity" is after all the name of a single phenomenon, not merely a verbal coincidence between distinct projects of ideological critique and philosophical ethics. Further, if I am right that this is truly an antinomy rather than a resolvable conflict, then we have found in the structure of agency itself a source of the grip ideological regimes have on those who inhabit them, as well as a reason why the formation of agency and subjectivity through the internalization of ideology must always. remain fragile and porous to that which ideology cannot formulate. This is why I claimed in the introduction that a satisfying account of normativity must rely on the irreducibility of the perspective of agency: for this source of ideology and its discontents issues from the ontology of agency rather than from any ameliorable set of social-historical conditions; and it can only be seen by attending directly to questions concerning agents' reasons for acting and desiring and believing, rather than solely to the historical causes of their formation as subjects.

Let me conclude this section by returning to the psychology that emerges from Boethian theory. Much of my argument in this chapter has been a gloss on the central Boethian tropes of imprisonment and exile: for an agent to embrace attitudes conditioned by accidents of her history, her habits, and her culture is for her to embrace features of her will that mark her imprisonment in the pathological, and mark her as in exile from her autonomy. Boethius's mentor Augustine captures the pathos of this condition succinctly in a passage I cited in the introduction: "Surely I have not ceased to be my own self . . . and yet there is still a great gap between myself and myself . . . Oh that my soul might follow my own self . . . that it might not be a rebel to itself." As Augustine and Boethius attempt to make sense of the aching gap in agents' relations to themselves and their longing to be at one with themselves, they repeatedly produce plots with nostalgic structures: as representations of psychological and moral alterity, imprisonment, exile, and rebellion get their punch from imaginary references to a lost freedom, homeland, and peace. The *Consolation* is full of such nostalgia, from its notions of the human creature as dreaming of its origin and drunkenly searching for its home, to its lyrical evocations of the Golden Age and of the radiance and harmony of the divine mind dimmed and scattered by our attempts to grasp it. It is easy enough to locate this nostalgia culturally, for it is clearly present in the Platonist myth, cited by both Boethius and Augustine, of the descent of an originary unity into corruptible materiality; in the biblical narrative of the Fall that so concerned Augustine, and that can never be far from Boethius's mind even if he does not invoke it explicitly here; and in the theological-moral notion of original sin that develops from the Fall narrative, a notion that locates the human as a creature whose identity, agency, and subjectivity are constituted through a founding self-estrangement that somehow retains a narrative structure, and for which the creature somehow remains responsible. The engagements with normative longing produced by Boethius, Augustine, and the Judeo-Christian and Platonist traditions that inform their thinking are thus heavily inflected by their imagination of states that would be free of it and by their sense of the pollution and guilt attending its necessary compromises.

A fastidious nostalgia is thus a deep part of the inheritance of western thinking about normativity, and it continues to have a life in intellectual traditions that have long since rebuked theological metaphysics, for instance in some traditions of Marxist theory and in various movements for a liberatory sexuality. But the power of normative nostalgia does not simply stem from the cultural weight of Judeo-Christian and Platonist myth. Rather than taking that weight as the resting place for analysis, we need to ask what makes nostalgic narrative of this kind seem like an explanation of something. And the Augustinian-Boethian tradition gives us resources for doing just that, even if neither would have used those resources to analyze his own nostalgia. Augustine's sense of a true self by which he is drawn and the Boethian sense of an authentic identity associated with the reflective drive have their source in an identification with autonomy, the capacity freely to choose one's own ends, not merely to be compelled by ends one happens to have. If a pure autonomy cannot be *narratively* prior to our ordinary condition of self-estrangement – if there never was an agency fully in possession of itself – there is a certain *ontological* priority to the sense of self associated with autonomy; for ends we freely choose are in a sense the only ones that are truly ours, the only ones that are not shadowed by a sense of enslavement or imprisonment. But, as the *Consolation* also reveals, what is ontologically prior in this sense is perpetually forgone, not by any particular act or decision on the part of an agent, but by the necessity of having and wanting some specific character, a distinctive voice, ends that are particular to you just because of the person you happen to be and the social world you happen to live in. It is of the nature of the human creature, then, to long for a freedom whose possibility is perpetually foreclosed, even as the completion of the movement towards that freedom would involve its dissolution as a distinctive inhabitant of the world, an agent with some specific set of habits and a character of its own. Normative nostalgia may find its most direct expression in literalized narratives of loss, but those are always at the same time phantasmatic narratives, attempts to render the antinomy at the heart of agency in familiar, graspable terms.

If the ache of normative nostalgia has its ultimate source in the way agency depends on irreconcilable demands, the same can be said for the other dominant feature of the moral psychology we have been exploring here, the sense of guilt and pollution that does not have its source in anything particular the agent has done, but whose taint spreads across all action as an inevitable condition of it. For while a pure autonomy is forgone not by any particular act but by virtue of the necessity of having and wanting a specific character, that necessity is not a causal one but a necessity of the will. To persist as ourselves we must resist the call of the reflective drive, and so resist the conditions of our autonomy. This attachment to self-division and to an agentive implication in unfreedom is what Boethius and Augustine express in their tropes of a desiring, motivated "loss" of ourselves and of a willful "fall" into imprisonment and abjection. The psychological fallout of the antinomy I have been describing is thus a kind of double death wish. On the one hand, in wanting to follow "its own self," to heed the call of the reflective drive, the human desires its death as the particular one it is, for that existence seems like an impediment to its autonomy; and since it still desires and wills that existence, it feels marked as guilty, unworthy of freedom. On the other, in wanting to maintain the particularity of its attachments and the solidity of its sense of itself, the human desires the death of its autonomy, and in so doing embraces the unworthiness that marks it.

A creature whose will is built around simultaneous desires for abject particularity and self-dissolution: one way of putting this is to say that such a creature is constitutively masochistic. To some, such a suggestion will no doubt seem excessive; to others, it may seem rather late in coming, something already theorized well enough by psychoanalysis, and in no need of the philosophical derivation I have given it. Let me then take a minute to explain what I mean by the term *masochism*, my reasons for using it and others that have psychoanalytic resonances, and more broadly the relation between the kind of analysis I pursue here and throughout this book and the kind, or rather kinds, properly classified as psychoanalytic.

On an initial definition, the term *masochism* as I am using it refers to a range of phenomena constituted by a willing investment in suffering, that is, a relationship to suffering which involves taking pleasure in it and identifying with it. Some such definition reflects the way the term has passed from what was once a technical psychoanalytic usage into ordinary language, where it is frequently invoked in ways that do not depend on any particular theory, and that need not refer to sexuality, much less to a sexuality judged to be "abnormal." So we speak, for instance, of the masochism of the ultramarathon runner without necessarily thinking that running 100 miles through the desert represents a sublimation of sexual urges; and we speak of the masochism of someone who enjoys being bound and whipped by his partner without necessarily thinking that his tastes reflect a state of mental unhealth, or that they issue from unresolved Oedipal anxieties. One might insist that such usage is the sloppy-minded misapplication of a scientific term that should only be invoked consistently with a technical psychoanalytic definition of it. But I think that the ordinary usage has something to say for it, since it locates the historically and psychologically specific case of a sexual taste for leather, whips, and fur as one instance of a broader phenomenon, without assuming that a particular theory owns the use of the term, or that the contours of that specific case constitute the core of the phenomenon and the basis for explaining it.

I have meant for the topic of masochism in this broad sense to be in play throughout this book, from the claim in the book's introduction that a willing investment in suffering attends all normative phenomena, to the discussion in chapter one of the punishments the Miller brings on a masculinity he associates with his agentive capacities, to the link made in chapter two between the conventional rhetoric of the wretched lover "slain by desire" and the Knight's longing to both complete and obliterate his agency by being taken up into the stasis of a beautiful formal stucture. In both Chaucerian instances, as in those I will discuss in later chapters of this book, sexuality provides central scenes for fantasies of the undoing and violent remaking of the self and for explorations of the pleasure to be found in suffering. As I will argue in the next chapter, this conjunction of topics emerges partly from an analysis of courtly or romantic sexuality Chaucer learned from the *Roman de la Rose*. Masochism becomes a convenient shorthand for this conjunction because of the way the social and psychological form that goes by its name – Masoch adoring his icily cruel mistress, the hard-nosed businessman stopping in for a quick whipping from his dominatrix during lunch – inherits and allegorizes a split in romance masculinity of which Chaucer and the writers of the *Rose* were very much aware.

One of the main purposes of this chapter has been to argue that while this collection of cases should be understood as bearing some family resemblance to, and standing in a genealogical relationship to, what we ordinarily call masochism, the abjections and thrills of hegemonic masculinity do not provide the stopping point for an explanation of them. In order to understand what drives these cases, we need to see them as ways of instantiating and representing something much more general, a drive to self-violation and a willing investment in suffering that does not reduce to *any* set of empirical instances of it, and cannot be fully understood through a focus on sexuality, but is rather a constitutive condition of agency as such. On the account I am proposing, masochism in this further sense is thus not an aberration, and not even something that picks out one group of people with a distinctive kind of desire. The masochist as a distinct type is rather someone who, to use Leo Bersani's term, is attached to a "melodramatic" expression of the self-violation intrinsic to agency.[28]

To see more fully how this argument engages with and differs from psychoanalysis, we need to expand the scope of the discussion to include not just the theory of masochism but the question of what psychoanalysis is in the first place. I will use as a touchstone a recent critique of psychoanalysis and its use in medieval studies, Lee Patterson's essay "Chaucer's Pardoner on the Couch: Psyche and Clio in Medieval Literary Studies."[29] Patterson follows critics of psychoanalysis such as Frederick Crews and Adolf Grünbaum in arguing that if psychoanalysis has any explanatory value, it must be understood as a scientifically verifiable theory of the causes of human behavior.[30] The core of that theory, in turn, resides in the centrality of the Oedipus complex and castration anxiety to Freud's analysis of infantile sexuality and sexual development. Patterson argues that there is no scientific or clinical evidence for these theories, and that since psychoanalysis has never had any evidentiary basis for its central claims, it proceeds preemptively, by assigning preordained significance to all data and refusing to rethink its premises, thus giving "an impression of immense explanatory power while concealing empirical emptiness."[31] If Patterson's account of psychoanalysis is accurate, then surely he is right that the entire enterprise, including psychoanalytic readings of medieval texts, is deeply flawed; and indeed, like Crews, Patterson is responding to some of Freud's most basic and repeated claims about the nature of his project. These claims belong to what we might call the technological ambition of psychoanalysis, the goal of providing, in Foucault's term, a "scientia sexualis," a transmissible and professionalized epistemology of sex.[32] But that technological ambition is not the only thing animating Freud's writings; as Bersani among others has argued, there is a profound tension in Freud between "the ambition of elaborating a clinically viable theory" and an impulse towards radical speculation that resists the normalizing and institutionalizing aspects of that theory.[33] Partly as a result of Bersani's readings of Freud, I am less convinced than Patterson is that psychoanalysis as a whole stands or falls on the explanatory value of the Oedipus complex, particularly insofar as what gets called "the Oedipus complex" refers to a literalized family romance that serves as a universal source of psychic trauma and the basis for the production of all sexuality and gender identity. Much of Freud amounts to speculative phenomenology rather than pseudoscientific theorizing, and we can learn a good deal from his brilliant reflections on such matters as the combination of affection and aggression in the child's game of fort/da, the interpenetration of mourning and melancholia, and the distinction between the sexual instinct and its socially produced "soldering" to sexual aims, without signing off on the idea that such reflections ultimately depend on a theory of Oedipal conflict.[34] The same holds for later writers in the psychoanalytic tradition, such as Lacan, Laplanche, Bersani, and Žižek; Bersani's writings on masochism, for instance, exist well to the side of Oedipal theory.[35] Within medieval studies, Aranye Fradenburg's work, particularly her recent book *Sacrifice Your Love*, is a luminous psychoanalytic meditation on the enjoyment surrounding the cultural and psychic drive to renunciation, which never as far as I can tell depends even implicitly on the Oedipus complex. And even when the Oedipal does appear in these writers, it often functions, as it sometimes does in Freud, not as the basis of a scientific explanation of anything, but as an allegory of much more general questions concerning how subjects come into being through the internalization of others and the identification with authority. In short, psychoanalysis as I understand it is not a unified theoretical edifice grounded in a set of core propositions, but is rather a live project of thinking that grapples with a set of problems that it sometimes powerfully illuminates, and sometimes formulates in problematic ways whose very problems can offer us opportunities for further thought.

As these comments suggest, I think that Patterson is wrong in declaring psychoanalysis intellectually bankrupt, partly because psychoanalysis has always been more than the theory and procedures of analysis Patterson critiques, and partly because psychoanalysis itself has pursued versions of some of those critiques. That being said, I am in wholehearted sympathy with what I take to be two central motives of Patterson's essay, a desire not to shortchange the self-understandings of the past, and a belief that simply adopting some theoretical and interpretive scheme – or, as I would put it, taking an intellectual tradition such as psychoanalysis to provide such a scheme – cuts short the work of theory. The two motives are closely linked, since it shortchanges the self-understanding of the past to think we can articulate it absent the work of theory, and since that work is bypassed just as effectively by the dogmatic thought that we already have a theory as by the empiricist thought that we do not need one. Patterson sums this up wonderfully in a closing slogan of his essay: "our task, in short, is not to become less but more theoretical."[36] Quite apart from the question of whether there is more in psychoanalysis than Patterson sees there, then, I think he is right that one way to be more theoretical is to ask how we might understand complex psychological structures, such as those he explores in the Pardoner, without invoking what is after all one main line of psychoanalytic theory, features of which are shared by psychoanalysis even at its most revisionary. That line pursues a causal analysis of psychological phenomena, locating their sources in terms of a developmental narrative centered on the polymorphous perversity of infantile sexuality and the various biological and cultural demands – sometimes, though by no means always, those surrounding the Oedipus complex – that lead to the renunciation of infantile pleasures and to attempts to recapture them in other forms. Whatever the value of such analysis, it is a mistake to assume that it is necessary for, or always the best path into, discussions of psychological complexity, even ones that focus, as this book does, on misrecognition, gender anxiety, and the ambivalences that haunt sexual desire.

One of the great values of studying Chaucer and the premodern intellectual and literary traditions in which he was steeped is that it makes available to us an alternative path of analysis that is obscured by a tendency to see psychological complexity as the exclusive province of psychoanalysis, a path that reveals features of misrecognition and of sexuality that do not clearly emerge from a psychoanalytic discussion. As I have argued, this alternative path leads not to the causal sources of psychological phenomena but to the structure of reasons that informs them; and as I have suggested and will continue to do so, it can help us provide an analysis that resists an impulse much medieval thought shares with some versions of psychoanalysis, that of locating the sources of moral and psychological alterity in traumatic narrative. Further, this alternative path of analysis inverts the procedure psychoanalysis sometimes follows, or seems to follow, of locating sexuality as the inner secret that determines human behavior and psychology.[37] My argument is that sexuality is important to Chaucer not because he sees it as the source of agency and misrecognition and self-violation, but because sexuality provides him with a rich site for exploring the misrecognition and self-violation that inevitably attend the antinomy structuring practical reason and an agent's sense of herself and her projects. No causal analysis, psychoanalytic or otherwise, can capture that antinomy, since a causal analysis necessarily sets the perspective of practical reason and agency to the side.[38]

Boethius has helped us formulate this account because of the way he pursues questions of misrecognition and an agentive investment in suffering in ways that were clearly influential for Chaucer, but that in themselves have nothing to say about sexuality. To understand the relation between this argument and Chaucer's representations of erotic life, then, we need to ask how a Boethian account of masochism that is in the first instance agentive and moral can illuminate the constitution of sexuality. I will pursue that question in depth in the next chapter by turning to the *Roman de la Rose*. Before doing that, however, I want to address more directly the question of what it means to think of Chaucer as a Boethian poet – which means, in this context, how Chaucer developed a poetic project out of Boethian interests in dialectic, the aporetic structures of thought and desire, and the willing self-division with which agents confront their desire for autonomy.

BOETHIUS, CHAUCER, AND NORMATIVE NOSTALGIA

It is often thought that Boethius's influence on Chaucer's poetry can best be seen in passages that cite the *Consolation* or, more broadly, in any way that Chaucer might be said to hold a set of views characterized as "Boethian doctrine," which usually means the positions staked out by Philosophy in the course of the dialogue. My argument is that Boethius's influence is at once less direct and more pervasive than that. I do not deny that Chaucer thinks the positions Philosophy articulates are correct; there is no question of irony or critique here, any more than there is within the *Consolation* itself. But for Boethius and for Chaucer, the articulation of a philosophically correct position is not the final goal. The fundamental philosophical interest of both writers is not to be found in positions, or even in arguments, but rather in problems; and the basic question to ask of each is not "What do they believe?" but rather "How do they investigate the problems that animate them?" For both, in other words, philosophy is not a set of doctrines or arguments but a project of inquiry. And the best way to see Boethius's influence on Chaucer's poetry is to see how Chaucer engaged the problems Boethius has brought us to, and how Chaucer developed and redirected inquiry into them.

I have argued that in the *Consolation* Boethius uses an explicitly dialectical mode of representation to explore the aporias that structure our thinking about happiness, desire, freedom, and justice. Early in his career, in the *Book of the Duchess*, Chaucer experimented with dialectical form by writing a dialogue between interlocutors in need of a therapy neither could provide; in doing so, he explored aporetic structures of thought informing mourning and erotic stasis. But Chaucer – unlike Langland, the *Pearl*-poet, Gower, Jean de Meun, Guillaume de Machaut, Dante, and other writers important to or contemporary with him – lost interest rather quickly in the philosophical dialogue in any version, abandoning extensive use of it with the exceptions of a deeply parodic experiment in *The House of Fame*, and a late return to it in *The Tale of Melibee*. That does not mean, however, that he lost interest in dialectic. I have already argued that dialectical structures inform the *Miller's* and *Knight's Tales* in the absence of any explicitly dialectical representation, and even in the absence of any direct reference to philosophical topics. Two relatively minor poems, "The Former Age" and "Lak of Stedfastnesse," will help to focus this argument further.

"The Former Age" and "Lak of Stedfastnesse" belong to a loose group of short poems often referred to as "Boethian lyrics," poems written in a direct authorial voice with no intervening narrator; here, it would seem, we have Chaucer's Boethianness in its purest and rhetorically simplest form. These poems imagine the "blisful lyf" (FA, 1) of a Golden Age in which excessive desire was unknown – people "helde hem payed of the fruites that they ete" (FA, 3) and "ne were nat forpampred with outrage" (FA, 5) – and in which everyone unfailingly obeyed the dictates of moral duty, for "mannes word was obligacioun" (LS, 2) and all were "wed . . . to stedfastnesse" (LS, 28). Chaucer says of these folk that "hir hertes were al oon" (FA, 47), by which he means that they were both individually and collectively wholehearted, suffering neither psychic nor social conflict. By contrast, the present is marked by "doublenesse" (FA, 62), by multiple forms of individual and collective self-division: war, tyranny, envy, covetousness, pride, a whole array of familiar ethical and political pathologies. In short, "the world hath mad a permutacioun / Fro right to wrong" (LS, 19–20). There is in Chaucer's poetry no simpler and more direct expression of the longing for a will perfectly at one with itself, a condition from which Chaucer imagines us to have lapsed into "wilful wrecchednesse" (LS, 13), a wicked indulgence in willfulness which is at the same time a miserable suffering we embrace as though it were our heart's desire.

In the compact form of these lyrics, then, Chaucer pursues Boethian interests in the desiring, agentive attachment to suffering; in a reflective viewpoint from which the possibility of an authentic, undivided self-hood appears bound to the drive to autonomy; and in the normative nostalgia that locates such autonomy in an irrecoverable past whose claim on the present cannot be erased. And Chaucer's pursuit of these interests begins to look as dialectical as Boethius's – though in an entirely different rhetorical mode – when we ask what exactly in these poems gives their longing its distinctive ache, and what would be required to assuage it. As Andrew Galloway has argued, "The Former Age" is not a poem that asks us simply to imagine the desirability of returning to the idyllic state it represents: that state is too thoroughly marked by what can only appear to us as sheer privation rather than a pleasingly Edenic simplicity.[39] If the inhabitants of the Former Age were not "forpampred with outrage," this is because they lacked the technology to produce food any better than pig fodder: "unknowen was the quern and ek the melle; / They eten mast, hawes, and swich pounage" (FA, 6–7). While grain may spring up unsown, this turns out to be a sign less of Golden Age abundance than of the inability to cultivate, for of this grain "they . . . eete nat half ynough" (FA, 11). And, in lines that comically reverse the rhetorical effect of Diogenes's tag concerning poverty's safety from depradation, Chaucer describes the unwillingness of tyrants in the Former Age to set out on campaigns to conquer wilderness and "busshes" (FA, 33–34), a description compli-cated by the fact that there should by definition have been no tyrants in the first place. What is important to see here is that none of these rhetorical complexities works to undermine the normative longing the poems voice. They rather work to divide us against our identification with an imagined past in which we would have been free of such longing by making us feel the claim of a "doublenesse" that yearns for "trouthe" and of a picture of "trouthe" that remains embedded in "doublenesse." For we could only assuage our longing for the Former Age as these poems represent it if we no longer desired to have enough to meet our most basic material needs, and no longer understood that a creature deprived of enough is free from tyranny only because its possessions are so undesirable.

"Lak of Stedfastnesse" provides some terms to drive this point home. To live in the Former Age as Chaucer depicts it would not be to attain the moral perfection of "steadfastness," but rather to suffer a peculiar kind of lack of steadfastness. This would not be the kind Chaucer depicts in the present of the poem, in which we fail in our reach for autonomy because we cannot bring ourselves to be true to our deepest convictions and most important obligations. It would rather be the lack involved in having nothing to be steadfast about: there would be no need for "trouthe" in relation to ourselves or in our bonds with others because no one would realize they lacked anything, and even if they did, there would be nothing worth breaking one's trouthe for. But then this condition could not begin to assuage the longing Chaucer so evidently feels. The longing for the Former Age rather involves a wish to obliterate the conditions in which any possible longing could ever arise, and to establish amnesia about the very thing that made it attractive in the first place. What makes Chaucer's poems so powerful is the way they resist such amnesia and show the impossibility of its ever being complete. They do so through their appeal to a notion of steadfast commitment that the fantasy of the Former Age cannot sustain; through their reminders that, unlike our imagined ancestors, we *are* creatures of deprivation and desire, and we know it; and through the paradoxical appearance of the figure of the tyrant, the one inhabitant of the Former Age who is *not* happy with "less than half enough," and so who functions as a kind of reservoir for the consciousness of deprivation on which the very possibility of steadfastness depends, but which cannot be an acknowledged part of Golden Age fantasy, and so must appear there only in displaced, demonized form. In each of these ways Chaucer's lyrics work to exhibit the way normative nostalgia erases the very possibility of the perfection it imagines, and depends for its tug on this very erasure. To invoke Susan Stewart's memorable phrase, the nostalgia of these poems is "a sadness without an object."[40]

Here, we might think, we have at last come across a deep difference between Chaucer and Boethius, a place where Chaucer substantially differs from Boethian doctrine and subjects it to critique. For we have just seen that Boethius remains subject to normative nostalgia in his metaphysics and theology, as well as in the account he would give of the ultimate source of moral failure; whereas we have seen, not only in the *Knight's* and *Miller's Tales*, but even in poems that lack an intervening narrator, that Chaucer again and again makes nostalgia an object of analysis, investigating its self-contradictions and, especially in the *Tales*, its implication in the blindness and violence of various social ideologies.[41] And, we might think, this difference reflects an even deeper one concerning each writer's relations to the ideal of philosophical truth. The aporetic structure of Chaucerian nostalgia may link it to Boethian dialectics, but for Boethius, dialectical investigation seems ultimately to stop in the articulation of philosophical truth, while Chaucer seems a more modern and skeptical figure who keeps his distance from any such claims, always complicating them rhetorically, placing them back in the realm of situated, interested, "doubled" discourse. To put the thought being entertained here in a nutshell, while Boethius places metaphysics in the mouth of Philosophy, Chaucer places Boethian metaphysics in the mouth of Theseus, a ruler with a distinct political agenda who is himself the imaginative product of a narrator whose moral, political, and erotic attitudes are shot through with ambivalence and misrecognition.

Such a thought would return us more or less to the prevalent view of both Chaucer and Boethius, and it would respond to much of what I have been arguing, but while I find it preferable to a Robertsonian view of Chaucer as a dogmatic poet, I think it shares with Robertson a tendency to garble questions of how to read Chaucer's analytical habits of mind with broad issues of skepticism and belief to which they are unrelated. Let us begin with Boethius. As we have seen, the *Consolation* begins with nostalgia, in the Prisoner's lament for a lost past of freedom and pleasure which Philosophy claims is only the perception of a change. Nostalgia is itself here an example of misrecognition, an attempt to narrativize a lack that is finally not historical. Golden Age nostalgia appears later in the first half of the dialogue, shortly before Philosophy begins the happiness argument; but while the invocation of the Golden Age appears now in the voice of Philosophy, it too functions as an expression of something else that it cannot quite formulate, suited to a moment in the dialectic in which historical narrative seems the only way to capture what will later be revealed as an atemporal metaphysical structure. And while that structure itself later gets expressed in narrative form, as a story about the workings of the cosmos rather than a sequence of historical ages, the reason for the production of that story is that the atemporal metaphysical structure towards which Philosophy points is scarcely conceivable except in mythical narrative form.[42] Even in metaphysics, then, narrative is not literal but phantasmatic, a way of trying to give imaginative form to something that, strictly speaking, cannot be represented. That is part of the point of Philosophy's distinction, late in the dialogue, between cognition and intellection: because cognition is always temporally and linguistically mediated, it can never grasp the truth complete and plain, but breaks what is whole and simple into reified parts; and while intellection involves direct contact with the essence of a thing, for that very reason it must be nonrepresentational.[43]

It is perfectly Boethian, then, for Chaucer to think that all representation carries doubleness and misrecognition within it – or, to put the point in terms from earlier in this chapter, to think of representation as essentially fetishistic, as reifying one's relationship to an unrepresentable object of thought and desire which it simultaneously points to and conceals. And it is equally Boethian for Chaucer to understand the production of narrative as a paradigmatic site for fetishistic reification. But it goes along with this way of thinking that if fetishistic reification involves a kind of false consciousness, then poetry, like all other representational forms, cannot supply a superior vantage-point from which such reifications can be subjected to a disinterested critique. The last thing a Boethian poetics would pursue, then, would be a Robertsonian moralism; and Chaucer's interest in the investigation of false consciousness from within, with no recourse to a discursive ground outside ideology, far from being protomodern, belongs quite centrally to the medieval intellectual tradition we have always placed him in.

The same can be said when we turn, as the Boethian lyrics do, from metaphysics to morals. Through the doubled rhetoric of these poems – through their way of distancing us from a longing to which they continue to give powerful and unironized expression – Chaucer pursues a critical investigation of something to which he finds himself deeply subject. And here too Chaucer is quite close to Boethius's intellectual commitments. For the force of Chaucer's appeals to trouthe and stedfastnesse suggests that, if no sense can finally be given to the idea of a prior state in which all were wed to those ideals, the appeal to a narrative priority misrecognizes another kind of priority, the ontological priority of the sense of self associated with autonomy, that is, with a nonpathological attachment to freely chosen ends. And what is more, the poems include in the realm of pathological attachment such things as the taste for human food rather than pig fodder and the desire for adequate material sustenance, both of which mark our desiring participation in a world of covetousness and tyranny, even as it is impossible to imagine a life without them, or at least a life anyone could want. Chaucer's rhetoric thus points to something it does not directly represent: a Boethian antinomy of the will, a conflict between the normative authority of autonomy and that of a way of life determined by practical and historical necessities. For both Boethius and Chaucer, such a conflict is constitutive of the human, and definitively marks the human as a creature of normative longing. Chaucer's Boethian lyrics present nostalgia as a way of trying to picture this fundamental deadlock by rendering it into fetishistic narrative, producing as its desired object a reified state that both expresses and diverts us from the problem for which it imagines a solution.

While Chaucer's Boethianness is not to be found in his poetry's exemplification of Boethian doctrine, then, neither is it true that the differences between Chaucer and Boethius are to be found in doctrinal disagreements. For all his interest in psychology and the limits of discursive knowledge, Boethius retains a commitment to making arguments about philosophical topics and to trying to say what is true about them. Chaucer's lack of interest in making arguments and in aiming at philosophical truth, on the other hand, is the sign not of an anti-Boethian skepticism, but of a much more powerful interest than Boethius has in exploring the social and psychological specificities of persons' inhabitation of philosophical problems. As I have argued with respect to the Knight and the Miller, and will argue with respect to the Wife of Bath and the Clerk, Chaucer deliberately produces a poetic rhetoric that invites the philosophical work necessary for such exploration. In this he participates in the larger intellectual and poetic culture I sketched in the book's introduction – the culture of Jean de Meun, Dante, and Langland, among others – although Chaucer's is perhaps the most subtle contribution to that culture, as it moves far afield of any explicit philosophical references or themes. But that subtleness should not be mistaken, as it often is, for a move to a realist poetics that rejects philosophy in favor of social and psychological portraiture. To think that is to deny ourselves the resources Chaucer assumed for a reading of his portraits.

CHAPTER 4

Sadomasochism and utopia in the *Roman de la Rose*

The purpose of this chapter is to extend and elaborate two closely linked arguments from the previous chapter. The more local of the two arguments concerns a reading of the intellectual tradition within which Chaucer developed his interests in gender and sexuality and his sense of those interests as central to a project of philosophical poetry. The larger of the two arguments concerns the recovery of a medieval idiom for understanding psychological phenomena such as repression, fetishism, narcissism, sadism, and masochism. The two arguments dovetail in a resistance to taking either set of concerns as distinctively modern, or as requiring a modern conceptual apparatus such as psychoanalysis to understand.[1] Rather than turning to speculative biology, traumatic narrative, any of the various developmental models of the psyche, or any of the various psychic topographies advanced by Freud or Lacan, my argument focuses on the perennial link the Christian tradition has made between problems of sexuality and problems of autonomy, a link which, as Peter Brown has argued, was central to Christian thinking about morality and sociality from Paul to Augustine, and which remained so throughout the Middle Ages and beyond. Partly to indicate the differences between the place of sexuality in this tradition and in psychoanalysis, in the previous chapter I bracketed sexuality completely, arguing that a sufficiently supple reading of dialectical form in Boethius's *Consolation of Philosophy* both provides a philosophical account of repression and fetishism and leads to the conclusion that agency is constitutively masochistic. The present chapter extends this argument concerning a constitutive masochism to include accounts of sadism and narcissism, while returning the discussion to the territory of erotic life. I do so through a reading of the *Roman de la Rose* that will attend to that text's engagements with Boethian dialectic, Aristotelian psychology, and the conceptions of utopian sociality at work in Cicero's analysis of friendship and in the Christian ideal of *caritas*. The two chapters together thus provide a context for understanding Chaucer's interests in gender and sexuality as thoroughly philosophical and thoroughly medieval. The eroticized punishments that Chaucer's Miller brings on a masculinity he wishes to imagine as a site of pure unimpeded activity; the combination of ethical admiration and voyeuristic, objectifying desire in both the Miller's and the Knight's representations of their tales' central female characters; and the Knight's abjected and ambivalent attempts to imagine a formalized ground for erotic conduct; these and other features of Chaucer's representations of gender and desire repeatedly open into broader considerations in ethics and theory of action because they are such powerful sites for exploring the masochism constitutive of agency.

This chapter's returning of the topic of masochism to a sexual context suggests another way of framing my argument that will help to clarify its historical and theoretical stakes. Both Chaucer and the authors of the *Rose* are deeply interested in a masculine eroticism that simultaneously elevates the feminine love object to sublime status and subjects it to an aestheticizing voyeurism, and that predicates its own desire on an immersion in suffering.[2] This erotic form commonly goes by the name of "courtly love," and as such it has come in for considerable discussion in recent years, most powerfully in the work of psychoanalytic theorists and critics.[3] The thought that courtly love is inherently masochistic is, however, hardly new. To be reminded of its familiarity one need only think of C. S. Lewis's famous description of the lovers in medieval allegory as

> "servants" or "prisoners" . . . who seem to be always weeping and always on their knees before ladies of inflexible cruelty . . . The lover is always abject. Obedience to his lady's slightest wish, however whimsical, and silent acquiescence in her rebukes, however unjust, are the only virtues he dares to claim.[4]

Here, it seems, we are not far from the masochistic contract. In one of the contracts between Leopold von Sacher-Masoch and "Wanda," for instance, Sacher-Masoch has his mistress declare in my hands you are a blind instrument that carries out all my orders without discussion . . . I shall have the right to punish and correct you as I please, without your daring to complain . . . although I may wallow in luxury whilst leaving you in privation and treading you underfoot, you shall kiss the foot that tramples you without a murmur.[5]

However distinct the erotic practices involved may be, courtly love and masochism in its modern form share more than just a lacing of eros with the pleasures of suffering. They also share a peculiar ideological reversal. Both are resolutely masculinist erotic forms, in that it is the man who is "really" in control, insisting on the code of conduct, as it were dressing up his love object in her cruelty; but the masculine fantasy at issue here elevates the feminine love object to the status of a capricious and judgmental tyrant and demands the utmost extremes of abjection in the desiring subject. In both courtly love and masochism, then, the routine pains of romantic love – the delectation of such questions as "Will she love me or not?", "Dare I love her?" and so on – have been elaborated, formalized, and radicalized into something like allegory. The question is how, in each case, we are to read such allegory, and how far each allegorical form can help us understand the other.

Lewis, of course, avoids the term masochism; had he considered the question of its use at all, he would probably have considered it an impediment to recapturing the historical specificity of courtly desire and the poetic forms in which it found its most elaborate expression. On the other hand, for at least some recent critics courtly love is the symptomatic expression of a structure of desire which medieval culture itself had no terms for understanding: as Žižek puts it, "it is only with the emergence of masochism, of the masochist couple, towards the end of the last century that we can now grasp the libidinal economy of courtly love" (*Metastases of Enjoyment*, 89). The apparent contrast between Lewis's careful effort to reconstruct a "long-lost state of mind" (*Allegory of Love*, 1) and Žižek's provocative claim that "history has to be read retroactively" (*Metastases of Enjoyment*, 89) would seem to depend on crucial disagreements concerning historical method and the substance of an account of courtly love. Should we maintain respect for the alterity of the past, or should we dispense with the necessarily limited self-understandings of the past in favor of an analytics for which we are only now developing the intellectual tools? I do not think we need to choose between these options – and *not* because the truth lies "somewhere in between," in a moderation of both positions. The problem with "careful historicism" is not that it shows an overly pious regard for the self-understandings of the past, but that, insofar as it imagines its task to be separable from that of theoretical speculation, its respect for the past is not radical enough; while the problem with "theory" is not that it courts anachronism and allows itself to play fast and loose with the interpretive object, but rather that, insofar as it imagines its task to be that of deploying an interpretive technology clearly distinct from the self-understandings of the past, it reifies its object and so is not theoretical enough.[6] In saying this, I do not mean to direct a polemic against Lewis and Žižek; these purposely exaggerated characterizations of historicism and theory fit neither. Instead I want to note the way certain features of their rhetoric, to which they may well be deeply committed but on which their deepest insights do not depend, makes it look as though they disagree about some substantive methodological issue, and so contribute to a limiting but widespread view of the interpretive options. In contrast to the idea that we need to choose between historicism and theory, my sense is that in order to do good history, we have to do good theory; and in this case that means neither adapting psychoanalytic categories from the outset nor polemically refusing to think about the topics and problems psychoanalysis engages.

Let us then take as a point of departure a more general narrative on which Lewis, all of the psychoanalytic critics I have cited, and for that matter quite a number of other literary and cultural historians would agree.[7] From roughly the eleventh century on, a rich tradition of literary interest in the sufferings of love developed in Spain and France and then spread throughout western Europe. This tradition came to include both Chaucer and many of the poets of most interest to him, including Guillaume de Lorris, Jean de Meun, Guillaume de Machaut, Dante, and Petrarch. Further, this tradition helped to produce, and was influenced by, the broader cultural phenomenon of an eroticism that included but was not limited to courtly love, and which bore many of the characteristics of what came to be hegemonic western romantic love. These features include the sweeping up of the erotic subject into a state of utter devotion; the staking of one's life and self on the love object; the intensification of the couple around the thrills and abjections of enamoration; and the production of a paradoxical erotic structure in which the feminine love object is constituted as a space of contemplation and delectation for the masculine subject and yet elevated to quasidivine status, while the masculine subject finds itself simultaneously in a position of sadistic mastery and lowered to the status of an insignificant worm undeserving of its object's attentions. In what follows I will argue that the *Roman de la Rose*, through its development of a rich allegorical mode of representation and its engagement with Boethian dialectics and philosophical psychology, provides a more powerful analysis of this form of eroticism than we have so far been willing to attribute to medieval culture. I hardly think the *Rose* was alone in this. But I restrict this chapter to a single text because I agree with Lewis that, partly because of our historical distance from allegory, it remains a difficult mode of representation to read; and the effort of historical imagination required here demands the kind of sustained close reading the *Rose* consistently rewards. I focus so tightly on the *Rose* also because it is the text other than the *Consolation* with which Chaucer maintained his most persistent intellectual dialogue, and with its explicit commitment to adapting Boethian dialectic to something like a character-based poetics it offers both Chaucer's closest model for philosophical poetry and a helpfully proximate contrast with his mature poetics. The chapter's larger theoretical-historical argument and its more local literary-historical one converge in a single question, to which I will now turn: how does the *Roman de la Rose* elaborate a Boethian concern with the masochistic constitution of agency into a concern with the sadomasochistic constitution of sexuality?

EROTIC PATHOLOGY AND THE SCENE OF FANTASY

In claiming that the *Roman de la Rose* is concerned with a sadistic eroticism, I initially mean only to be drawing a fairly straightforward consequence of what has long been seen as the misogyny of the text's dominant erotic representations.[8] Throughout the poem, masculine eroticism is figured in terms of violently appropriative desires to invade or penetrate the desired other, to objectify, commodify, and aestheticize her, to possess her and establish mastery over her. The initial cluster of figures for male erotic satisfaction allegorize this sadism quite explicitly: to penetrate the rose's enclosure, pluck the rosebud, and hold it in one's hand is to subject it to death, for, as the narrator well knows, a plucked rose will wither in a matter of days: "les roses overtes et lees / sont en un jor toutes alees, / et li bouton durent tuit frois / a tot le moins .II. jors ou trois" (1643–46) ("the broad, open ones are gone in a day, but the buds remain quite fresh at least two or three days [53]").[9] Friend's cynical advice to "cuillez la rose tout a force / et moutrez que vos estes hon" (7660–61) ("cut the rose by force and show that you are a man" [144–45]) links the violence of such desire to the shoring up of a threatened sense of virility in a familiar way, and justifies the violence in an equally familiar way through a supposed feminine desire for it: "il veulent par force doner / ce qu'il n'osent abandoner" (7667–68) ("they want to be forced to give what they do not dare abandon" [145]). And, to skip the many instances in between, the poem concludes with an elaboration of the initial rose-plucking trope into that of a full-bore assault on the "tower" of the woman's body, an assault whose purpose is "por tout prandre et metre par terre" (20680) – a line that hovers between the preparatory mechanics of conventional male-on-top lovemaking ("to take everything and place it on the ground") and, as Dahlberg translates it, a murderous rapacious-ness ("to take everything and level it to the earth" [339]). In what follows I will argue that the *Rose* itself, despite what Christine de Pizan and many since have seen as its misogyny, does not endorse such an eroticism; the poem is about misogyny rather than an uncritical instantiation of it, and it casts the eroticization of misogyny as pathological.[10] In making this case, however, I will finally be interested in something a bit more unsettling than a moral evaluation: for, as I will argue, the text also suggests that there are real problems in saying just what is being desired here, as well as in saying how this pathology is distinct from "normal" sexuality.[11] As in the previous chapter, then, my ultimate argument will not concern a distinct, minoritized disposition. Just as masochism there was a name for a structuring feature of agency, so sadism and masochism here will be names for structuring features of normative sexuality, features that derive from the ontology of sexuality, and ultimately from the ontology of agency itself.

One problem in distinguishing the normal from the pathological here emerges from the narrator's desire for an erotic satisfaction that he knows to involve the imminent death of the precious love object.[12] This desire suggests that implicit in the dreamer's attraction to the erotic object is an equally powerful aversive impulse, a wish for the removal or erasure of the desired one; and if we connect this to the objectification involved in imagining her as a rose, it seems as though both her objectification and the desire for her death point to something unbearable about her considered as an agentive being, something sticking out from the world of natural objects and strictly possessable things. Read allegorically, the beauty of the rose might then be understood as a way of trying to imagine the erotic other as part of a natural world which is itself the object of an instrumentalist fantasy, a dream of perfect manipulability – a way of imagining, in other words, her "death" as an agent and subject of desire. And since the death of the desired object entails its loss for the one who desires it, the wish for that death might also be understood as a wish for the frustration of desire and the suffering of loss. This returns us to the masochism of courtly love, and also helps to make sense of the dreamer's rather peculiar invocation of his own embalmed body just at the moment when he first contemplates plucking the rose: "et bien sachiez, quant je fui pres, / l'odor des roses savoree / m'entra jusques en la coree, / que por noiant fusse enbasmez" (1624–27); "Mark well: when I was near, the delicious odor of the roses penetrated right into my entrails. Indeed, if I had been embalmed, the perfume would have been nothing in comparison with that of the roses" (52). If masochism, so far at least, is less transparently allegorized by the text's dominant representations than is sadism, it is perhaps even more important to our understanding of the desires at issue here, since it would speak to the depth with which aversion and attraction, and suffering and desire, overlap.[13]

The sense of an overlapping or perhaps even mutually constitutive aversion and attraction gains support from reflection on what it means to desire, as the narrator does, the plucking especially of those "boutons petiz et clous" (1637), those small, tight buds, as opposed to the attractive but less hyperbolically pleasing "roses overtes et lees" (1643). Most obviously, this figures the desirability of "deflowering" a virgin; but "plucking the bud" is not just a figure for penetrating the virginal intactness of the love object. The dreamer is devoted to the bud – *that* is what he wants to hold in his hand – and if the bud is a figure for the virginal love object, then to pluck the bud is also to keep her from growing into that later state of full floral openness, and so to *preserve* her in her unviolated intactness. In this sense, the desire to possess the love object in its self-enclosed, budlike state is a desire to possess her as aseptic and free from change, perhaps even free from death. This desire for a changeless love object circulates in rather unstable form through various sites of erotic objectification in the text, and in ways that give that objectification a particularly aestheticizing valence, as for instance in the earlier figuration of female genitals in the artifactual enclosure of the Garden of Love, or in the later apparent digression on Pygmalion and his fetishized feminine art object. And if this aestheticizing wish to preserve the rosebud's intactness seems distinct from a violating sadism, it does involve its own form of aversion, this time an aversion towards the sexual act altogether, at least in its genital heterosexual form. The elevation of the erotic object into the asepsis of art – and, as both the dreamer and Pygmalion will experience it, into the art object's indifference towards her lover's attentions – suggests, no less thoroughly than the desire for its death, a masochistic wish to keep at a distance, and even to lose, the very thing whose possession it means to guarantee.

Sadism and masochism are of course my terms, not the poem's. The central term the *Rose* provides for the erotic pathology at issue here is narcissism: the dreamer falls in love with the rose while gazing into what the text variously refers to as the Fountain of Love and the Fountain of Narcissus, and an Ovidian interest in narcissism pervades the text well beyond its explicit invocation of the Narcissus and Echo narrative.[14] Let me proceed then by saying what I take narcissism to involve in this text, and how sadomasochism might be understood as essential to it. Minimally, narcissism involves the notion of an erotic withdrawal and self-enclosure: Narcissus falls in love with an image of himself to the exclusion of any other love object.[15] I will elaborate this purposely bare and literal characterization in a moment. But before going too far with the Ovidian story or its specific location in the *Rose*, I want to back up from the figure of Narcissus to suggest how Guillaume provides some terms for understanding it with an already quite elaborate representation of erotic self-enclosure earlier in the poem.

The text's central figure of an erotic enclosure, if not immediately of a self-enclosure, is the Garden of Love itself. But the distinction between erotic immersion in the *locus amoenus* and erotic withdrawal is blurred by the location of the Fountain of Narcissus at the center of the garden, which suggests that narcissism and love may not be fully distinguishable here. What is more, the notion of erotic enclosure is echoed, less as a danger than as a positive ambition, in the narrator's description of the poem itself as a kind of place "ou l'art d'Amors est tote enclose" (38), which we might translate either as "where the art of love is entirely enclosed," or, as Dahlberg does, "in which the whole art of love is contained" (31). The ideal of a totalized art of love, and of a poem that might fully specify and delimit that art, already implicates the narrator in a kind of narcissistic withdrawal from the erotic other's agency, as though one might guarantee one's possession of a lover through the possession of a complete and perspicuously representable theory of loving.[16] "Allegory" might be thought of as the literary form of such an ambition, and "courtly love" might be thought of as its social form.[17] The *Rose*, however, supports neither a view of allegory as a totalized art, a coherent system of correspondences between literary representations and abstract ideas, nor a view of loving as formalizable within a set of rules. The problems in saying what "plucking the rose" is supposed to "mean" already suggest this, and a close reading of almost any of the poem's central figures produces similar problems.[18]

The case of "Bel Acueil" ("Fair Welcoming") is particularly telling in this respect. At first glance, Fair Welcoming seems to be little more than what Lewis took him to be, one of a group of figures representing the Lady's inner conflict over how to respond to the lover's pursuit of her – in this case, a figure for her disposition to respond favorably. If we read Fair Welcoming strictly in this way, it may seem possible to explain away his masculinity as a grammatical accident, since on such an account it looks merely paradoxical: "acueil" is a masculine noun in Old French, so of course the text refers to the personification of this attribute with the masculine pronoun, even if a woman is doing the welcoming. But if we remember that everything in the narrative is part of the narrator's dream, and so constitutes his representation of the scene of his desire, this grammatical oddity begins to look more significant. For all the violence of the *Roman de la Rose*, it is not supposed to be a rape narrative; it is supposed to be a story that encapsulates the art of love, where it is presumed that that art pertains to a male lover whose desire is trained on a female object. For such a story to go forward in a way that does not collapse into rape, it has to find space for representing the love object's potential desire as well as the lover's. But according to the story's initial premises, the desirability of the feminine object is predicated on her being just that: an object, passive in the face of the lover's desire, a site on which his desire can work and display itself. The gender ideology in which this story participates – familiar to us from the Chaucerian texts already discussed – is what makes the Lady's representation as a rose appropriate; this ideology is also what makes it so much as possible to imagine that there could *be* an "art of love" that would formalize the male pursuit of an erotic object in such a way as to guarantee its success.[19] But in imagining the scene of his desire in such a way the dreamer now has a problem: if the feminine object is supposed to be a passive site on which he deploys and displays his art, then in order to imagine her activity in returning his desire, he has to imagine her as being "like a man."[20] Moreover, insofar as the dreamer's desire lodges in her *not* merely as a passive object but as an agent capable of desiring and loving him, her masculinity becomes the very target of his desire. In order for this heteronormative and antifeminist dream of desire to give expression to nonnarcissized erotic energies, and to avoid collapsing into pure erotic withdrawal, it must produce a homoeroticism at its very center. The masculinity of Fair Welcoming, then, far from being a minor grammatical embarrassment that both Guillaume and Jean somehow either failed to notice or were incapable of avoiding, is essential to that figure's allegorical function.

I have meant the parallel between this argument concerning Fair Welcoming and the argument I made in chapter one concerning Alisoun in the *Miller's Tale* to be fairly obvious: it is the sign, I think, of a proximity between Chaucer's writing and the *Rose* that extends beyond any moments of direct textual citation to include both broad conceptual purposes and the literary methods for pursuing them. One way of putting this is to say that I was reading Alisoun allegorically, as part of the Miller's dream of desire. But putting the point that way requires noting that when we look closely at more familiar examples of allegorical representation such as those of Fair Welcoming or "plucking the rose," we should dispense with the notion of allegory as a static mode of representation and see it instead as a remarkably powerful way of representing the mobility of fantasy.

In saying this I do not mean to appeal to a distinctively psycho-analytic technique for reading that mobility. By fantasy I rather mean something familiar to the Aristotelian tradition of psychological theory which a number of critics have located as essential to medieval alle-gory.[21] On Aristotle's definition *phantasia* is "that in virtue of which we say that an appearance (*phantasma*) occurs to us."[22] I have translated *phantasma* as "appearance" rather than, as it is sometimes rendered, "image," for two reasons: first, to remain closer to the Greek, in which *phantasma* is a noun related to the verb "appear," *phainesthai*; and second, to help avoid a common modern misconception of *phantasia* as referring fundamentally to the capacity to form mental images, a misconception largely driven by our inheritance of an empiricist psy-chology quite different from Aristotle's.[23] What Aristotle is after here is the capacity to see something *as* something, to have it appear to you, as it were, under a particular description. In contrast to the faculty of sensation, whose data have not yet been organized into anything perceivable, *phantasia* produces the synthesized appearances that are the proper objects of perception, thought and affect, such as a delicious ice cream cone or a hungry lion, or for that matter a beautiful rose. In a sense, *phantasia* is something that acts on us, and our capacity to be acted on by it is part of what makes us capable of action ourselves. It is an essential feature of the appearance of the hungry lion bearing down on you, for instance, that you fear it and are inclined to run away, and only an animal with sufficiently complex perceptual capacities can be acted on in such a way. As Aristotle puts it, *phantasia* is a "move-ment . . . enabling its possessor to act and to be affected in many ways."[24] To this extent humans can be said to share the capacity for producing phantasms with many other animals. What makes human *phantasia* constitutively different from that of other animals is its relation to our higher cognitive capacities. This relation has two aspects. On the one hand, in humans *phantasia* never gives a neutral representa-tion of a state of affairs, but is already loaded up with interpretation and desire.[25] On the other hand, as Aristotle puts it, "to the thinking soul phantasms serve as sense-perceptions . . . Hence the soul never thinks without a phantasm."[26] To this Aristotle later adds that we are "not capable of desire without *phantasia*."[27] In thinking and desiring, then, fantasy continues to be something that acts on us: the things we think about and desire are delivered to us by *phantasia*. But if no thought or desire is ever free of fantasy, *phantasia* is also something we make, since it is itself continually shaped by thought and desire. Fantasy – the faculty by which the creature represents objects of thought and affect to itself – is the interior space in which scenes of belief and desire get made.

The dialectical method of the *Consolation of Philosophy*, the allegorical method of the *Roman de la Rose*, and Chaucer's apparently more realist poetics are all predicated on such a psychology.[28] And all of these texts, as I have argued, work both to reveal the essential indeterminacy of scenes of thought and desire and to explore the drive to reify those scenes and declare them determinate. If the desire for totality is never far from view in the *Rose*, then, that text's allegorical method provides a means for examining how the desire for totality and determinacy gets produced within the conditions of its impossibility. Further, if a narcissistic desire for totality cannot be the allegorical "truth" of the text, while narcissism may inflect "normal" sexuality here quite deeply, it cannot do so as the secret truth within the normal. Rather, the narcissistic wish for totality already has the status of an ideological fantasy, an incoherent structure of thought and desire that provides the conditions for the modes of subjectivity represented in the text, but that always does so in relation to something else that it cannot figure.[29]

I will suggest what that something else is, and the form of its relation to narcissistic fantasy, in a moment. But first I want to explore more fully the local texture of the fantasy itself, to see what further terms of analysis it provides. While the opening of the poem announces a narcissistic totality as its ambition, the opening scene of the dream itself seems to be anything but one of enclosure. It is rather a scene of erotic expansiveness, one of the great instances of the familiar medieval literary *topos* of the springtime regeneration of the natural world:

> Avis m'iere qu'il estoit mais,
> il a ja bien .v. anz ou mais,
> qu'en may estoie, ce sonjoie,
> el tens enmoreus, plain de joie,
> el tens ou toute rien s'esgaie,

que l'en ne voit buisson ne haie
qui en may parer ne se veille
et covrir de novele fuelle.
(45–52)

I became aware that it was May, five years or more ago; I dreamed that
I was filled with joy in May, the amorous month, when everything
rejoices, when one sees no bush or hedge that does not wish to adorn
itself with new leaves. (31)

Far from turning away from this erotically charged landscape, the narrator finds himself moved by the joyful desire of the bushes and hedges for
their new growth, by the earth wanting a beautiful new robe of grass and
flowers, by birds bursting into song from sheer joy, and by the way young
people are enjoined by all this sweet beauty to a kind of mimetic erotic
activity.[30] But the notion of enclosure, or anyway of a kind of withdrawal,
gets reintroduced when the speaking voice of the poem reintroduces
himself as a character inside his dream and the poem begins to shift
from sheer lyrical expressiveness towards narrative. Not that the narrator
is unattracted to this scene: he is filled with the desire to run out of town
to listen to the birdsong, "hors de vile oi talant d'aler / por oïr des oisiaus
les sons" (94–95). But this is strikingly unlike the way he has just said that
young people tend to be moved by such a scene, when "mout a dur cuer
qui en may n'ame / quant il ot chanter sus la raime / as oisiaus les douz
chans piteus" (81–83), "he has a very hard heart who does not love in May,
when he hears the birds on the branches, singing their heart-sweet songs"
(32). For the dreamer is not, apparently, moved to love, or even to
sociability, by this sweet piteous birdsong. Instead he runs out "tot sol"
(99), all alone, not to be gay and amorous – or at least not directly – but
rather to immerse himself in the beautiful expression of an eroticism he
will not pursue directly. What we still ought to call his amorousness
seems then to be constituted by the pleasures of a contemplative distance
on this beautiful expressiveness. And in contemplating this beauty, he has
deflected the impulse towards erotic connection which he has just figured
as natural and necessary into a peculiarly solitary activity, the reverie of
a listening that precludes a fuller form of sexual participation.

This combination of hyperbolic attraction to an erotic scene and
contemplative withdrawal from it becomes a kind of running joke on
the dreamer throughout the poem. In coming upon the refined courtly

eroticism of the dancing allegorical figures inside the Garden, for instance, the dreamer declares

> Dex! com menoient bone vie!
> Fox est qui n'a de tel envie!
> Qui autel vie avoir porroit,
> de meillor bien se soufreroit,
> qu'il n'est nus graindres paradis
> d'avoir amie a son devis.
> (1293–98)

> God! What a good life they led! He who does not long for such a life is a fool. He who could have such a life might dispense with a greater good, since there is no greater paradise than to have one's beloved at one's desire. (48)

Leaving aside for the moment the confusing thought of an unspecified dispensable good that is somehow greater than an erotic repletion which is itself greater than any other paradise, the joke comes with the utter deadpan *non sequitur* of the immediately following lines. It may be utter folly not to long for such a life, but rather than trying to join in it, "D'ileques me parti atant, / si m'en alai seus esbatant / par le vergier de ça en la" (1299–301), "At this point I left there and went off alone to enjoy myself here and there throughout the garden" (48). Perhaps the translation should read: "I went off alone to pleasure myself here and there throughout the garden."

In speaking of a kind of self-enclosure, then, I do not mean to suggest that the dreamer is fundamentally averse or unresponsive to the joyful energy of the season. He is drawn to contemplate an expression of this joy, and he is also moved to a beautifully lyrical expression of it himself in this poem of love. In a sense, then, the production of the text replicates the expansiveness to which he is attracted. But there is a crucial difference between the dreamer and the birds. For his literary activity is born out of his *not* just heeding nature's call as the bushes and the birds do; the full joyfulness of the scene for him can only be captured by his establishing enough distance on it to have something to *say* about it. As the dreamer has already indicated, this will mean more than just engaging in lyrical rhapsody; it will require of him the much greater reflective distance necessary for a total declaration of the truth of the matter, the linguistic enclosure of the whole art – the craft, but also the artfulness, the artifice – of love. And while this reflective ambition seems to drive the production of the narrative, it is hard to see how he could fulfill it while charging ahead towards some orgasmic goal. The nature of that ambition rather threatens to stall the very narrative it engenders, to transform it into the sheer lyrical reflectiveness of the dream's beginning, or perhaps of Narcissus's enraptured gaze.

Still, as we know, the dreamer will soon get directed upon the narrativized goal of actually being a lover. The moment he faces, then, is in a sense that of any young person in this season, or for that matter of any bird: he wants to *do* something, not just to reflect on it. The problem of the dreamer's ambivalent impulse towards erotic self-enclosure – which is also, as I have been suggesting, the problem of the relation between the normal and the pathological here – can then be reformulated as follows. The opening of the *Rose* poses the problem of how to understand the relations between two desires that seem to drive in different directions but at the same time to inflect each other: the desire to be a lover, to pluck the rose, to possess an erotic object, to practice the art of love; and the desire to contemplate being a lover, to enjoy the birds singing love and the bushes blooming it, to write poetry about it, to theorize that art and to produce it *as* art. The birds become so central to the poem's opening, I would suggest, because they provide an attractive figure for a perfect alignment of these two impulses. Their singing expresses their joy, it can be seen as a kind of aesthetic reflection that produces an excessive, gratuitous beauty; and it also serves quite directly and pragmatically to attract a mate. The human case, however, is more complex. For the reflective or aestheticizing impulse heightens the pleasure of loving, making it into something more refined, more beautiful, more artful, like the caroling the dreamer encounters in the garden; but in doing so it also defers that pleasure, driving a reflective wedge between the desiring creature and the target of desire, and making this reflective wedge central from the very start to the production of desire and to the creature's seducibility by the erotic.

I would suggest that we read the figure of Narcissus in the *Rose* as a kind of allegorical limiting case of this pleasurable reflective gap. Narcissus is in the position of pure speculation, wanting nothing so much as a look that perpetually frustrates the very desire for erotic satisfaction that gives rise to it. We should remember who Narcissus is: the one who could not respond to the love of Echo, because he was too enamored of his own beauty. The point of Echo being the one he refuses, in Ovid as well as the *Rose*, is to cast the love Narcissus finds to be too alien as itself something very close to narcissism: hers is a voice that would respond perfectly to his own, never offering resistance or alterity, just "reflecting" his. Or almost: for unlike Narcissus's image in the fountain, Echo is at least another, she is at least *separate* from him. What Echo figures, then, is the voice of the erotic other stripped down to the minimum, made to carry no content except that of her separateness, and of the fact that, as Guillaume puts it, "l'avoit amé plus que rien nee" (1443), she loved him more than anything born. What Narcissus cannot bear is the sheer weight of that love, the demand made on him by the call of another who asks him to speak words of love and offers him nothing but a faithful return. Narcissus's inability to bear this demand is what makes his punishment so appropriate: for he is given a love that does *not* call him, a love that has no other in it, and so one that can never threaten him with the possibility of consummation. In a sense, then, he is not even punished, at least not by any agency external to him. For Narcissus is quite literally given the fulfillment of his desire, and in two seemingly opposite ways. On the one hand, Narcissus is the figure in whom the desire for an impossibly perfect possession of the erotic object has been gratified: there is no chance that the object will move, or even look away from him; it will always remain fixed in and by his gaze. But by the same token he dies of an unanswerable longing for something that can never be possessed, never even touched or heard, since it is only a reflection, a specular image; and this fulfills his desire for a love object that is not so much as an echo. *Narcissism* becomes then Guillaume's term for an eroticism structured by these two interpenetrating longings, for a perfect possession of the erotic object and for an object necessarily removed from any contact with the desiring subject. And in the interpenetration of these longings we can read as well the sadomasochism of the narcissistic subject, the way its hatred of the love object fuses with its wish to destroy the possibility of its own satisfaction, to lace its pleasures with suffering, and, as the allegory of a punishing granting of its wishes suggests, to take vengeance on itself for its perversity.

This form of eroticism, as I have argued, should be understood as an allegorical limiting case of the dreamer's restless and fraught impulses towards violent appropriation of the love object, erotic self-enclosure, and the frustration of desire and the suffering of loss. I have also suggested that what is getting exemplified here is not a distinct, "minority" type of erotic pathology which Narcissus and the narrator happen to share, but rather an understanding of how sexuality is constituted for a reflective creature, a creature for whom desire does not just function, as it does for those birds, as a transparent natural demand. Allegory, in other words, functions here as a mode of literary speculation concerning the ontology of human desire, a way of making the implicit structures of even the most ordinary desire visible in particularly heightened form. But if we are to continue to resist a hasty schematization of this ontology in terms of some supposedly perspicuous theory – theological, psychoanalytic, or otherwise – this suggestion needs further testing, as well as further elaboration, from within the terms the *Rose* gives us.

I will draw those terms from Jean de Meun's continuation of Guillaume's poem, and mainly from the discourse of Reason with which Jean begins. In doing so, I do not mean to deny the much discussed differences between the two parts of the poem. But I think it is a mistake to exaggerate those differences by reading Guillaume as the idealistic (and therefore naïve) adherent of courtly ideology and Jean as the intellectual moralist and realist who exposes courtly love's theological absurdity and the seamy sexual underside of its erotic idealizations.[31] As my argument already indicates, Guillaume is more aware of the problems with courtly desire than any such account acknowledges; and as I will now argue, Jean saw in Guillaume's allegory of the impasse of courtly desire an opportunity not for deflationary irony but for elaboration, first through the form of dialectical philosophy, and then through the production of figures such as Amis, Faux Semblant, and La Vielle, who hover between the status of allegorical figures and something like Chaucerian characters.

In fact, what I have already said concerning the centrality of reflective capacities to an understanding of courtly desire points the way to Jean's Raison. But Raison may seem to be an unpromising place to turn, even if we grant Guillaume's intelligence and self-consciousness concerning the lover's impasse; for Raison almost entirely devotes herself to an antierotic diagnosis of the lover's errors, with the result that this section of the poem has met with boredom on the part of critics interested in sex, and to critics interested in Raison, it has lent itself to the kind of moralizing reading of perversion I am claiming is misplaced.[32] What is more, Raison has little directly to say about erotic life; she mainly expounds on such matters as economic life, civil conduct, justice, free will, and linguistic meaning, all of which seem far from the focus of the dreamer's interests. But we should not be surprised by this difference from what we might have expected in a figure so clearly meant to carry normative authority in this text. As I will argue, Raison is far from the garrulous figure she is sometimes taken to be, and Jean is not merely taking her discourse as an opportunity to show off his encyclopedic learning. Understanding the precision of Raison's focus is essential to seeing the terms she provides for an analysis of erotic psychology.

THE CLAIM OF REASON AND THE DEADLOCK OF UTOPIAN DESIRE

Reason, as is well known, is a figure derived from Boethius's *Philosophy.* In keeping with Philosophy's analysis of the Prisoner's self-frustration, Reason unites the various topics she engages through an analysis of how the human creature incoherently imagines its happiness in terms mediated by the trope of possession. Reason, however, is considerably more interested than Philosophy in the ways persons inhabit specific forms of desire and belief organized around that trope. This impetus towards phenomenological specificity can serve as a helpful bridge between the abstractions of Boethian argument and the case of the dreamer. For the sake of clarity concerning the scope of Reason's concerns, I will leave sex aside for a moment and take the example of money.

According to Reason, the only real value money has lies in its function as a medium of exchange. "L'avoir n'est preuz for por despendre" (5137), "wealth is profit only when spent" (107): money, as Reason will say about words later, is nothing more than a sign for something else, in this case, for its exchange value. But humans, according to Reason, cannot understand this; we reply "qu'avoir n'est preuz for por repondre" (5140), "wealth is profit only when hidden." In thinking this way we fetishize money, investing the sign with the affect that should be directed on the thing it represents.[33] We think of money as itself the locus of value, and want to secure our possession of it; so we hide it away, creating a territory of secret desire, as in the standard iconography of the miser locked away alone, gleefully counting his gold. To recall one of the core tropes of Guillaumean narcissism, we might say that the miser fantasizes the possibility of a totalized enclosure for the object of his desire, as though he could promise to offer himself the entire art of wealth. But Reason makes it clear that the miser figures a structure of desire to which everyone is subject: "il sunt tuit serf a leur deniers" (5131), "they are all slaves of their money" (107). The upshot of this structure of desire is anything but the repletion it holds out as its aim. For we are unable to bear the thought that money must be spent; its ordinary circulatory properties make it seem as though the object of our desire were perpetually slipping away from our grasp. So, among other things, we come to hate the fact that we have to spend money on such bare necessities as clothing and food. The necessities of survival start to look like terrible impositions – as we imagine, impositions made on us by our bodies. Thus we divide ourselves against our own corporeality, in order to imagine that the impediment to getting what we want is merely some set of external circumstances. At the same time we come to be tormented by what Reason refers to as the "remanant" (5047), the taunting remainder that escapes possession: "donc ja tant boivre ne pourra / que toujors plus en demourra" (5053–54), "he will never be able to drink so much that there will not remain more" (106). But this specter of a limitless remainder in the world which "le destraint en tel defaut" (5059), "torments him in his lack" (106), is really a screen for an interior remainder, an excess in the subject's desire that cannot be figured in terms of the possession of a fetishized object at all.

The psychic structure of an inner division held in place by the trope of possessing a fetishized object suggests a common ground between the miser and the dreamer and helps to clarify the dreamer's relation to the field of his desire. The dreamer wants to pluck the Rose, and he knows this entails the Rose's death. But since the Rose is what he wants, he cannot want it dead: the trope of plucking is not adequate to his desire. So his fantasy of the beloved as a pluckable thing produces the screen

remainder of a bunch of apparently external impediments to his possession of her – Dangiers, Male Bouche, Honte, Peor, and so on – which
are analogous to the miser's screen remainder of external impediments,
the tormenting sense that there is both never enough money for his
needs and, even in the absence of any identifiable need, always more
money to be had. While the figures of Dangiers, Male Bouche, and so
on most obviously allegorize the beloved's and her society's resistance to
her being plucked, when they are considered as features of the dreamer's
imagination of the scene of his desire – as figures in the fantasy of desire
he is representing – they are more properly understood as signs of his
own resistance to plucking, of his repressed and inarticulate knowledge,
like that of the miser, that the dream of a perfect possession is inadequate to his own desires and ends.

While the vicissitudes of the trope of possession suggest a line back to
Boethius, I want to focus here on a topic the *Rose* engages much more
fully than Boethius does, that of intersubjective relations: this will lead
us to the horizon of utopian desire to which my title refers. According
to Reason, what really torments both the miser and the dreamer is that
their entire picture of possession and lack is itself a diversion from
a deeper lack they wish to repress, their lack of that perfection, at once
psychic, moral, and social, which is expressed in Reason's ideal of
a friendship consisting in "bone volanté conmune / des genz antr'els, sanz
descordance, / selonc la Dieu benivolance" (4656–58), "mutual good
will among men, without any discord, in accordance with the benevo-
lence of God" (100). This is an adaptation of the Ciceronian formulation of friendship as "omnium . . . rerum cum benevolentia et caritate
consensio", "accord in all things, with mutual good will and benevo-
lence"; and while the differences between the two accounts are important, Cicero's lengthier treatment of the common ground can help us see
what is at stake in it.[34] According to Cicero, among true friends there is
no space of self-interested privacy within which notions of possession
and lack could take hold. Friends have no private property from each
other, and can in principle do nothing to incur or impose debts on each
other. Nor do they wait on a return for their actions or gifts; in a sense
they cannot even give each other gifts, since they already hold everything in common. They have no subjective private property either:
friends have no secrets from each other, and can feel no shame before

each other, nor do their fundamental interests, values, or desires diverge. This is because, as Cicero puts it, a friend is like another self, an *alter ego*, by which he quite precisely does not mean that a friend is a narcissized replica of the ego, since the notion of a primary, self-cherishing relation to the ego is completely out of place here. An *alter ego* is rather someone who occupies the most intimate space of your selfhood, someone whose alterity constitutes not a break with your ego but a constitutive extension of it.

The difficulty of giving the notion of an *alter ego* a positive articulation that does not seem to lapse back into the very narcissism with which it is meant to contrast indicates how hard it is to imagine what such a relationship would be like. It would not be like even the most self-sacrificing of relationships, since it could in principle involve no sacrifices: in a state of accord in all things, there is nothing to give up. But neither would it be a gratification of the wish for a relationship in which you would never need to give up anything, for anything and everything might be required of you in it. It is just that, in the case of true friendship, anything and everything would not be a sacrifice, would not register as an imposition: as Cicero puts it, "nullo loco excluditur, numquam intempestiva, numquam molesta est" (132). This would seem to exclude most, if not all, of what we ordinarily call friendship, as Cicero acknowledges in saying that there have probably been only three or four true friendships in history. We might be inclined to say that this involves an overly stringent judgment of ordinary amicable relations. But Cicero's project is less to level a moral accusation than simply to analyze an attitude. In *De Amicitia* Cicero attempts to isolate the conceptual and motivational structure of a notional relationship in which neither party seeks some advantage from the other, nor draws a line at some point when the disadvantages brought by the relationship become too great; and he claims that this is what we mean by the term *friendship*. It is clear from the dialectical structure of Cicero's argument that he thinks it is hard to see what is involved in such a relationship. Any description of it threatens to collapse into sentimental platitude, or to generate misunderstandings that slide back into the view that what we really always want is egoistic gratification, and what we really always have at heart is self-interest. But Cicero argues that in fact the opposite is true. The desire for friendship underlies every way in which we reach for relational bonds with others, no matter how narrow our purported self-interest may be: insofar as we lapse from the form of relations with an *alter ego* we are betraying our fundamental desire for the other. The point of Cicero's stringency in insisting on the impossibly small number of true historical friendships is to save this claim from the sentimentality it seems to court. For as it happens we always do betray this desire; it remains strange to us, unaccommodatable to the ways we ordinarily have of inhabiting and imagining even our most intimate relations with others, a site of inner alterity as alien as any external "other" could ever be.

By adapting the Ciceronian discourse of friendship to the field of erotic relations – a field not particularly important in *De Amicitia* – Reason in effect suggests that the desire for friendship is what I earlier referred to as the "something other" than the fantasized appropriability of the love object, in relation to which narcissistic desire is always articulated.[35] Friendship in its ideal form is so easy to mistake for narcissism because it answers to so many of the desires narcissism configures. The desire for a relation of perfect resemblance, figured in narcissism as "reflection," is realized in friendship in a way that strips it of any egoistic content: narcissism in effect wants to take the ego as antecedently given, and then find that ego replicated in the world, while in friendship the ego has no primary relationship to itself, but is so fundamentally constituted in the relationship with the other that there is in a sense only one soul there, present in two bodies.[36] The desire for unbreakable contact with the other, figured in narcissism as a perfect possession, is also realized in the extended interiority of friendship, although in a way free of any reification of the love object, since the other in friendship is no more a static object than is the ego. And friendship also answers to the desire for an intimacy that reaches all the way through the other, leaving nothing in them that establishes a secret reserve or that turns away from the desiring subject, a desire figured in narcissism by the reduction of the other to a pure surface that cannot look away. Friendship, in other words, is the truth of narcissism, the realization of narcissism's aim, even as it is also that which narcissism definitively refuses.

To say that the dreamer's sadomasochistic sexuality is a perverse expression of the desire for friendship might seem strange enough – and it certainly seems strange to the dreamer, since it dispenses with so much of what constitutes his desire as he lives it. But Reason does not stop there, and the further trajectory of her analysis breaks from Cicero in a way that establishes the properly utopian horizon in relation to which all desire in the *Rose* is articulated. When Reason diagnoses in the dreamer a "fainte volenté d'amer / en queurs malades du mahaing / de couvoitise de gaaing" (4742–44), a "simulated desire of loving in hearts sick with the disease of coveting gain" (101), she further remarks that "ne peut bien estre amoreus / queurs qui n'aime les gens por eus" (4749–50), "the heart which does not love people for themselves can never be a loving one" (102). This follows straightforwardly enough both from Reason's discourse on friendship and from the poem's earlier representation of the dreamer's sexuality. It also leads Reason directly to her discussion of money. But Reason aims at more than an account of how the trope of possession structures economic life and erotic love. While living in a world of money means that we inevitably fail to love people for themselves, turning them into opportunities for our diseased gain-seeking, Reason also wants to picture an alternative: if "bone amor par tout resnast . . . el monde nul povre n'eüst / ne nul avoir n'en i deüst" (5109–18), "if right love reigned everywhere . . . then there would be no poor man in the world, nor ought there to be any" (107). Here we are catapulted far away from the local problem of objectifying an erotic other or the goal of loving a friend in a way that frees love of its self-seeking tendencies. Friendship, like the erotic desire for something other than a merely possessable object, demands that we love some specific other "for themselves" in a context of intimate desire, which means not treating them as a utilitarian means for some sort of gain. The turn to money radicalizes this analysis. Now the dreamer's erotic pathology turns out to be just one instance of narcissized utilitarian relations which take many forms, and which obtain not just in concrete interactions among persons but also systematically, in the structure of a society that builds the prosperity of some on the poverty of others. And desire will remain hostage to this systemic drive to victimization until love of all kinds – erotic love, love of money, love of the usefulness of others – is transformed into *caritas*, in which we love with "l'amor dou conmun" (5420) – the love, that is, of only those goods that all hold in common, and the love of that in each person which is common to everyone, the bare fact of their humanity.

According to Reason, then, the final truth of love's desire is not just friendship but *caritas*; that is what the dreamer has been aiming at all along, and it is what he would in fact pursue if his will were purged of the repressions, self-deceptions, and self-punishments that characterize its dominant dispositions. Again, this is a claim that threatens to slide into facile moralism, partly because it is in fact the subject of much moralizing in medieval culture, and partly because modern western culture has tended to replace the muscularity of the patristic notion of *caritas* with the moral sentimentalism of "charity."[37] But what makes this claim hard to swallow, and what no platitudinous expression of it can capture, is the way *caritas*, much more than friendship, involves a massive refiguration of the desire that so evidently continues to motivate the dreamer. For, as the formula "l'amour dou conmun" suggests, everyone is a proper object of *caritas* regardless of the particular relations in which one stands to them; as Reason says, the dreamer must love "en generalité / et lest especialité" (5413–14), "love generally and leave particular loves" (111). *Caritas* thus involves the utter disappearance of an erotic object, and even more – and here it contrasts strikingly with friendship – the utter disappearance of any desire that picks out persons as the particular ones they are. To respond fully to the claim of *caritas* one could have no bonds with others that would make of them privileged loci of value and would therefore encourage the preferential treatment and concern that allow for erotic or amicable intimacies, for this very "especialité" also lays the groundwork for inequitable social relations. Nor could one love in others anything that makes them something other than an instance of "the common." Reason's appeals to friendship and to *caritas* may work together to problematize the dreamer's fantasy of a narcissized kernel to his own subjectivity, but *caritas* is finally unamicable, for it requires the erosion of much of what binds us to the particular others we care about and much of what constitutes us as creatures that care about anyone at all.[38] To return to the language of the previous chapter, the desire for *caritas* involves a desire that both its subject and its objects be characterless: in aiming at *caritas*, the identity towards which one aims and that which one loves in others is the "characterless moral self."

I initially turned to narcissism as the term the *Rose* proposes for a sexuality constituted by sadomasochistic wishes for the destruction and loss of the love object, and for its transformation into something necessarily removed from the desiring subject – an unapproachable Lady, a virginally intact bud, a perfect aesthetic object, an insubstantial specular image. I then suggested that, far from being a specific pathology local to the psyche of the dreamer and anyone else unfortunate enough to suffer from it, narcissism is this text's way of figuring the ontology of erotic desire for a reflective creature. The discourse of Reason has now allowed some specification of this ontology. Being a reflective creature means being a creature of instrumentalist fantasy, for whom a reflective distance on the world allows for the positing of an ego ontologically distinct from the objects it possesses and manipulates; it means, as Aristotle puts it, being a creature of the hand, "the instrument of instruments."[39] But it also means being a creature for whom a reflective distance on itself makes it, to recall Augustine's phrase once more, "a problem to itself." The nature of this problem in the context of erotic life emerges from the utopian drive in Reason's claim. Given that in order to follow through on this claim it would be necessary to undertake a fundamental reconstruction of the dreamer's motivational structure, a reconstruction that would make him unrecognizable to himself and perhaps unrecognizable as a human, it is no wonder that the dreamer asks Reason to be silent and turns to the more amenable advice of Amis. What brought the dreamer to the point of listening to Reason, after all, was not the ambition of a sociability cleansed of all self-interest, but the more local and obvious frustrations of his erotic project. Here we return to the kind of dialectical *aporia* we saw in the *Consolation of Philosophy*. For the claim Reason exerts on the dreamer emerges from nothing more than his desire to rid himself of the sufferings and incoherences that beset him. Reason herself, for that matter, is nothing more than the allegorical embodiment of the dreamer's own capacity to reason about his desire, to ask what might be the conditions under which it would be free of the lack that torments it. It is clear from the dreamer's whole way of configuring the scene of his desire that simply succeeding in "plucking the rose" would not do the trick; otherwise there would be no place in the poem prior to Reason's appearance for the dreamer's aversion to sexuality or his desire to lose the love object, each of which challenges the dreamer's sadistic picture of erotic satisfaction, if rather more implicitly than Reason does.

Reason's claim is thus already there in the dreamer well before her appearance as an independently represented figure. If following through on Reason's claim would make the dreamer unrecognizable to himself, that unrecognizability has already been internal to every way the dreamer has of understanding himself and his projects. The discourse of Reason thus serves to make explicit an ontological deadlock that has always been at the heart of the dreamer's desire. The conditions of love's possibility – what it would take to realize it fully, to purge it of its self-ravishment – coincide perfectly with the conditions of its impossibility, for they are conditions in which love can no longer specify either its object or anything like its libidinal bond to that object.[40]

While the *Roman de la Rose* endorses a set of Boethian doctrines and adapts the figure of Philosophy in that of Reason, then, the text's Boethianness does not reduce to any such local resemblances. What finally makes the *Rose* Boethian is the way it extends the aporetic structures of the *Consolation* into territory Boethius himself had little to say about; for the *Rose* represents sexuality as a "sadness without an object," a form of desire that, for reasons internal to its own structure, has always already forgone the possibility of its own fulfillment. Sexuality in the *Rose* is constituted at the intersection of incompatible normative demands, none of which the erotic subject can simply forgo: the demand to reify sadistic desires and fetishize the possessable object, a demand to which the dreamer gives voice when, dismissing Reason, he plaintively confesses "ne peut autre estre" (6871), "I can be nothing other than I am" (132); the demand to transform a narcissized sexuality into the friendship-like loving it both expresses and represses; and the demand to realize the utopian horizon of a loving which transcends all pathological attachments and dissolves anything in the erotic subject and its objects that particularizes them. As was the case with the antinomy of the will exhibited in the *Consolation,* a sense of authenticity and freedom attaches to each of these imperatives. Each promises to reveal the truth of desire; and each in its conflict with the others brings with it an inevitable loss of that which also seems to constitute the truth of desire. The desire for each is therefore inflected by a desire for loss, and for the dissolution of the identity bound up with the others.

What would it mean for such a creature to be normal? This is a question in which both Guillaume and Jean were deeply interested:

most of the *Rose* is devoted not to articulating an ontological deadlock, but to exploring the ways agents constitute their wills by occluding that deadlock, and even by mobilizing it as a source of erotic energy. And for Jean in particular, this is an interest best pursued by investigating the specificities of cases. I think that Chaucer found the most important model for his own poetic practice in Jean's devotion to case studies that always refer back to an ontological argument they never explicitly make. Arguments about degrees of literary realism have mostly derailed our efforts to understand Chaucer's indebtedness on this score, or for that matter our efforts to understand the relations between Jean's and Guillaume's sections of the *Rose*. There is, to be sure, something like a scale of realism in literary portraiture, on which Jean occupies a middle position between Guillaume and Geoffrey. But the analytical mode with which both Jean and Geoffrey engage "the real" remains considerably closer to allegory than we have generally supposed. The rest of this chapter will suggest how this is so by examining two instances of Jean's case study mode which themselves occupy rather different places on the realist continuum, and by placing those case studies back in the context of Guillaume's allegorical mode.

BEING NORMAL

I begin with the discourse of Amis, a figure who is clearly in some sense a personification of an abstraction, yet to whom Jean also gives a biography, if a somewhat more truncated one than the one he will give to La Vielle. At first glance, Amis seems to be a figure diametrically opposed to that of Reason, a mouthpiece for views utterly incompatible with hers. In this, Amis resembles somewhat Chaucer's Miller, as a figure for the turn away from philosophy; and in fact I think that when Chaucer began the *Canterbury Tales* with the Knight and the Miller, he had in mind a rather loose association with the way Jean began his part of the *Rose* with Reason and Amis. If the *Rose* investigates the deadlock of desire even in the absence of a philosophical interlocutor, then, Amis will provide a good test case for examining how this is so, as well as a helpful comparison with Chaucer's own representation of a "normal" masculine subject.

Amis seems so thoroughly to refuse Reason's claim because he assumes from the start that there is no question concerning the nature of the dreamer's desire. It is obvious that the dreamer wants to pluck the rose, and Amis promises to help him attain this eminently practical goal. What is more, the cynical advice Amis offers for manipulating social appearances and the beloved's desire takes the discussion back into the territory of the instrumentalist egoism that dominates both the poem's central cluster of tropes and Reason's diagnoses. The dreamer is to avoid his beloved, and if he sees her he is to pretend that her attentions mean nothing to him; he is to buy off all of those allegorical representatives of the beloved's and her society's resistance to him with false praise, gifts, and promises of service, creating a sense of obligation within a network of exchange; and finally, these psychological machinations are supposed to pave the way for a display of force:

> Tout voiez vos Poor trembler,
> Honte rogir, Dangier fremir,
> ou tretoz .III. pleindre et gemir,
> ne prisiez tretout une cocoree,
> cuillez la rose tout a force
> et moutrez que vos estes hon,
> quant leus iert et tens et seson,
> car riens ne leur porroit tant plere
> con tel force, qui la set fere.
> (7656–64)

Although you see Fear and Shame blush, and Resistance become agitated, or all three lament and groan, count the whole thing as not worth a husk. When place and time and season occur, cut the rose by force and show that you are a man, for, as long as someone knows how to exercise it, nothing could please them so much as such force. (144–45)

The beloved's interiority seems now to be of interest solely for the purposes of calculation and self-justification. Her agency and desire matter, that is, insofar as they provide the dreamer with potential mechanisms for advancing his project of erotic possession, or insofar as they provide a screen on to which he can project her receptivity to the most violently objectifying of his intentions. At the same time, masculine violence gets reimagined as technical expertise: the successful lover is the one who knows how to exercise force correctly and at the right time, that is, in a way designed to produce the apposite feminine desire that licenses it. In any case the other's desire and agency do not exert the claim on the subject's sense of what he wants, or his sense of what it would mean to get it, which was so central to Reason's attempted redirection of the dreamer's will.

That, at least, is how Amis seems to understand the erotic agenda to which he subscribes and which he offers in answer to the dreamer's dilemma. That this agenda hardly rests on a stable package of beliefs and desires becomes clear, however, when we notice how much of Reason's utopian agenda remains alive, if in peripheral or hybridized form, in Amis's discourse. Amis's utopianism appears quite clearly, for instance, in his nostalgia for the Golden Age when "furent amors leaus et fines, / sanz covoitise et sanz rapines" (8329–30), "loves were loyal and pure, without greed or rapine" (154). The digression into Golden Age talk emerges, predictably enough, out of a lament over the difficulties men have in keeping hold of their women: Amis tells the dreamer that "quant l'en a la chose aquise, / si recovient il grant mestrise / au bien garder" (8227–29); "when one has acquired something, he must exercise great mastery in keeping it well" (153). The difficulty in keeping women immediately expands into the difficulty of satisfying the ravenous feminine appetite: "sunt eles voir pres que toutes / covoiteuses de prendre, et gloutes / de ravir et de devorer" (8251–53); "women are nearly all eager to take and greedy to ravish and devour" (153). This ravenous appetite turns out to be directed not just towards the goods women want from their men, but towards the men themselves: for this nightmare of the devouring female is exemplified for Amis by Hibernia, who "nus seus n'i peüs soffire, / tant estoit de chaude matire" (8261–62), "was of such hot matter that no one man could satisfy her" (153). Amis's slide from women as hard-to-keep possessions to women as ravenous devourers of possessions to women as oversexed devourers of men indicates that he is less in the business of offering practical advice about a specific danger than in recoil from a more general anxiety concerning the place of feminine desire in a project of masculine mastery. Whatever it is one has to be on guard against here, the obvious undesirability for a man bent on erotic possession of a world filled with women "like that" suggests that nostalgia for a time when "sanz rapine et sanz covoitise, / s'entracoloient et besoient / cil cui li jeu d'amors plesoient" (8402–04), "those who were pleased by Love's games would embrace and kiss each other without rapine or covetousness" (155), is in some sense continuous with Amis's masculinist fantasy. But it is also a violation of that fantasy's basic premises. For the Golden Age is a time of a sexuality clear of the cunning manipulativeness that dominates Amis's advice, and more than that, a time of pure egalitarianism in all social relations, with no private property of any kind and nothing resembling a narrow self-interest in anyone's motive. This structure of an ideological continuity that overlaps with a conceptual violation is present as well in Amis's segue out of nostalgic fantasy. He concludes his discussion of the Golden Age with the slogan, "onques amor et seigneurie / ne s'entrefirent compaignie / ne ne demorerent ensemble" (8421–23), "love and lordship never kept each other company or dwelt together" (156), and offers as an example the self-defeating and self-consuming obsessions of a jealous husband. But the speech of the *mari jaloux* so overwhelms Amis's voice, continuing uninterrupted for almost a thousand lines of verse and replicating so nearly the terms of Amis's own announced understanding of gender and sexuality, that it is almost impossible to remember that he is supposed to be an example of something Amis is warning against.

The reason the contradiction between utopian idealism and cynical realism can seem to Amis like a noncontradiction is that he manages to narrativize it: the Golden Age is past, and now we have to make do in a world where everyone is out for their own. But the problem with a narrativized disposition of the contradiction is that the *desire* for non-instrumentalized relations is what gives Golden Age fantasy its appeal, while Amis's erotic program is predicated on that *not* being anyone's desire – not his, not that of men in general, nor for that matter that of the rapacious women men must constrain or the passive women longing to be forced. Amis's desire to narrativize a contradiction that remains internal to him thus allows us to see the ideological function of Golden Age fantasy here. Amis produces nostalgia as a necessary reservoir for the utopianism that the ideology of purely instrumentalized relations with others requires him to disavow: the desiring subject can thus give expression to the utopian drive while performing an act of segregation whereby that drive is not allowed to infect the agenda he sets for himself. In this way, nostalgic idealism and cynical realism, far from being irreconcilable opposites, function to sustain each other.

Besides nostalgia, how does an unassimilable utopian drive get articulated within the terms of Amis's ideological settlement? One way appears in the figure of the devouring female from which Amis recoils. That such a figure should appear here is, if unsurprising, nevertheless a sign of ideological strain: "woman" was supposed to be just a beautiful passive object, a rose. To risk then an obvious question: where does the figure of the devouring female come from? That feminine agency and desire enter into the picture at all, even in a calculative way, already violates the integrity of the central trope of thought that binds Amis and the dreamer together. That trope is strained further by Amis's insistence that women really want the show of force he urges; for why, if plucking is sufficient to masculine desire, should it even matter that women want it? The fantasy of women who want to be forced is, like nostalgia, a reservoir for the occluded claim of the other's agency and desire, a way of trying to give voice to that claim safely, without challenging the basic structure of a project of erotic conquest. In the female who would devour partner after partner both economically and sexually, we see the necessity for this reservoir to be continually expanded. If she wants to be plucked, that means that she wants something after all. And if she wants something, she might want anything: perhaps she wants to be plucked by many, and perhaps she wants to pluck many as well. The nightmare image of a rapacious and unsatisfiable feminine desire, as inimical as it is to the fantasy of masculine possession, is the price the masculine subject has to pay to keep that fantasy from collapsing completely. But it is a price that can never be adequately paid, for the fear of an insatiable feminine desire is partly the sign of a recognition, however repressed, that feminine desire cannot be satisfied by the terms the fantasy of plucking offers it.

While Amis's nostalgia and his various figurations of feminine desire function as reservoirs for the unassimilable claim of the other on his picture of masculine sexuality, they also give expression to a sense of that picture's injustice, its production of the feminine as a site of victimization. And they give expression as well to a sense that his picture normalizes a disposition of the will within the masculine subject which falls short of the subject's own desires and hopes for itself. This suggests that the sexuality given voice in Amis's advice is suffused with guilt and shame; and since this sexuality is supposed to answer to the dreamer's desire to get back on track in his pursuit of the rose, it suggests that what I have been calling the dreamer's sadomasochism is suffused with guilt and shame as well. It should not be surprising that Amis never overtly voices this guilt and shame with respect to his agenda. If he were to acknowledge it, he would have to direct his cynicism much more bluntly towards himself, and see his ideological compromises as precisely that. But the last thing Amis wants is to declare himself a hypocrite; he wants his story to be that of a wounded heart seeking self-protection in a hostile world.[41] So his guilt and shame must be displaced on to the longing for a lost utopia, the condemnation of a jealous husband who is little more than an exaggeration of his own views, and the nightmarish resurgence of a feminine interiority he both desires and wishes to imagine away.

What makes Amis a case study of the deadlock of desire is the way his discourse exhibits conceptual incoherences and psychological conflicts which overlap with practical functionality. However incoherent and strained his occupation of his views may be, they do serve to provide him with a way of recognizing himself and of moving forward in a recognizable social world. They serve, that is, as the basis for his constitution of a will; they are what gives him a characteristic *habitus*. Jean de Meun's interest in case studies of this kind, as exemplified also in the discourses of Faux Semblant and La Vielle, has for some time been seen as a literary model for Chaucer, who developed the investigation of *habitus* into something more like our modern conception of literary "character" in the *Canterbury Tales* by providing the pilgrims with concretely realized social locations and elaborate and distinctive psychological dimensions.[42] I think that some such account is right. But I also think that such an account tempts a false equation of the kind of analytical interest I have attributed to Chaucer and Jean with an interest in something like psychological realism, with the result that our sense of the representational means available for pursuing such an interest becomes unnecessarily restricted, as does our sense of what Chaucer might have found compelling in the *Rose*. This leads, among other things, to misplaced attempts to evaluate both the *Rose* and the *Canterbury Tales* in terms of criteria more suited to a nineteenth-century novel: so it is often suggested that the discourse of La Vielle is the best section of Jean's *Rose* because it gives such a compelling picture of a life, and some of Chaucer's more experimental tales, such as those of the Physician and the Manciple, get called failures because they do not. This entire book is, among other things, an attempt to suggest how misplaced this kind of evaluation is, and how deep the similarity is between something that looks to us like a familiar literary interest in character and something that looks like an unfamiliar allegorical mode of representation; for my whole way of proceeding interpretively with Chaucer's texts has been in effect to read them as allegorical *phantasia*, built around tropes that function as meditative sites in much the way the tropes of the *Rose* do. I will continue with such reading in the next two chapters. To conclude my discussion here I will turn to two obvious cases of allegory in the *Rose*, neither of which exhibits either biographical complexity or a highly individuated psychology, but both of which contribute to the text's exploration of how a normalized sexual subject gets made.

The first is one that has already served as a touchstone throughout this book, the apparent digression on Pygmalion that occupies the bulk of the poem's closing sequence. The context for the poem's turn to Pygmalion is the moment when the dreamer, after more than 20,000 lines of poetry, finally gets himself to the point of having sex. What makes the *Rose* such a searching exploration of sexuality is that it makes the apparently easy question of how the dreamer does this – a question that may seem to be answered by referring to the nearly irresistible force of a biological drive or a cultural norm – seem worth puzzling over. For the entire poem has been devoted to the exploration of a "blocked" sexuality, the sexuality of a creature that cannot distinguish love from narcissistic self-enclosure, and feels its desire to be a Fall from a utopian sociality it longs for but cannot imagine inhabiting. Under these circumstances, it is far from obvious that anything resembling an erotic encounter will happen. The question of how it does happen is only made more perplexing by the vicissitudes in the dreamer's imagination of a love object. If she is a reflection, a rose, or a rosebud, then one can gaze on her or pluck her. If, as in the poem's late phantasmagoric proliferation of tropes, she is a tablet, an anvil, a field, a tower, a shrine, or an enshrined image, then one can write on her, or hammer her, or plow her, or raze her to the ground, or enter her sanctuary, or fall on one's knees before her. But, as obvious as the applicability of all of these tropes is, one thing one cannot quite do in any of these cases is make love to her. This is where Pygmalion comes in. For the dreamer, right at the point of doing – we do not know quite what, but *something* – declares that his image is like Pygmalion's, and proceeds to discuss Pygmalion's case for 400 lines, after which he declares mysteriously "Mes c'est trop loign de ma matire, / por c'est bien droiz qu'arriers m'an tire. / Bien orroiz que ce senefie / ainz que ceste euvre soit fenie" (21181–84), "But this is all very far from my matter, and I must draw back from it. By the time you have finished this work you will know what it means" (346). What could this mean?

One obvious relevance of Pygmalion is that he allegorizes the problem of the dreamer's blocked "courtly" sexuality. If the erotic object is Pygmalion's perfect statue, more beautiful than Helen or Lavinia and the sign of her maker's artistic powers, then the erotic subject can admire his handiwork, kiss her and fondle her, dress her up and stage a mock wedding and even take her to bed, but her kisses, not to mention everything else about her, will always remain cold. And, as Pygmalion well knows, the source of this dilemma lies in the masculine subject who, in desiring this way, feels himself to be an apostate from nature: "ceste amour est si horrible / qu'el ne vient mie de Nature... Nature en moi mauvés fill a... Si ne l'an doi je pas blamer / se je veill folement amer; / ne m'an doi prandre s'a moi non" (20832–39), "this love is so horrible that it doesn't come from Nature... Nature has a bad son in me... But I should not blame her because I love insanely, nor should I put the blame anywhere but on myself" (341). What is being represented in all of the poem's figures for the love object, after all, are not literal attributes of women, but a masculine fantasy that places a bar on the consummation for which it constantly fuels the desire. The mutually productive relation between desire and its prohibition in this fantasy emerges clearly in Pygmalion's response to his frustration. Comparing himself to Narcissus, he declares that he is better off, "car, quant je veill, a ceste vois / et la praign et l'acole et bese, / s'an puis mieuz souffrir ma mesese" (20854–56), "for, when I wish, I go to this image and take it, embrace it, and kiss it; I can thus better endure my torment" (341). But given the cold unresponsiveness of his statue, what enables his endurance is more the enjoyment of a masochistic suspension in torment than anything that provides him with real relief.

Given the depth of this fixation, it is unsurprising that it takes divine intervention to free Pygmalion of his blocked sexuality. Venus hears his entreaties and brings the statue to life, after which both Pygmalion and his newly living "sweetheart" offer each other love, pleasure, companionship, and friendship, and, in the kind of symmetrical formulation to which Chaucer has the Wife of Bath and the Franklin appeal, neither refuses anything the other might desire. But if Venus provides a miraculous transformation in the love object, the real miracle happens before the goddess appears, and is in fact the reason she is willing to intervene. In praying to Venus for her aid, Pygmalion asks that his statue "deviegne ma leaus amie, / qui de fame ait cors, ame et vie" (21069–70), "become my loyal friend and may have the body, the soul, and the life of a woman" (344). Venus's transformation of the statue does no more than literalize the prior transformation in Pygmalion's phantasmatic image of the love object, by which he becomes capable of imagining his desire as targeting a creature with a soul, who might be his friend. But how does this prior transformation happen? What makes this miracle possible?

The text gives us no answer; indeed, that is the very point of having the apparent cause of transformation follow the real change. This unanswerability marks the Pygmalion episode as rather less of a redemptive fantasy than at first it seems; for it leaves us with exactly the same question we had before, that of how the masculine desire under investigation here could ever get past the barriers it erects to its own consummation. But the episode's function in the poem's closing sequence does help us answer this question. The narrator is drawn to the Pygmalion story because it seems in some sense "like" his own. In pursuing that likeness, he finds himself giving voice once again to the desire for a utopian mutuality cleansed of any self-interest. But as soon as he does so, he recoils: "this is all very far from my matter, and I must draw back from it." And draw back he does: the love object is just a rose once more, and the dreamer is bent on poring over its petals and plucking a flower. The placement of the Pygmalion episode suggests, then, that in order to produce the erotic energy necessary to move towards consummation, the masculine subject must mobilize both the desire for utopian intimacy and the desire for its rejection. To see how this is possible, we must return to the poem's central erotic trope, and in so doing return squarely to the meditative function of allegory.

How can the inescapable and unrealizable utopian horizon of desire that keeps emerging in this text help us understand more fully the psychic work involved in imagining the erotic goal as that of plucking a beautiful rose? We can take our start from the way the *Rose* represents that goal as involving a narcissistic aversion to the subjectivity and agency of the love object. In the context of Reason's argument, this aversion with respect to the object emerges as an expression of the dreamer's aversion to the utopian aspect of his own desire. A deadlock in the structure of a desire that both cannot and must be figured in terms of violent appropriation thus gets projected vengefully on to the love object, which must be destroyed for the desiring subject to maintain its phantasmatic integrity, its pretence of freedom from the mutilation it suffers and visits on itself. Sadism, for all its perversity, functions in this way as a mode of normalization, a way of declaring an ideological settlement that regularizes the subject's desire by occluding the deadlock that motivates it. But, as Reason has argued, any such normalization is inherently unstable, since it replicates the move by which the dreamer entrenches himself in narcissistic fantasy and so places his utopian desire under prohibition.

The depth of this instability begins to emerge if we return to the thought, expressed in the dreamer's knowledge that a plucked rose will soon wither, that a sadistic aversion to the other involves a wish for losing the love object. For now we should also be able to see in sadism, not just a digging in of the heels against utopianism, but a peculiar wish for release from the fantasy of erotic possession. Insofar as desire is stuck in the trope of possession, it might look as though the only way to escape a compulsion by the urge to possess is to put an end to the possibility of desire; and one way to do that is to ensure the death of the love object, thereby leaving the desiring subject with nothing to possess. But even this peculiar expression of the utopian drive within a sadism that prohibits it does not leave us with the truth of the dreamer's desire. Reason declares that it does, and the *Rose* goes some way towards suggesting that the normative authority of Reason cannot successfully be denied. But, successfully or not, the dreamer does deny it. The normative authority of the reified desires he most readily calls his own is itself undeniable: that is what makes the dreamer's deadlock a version of the Boethian antinomy discussed in the previous chapter.

As the dreamer tells Reason in dismissing her advice, "Et se je sui fols, ne vos chaille: / je veill amer, conment qu'il aille, / la rose ou je me sui voez, / ja n'iert mes queurs d'autre doez" (7181–84), "It makes no difference to you if I am a fool. However it goes, I want to love the rose to which I am pledged; no other will ever fill my heart" (137). The dreamer's urge to pluck the rose and hold it in his hand clearly expresses an urge to hold on to *this* particular object, to attach himself to the only one that will ever fill his heart. As the dreamer also tells Reason in rejecting her argument, "ne peut autre estre" (6871), "I can be nothing other than I am" (132); this is the desire that seems, to him, to make him who he is. The particularizing force of sadism suggests that, however death-dealing, such a desire should also be read as part of the dreamer's effort to secure an object that can withstand the utopian dissolution of preferential attachments, and around which he can secure a sense of the identity that goes with those attachments. If the dreamer can force the love object to yield itself up to him in all its particularity, perhaps the very violence and suffering that attends such force can establish an erotic bond that his own yearning for *caritas* could never break.

The dreamer's investment in the abjections of *fin'amors* suggests that the suffering by which a specific love bond gets established runs in both directions, towards the erotic object and the desiring subject. This brings us back to the masochism which I have been suggesting underlies the more obvious sadism in the *Rose*. Now we ought to be in a better position to understand why the *Rose* simultaneously represents love as involving the armored integrity of a narcissized self-interest and the humiliation of the courtly lover undeserving of his beloved's attentions. If a desire to suffer the loss of the love object involves a desire for something more than the object's fantasized appropriability – a desire, that is, for the other *qua* subject and agent – then the desire for that loss also involves a longing for a wounding opening in the hyperbolically self-enclosed sadistic subject, through which the otherness of the desired one could find entry. In the wish for a narcissistic wound the sense of guilt and shame accompanying sadism finds expression: masochism in effect becomes a name for the punishment the sadistic subject visits on itself for its betrayal of the other it so resolutely objectifies.

The text's investment in courtly love ideology – expressed, for instance, in the God of Love's advice to the dreamer in the garden – suggests that the inflection of a sadomasochistic eroticism by a sense of the guiltiness and shamefulness of sex is hardly local in the *Rose* to the trope of plucking. Perhaps the most widespread locus of such a psychic bar to the free enjoyment of a simple eroticism can be found in the text's imagination of the beloved as a kind of perfect aesthetic object. In the formalist aestheticism of the Garden of Love, of the aseptically closed rosebud, and of Pygmalion's statue, the beloved – like the "Unapproachable Lady"of *fin'amors* – is preserved from the impurity of the Lover's appropriating desire, uncontaminated by his guilt. She is also unable or unwilling to reach back to him with desire. It is as though, in imagining the desired other as aseptic art object, the lover wishes to preserve her not only from the impurity of his desire, but from what he cannot help thinking of as the impurity of her own desire, which would contaminate him if it touched him. The desire for her death in this respect expresses a wish to preserve her in her asepsis, to imagine her as a being that could neither receive nor offer love.[43] And, to return to the notion of sadism as a projection on to the love object of a deadlock in the lover's desire, the violence of the lover's need to "show he is a man," to tear down the embattled edifice or sanctuary of the beloved's body, emerges as well as a desire for revenge on her for this very asepsis – and even for her not being aseptic enough, that is, for her continued "invitation" of the desire she repels and the danger that she might cease to repel it. The instability of the desires swirling around the formal beauty of the love object are captured as well in Pygmalion's desperately apologetic entreaties of his beloved statue. As in the abject appeals to the beloved in *fin'amors*, this form of projection has as an essential component a desire for the very love it figures as polluting, together with a humiliating sense that one is not even worthy of being polluted.

The masochism of courtly love, with its attention to the claim of the other in the form of a wounding opening in the narcissistic subject, involves less of a frontal denial of the deadlock of desire than does sadism. But the example of Pygmalion and the text's intimations of a sexuality tinged with guilt, shame, and pollution are meant to suggest that this hardly locates courtly masochism as a site of the redemption of sexuality from its narcissistic tendencies. Masochism is as fully complicit in normalizing the deadlock of desire as is its cousin sadism, and this is particularly clear in the *Rose*, where sadism and masochism are less distinct modes of desire than mutually reinforcing components of a more general narcissized sexuality. Masochism's role in the process of normalization, as I have been suggesting, is closely tied to the production of sexual guilt and shame. By figuring the desire for the other *qua* agent and subject as a desire for being wounded or polluted, masochism reinforces the thought that the "normal" subject is the one for whom the other's agency and subjectivity just are fundamentally a wound and a pollution. Masochism thus endows the normalization of a sadistic narcissism with the pathos and dignity of ontological tragedy, the sense that the very essence of selfhood is violated by the self's need to turn to the other. This in turn ensures that sex will provide ample nourishment to masochism's appetite for guilty suffering. But it also produces the sense of thrilling mobility in the self necessary for the narcissistically fixed subject on display throughout this text to set itself in motion.

CHAPTER 5

Suffering love in the *Wife of Bath's Prologue* and *Tale*

In arguing for the convergence in Chaucer's poetry of his interest in philosophy and his interests in gender and sexuality, I have so far focused primarily on the ways Boethian philosophy can help us read the "courtly" or "romantic" scene of a masculine sexuality that is simultaneously objectifying and abject, and that takes pleasure both in the suffering of its object and in the suffering it inflicts on itself. In the previous chapter, however, I turned as well to the equally powerful interest Chaucer inherited from the *Roman de la Rose* and elsewhere in a utopian sociality that provides both a model for and a site of resistance to the small-scale intimacies available in erotic relations, friendship, and marriage. The final two chapters of this book will elaborate Chaucer's interest in the idea of a utopian intimacy in which "two become one," in the context of discussions that move beyond the relatively narrow sphere of courtly male desire to examine how ideologies of gender and sexuality function in the formation of medieval women as subjects and agents, and how those ideologies affect the dynamics of the intimate couple. My discussion will focus on the two texts in which Chaucer pursued his interests in these topics most thoroughly and powerfully, the *Wife of Bath's Prologue* and *Tale* and the *Clerk's Tale*. In keeping with my argument in the rest of the book, I will argue that for Chaucer the desire for utopian intimacy is always inflected by sadistic and masochistic urges, and that the internal relation between sadomasochism and utopian desire can best be understood by returning to Chaucer's interests in autonomy and the structure of agency.

Finally, I will continue, more by way of example than by explicit argument, my account of the proximity between Chaucer's poetry and allegory. This is itself an account with both literary and philosophical stakes. In the previous chapter I argued that in the *Rose* allegory functions not as the static embodiment of abstract concepts, but as a supple vehicle for speculation concerning the structure of fantasy. Allegorical tropes in that poem serve as meditative sites that embed dialectical structures of thought and desire, and that invite the work of a reflective engagement with what makes desire and agency problematic. As I have been arguing, this is precisely what Chaucer does in the *Canterbury Tales*; and while his literary means for doing so are hardly identical to those of Guillaume and Jean, we will exaggerate those differences unless we understand the kinship among their intellectual and literary projects. Another reason for turning next to the Wife of Bath, then, is that while she is clearly derived from the figure of La Vielle in the *Rose*, of all the Canterbury narrators she has been the most thoroughly identified with a supposedly realist, quasinovelistic, character-based poetics; what is more, her mode of autobiographical self-disclosure has been taken as an index of a Chaucerian privileging of "the subject" that amounts to an ideological and philosophical commitment as well as the basis for a poetics.[1] In this chapter I will argue, however, that the Wife provides Chaucer with an occasion for exploring the *myth* of "the subject" – the myth, that is, of subjectivity as a private interior space constituted prior to the person's engagements in the social. Chaucer pursues this exploration not merely to subject that myth to critique, but to understand what gives it its ideological power; and his attention to the Wife's troubled engagement with that myth, and the scenes of fantasy through which she ambivalently inhabits it, constitutes an elaboration of the allegorical imagination rather than an evolution away from it.

To begin unpacking the structure of the Wife's fantasy relation to intimacy, and the way that structure opens into broader concerns with the constitution of subjectivity, let us turn to one of the more striking moments in the Wife's *Prologue*, a moment that captures in quasiallegorical form the interlacings of suffering and desire that mark out the territory of the erotic for Alisoun.

BLOOD AND MONEY

Well into her account of the "wo that is in mariage" (III.3) the Wife of Bath reports a strange dream, a dream she says she did not really have, but which she used to seduce her clerk Jankyn, the man who would become her fifth husband.

> I bar hym on honde he hadde enchanted me—
> My dame taughte me that soutiltee—
> And eek I seyde I mette of hym al nyght,
> He wolde han slayn me as I lay upright,
> And al my bed was ful of verray blood;
> 'But yet I hope that ye shal do me good,
> For blood bitokeneth gold, as me was taught.'
> And al was fals; I dremed of it right naught,
> But as I folwed ay my dames loore,
> As wel of this as of othere thynges moore.
> (III.575–84)[2]

Alisoun reports using the dream as a sign of her erotic availability to Jankyn, given in the hope of arousing him and receiving signs of his desire for her. He is supposed to find this sexy, and since, in contrast to her first three husbands, Alisoun finds him sexy – he is the one with legs and feet "so clene and faire / That al myn herte I yaf unto his hoold" (III.598–99) – and since this is the way she thinks to initiate things between them, apparently she finds it sexy too. But what is supposed to be sexy about a dream in which her bed fills with blood as Jankyn "wolde han slayn me as I lay upright"?[3]

The trope of being slain by desire is of course common enough, and together with the dream's suggestion that masculine sexuality harbors a murderous intent, it links this passage to the sadomasochism and antifeminism I have been exploring throughout this book. But the erotics of this moment is rather different from anything I have discussed so far. Despite the differences among the *Knight's Tale*, the *Miller's Tale*, and the *Roman de la Rose*, each of those texts explores the erotic psychology of a narcissized masculine subject and agent, whose desire finds its immediate expression in voyeuristic delectation and an impulse to sadistic mastery. The Wife of Bath, however, is hardly peering in on Jankyn unobserved; she does not imagine him as a tasty morsel waiting to be consumed or a beautiful rose waiting to be plucked. Nor is the suffering embedded in this scene that of the voyeur's romantic abjection, his sense of the erotic object as turned away from him, oblivious to his demands. For Alisoun fully expects Jankyn to respond, and she is giving him the kind of erotic target she thinks will arouse him. What she thinks will arouse him is the thought of his own violent power, together with the belief that he is getting a glimpse at her desire for that violence. On Alisoun's view, then, Jankyn is the one whose desires amount to a species of sadistic voyeurism. Through the seduction of her dream she is offering herself up to the masculine erotic pathology we have been examining; she wants to be found desirable by someone who occupies the position staked out as masculine by her culture's dominant ideology of gender and sexuality.

One way of putting this contrast between Alisoun and the men would be to say that her desire takes its form from what that same ideology of gender and sexuality figures as the feminine position. The contours of her desire, in other words, are not to be explained by recourse to some peculiar feature of her psychology; Chaucer rather means the dream to allegorize some basic features of a much more widespread erotic form. The men seem to have been trained into thinking of themselves as in the first instance erotic subjects and agents confronting a world that consists of possible sources of gratification, and trained into thinking of women as in the first instance the objects that constitute that world. If, as I have argued, the masculine narcissist must imagine his erotic others to be subjects and agents as well, the structure of his desire depends on the way it refigures the demands such others make on him so that they seem to disappear, leaving him alone in a world of pure reflection. Alisoun's seductive gesture, however, proceeds directly from a sense of herself as addressing an erotic subject. That subject's demands do not get repressed or refigured, but immediately provide the terms by which she constitutes an erotics for herself. Alisoun seems, then, to have been trained into thinking of herself as in the first instance part of the world of objects that a man might want, and thinking of her existence as such an object as the basis for her elaboration of a subjectivity and an agency. Her own reading of the dream helps to specify some of the further contours of this self-conception. The blood that fills her bed, as she was taught, signifies gold, and the link between blood and gold leads her to expect that Jankyn will "do her good." Given that Jankyn, unlike the Wife's first three husbands, is not the one in this relationship with the money, and especially given her fantasy of Jankyn's murderousness, her blood would seem to be something other than the sign of her expected financial profit. But whatever else her blood signifies, she offers it to Jankyn as an item of exchange, something for which he will provide an unspecified "good" in return. As wisdom passed on to her from her mother, this offer recalls an earlier relationship between blood and gold, in which a 12-year-old Alisoun's virginity was exchanged for the "good" of being married to a rich husband. If this dream sketches the contours of an erotics for Alisoun, its sexiness would seem to be inseparable from the sexiness of imagining her blood and whatever it might stand for – the virginity she no longer has, her suffering or death at the hands of her lover, perhaps even her very desire – as interchangeable with money, as commodities that a man might want to buy and she might want or need to sell.

I begin with this passage because it directly links the topics of this book with what many critics have taken to be Chaucer's central concern in the *Wife of Bath's Prologue* and *Tale,* namely the exploration of what it would be like to come into a sense of oneself as a woman, where the terms of that self-understanding are largely given by the patriarchal construction of "woman" as, among other things, a commodified sexual object. I think this critical emphasis has been right. But my sense of this passage also helps to indicate some differences I have with the best recent accounts of the Wife's project and of Chaucer's interest in it. On one such account the Wife, and Chaucer through her, means to offer a critique of patriarchy, perhaps alongside a critique of nascent capitalism.[4] But while the notion of critique means to capture the suffering and anger to which the Wife so frequently attests, her overall posture is more one of triumphant recollection than critical resistance, or even for that matter uncritical resentment. Throughout the prologue she declares that she has mostly gotten what she wanted from the world – "Unto this day it dooth myn herte boote / That I have had my world as in my tyme" (III.472–73) – and in relating the dream she clearly intends to be celebrating her seductive powers. She seems, then, too deeply to have internalized patriarchal ideology, and to take too much pleasure in her occupation of the position it assigns her, for the notion that she offers a protofeminist critique to gain a very firm footing. Alternatively, a number of critics have argued that the Wife understands her own prospects for happiness quite thoroughly in patriarchal terms.

She may still be out to reform patriarchy – perhaps she is miming the operations of patriarchal discourse to make a space for her own desire, or perhaps she strategically deploys antifeminist tropes to lure in and reeducate prospective lovers – but even in those cases her desire itself remains that of the patriarchal wife, and thus leaves her, and possibly Chaucer too, fully complicit in patriarchal wish fulfillment.[5] But, as I have argued throughout this book, not even Chaucer's male characters are fully complicit in patriarchal wish fulfillment; patriarchy is far too incoherent for anyone to understand their prospects for happiness thoroughly in its terms, much less someone who knows as well as Alisoun does how much the patriarchal deck is stacked against her. What is more, in trying to account for the Wife's internalization of patriarchal ideology and her posture of triumph, this second position tends to exaggerate her identification with what that ideology tells her she is.[6] And while the view of the Wife as protofeminist loses hold of the pleasure she takes in her occupation of an ideologized femininity, this second view loses hold of the depth of her suffering. For if patriarchal ideology ultimately determines the contours of her desire, then her suffering appears as little more than a historical tragedy the Wife herself could not appreciate: we can see that she is imprisoned by the historical conditions of her strategy, but as far as she is concerned nothing is lost.

I will argue, however, that from the Wife's own point of view quite a bit is lost. Her dominant terms for understanding herself may be given to her by patriarchal ideology, but she inhabits those terms with a good deal of ambivalence; and that ambivalence is the sign not of a conflict between her autonomous desire and an ideology that threatens to exclude it, but of a conflict internal to her desire itself – or, to put the point more precisely, a conflict in her will. This conflict has multiple sources: in the incoherences of patriarchal ideology itself, in the conceptions of subjectivity and agency that ideology depends on, and in an ontological problem concerning love which, even if it can never *historically* precede the production of erotic ideology, nevertheless has a certain *ontological* priority as a source of ideology. Here, then, we will see Chaucer continuing to pursue a Boethian philosophical interest in the relations between history and ontology, in a context quite far removed from any of the technical philosophical concerns that occupy the *Consolation.* To begin to see the form that interest takes, let us return to the Wife's attempt to carve out a space for feminine agency and the conception of subjectivity that that attempt entails.

THE MYTH OF THE SUBJECT

I have said that throughout her prologue the Wife of Bath remains committed to declaring herself triumphant over her husbands and the antifeminist ideology that would deprive her of a voice. Before exploring the ambivalences in the Wife's project, I want to be clear about just what she thinks that project is and about what conceptual commitments it reflects. The Wife's triumphant posture is nowhere more clearly in evidence than in her declaration of a marital agenda.

> In wyfhod I wol use myn instrument
> As frely as my Makere hath it sent.
> If I be daungerous, God yeve me sorwe!
> Myn housbonde shal it have both eve and morwe,
> Whan that hym list come forth and paye his dette.
> An housbonde I wol have—I wol nat lette—
> Which shal be bothe my dettour and my thral,
> And have his tribulacion withal
> Upon his flessh, whil that I am his wyf.
> I have the power durynge al my lyf
> Upon his propre body, and noght he.
> Right thus the Apostel tolde it unto me,
> And bad oure housbondes for to love us weel.
> (III.149–61)

As critics have emphasized for some time, Alisoun means this declaration as a strike against both a clerical suspicion of sexuality and the antifeminist gender politics such a suspicion fosters.[7] The medieval Church, following Paul, taught that spouses have an obligation to have sex with each other because of the danger that erotic desire – the "tribulation of the flesh" – would drive people to commit adultery. If marital sex was a moral duty, then, it remained the lesser of two evils, a nagging reminder that you had failed to live up to the perfection of complete sexual renunciation. As Paul put it, "it is better to marry than to burn with desire," and the medieval Church made it clear that rendering the "marital debt" was supposed to involve as little desire as possible.[8] While this moralization of sex was directed at both men and women, since it was conducted mostly from an antifeminist perspective that associated the unruliness of desire and the flesh with "the feminine," the impulse to constrain sexuality involved an impulse to constrain women as well. But by claiming the free use of the instrument her maker fitted her with, the Wife recasts the marital debt from the sober doing of a moral duty into an ideal of the pure pursuit of erotic pleasure in marriage, an ideal for which Solomon serves as the presiding genius: "As wolde God it leveful were unto me / To be refresshed half so ofte as he!" (III.37–38). In keeping with this ideal, the Wife recasts the "tribulation of the flesh" from the fearful aching of unfulfilled desire into the quivering exhaustion of "having it" morning and night. Alisoun means the prospect to be both titillating and daunting, for any man who would seek such erotic repletion would also have to forego the antifeminism that fuels so much of the husbandly behavior she reports.[9]

The Wife's marital agenda suggests that her attempt to rehabilitate the feminine also involves attempts to rehabilitate pleasure, sexuality, and the body. Alisoun foregrounds the relations among those concerns from the moment she begins to speak, as she shouts down the Parson: "He schal no gospel glosen here ne teche. / . . . / My joly body schal a tale telle" (II.1180, 1185). Her voice, she implies, issues in a direct and unmediated way from her body rather than from the clerical activity of "glossing," a term for interpretation which in Alisoun's mouth carries a strong connotation of deceptiveness. "Glossing" may have the power of male institutional authority behind it, but Alisoun will have none of it:

> Glose whoso wole, and seye bothe up and doun
> That [our sexual "members"] were maked for purgacioun
> Of uryne, and oure bothe thynges smale
> Were eek to knowe a femele from a male,
> And for noon oother cause—say ye no?
> The experience woot wel it is noght so.
> (III.119–24)

"Experience" is a more reliable source of knowledge than "glossing," it would seem, because, like "the body," it constitutes a realm of authenticity free of the idealizing and prudish distortions that attach to a supposedly authoritative clerical hermeneutics. What is more, not only does the Wife claim that experience has an epistemic privilege over glossing, in the first words of her prologue she declares that experience would be a reliable source of knowledge even in the absence of any public authority: "Experience, though noon auctoritee / Were in this world, is right ynogh for me / To speke of wo that is in mariage" (III.1–3). In imagining a world with no authoritative discourse, but in which experience would still authorize her to speak, the Wife indicates the conceptual center of her attempt to carve out a space for feminine agency. If her experience would tell her all she needs to know even in a world devoid of "auctoritee," and if her voice issues directly from her body, that is because her experience of that body constitutes a private realm of subjective certainty, a realm whose deliverances of knowledge are completely independent of the public world in which authority is established and conferred.

I think that Patterson and Dinshaw are right, then, in describing the Wife's agenda as complicit in a standard package of binaries through which medieval culture imagines gender difference, although I also think that this only begins to describe the conceptual structure of the Wife's commitments.[10] In particular, I think that Patterson captures something essential in his idea that in the Wife of Bath's discourse "the realm of the *asocial* – of the internal, the individual, the subjective" gets represented as the realm of "the feminine," and that this representation involves an implicit claim that "the basic unit of social life is a socially undetermined selfhood."[11] Patterson's first formulation gets its grip from the way Alisoun imagines that the contrast between masculine and feminine involves a series of parallel contrasts: between authority and experience, duty and pleasure, a denial or suspicion of the body and an identification with the body, an unreliable interpretive discourse and authentic self-expression or straight talk or the literal text. The feminine gets associated with an essentially subjective interiority because each term on one side of the series figuratively resonates with the others. But then, as I just suggested, the consequences of this figurative resonance go well beyond what Alisoun or anyone else thinks about gender difference. While a subjective experience that stands in need of no interpretation gets figured, along with pleasure and the body, as feminine, by the same token the body gets imagined as the site of "the literal," that is, of a nonidealized materiality that comes before interpretation; doing your duty is taken to require the denial or glossing over of your true pleasures; and experience is taken not to involve or require interpretation, but rather to be a realm of subjective immediacy whose deliverances are not open to doubt.

We can see the grip of Patterson's second formulation concerning the basic unit of social life if we return to a topic raised by Alisoun's seduction of Jankyn, her closely linked interests in power and in the commodification of marriage and sexuality. We see that link, for instance, in her declaration that her husband will be her debtor and her thrall, and that the marital debt gives her power even over his own body; in her complaint concerning the husbandly wish to assay women at market before marrying them, as one assays "oxen, asses, hors, and houndes" (III.285) before a purchase; and in her admonition "And therfore every man this tale I telle, / Wynne whoso may, for al is for to selle; / With empty hand men may none haukes lure" (III.413–15). These and other similar comments suggest that the Wife's interest in the commodification of marriage and sexuality, and the violence involved in this commodification, is informed by a much broader picture of what sex and marriage essentially are, namely that they are relations of exchange in which power ultimately rules the day – or, to put the point even more broadly, that they are relations between essentially self-interested parties. The language of commodity exchange appears when each party thinks that, at least with respect to some particular event, their interests are served by their relation, as when the Wife allows her husbands the use of her "instrument" in exchange for money or land: "[When] he had maad his raunson unto me; / Thanne wolde I suffre hym do his nycetee" (III.411–12). But, as Alisoun makes clear with the immediately subsequent lines concerning the luring of hawks, even in such cases there is always profit to be had. Relations of exchange, that is, always have power and even violence at their core; or, to reverse one of the Wife's tag lines, gold signifies blood.

In this connection, the idea that the Wife lays claim to a "socially undetermined selfhood" becomes relevant not only as a thought about her relations to gender ideology, but also as a much broader thought about the conceptual relationship between social units and their con-stitutive parts. On the view the Wife expresses in these passages, people come into social relations prepackaged, as it were, with a set of desires, interests, hopes, fears, and so on – with, that is, an "individuality" and a "subjectivity" – that determine their aims in participating in social life. We might describe such a view of social life and its basis as atomistic. On such a view, social units – marriages, families, friendships, gossip groups, towns, and so on – are made up of discrete parts, people whose identities are determined first, prior to their engagement in the social unit. The self would then be socially undetermined in the sense that individual people would be the atoms of which social units are composed, and descriptions of social life would be descriptions of how these antecedently determinate parts get put together and interact. This view of social life functions as a reformulation of a claim about subjectivity because in fact they present versions of the same thought. For if one thinks that a person's subjectivity is determined independently of the intersubjective space of interpretation, it is a small step from there to thinking that the contents of that subjectivity – a person's desires, interests, and so on – are determined independently of the desires and interests of anyone else; and it is an equally small step from there to thinking that everyone's only true interest is self-interest.

I do not mean to suggest that this provides the final word on the Wife's structure of belief and desire; the *Wife of Bath's Prologue* and *Tale* are not, as Patterson would have it, about "the triumph of the subject."[12] I mean rather to be sketching a picture in which the Wife is deeply invested, a way she has of representing herself not only to others but to herself – or, in the terms of Aristotelian psychology, a *phantasm*.[13] And to keep a focus on the allegorical generality of this self-representation, we should remember at this point that Alisoun is hardly alone in being held captive by this picture. I have been arguing throughout this book that at the center of the philosophical interests both of Chaucer and of the intellectual tradition to which he belonged is a powerful myth concerning personhood: that the essence of personal identity resides in an essentially private subjectivity, and that what is to be found in that subjectivity is a primary concern with the self that precedes the person's concerns with everything and everyone else.[14] This myth is at the core of the Miller's naturalism, of the fratricidal Theban polity the Knight set out to critique, of the Prisoner's resistance to philosophical therapy in Boethius's *Consolation of Philosophy*, and of the narcissized masculine sexuality on display in the *Roman de la Rose*. But even in cases, such as that of the Miller, when this myth so dominates a person's imagination that he is prepared to avow it wholesale as the truth of what we are and the secret of happiness, its grip is never total. As each of these texts in a different way has helped us to see, our engagement by this myth is necessarily both deep and deeply ambivalent. And this is no less true for the Wife of Bath than for her masculine counterparts.

We can begin to chart the territory of the Wife's ambivalence by turning to one of her favorite topics, the body. "In wyfhod I wol use myn instrument": this is just one example of the Wife's habit of figuring both her and her husbands' genitals as an "instrument" (III.132, 149), or a "harneys" or apparatus (III.136), or a "thyng" (III.121; see also "bele chose," III.446, 510, and "quoniam," III.608). Again, this is a common enough set of tropes, and it fits relatively easily with the Wife's picture of the self as metaphysically private, a subject inside a body. It also fits well with the social atomism that that picture encourages. In imagining sex and marriage as relations of power and exchange, Alisoun figures the sexual organs as instruments or things, and even, as we have seen, as commodities: they are the tools of the trade, or things to be traded. But if the Wife figures her genitals, or more broadly her body, as an instrument or apparatus, a thing to be used by her in achieving her ends and by her husbands in exchange for money, land, and power, then she cannot identify as fully and directly with her body as her picture suggests she does.[15] Our relation to an instrument or tool – a hammer, say – is a relation to something we use to effect our will; something that is separable from us, external to us; something we can pick up and put down. If, as would be the case with the body considered as an instrument, we cannot pick it up or put it down, we might, as Alisoun seems to do here, imagine it to be an inalienable tool, some-thing external to the self which nevertheless must always obey our wishes; but even here we are still far from something that can serve as the ground of a person's authority and self-presence. What is more, since instruments can break or fail, and since, as Alisoun intimates at several points, the body must inevitably grow old and die (cf. III.474–75), this instrument that cannot be put down will at times feel less like an inalienable tool than like something to which we are stuck, or, as the more common trope has it, something *in* which we are stuck, as in prison. I will return to this thought later; I know that

Alisoun's avowed identification with the body makes it seem as though this particular trope is quite far from her mind. For now, I only want to suggest that, coexisting uncomfortably with the Wife's identification with her body as a locus of subjective self-presence, is a counterthought, itself closely allied with the very same picture of the metaphysically private self, that her body is only an instrument of her will, an object or even a space of commercial transaction, an apparatus from which she is absent or behind which she recedes.

The body is not the only site of the Wife's ambivalence, although it is the one that most directly problematizes the sense of her that prevails in current criticism. A site of ambivalence that brings us back to the Wife's concern with eros can be seen in a comment she makes about Jankyn's sexual prowess:

> But in oure bed he was so fressh and gay,
> And therwithal so wel koude he me glose,
> Whan that he wolde han my *bele chose*;
> That thogh he hadde me bete on every bon,
> He koude wynne agayn my love anon.
> (III.508–12)

Consistently with her agenda of reclaiming sexual pleasure from clerical suspicion, the Wife links skill in bed, not just the sober doing of a duty, to the production of love and the promotion of marital concord. But by describing Jankyn's sexiness as a capacity for glossing her, she also links it to the antierotic realm of clerical *auctoritee*, and more broadly to the unreliable interpretive discourse that belongs to the realm of the mediated, the idealized, and the public. And if glossing is what excites her and wins her love, then the possibilities of sexual pleasure and marital happiness are not finally articulable for her in terms of a metaphysically private experience, an atomized self, or a grounding materiality, however deeply she may wish to imagine them as being so.

A similar ambivalence, and the last one I will mention for now, appears in the representations of utopian married sociality that conclude the Wife's prologue and tale. On the one hand, feminine "maistrie" becomes the precondition of marital concord in both moments of narrative closure, and the answer to the question of what women most desire in the tale. This is hardly surprising, since according to her picture of the self and its engagements in social life, what everyone most desires is "maistrie," and in the state of affairs she wants to redress it is mostly men who have it. Yet Alisoun's description of these utopian marriages as spaces of mutual obedience, kindness, and *trouthe* has made it a critical commonplace that, as Dinshaw puts it, "what she wants is reciprocity, despite her talk of 'maistrie'; she most wants mutual recognition and satisfaction of desires."[16] The standard critical response to this ambivalence has thus been to erase it: the Wife *says* that her, or women's, or everyone's fundamental desire is for domination, but that is just part of her rhetorical strategy; her *real* fundamental desire is for reciprocity.[17] Given the centrality of the Wife's social atomism to her whole way of imagining the self, however, the thought of a fundamental desire for domination cannot be so easily set aside. The critical task here, it seems to me, should not be that of saying how the Wife reconciles the conflict between her desires for domination and for reciprocity, but that of saying why she cannot. The rest of this chapter, then, will pursue the question of how an unassimilable desire for utopian intimacy intersects with a dominant self-conception in which others are imagined as alien to the self, and one's relations with them are imagined as fundamentally determined by power.

THE EROTICS OF AMBIVALENCE

The body provides a good place to begin because of its centrality to the Wife's agenda. Why does she imagine the body as an instrument, given that doing so compromises her identification with what she also feels to be the ground of her experience and her agency? We can get an idea from the way the Wife's confident assertion of perpetual profit in bed modulates into something closer to a confession of anger and disgust:

> Namely abedde hadden they meschaunce:
> Ther wolde I chide and do hem no plesaunce;
> I wolde no lenger in the bed abyde,
> If that I felte his arm over my syde,
> Til he had maad his raunson unto me;
> Thanne wolde I suffre hym do his nycetee.
> And therfore every man this tale I telle,

Wynne whoso may, for al is for to selle;
With empty hand men may none haukes lure.
For wynnyng wolde I al his lust endure,
And make me a feyned appetit;
And yet in bacon hadde I never delit.
That made me that ever I wolde hem chide.
(III.407–19)

Alisoun claims that chiding, sexual withholding, and making herself sexually available while pretending to enjoy it were the means by which she "hadde the bettre in ech degree" (III.404) over her husbands: this was all just part of her strategy for power and profit, and so fits quite well with her marital agenda. But the passage ends with her chiding her husbands because she is angry and disgusted at the shrivelled old meat that never gave her pleasure. And while that anger and disgust is partly directed at her husbands for being so monumentally undesirable, it is also directed at herself. For in pursuing her strategy she trades away her pleasure in exchange for a claim to victory; she centers this strategy on a willingness to "suffer" sex, to undergo it or be passive in the face of it; and in doing so through a "feyned appetit," a false representation of her desire, she places herself on the side of the "gloss," of what she figures as the realm of the inauthentic and the denial of bodiliness and pleasure. In all these ways, her basic conception of her agenda and of the strategies through which she might put it into practice requires that she surrender the very things which it is the whole purpose of her agenda to reclaim, and requires as well that she align herself with the forces that have dispossessed her.

While Alisoun's anger and disgust at her husbands is real, then, and while they richly deserve it, her chiding also has the function of diverting attention from the sordid compromises her agenda necessitates: "husbandly bacon" represents an external source of pollution that can contain a potentially more damaging sense of inner pollution. One of the principal advantages of the Wife's instrumental view of the body is that it defends her against both of these sources of disgust. If her body is not just *her*, but is rather her instrument, something she owns and uses, then even the most sordid of her marital and erotic compromises hardly amount to anything. All that she trades away, all that can become polluted or possessed, is her body; it isn't *her* there, bearing up under her husband's desire; in fact, since his desire is for her body, that desire can make no claim on her at all. She remains behind the scene, arranging and controlling it for her profit; she is untouched; she preserves, we might say, her chastity.

The instrumentalization of the body, then, is essential to the Wife's ability to maintain a functional agenda, for it allows her to imagine her immunity to suffering and pollution, through the thought that there is something that is unqualifiedly her, fully intact, not passive in any way; something that is fully distinct from the territories of marital and erotic exchange. Her agenda had already promised such a thing, and called it the body: on this view, the territory of exchange is that of social life, and the body was supposed to be distinct from that territory in part because it was supposed to mark out the unity of her subjectivity and the locus of her self-interest. But we have seen that this view by itself does not hold up, for her agenda requires that her body itself become both a territory of exchange and an instrument whose use is up for sale. So she has to imagine that this intact, distinct something that is "really her" is more "internal" than her body – call it her soul. The Wife's social atomism is thus tracked by an atomism with respect to herself, a way of seeing herself as made up of discrete parts, one of which is inside the other. And here the Wife's attitude turns out to be less distinct from the Platonist and Christian myths than is typically supposed. For if the body she is inside on this view is a site of disgust and loss, then her body is after all a kind of prison for her soul; and if she wants to distinguish herself from that body's erotic transactions to preserve an interior chastity, then a Pauline renunciation of sexuality is perhaps closer to her heart than she would care to admit.

The Wife of Bath's need to imagine an immunity to suffering and pollution is a powerful one, particularly in the context of the gender politics the prologue sketches. But it brings with it even more powerful costs. We see these costs first of all in the very fact that the Wife has two ways of imagining her immunity, which involve two ways of imagining the scene from which she recedes and the person she is apart from that scene. This does more to trouble the question of her identity than to answer it: is her body essential to who she is, or is she merely in it? We might well wonder, after such a double receding, after she has given up what otherwise seems to her to be the ground of her identity, what is to stop her retreat from suffering and pollution at the site of her soul; for, as her internalized disgust suggests, her sense of pollution does not stop with the body. Perhaps, then, her soul is not far enough away from the scene of suffering, pollution, and compromise, and she is even further inside – only where would that be? What could be far enough away? Perhaps all really *is* "for to selle," and there will be no one left to reap the profit.

But as disturbing as the threat of a potentially infinite dwindling away of identity may be, it is not the only problem the Wife faces here. Let us assume that an erotic territory of the kind the Wife wishes for could exist – one whose sufferings would either be unreal or would attach to something external to her, like a body, and so in either case would leave her untouched. Such a territory would also leave her untouched by its pleasures and any other satisfactions of desire; they, like the sufferings, would either be unreal or would happen only to her body. But this is not what Alisoun wants or wants to claim. It is not that her instrument has had pleasure, *she* has; and in satisfying her desires, she was right there, not behind the scene but in it. Unlike her identification with the body, this is one thought to which the Wife seems unambiguously committed. But what is the pleasure of being in the erotic scene like for her, given the suffering and pollution she associates with it?

Consider again the false dream by which Alisoun seduced Jankyn. A consequence of the Wife's social atomism, and a way of reading Jankyn's wish for her death and the flow of her blood in the dream, is that she sees Jankyn's desire as a violent objectification she suffers or undergoes: she is passive with respect to it, merely its object. The puzzle then is that she seduces Jankyn at all. She desires his desire for her, *this* desire for her. Given her impulse to recede from the erotic scene, one advantage to the thought of a violent objectification is that it allows her to imagine that the target of Jankyn's desire is merely an object rather than her. Maybe what he wants and gets is her body; maybe it is her phantasmatic projection into the territory of exchange; in any case it is something she can treat as distinct from her. His desire, in other words, cannot threaten her chastity; it cannot invade the privacy of her subjectivity; it cannot disturb the thought that her interests and desires precede her social relations and provide her with a determinate basis on which to act. We have seen why the Wife would want to hold to such a fantasy, but it hardly explains why she would want to seduce Jankyn; it hardly suggests anything erotic. As I have said, it also requires her to wish her suffering away: she can only have this fantasy to the extent that she ignores or denies the existence of the very thing that motivates it. So there must be some other desire involved here.

A more properly erotic desire is suggested by the Wife's ambivalence over the body. She wants to imagine that the body serves as the experiential source of her autonomy and pleasure; but she also thinks of the body as an instrumentalized and commodified object. To the extent that she remains identified with such an object, then, her desire to lay claim to her autonomy and pleasure cannot be separated from the thrill of imagining her own instrumentalization and commodification. The thought that she finds pleasure in being the target of an instrumentalizing and commodifying desire gains further support from her other ambivalence over glossing. If she is aroused by glossing, then she remains attracted to something she associates with the denial or destruction of the body. And if we follow through on the association of glossing with violence, then it looks as though Jankyn's ability to give her pleasure in bed and his habit of beating her on every bone function for her less as the opposites she says they are than as mutually constitutive features of a single eroticism. If Alisoun thinks of the self as a body, and the body as an instrument, then that is partly because she equates being loved with being violated, or more broadly with being used. In this sense, she wants to take up the place reserved for her in a familiar patriarchal fantasy, and to mark herself as an appropriate object of masculine narcissism. Unlike her desire for sheer absence from the erotic scene, this desire does define an erotics, a masochistic one in which sexiness lies in being violently made into an instrument of the other's pleasure, a suffering passive thing.

This is still hardly a desire for utopian reciprocity; but I would suggest that it is closer to such a desire than it may seem to be. The Wife's desire to be used, and more broadly the idea that she desires Jankyn's desire, implies that at least in this case she does not simply want power over a passive husband, since if she did what he wants would not be in question. Similarly, the thought that the Wife desires *Jankyn* suggests that she does not simply want either a profitable exchange or the instrumental use of him for purposes of gratification, since if she did she would really only want something *from* him, and *he* would not be in question. And the same goes for what she looks for in him: if she wants him to desire *her*, then she cannot simply want him to see her as some substitutable commodity or instrument. But her picture of the self and its entrance into social life does not allow for any other way of conceiving desire, and however ambivalent her commitment to that picture is, she is so deeply invested in it that without it her marital and erotic agenda would collapse. To let that picture go would be hard; it would involve suffering, and it would require her to identify with her suffering rather than assigning it to some imagined or projected "exterior." Letting go her picture of the self would even feel like a kind of death. But it would be a death she would also desire, for, as I have argued, that death is essential to the very possibility of the erotics she wants to claim. And now we can say what the content of that death wish is: it is a wish for the death of the self configured around the myth of the subject, a wish that is for everything in her that clings to that myth, everything that resists the pleasure and pains of a utopian reciprocity, to be stripped away or purged.

I have argued that the Wife clings to the myth of the subject in an attempt to reclaim her autonomy from a patriarchal ideology that threatens to make it illegible, and that a central feature of this attempt is an ambivalent attitude towards a body that seems at once to ground and threaten her autonomy. I have also argued that her identification with the body is closely associated with her social atomism, her sense of her desires and interests as given prior to her relations with others. One thing the Wife would have to imagine as being purged in her death wish is thus the phantasmatic instrumental body, the tool she finds at once so inalienable and polluting – as though the body sown in corruption might pass away, to be replaced by a new body redeemed of its sufferings. The Wife's masochism, I would suggest, involves a deeply Pauline desire for the corruptible to put on incorruption, and so to be transformed. Masochistic suffering and death, however, are no more the final objects of her desire than is domination: if Alisoun imagines a "death of the body," that is a way of imagining what is involved in entering into a new life of utopian intimacy. But how are the dead raised up? And with what body do they come? These are questions the Wife addresses in her tale, and I will conclude this chapter by turning to them.

THE RESURRECTION OF THE DEAD

The *Wife of Bath's Tale* concludes with a promise of utopian intimacy predicated on the appearance of a transfigured body: the hideous old hag who has rescued the rapist knight of the tale from punishment becomes fair and young, and the two "lyve unto hir lyves ende / In parfit joye" (III.1257–58). Magical transformations aside, there is a clear parallel here to the resolution between Alisoun and Jankyn at the end of the prologue: "After that day we hadden never debaat. / God helpe me so, I was to hym as kynde / As any wyf from Denmark unto Ynde, / And also trewe, and so was he to me" (III.822–25). But the language of reciprocal kindness and *trouthe* is more jarring in the prologue than that of perfect joy is in the tale, and not only because the former lacks a fairy-tale setting to shield it from the hard edge with which the Wife has narrated her own history. For the resolution of the prologue is predicated on Alisoun's gaining from Janykyn "the governance of hous and lond, / And of his tonge, and of his hond also" (III.814–15); and her control over a tongue and hand that fill out the list of Jankyn's major possessions pulls the moment back into the orbit of her picture of the self and social life. It seems as though Jankyn's body has become an instrument of her will after all, and this has the effect of suggesting simultaneously that he is a slave rather than a loving partner and that her control of him only goes so deep, to those things that can be represented as his possessions but perhaps no further. The perfect reciprocity of the prologue's conclusion can be no more than the reciprocity of atoms in social space, an exchange of kindness and *trouthe* between partners whose wills remain utterly discrete.

The conclusion of the tale shares with that of the prologue the narrative structure of a granting of feminine "maistrie" that precedes the final cessation of hostilities. But the differences in how the granting is cast provide the key to understanding the appearance of that celestial body in the tale. The rapist knight, faced with the fairy-tale choice of having his wife young and beautiful but perhaps unfaithful, or old and ugly but always faithful, gives over his choice to her:

> My lady and my love, and wyf so deere,
> I put me in youre wise governance;

Cheseth youreself which may be moost plesance
And moost honour to yow and me also.
I do no fors the wheither of the two,
For as yow liketh, it suffiseth me.
(III.1230–35)

The knight promises that he will wait on his wife to specify what will give pleasure and honor to both of them, and that he will find his satisfaction in whatever pleases her. Unlike Alisoun's sovereignty over Jankyn, then, the governance the knight grants his wife does not stop at the tongue and hand. It reaches all the way through him, leaving no possibility of an inner reserve that goes untouched. But while this governance is more complete than that imagined in the prologue, it is also less tyrannical. The knight does not forego his desire or become an instrument of his wife's will: in offering the promise he is still laying claim to his own satisfactions and to the fulfillment of his own pleasure and honor. The knight's promise, then, is the one moment in the Wife of Bath's discourse in which clear and unambiguous voice is given to the desire for intimacy as Cicero and Jean de Meun understand it, namely as the desire for relations with an *alter ego* who occupies the deepest sites of one's selfhood, someone whose alterity constitutes not a break with one's ego, but a constitutive extension of it.

It is remarkable that the knight should be the figure to give voice to such a desire, for he is the single figure in the Wife of Bath's discourse for whom the possibility of such a desire is most alien. Up to this point the knight has served as an allegorical representation of patriarchy at its worst. His desire takes aim at its object in a purely instrumentaliz-ing way, and so registers as pure threat, pure violation:

And happed that, allone as he was born,
He saugh a mayde walkynge hym biforn,
Of which mayde anon, maugree hir heed,
By verray force, he rafte hire maydenhed.
(III.885–88)

The casualness of this description is striking: it just happened that the knight raped a young woman, as though it were the most routine of acts, as though when he sees her walking before him she exists for nothing other than the immediate gratification of his desire. It is appropriate, then, that in order to save his life from the just retribution of the law he must discover what women most desire, for it has seemingly never occurred to him that there might be a question worth asking about feminine desire. Or, to put the point as Alisoun does in another allegorical moment in the tale, it is as though the knight's violence stems from a feeling that he cannot approach what seems to him to be the mysterious otherness of women, a self-enclosed dance that excludes him; for even when he wants to draw near to such a dance, it vanishes under his approach, to be replaced by the sheer loathsomeness of an ugly, aged femininity (III.991–99). The knight, then, is a figure not so much for blindness to the bare existence of a feminine other or feminine desire as for a fear of this otherness, a suspicion that it constitutes a magic circle that excludes him, or that if he should come close to this otherness he would find it repulsive.

So far I have discussed the tale's ending as though the miraculous transformation that occurs there is the one that befalls the ugly old hag. But the conceptual structure of the narrative is, I think, closer than such a reading would suggest to that of the Pygmalion episode at the end of the *Rose*, in which the transformation of the love object is preceded by a change in the erotic subject. Given the knight's figurative function in the tale, the hag's transformation looks more like the expression provided by the narrative machinery of romance to an earlier, more inexplicable change, whereby the knight is suddenly able to address her as "my lady and my love, and wyf so deere." That any woman, much less this one, appears to him as dear rather than alien and frightful; that he can regard her with a loving gaze, rather than one of appropriation, suspicion, or repulsion – this is a change that truly would seem to require a miracle. And once it has occurred, the woman in question is already beautiful; she has no transformation to undergo, the knight need only "cast up the curtyn, looke how that it is" (III.1249). According to this trope of casting up the curtain in bed, seeing how it is with another depends on seeing her with the eyes of love. If you do not, the curtain remains drawn, you cannot know what is there, and you will be condemned to imagining that behind the veil lies only frightful deformity. Once you do, the curtain has been lifted not only from between you and the other, but from between you and yourself: for what is revealed to the knight is not only the beauty of the other but the truth of his own heart's desire. His fearfulness has not only objectified and instrumentalized the others in his world, it has shielded him from himself.

As I said in discussing the Ciceronian account of friendship to which this package of tropes refers, it is almost impossible to think this way without indulging in sentimentality, even though a sentimentalizing reading of such an account gets it precisely wrong. The question then is what produces this sentimentalizing impulse. Alisoun's own sentimentality – the flipside of her *Realpolitik* desire for power – appears in the thought, expressed in the old hag's transformation, that love might free her from the pollutions and sufferings of her erotic life, free her, that is, from the phantasmatic "ugly body" to which patriarchy has bound her. Here again the Wife gives voice to a repressed Pauline longing: "Who will deliver me from this body of death?" Her senti-mentality thus resides in her way of imagining her desire for freedom, as a wish for deliverance from the imprisoning, "dead" stuff of which she is made, and deliverance by a redeemed version of the very agency of her imprisonment.

But the freedom the Wife seeks here goes beyond that which patri-archy and her husbands have denied her. The other as separated from you, as though by a curtain: this trope is a version of a thought that dogs the Wife's picture of the self, the thought of the body as a site of exterior stuff, instrumental or imprisoning as it strikes you, either way some-thing that shadows the one inside, the one who can never be reached. The other as self-enclosed, excluding you, harboring frightfulness or threat: this trope too is a version of the thought of subjectivity as an essentially private realm in which each person nurses the fundamental motive of a narcissized self-interest. The rapist knight, then, allegorizes not only the men in Alisoun's life and the world they have made, but also the dominant terms of her own self-understanding, the myth of subjectivity by which she hopes to snatch pleasure and freedom from that world; and his redemption is as much a figure for her own redemption from that myth as it is for the redemption of patriarchy from its worst excesses.

Perhaps the sense that a sentimentality inevitably attends talk of utopian intimacy is itself a product of that myth. The charge of sentimentality stems, I think, from the idea that a utopian intimacy would be a state of bliss, that the perfection of such an intimacy would consist of a subjective state of pure pleasure and total gratification. That is why the conclusion of the tale reads so easily as a wish fulfillment, either Alisoun's wish to be young and beautiful and loved, or the masculine wish for a beautiful, young, and faithful wife: we are inclined to suspect that the drive to narrative closure is driven by some wish for a subjective gratification that the conclusion promises to supply.[18] But to think this is to repress the pairing in Cicero's account of the happiness of friendship with its totalizing demands; and in the contexts of the *Wife of Bath's Prologue* and *Tale*, there is something chilling about such demands, and something fearful about wanting an intimacy that includes them, something quite far from anything that could function as a wish fulfillment. To return to the Pauline imagery that hovers over this scene: if the ugly body, old and bound for death, is sown in the corruption of instrumentalizing desire and fear, the dead are resurrected, in the twinkling of an eye, with a new celestial body sown in the incorruption of love. Such Pauline language is beautiful and moving; but this is still talk of death. And it would be a terrifying prospect, and a kind of death, to look at another who appears to you as an ugly and frightful threat – as men must appear to Alisoun, but also in a sense as women appear to the men we have been discussing, both here and throughout this book – and see them as beautiful, see your relations with them as a place for a transformative fulfillment. It would seem to require, that is, the death of your "body" or your "matter"; or, to put the point in terms that can help explain the Wife's hyperbolic metaphors, it would require a willingness to forego the identity your history has given you, and in that sense to suffer the death of the stuff you are made of. In order to understand the desire for the incorruption of love, we would have to imagine our way into such a willingness much more fully than Alisoun's tropes of masochistic harrowing and magic transformation can allow.

The place Chaucer most powerfully pursues such an imagining, I think, is the *Clerk's Tale*. It may seem odd to mention the *Clerk's Tale* here, for in its representation of Walter's tyranny and Grisilde's victimization it would seem to leave utopian intimacy far to the side. But the Clerk's focus on Walter's obsessive inflicting of pain on Grisilde and her equally obsessive embrace of it belongs, I will argue, to a radically antisentimental account of love, one that will lead us to the ontological problem concerning love that, I think, underlies the ideological and erotic ambivalences we have been examining. And the Clerk quite directly picks up on the Pauline tropes I have been exploring here. When Walter marries Grisilde and brings her from her "throop" into his palace, he has her stripped from her "povre weedes" and reclothed in royal garb, as though having borne the image of the earthy she should now bear the image of the heavenly; and Grisilde greets this not as an imposition but as something she herself wills. What is involved in Grisilde's willingness to do this, and Walter's desire to have her do it? These are questions to which I will now turn.

CHAPTER 6

Love's promise: the *Clerk's Tale* and the scandal of the unconditional

Throughout the history of its modern critical reception, the *Clerk's Tale* has been marked by a powerful but obscure sense of scandal.[1] It is not hard to see why. The Clerk's story of Walter and Grisilde is that of a wife's unconditional love for her husband which compares her loving virtue to various models of Christian heroism such as Abraham, Job, Mary, and even Christ. But the husband she loves is a paranoid despot who puts her through the most terrible trials, leading her to believe that he has ordered their children killed and finally ejecting her from the palace and staging a fake wedding to a new bride, all to see if there are in fact conditions under which her love for him might come up short. In such a context, the very idea of unconditional love begins to look tarnished, by its seeming indistinguishability from sheer subjection, by its fueling of sadistic hunger, by the implication of that subjection and hunger in the nastiest of gender politics, and by the sheer ugliness of what gets done in its name.

Some critics have insisted that any such reaction to the tale is nothing more than an anachronistic projection of modern concerns on to the text, fueled by a failure to appreciate the Christian ideals to which the Clerk adheres.[2] But, as a number of critics have argued, the tale's generation of moral unease is not the product of a modern reading, and Chaucer's revisions to his sources suggest that he wanted such a response, since he enhanced or added the features of the tale that have helped produce it.[3] In one of Chaucer's most pointed additions to the tale's Petrarchan source, for instance, the Clerk frames the onset of Walter's desire to test his wife by declaring his own feelings of outrage:

> Ther fil, as it bifalleth tymes mo,
> Whan that this child had souked but a throwe,
> This markys in his herte longeth so
> To tempte his wyf, hir sadnesse for to knowe,
> That he ne myghte out of his herte throwe
> This merveillous desir his wyf t'assaye;
> Nedelees, God woot, he thoghte hire for t'affraye.
>
> He hadde assayed hire ynogh bifore,
> And foond hire evere good; what neded it
> Hire for to tempte, and alwey moore and moore,
> Though som men preise it for a subtil wit?
> But as for me, I seye that yvele it sit
> To assaye a wyf whan that it is no nede,
> And putten hire in angwyssh and in drede.
> (IV.449–62)

The Clerk makes it abundantly clear that the subsequent narrative should not be taken as an endorsement of Walter's conduct. But the very effort to secure a sense of scandal here raises questions which the tale gives us no easy way to resolve. The passage seems to describe the sudden upsurge in Walter of a strange, terrible, and irresistible desire to tempt Griselde to betray him, so that he might know the strength of her commitment. But the Clerk also casually remarks that this is the kind of thing that "bifalleth tymes mo," as though husbands were routinely vulnerable to desires of this kind, as he later claims they are: "wedded men ne knowe no mesure, / Whan that they fynde a pacient creature" (IV.622–23). Is Walter then an exceptional case or the husbandly rule? For that matter, is his "merveillous desir" an exceptional event in his own psychic life, the initiating moment for the awful events to follow, or does it simply accompany the latest in a series of ever escalating tests that ought to have been enough and by now have become needless? These questions together point to a tendency in the passage to normalize Walter's behavior. It might just be the usual thing husbands do; what is more, if it is the kind of thing that should not be done to excess or needlessly, that implies that some form of Walterish testing might be just enough, and might even be necessary. This normalizing tendency, however, sits uncomfortably against the Clerk's outrage; after all, the acts he is getting ready to relate are supposed to be both unusual and horrible, not merely needless exaggerations of normal practice. In the face of such confusions, the Clerk retreats into a shrill attempt to secure his *bona fides* by conjuring a nameless enemy with whom to contrast his own views of Walter's actions: *some* men may see Walter's method as the work of a refined intelligence, but as for *me, I* say it's unseemly – at least when there's no need for it.

The Clerk never does address the question of when there would be a need for the course of action Walter pursues, or that of who could be inclined to praise its subtlety; in fact, he works hard in what follows to make such considerations morally repugnant. Nor does he do anything to clarify the sense of an obscure history of temptation and betrayal, or the discrepancy between Walter's perverse exceptionality and his approximation to a husbandly norm. That is part of what gives this passage, and the tale as a whole, its sense of *scandal*, of being a collecting site for a powerful sense of shame and disgrace that can never quite be located or localized, even as it demands to be named and spoken of. The peculiar psychic and social power of this sense of scandal depends on its disavowed ambivalence between two incompatible moral postures: one of knowing resignation in the face of an all too familiar sordid state of affairs, and one of shocked affront in the face of a terrible anomaly that nearly escapes our capacity to understand it.[4] The urge to name scandal's object in each of these ways is only intensified by the self-contradiction of doing so, which is one reason why scandal tends to feed on itself as much as on the news it devours so eagerly. Within the tale, the Clerk describes just such a circular production of the appetite for rumor and judgment as "the sclaundre of Walter ofte and wyde spradde" (IV.722): "for which, where as his peple therbifore / Hadde loved hym wel, the sclaundre of his diffame / Made hem that they hym hatede therfore" (IV.729–31). What makes Walter's people come to hate him is not simply what they think he has done – which, as it happens, is not even anything he *has* done, since his spreading infamy revolves around the false belief that he has murdered his children rather than his actual ill-treatment of his wife. Nor is it even the spread of Walter's infamy that brings about his people's change of heart; rather, in an oddly doubled formulation, they come to hate him for "the sclaundre of his diffame," literally "the scandal of his infamy," which very nearly amounts to saying "the scandal of his scandal."[5] This formulation marks the public response to Walter's conduct as a site of opacity and repetition: as with the Clerk's own response, the production of moral judgment gains a momentum of its own, in no small part because of the lack of any clear set of terms linking that judgment to the scene it purports to evaluate.

This phenomenon of a powerful sense of scandal joined with a deep unclarity about the location of the moral problem has continued in the modern critical response to the tale, as opprobrium has spread from Walter to take Grisilde, the Clerk, and Chaucer as its targets as well, with little collective agreement about what the criteria of moral judgment should be here. So some have seen both Walter and Grisilde as peculiarly perverse, his cruelty and her obedience so pathological as to be nearly unintelligible; others have produced intelligibility by denying any human or characterological dimension to the tale, shifting the moral focus to the Christian lessons exemplified in the narrative; and others have produced other forms of intelligibility by reading the narrative and its characters as exemplary of various political and gendered pathologies and virtues.[6] What almost all critics share is individual certainty about where the moral problems of the tale are to be located – in crazy sadistic urges and crazier passivity; in the difficulty of owning up to the heroic self-abnegation demanded of the medieval Christian subject; in the tyrannical or patriarchal gaze and the production of the feminine as a site of self-sacrifice – while all this certainty about location occurs in the context of a collective uncertainty more powerful than that produced by anything else Chaucer wrote.

In this chapter I will argue that the Clerk is right to be worried about Walter's exemplarity, and about Grisilde's too; he is also right to be worried about his own good faith. In this he anticipates the collective, if not the individual, critical response to the tale, which rightly insists at once on Walter's exceptionality and his normalness, on Grisilde's heroism and her pathology. Chaucer means the tale to produce all of these responses, and not as false lures to be resisted by the properly armed reader, but as substantive engagements with what the tale is about. This does not imply that the tale is merely incoherent or a product of the Clerk's confusions, or that the questions the tale raises, or the concepts that inform those questions, are "undecidable." Chaucer rather intends the *Clerk's Tale* to throw into relief what is simultaneously deeply attractive and deeply disturbing about unconditional love. Further, conflicting attitudes towards unconditional love in the tale are of interest to Chaucer partly because of how they open into a broader ambivalence concerning autonomy and the ideal of an unconditional will. In this chapter, then, I will return to the argument concerning eros and autonomy that has preoccupied me throughout this book. Here, however, I will be focusing less on the romantic contexts of enamoration and desire that have been central so far, and more on love's promise: both the promise it entails of unconditionality, and the promise it holds out of a redemption of the conditions within which it comes into being and endures or fades. That is not to say that the tale offers some kind of object lesson on the value, or for that matter the dangers, of unconditionality and redemption: Chaucer does not intend the *Clerk's Tale* to illustrate a doctrine or impart a lesson. Here as elsewhere in the *Canterbury Tales*, Chaucer makes a contribution to philosophical inquiry by exploring the way a deep practical commitment opens into a set of conceptual problems, and by clarifying what makes those problems hard.

THE POLITICS OF NARCISSISM

What does it mean for Walter to test Grisilde with such grim resolve, and for Grisilde so doggedly to stand up to his ordeals? Why do these two exert such a powerful fascination on each other that, through their long story of violent betrayal and faithful commitment, neither flinches until the rather awkward and unconvincing anticlimax of the tale, in which Walter, seemingly for no reason, declares an end to his tests and reunites Grisilde with her children? And what does it mean for Chaucer and the Clerk to build an investigation of love's promise around this claustrophobically obsessive pair?

The place to start with these questions is with the tale's representation not of love's promise but of its politics.[7] Walter's early portrait as a political leader sets the stage for the tale's love narrative; and in that narrative it is no accident that Walter is Grisilde's lord and she his subject, nor that he is the husband and she the wife. For the Clerk, then, love's promise is imbedded in its politics, and love's politics are imbedded in the structure and motivations of larger political arrangements. The Clerk lays out the rough form of these imbeddings when he diagnoses what he calls Walter's one major moral and political fault: his failure to consider "in tyme comynge what myghte hym bityde" (IV.79), a failure that attends his fixation on "his lust present" (IV.80), and which finds its paradigmatic expressions in his attraction to hawking and hunting (IV.81) and his aversion to marriage (IV.83–84). Walter's people voice the most immediate link between what will happen to him in "tyme comynge" and his refusal to marry when they beseech him to choose a wife. As their nameless spokesman says,

> thenketh, lord, among youre thoghtes wyse
> How that oure dayes passe in sondry wyse,
> For thogh we slepe, or wake, or rome, or ryde,
> Ay fleeth the tyme; it nyl no man abyde.
>
> And thogh youre grene youthe floure as yit,
> In crepeth age alwey, as stille as stoon,
> And deeth manaceth every age, and smyt
> In ech estaat, for ther escapeth noon;
> And al so certein as we knowe echoon
> That we shul deye, as uncerteyn we alle
> Been of that day whan deeth shal on us falle.
> (IV.116–26)

What the people have in mind here is the danger that Walter will die without an heir, in which case they will be vulnerable to foreign rule. But the ominousness with which this spokesman drives home his point about death's inevitability, describing death as a lurking, creeping menace whose certainty is only matched by the uncertainty with which we await the moment of its blow, suggests that more is at issue here than a failure of political prudence. If part of Walter's marriage resistance stems from avoiding the problem of political succession, the shadow of death looming over this passage suggests that marriage and reproduction bear with them broader intimations of mortality and replaceability. In resisting marriage and ignoring the problem of succession, Walter in effect reverses the position of Nature in the *Roman de la Rose*, who argues that sexual reproduction provides a mortal creature with a version of immortality through its ability to replace itself: for Walter, refusing reproduction allows him to repress the need for his replacement and so to imagine himself immortal.[8]

While the people's complaint focuses on Walter's lack of political prudence, the Clerk's broader diagnosis focuses on a more fundamental prudential failure. To fail to consider the future through a fixation on immediate pleasure is to indulge in an extremely narrow and ultimately self-defeating picture of desire, pleasure, and freedom: freedom consists in doing whatever you want whenever you want to, heeding only the call of your pleasure, allowing nothing to stand in the way of your enjoyment. This is a picture of freedom as wantonness, as the sheer unplanned enjoyment of being moved by whatever desires happen to arise in you. But, as almost any moralist's discussion of prudence will tell us, there are plenty of cases in which pursuing your immediate pleasure is not only wrong, but will lead to a catastrophic result even from the perspective of your own narrow self-interest. To live as Walter does, then, is to indulge in a peculiar fantasy of immortality – literally, since it requires ignoring that the pursuit of some pleasures could get you killed; but also figuratively, since it requires ignoring the "death" in your own desire, the rift that is always there between your desire for immediate pleasure and your desire to pursue ends that may be incompatible with your immediate pleasure, such as (leaving moral considerations to the side), your middle- or long-term self-interest. The Clerk captures Walter's indulgence in such a fantasy of immortality in the list of his paradigmatic activities of hawking and hunting, riding and roaming. One's goal in pursuing such leisured aristocratic activities just is to do them in a pleasurable way, to reside as it were immortally in the timeless present of the pleasure they produce.[9] In keeping all his thought on his "lust present," then, Walter's problem is not simply that he ignores the need to plan for the future, as though he were Aesop's irresponsible grasshopper; it is that he does so in a way that allows him to imagine his pleasures – and so, by extension, *himself* – as utterly present and whole, free of any deferral, opacity, or self-contradiction. But far from escaping the thought of death, Walter is haunted by it, seeing death's shadow in every renunciation of pleasure, every difference in his own desire, everything that projects him forward in time one step closer to his inevitable end.

By itself this says little about politics, marriage, or love, except that all are, for Walter at least, tainted by an association with death which he attempts to repress. The political and erotic import of this taint begins to come out when Walter asks Grisilde to marry him:

I seye this: be ye redy with good herte
To al my lust, and that I frely may,
As me best thynketh, do yow laughe or smerte,
And nevere ye to grucche it, nyght ne day?
And eek whan I sey "ye," ne sey nat "nay,"
Neither by word ne frownyng contenance?
Swere this, and heere I swere oure alliance.
(IV.351–57)

Even as prenuptial agreements go, this is rather ominous. If there is to be a union here, it will be predicated on an extremely sharp contrast between Walter's husbandly lordliness and Grisilde's wifely subjection, a contrast strong enough to support and require Grisilde's readiness to Walter's every pleasure and his freedom to cause her happiness or suffering. Walter wants to be assured of Grisilde's "good herte" – on a very pointed formulation of how a good wifely heart should be understood – while offering her no such assurances about himself, since doing so would constitute a boundary on his freedom. Perhaps his pleasures will be anchored in his doing well by her; but they may just as well be anchored in his causing her pain. The Clerk looks back to Walter's terms here, and offers a gloss on them, when he later speaks of the impropriety of married men knowing "no mesure" in the face of patient wives: husbandly pleasure lies in the sensation of unbounded-ness, produced by the violation of the boundaries of propriety and by the violation of those boundaries marked out by wifely pain, the most basic sign of her otherness to him, of her potential for resistance to his desires even in the form of an unwilled animal flinch.

The gender politics of Walter's demands are explicit enough, but, as the background portrait of Walter the marquis suggests, the Clerk has a broader political horizon in mind as well. In asking Grisilde to make herself "ready to his desire" while never exhibiting resistance to his commands in her words or facial expressions, Walter echoes his expec-tations of all of his subjects, whom he commands to revere his wife "in word and werk" (IV.167), and whom the Clerk describes as "obeisant, ay redy to his hond" (IV.66). Walter wants from Grisilde an extension of what he wants from others generally: to be unresistant, transparent to his desires, ready-to-hand as though they were his instruments. The wish to reduce the world of others to a field of instruments finds expression in Walter's peculiar restriction of the obedience he demands to words, expressions, and actions, a restriction thrown into sharp relief when Grisilde alters his terms, much more ambitiously promising "as ye wole youreself, right so wol I" (IV.361). Grisilde's promise would seem to offer an attractive development to Walter's hunger for control: his power will now extend beyond the observable phenomena of behavior, any of which could be mere performances masking an inner resistance, to include her will itself. It is clear from Walter's subsequent fascination with establishing the truth of Grisilde's inner obedience that he finds such power alluring. It might be surprising, then, that Walter does not ask for such power in the first place, that he predicates his politics on the demand for an obedience that, as it were, stops short at the skin, leaving the interior world of his subjects unaccounted for. But the logic of instrumentalist reduction precludes any talk of inner obedience; an instrument, after all, does not have a will, so all you can ask of it is that it perform properly in clearly observable ways. Of course, in the case of an instrument, it makes no sense to think of this as a restriction, since there is no interior life being left out of account. In restricting his demands of others to such observable performances, then, Walter is not revealing a fundamental view of them as his instruments so much as he is working to assimilate them to the condition of instruments, as though by doing so he could fastidiously keep his subjects' wills out of the picture entirely.

In Walter's politics, then, we see another example of Chaucer's interest in the myth of the subject, and of the grip of that myth on a narcissized masculinity for which the presence of another's will, even in the form of a Grisildan Echo, is unbearable – so for which instrumentalist fantasy serves as a way of imagining a world, like the one Narcissus sees in his pool, emptied of others except in the form of a surface reflecting back his own image, his own will. In the aseptic immortality of Narcissean suspension, Walter seems to think he can escape everything that has the stink of death: the inexorable forward march of time, the claims of prudence, all signs of a world of others and of his own inner fragmentation. As the Clerk says and Walter's people sense, more than anything else this means avoiding the pollutions of marriage, with its twin demands of intimacy and of self-replacement; or, if marriage there must be, it must be accommodated as fully as possible to the politics of narcissism, the intimate other reduced to an instrument and all offspring removed from the scene and declared dead. The tale's later invocation of the incest motif in Walter's staging of a fake wedding to his daughter highlights this feature of his psychology: his children are allowed to return, but only in a context that denies their status as his replacements, a context in which he can pretend to reclaim immortality by reinserting himself in the subsequent generation.

But, as we have already seen, Walter's request for a perfect instrumental obedience produces something else, Grisilde's promise of a union of wills. While Walter had always demanded of his subjects a perfect but external conformity, Grisilde, in forcing the issue of her will on to the scene of their marriage, opens up a vista on the interior life of his subjects, and on his own desires, that his instrumentalist picture had always served to occlude. This vista helps to account for Walter's strange yet familiar inability to resist the urge to test Grisilde. Now he must "know her sadnesse" – know, as it seems, not just the observable fact of her loving obedience, but the interior fact which backs that obedience up, making it a durable reality rather than an ephemeral veil. But after Grisilde twice remains firm while having their children seized from her and, as far as she knows, murdered at his command, Walter's thirst for such knowledge only becomes more vampiric and epistemically extreme: he longs "to tempte [Grisilde] moore / To the outtreste preeve of hir corage, / Fully to han experience and loore / If that she were as stidefast as bifoore" (IV.786–89). But what could "the outtreste preeve of hir corage" possibly be, if it has not been reached already? And what could possibly constitute full and direct experiential knowledge of her steadfastness? According to the logic of Walter's obsession, Grisilde's obedience at any moment can only show that she will go *that* far; there could always be some further point at which she would balk. What's more, her will may never have been on display at all; any of her "successes" could always have been mere performances. Or, if her will was on display at least at the moment of her promise, she may have been so crushed by Walter's punishing tests that there is nothing of her left, her interiority become an insensate mass, like the interior of the instrument Walter first asked her to be. In fact, how could her acts of obedience be anything other than performances or signs of her insensateness, given what she does at his command? Even if she meant her pronounced love of him before, how could she possibly do so now, given the monster he has proven himself to be? Since Walter's tests can only tantalize him with the prospect of a certainty none of them can provide, Grisilde becomes for him "ay sad and constant as a wal" (IV.1047), her obedience an impenetrable surface keeping Walter out and keeping her interiority hidden from view.

More is at issue here than the desire for knowledge, of course. As Walter said at the contractual moment, he has wanted all along the freedom to cause Grisilde pain, and in this respect as well Grisilde's obedience frustrates him even as it seems to grant his wish. Throughout the tortures Walter inflicts upon her, her pain seems hidden behind her wall-like impenetrability. Or perhaps he has not even been so successful as to cause her an invisible pain: since everything he does to her and forces her to do is by her declaration something she wills, she may not be suffering at all, at least not suffering anything she does not want to. How, then, can Walter luxuriate in the pleasure of feeling his power wash over Grisilde, violating all boundaries between them, violating even the otherness of her animal resistance, if there is no resistance, no otherness, to overcome? Here, as in the *Roman de la Rose*, the sadism of narcissized masculinity both frustrates itself and seeks vengeance on the object that provokes it. Maybe, if he causes her enough pain, Walter can break through that wall and see the suffering behind it; if he cannot do that, maybe he can break her, destroying the otherness that so stubbornly refuses to show itself; and if even that proves impossible, at the very least he will punish her for the excessive devotion that violates the instrumentalist contract and so insistently refers to the Grisildan will he wishes to repudiate.

The thought of Walter's tests as attempts to break through the wall of Grisilde's obedience helps to explain an otherwise odd detail, the Clerk's use of the term "tempt" seemingly interchangeably with "test" to describe Walter's provocations of his wife. Much of the critical discussion of Walter relies on the idea that he wants Grisilde to pass his tests and so to prove her obedience, which is his truncated way of imagining her proving her love for him. That idea is right as far as it goes. But the idea of tempting someone to do something ordinarily implies that in some sense we want them to do it; while for Grisilde to succumb to Walter's temptations would be for her to *fail* his tests, to show, as he sees it, that she does not really love him and probably never did. If, however, Grisilde's devotion registers for Walter at least partly as an unwanted excess, then in some sense he does want her to fail, and temptation is precisely what is at issue. For if Walter were to break through the wall of Grisilde's obedience and she were to fail his tests, showing signs of an inner reserve or resistance to him, then it would turn out that she had been suffering under his commands after all. His power would have produced visible signs of a pain that he would have reason to presume had been there all along, and that would mean that even in her previous obediences there would in fact have been boundaries violated and otherness overcome. It would also mean that she was not in fact an insensate mass, showing no sign of pain only because she had so closely approximated the pure instrumentality Walter had wished for her. Walter's sadistic pleasures would then be confirmed, if only in the moment when the guaranteed obedience he seeks is lost to him.

Again as in the *Roman de la Rose*, "sadistic narcissism" here names an unstable, fragmented *habitus* of thought and desire, a phantasmatic structure that needs understanding rather than the stopping point of an explanation. Walter's instrumentalism is central to his narcissism, but his sadistic pleasures can only find confirmation through the abolition of the instrumentalist contract; and no matter how deeply the asepsis of narcissism appeals to Walter, he wants, like other sadists, to get dirty – if not literally to have Grisilde's blood wash over him, then perhaps more profoundly to feel her suffering soak into his pores. And even this desire, it turns out, is not born of some fundamental hatred of the other or love of causing pain. Walter's sadism is linked to the desire not for Grisilde's death, but for her life: torture is his way of trying to reach Grisilde, to break through the wall that separates them and end his narcissistic solitude. One might even say – in fact I think we *should* say – that torture is his way of loving Grisilde. To see how deeply related torture and love are here, we will have to turn more squarely to an account of the tale's representation of love's promise in the figure of Grisilde. For now let me conclude with the politics of narcissism by noting that the Clerk quite explicitly links something he comes very close to calling Walter's love for Grisilde to the very attributes in her that make her such perfect fodder for Walter's lust for power.

Before Walter's people approach him with their plea that he marry, when he is apparently still in the thick of his marriage resistance, the Clerk describes him coming to a curious resolution: he "disposed that he wolde / Wedde hire [i.e., Grisilde] oonly, if evere he wedde sholde" (IV.244–45). The oddness of such a decision – however common decisions like it may be in "real life" – resides partly in the direct conflict between Walter's choice of an object and his thinking that under no circumstances will he marry, "for noght that may bifalle" (IV.84). Walter's resolution to choose Grisilde thus takes the form "if I ever do this thing that I will never under any circumstances do." However deeply ingrained and genuinely felt Walter's principled resistance to marriage is, he already entertains the thought of marrying *Grisilde* in particular, and he can do so partly because he "knows" in principle that he will never make this thought a reality. There is also something about Grisilde that provokes Walter's resolution. While she is only fairly good-looking, the beauty of her virtue exceeds that of almost any other; her heart is free of all sensual desire; she never gives over labor for idle ease; and "in the brest of hire virginitee / Ther was enclosed rype and sad corage; / And in greet reverence and charitee / Hir olde povre fader fostred shee" (IV.219–22). This may seem a rather too clerkly portrait of a woman's attractions, and later we will turn to the Clerk's interests in casting Grisilde as a figure of such spartan virtue and in shielding both her virtuous beauty and Walter's attraction to it from sensual desire. For now we can say that when Walter, gazing on Grisilde, "noght with wantown lookyng of folye" (IV.236), but rather "commendynge in his herte hir wommanhede, / And eek hir vertu" (IV.239–40), decides in his provisional way to marry her, her asexual womanliness and virtue carry with them a particular charge for him. His desire for patriarchal domination could hardly find a better target than this dutiful, hard-working daughter, this virginal enclosure for a steadfast heart; and if she is a rather plain girl with no "likerous lusts" of her own, this only makes her more suited for domination, as it frees Walter of the burden of a sexy wife whose eroticism could give her a measure of power over him and could make her a prize rather hard to guard.

There is more to Grisilde's virtue, however – and more to Walter's attraction to it – than its status as the object of patriarchal fantasy. If

Grisilde works hard instead of idly pursuing sensual desire, and if Walter is attracted to her not out of wanton folly but out of admiration for her virtue, that is also because she is a figure for the prudence Walter repudiates in his riding and roaming. In the midst of his wanton pursuits, Walter is struck by his admiration for and attraction to Grisilde's steady attention to the demands of "tyme coming"; and this provokes in him a resolution that, however odd, is also clearly prudential: in case he should ever change his mind about marriage, this is the person he wants to marry. What is finally odd about this scene of enamoration, then, is that the same features of Grisilde's representation invoke both Walter's entrapment in the fantasies of power that attend his wanton picture of freedom and his attraction to the prudential virtue that that picture must repress.[16] Walter wants Grisilde because she simultaneously seems able to fulfill his patriarchal fantasies and to free him from them. For Walter, at least at first, that may be love's promise.

GRISILDAN UNCONDITIONALITY

If Grisilde is an object of intense admiration and equally intense suspicion for Walter, it remains to be seen why. It is already clear that we cannot invoke Walter's sadistic narcissism as the basis for an explanation, since that condition involves misrecognitions that themselves stand in need of explanation. Besides, as the critical history of the tale attests, Walter is hardly alone in his attraction and repulsion; and what is more, the Clerk seems to want to ensure this double movement. On the one hand, he compares Grisilde's loving self-sacrifice to Christ's, her willingness to sacrifice her children to Abraham's, and her patient suffering to that of Job and the Saints; on the other, he makes it clear that those very virtues entail her complicity in her victimization and in the victimization of those who most depend on her. The Clerk's proposed moral only makes muddy waters muddier. Grisilde, he says, should not be taken as a model for wifely behavior; such a life would be intolerable and ill-advised. She should rather be seen as a model for a generalized constancy in the face of adversity (IV.1142–47). But this moral, which could be the moral of many tales quite different from this one, erases the marital scene that the whole tale has been built around.

As the Clerk goes on in very precise language to distinguish the adversity God sends our way from what Walter has done to Grisilde – God never *tempts* us, nor does he seek to *know our wills*, since he already does (IV.1153, 1159) – it seems that, in order to make this generalized moral fit the tale, the Clerk must declare irrelevant the entire first part of the narrative, his interest there and subsequently in Walter's political and marital narcissism, and everything that interest means for an understanding of Grisilde's loving obedience. But the pointed way this moral's erasures refer us back to the tale's interest in paranoid fascination and marital desire, together with the Clerk's immediate return to gender politics in his subsequent Envoy, suggests that he wants us to notice what his moral leaves out. However admirable he and his audience may find an unswerving devotion to the divine will, and however much the love of God and the love of a spouse may seem to them comparable, the attempt to bring that comparison to bear on this story produces as many questions as it does answers.

To see how deep these questions go, let us turn to one of the scenes that generates them most urgently, Grisilde's giving up of her daughter at Walter's command to what she believes to be a cruel death. In this scene Grisilde sits "meke and stille" "as a lamb" (IV.538) while Walter's "suspect" sergeant (cf. IV.540–42) seizes her daughter with an ugly, fierce expression, as though he were going to kill her then and there. At this point the Clerk, who tells most of the tale with a spareness and emotional reserve which Muscatine characterizes as "fine astringency," shifts into an uncharacteristic rhetorical mode somewhere between melodrama and the high pathos of the Pietà:[11]

> But atte laste to speken she bigan,
> And mekely she to the sergeant preyde,
> So as he was a worthy gentil man,
> That she moste kisse hire child er that it deyde.
> And in hir barm this litel child she leyde
> With ful sad face, and gan the child to blisse,
> And lulled it, and after gan it kisse.
>
> And thus she seyde in hire benigne voys,
> "Fareweel my child! I shal thee nevere see.
> But sith I thee have marked with the croys

Of thilke Fader – blessed moote he be! –
That for us deyde upon a croys of tree,
Thy soule, litel child, I hym bitake,
For this nyght shaltow dyen for my sake."

I trowe that to a norice in this cas
It had been hard this reuthe for to se;
Wel myghte a mooder thanne han cryd "allas!"
But nathelees so sad stidefast was she
That she endured al adversitee,
And to the sergeant mekely she sayde,
"Have heer agayn youre litel yonge mayde."

"Gooth now," quod she, "and dooth my lordes heeste;
But o thyng wol I prey yow of youre grace,
That, but my lord forbad yow, atte leeste
Burieth this litel body in som place
That beestes ne no briddes it torace."
But he no word wol to that purpos seye,
But took the child and wente upon his weye.
(IV.547–74)

This touching domestic scene of a mother kissing and gently cuddling the little child she must allow to be borne away to death – the kind of thing apt to fill a nurse with pity or cause a mother to cry out in sorrow – gains a good deal of its gravity from its invocation of that other mother holding in her lap a child "marked with the croys / Of thilke Fader." But the scene's invocation of the Pietà also gives it a perverse edge that the Clerk highlights through several pointed details.[12] In many Marian lyrics, as well as in many Pietàs in painting and sculpture, Mary is tormented by her sorrow, crying, gently cradling her son as though to provide the nurture and comfort his dead body can no longer receive; or, in another standard scene of Marian piety invoked by this passage, she holds the Christ child in her lap, full of sorrow at the coming Passion, even as she knows that he is destined to die for her sake and for that of all humanity.[13] By contrast with such scenes, Grisilde shows no signs of pain as she holds her child: well *might* a mother cry out "alas," but Grisilde does not. Further, when Grisilde tells her child "this nyght shaltow dyen for my sake," she reverses the direction of

Christ's sacrificial announcement to his mother in poems like "Stond wel, moder, under rode," thus replacing its consolatory effect with something closer to cold selfishness. While the crucified Christ offers his grieving, incredulous mother consolation with the good news of his redemptive death, Grisilde's child is hardly going to her death, as Christ went to his, knowingly and willingly; nor is there anything redemptive about this death, which is "for Grisilde's sake" not because it is part of some divine providential plan, nor even because it will somehow redress the pain and injustice Grisilde suffers, but only in the sense that in sacrificing the life of her child, Grisilde is able to maintain something she apparently values more, the purity of her will in its commitment to Walter. The moment's invocation of another sacrificial scene between parent and child, that of Abraham and Isaac, makes matters worse; for Grisilde sacrifices her child not, like Abraham, at the command of God, but at that of a husband the Clerk regards as perverse and cruel. As with the tale's moral, the effect of these references is oddly double: while they compare Grisilde's love for Walter with Christian piety, they do so in ways that throw into relief the self-regarding obsessiveness of Grisilde's marital commitment and her desire for a pure will, their requirement of an inhuman detachment from maternal suffering and a monstrous dereliction of maternal duty.

Both the melodrama of this scene and its invocation of Marian piety arise in response to one of the most basic dramatic difficulties the Clerk faces. He means Grisilde to embody the perfection of patient fortitude and of her promise of a unity of wills with Walter. She must not then be seen weeping and wailing or wanting to resist Walter's commands, and in a sense she must not even be understood to *suffer* them. Like a Ciceronian friend, she must find the demands of her intimate other to present no imposition on her – "numquam molesta est" – otherwise she will have achieved, not union with Walter's will, but only a willing endurance of it. Yet if she should seem devoid of suffering, like some cardboard personification of virtue, her perfection would be empty, her "patience" more stone-like than Job-like. The Clerk must find ways, then, to allow her suffering to register without it appearing constitutive of her, without it impinging on the unity of her will. One way he does this is by using this strange mixture of melodrama and Marian piety, not to show us Grisilde's pain directly – "she neither weep ne syked, /

Conformynge hire to that the markys lyked" (IV.545–46) – but to generate pathos around her and on her behalf, and to use that pathos to create a vicarious identification between the tale's audience and the maternal suffering Grisilde manages not merely to bear but to negate.

This indirection ensures that the suffering Walter causes is not made to disappear by what Grisilde does with it. But it also ensures that just when our identification with maternal pathos reaches its height, Grisilde divorces herself from it. That is one reason so many readers have found Grisilde's actions and her affect to be monstrous, and why they have not been making aesthetic or historical mistakes in doing so. This becomes even clearer when we attend to the other way the Clerk allows Grisilde's suffering to register while maintaining her detachment from it, that is, in the way he shows the work by which she takes a deep and real pain and disidentifies herself with it, forcing it to function in her own psychic life as an unwanted intrusion that will not speak for her. The Clerk shows this most directly in the speeches in which Grisilde responds to Walter's various tests, as we see her struggle with impulses of grief, resistance, and regret as she works her way from bewilderment back to resolute oneness with her husband.[14] In the scene in question here, we see less the struggle itself than signs of Grisilde's attempted emergence from it, as when she tells the sergeant "have heer agayn *youre* litel yonge mayde," and begs him to bury "this litel *body*." To mark her freedom from the conflict in her commitments and passions, she must refer to her daughter as no longer hers, and even in a sense as no longer alive, as though, in keeping with the scene's invocation of the Pietà, the child were already a body awaiting burial. If, as Grisilde believes, the sergeant will commit the actual murder, in order to distance herself from her loss she must figuratively kill off the child first, declaring it dead in her heart and thereby declaring herself no longer a mother, no longer someone who *can* lose a child. This need gives a double edge of protectiveness and aggressivity to her marking the child with the sign of the Father, and gives an unpleasantly necrophiliac whiff to the kiss with which she bids it goodbye, a kiss now rather too close for comfort to the kiss of death.

If, however, the Clerk means us to recoil, not only from Grisilde's dereliction of maternal duty but from what she does to divorce herself from her own attachments, he does not mean us to stop there. The point of the tale's rhetoric in such moments is not simply to cast Grisilde as a monster, but rather to break through the amnesia of sentimental pieties concerning unconditional love through which we protect ourselves from love's radical dimension.[15] It is all too easy to feel an emotional attraction to the idea of unconditional love as long as that idea is left fairly vague, contrasted, say, with the conditions we think we discover in standard melodramas of love's collapse, as when we imagine that one partner has implicitly thought "I love you as long as you do not become fat, or seriously ill, or poor, or depressed." But the implicit conditions that emerge around Grisilde's negation of them are harder to view with such condescension: "I love you as long as you do not undergo a terrible change into a sadistic monster"; "I love you as long as it does not require the death of others I love"; "I love you as long as it does not require me to become the kind of mother who would willingly send her children to be murdered at your command." The gender and class politics of the tale, far from compromising Grisilde's embodiment of unconditional love, help to reveal how muscular the Clerk's notion of it is, for in placing Grisilde in a position of political disempowerment and dependency, the Clerk distinguishes her love from the conditions implicit even in standard pictures of ideal intimacy, such as those imagined by the Wife of Bath and the Franklin: "I love you as long as we are on an equal footing and our love is mutual, as long as I am not the politically and ideologically abject, as long as there is room for negotiation and compromise."

I have argued that, contrary to one tradition of reading the tale, the Clerk does not intend his comparison of Grisilde to Abraham and Job to erase what is disquieting, and even revolting, about her; I have also argued that this very disquiet and revulsion is essential to the Clerk's effort to distinguish unconditional love from a sentimental approbation of love that remains fraught with potential conditions, waiting for the right circumstances to be actualized. In this respect, it is the very monstrosity of Grisilde that makes the stories of Job and Abraham and Isaac relevant to her case. The point of those stories is to exemplify an unconditional love for God that requires bearing up under sacrifices that can only appear horrible and even incomprehensible by ordinary standards, a love that, measured by those standards, is monomaniacal, requiring an inhuman detachment from all other bonds and a monstrous dereliction of the duties that attend those bonds. The fact that God rather than Walter is the object of such love for Abraham and Job is in a sense beside the point, for those stories work to carve away everything about God that might make him appear worthy of devotion, so that the only thing that supports a love for him is the bare fact of one's commitment to it. We need not, then, leave the domestic scene of the tale aside to understand Grisilde's exemplary function within the Clerk's religious framework. For the Clerk, to engage in an unsentimental, nonamnesiac way with the desire to love with a whole will requires heeding the muted call of the old biblical ideal whereby a sacrificial commitment must survive the loss of one's deepest attachments; or, to put it another way, it requires a return to the primitive Christian ideal of apostolic integrity, of a purity of heart to be found in willing one thing – a purity that, as Christ declared, requires the renunciation of all intimate associations that might compete with one's commitment.[16] But such a return cannot happen through naïve idealism or conventional pieties that leave intact the settled compromises of daily life. Since those compromises are the very fabric of the normal, to begin to break them and reach towards the life of a pure, devoted will we must confront the abnormality, the repulsive excess, of the effort to be whole.

The preceding formulations stress the Clerk's moral suspicion of sentimentality; but the idea that Grisilde's love, like that of Abraham and Job, is supported only by the bare fact of her commitment to it suggests a further, more technical sense in which the Clerk's account of love is antisentimental. For the Clerk, to understand love as an unconditional disposition of the will, it is necessary to understand that love is not a sentiment; more broadly, it is not a feeling or passion or state of affect, or for that matter any other kind of subjective state.[17] There may be subjective states that paradigmatically accompany love – feelings of fondness and care for the love object, for instance – but such states are not what love essentially is. The link the Clerk makes between love and autonomy can help us see why this is so. An autonomous will is one that "gives itself a law": it is not dependent on any law outside itself, not in that sense passive or caused. But if love is fundamentally a sentiment or feeling, then the will of the person who loves can be said to be passive, in the sense that their disposition to love has its source in something else, a subjective state that they do not choose. Such love is in the technical sense sentimental because it is *pathological*, a form of *pathe*, an affect or movement of the soul. An autonomous disposition of the will, by contrast, must be nonpathological: for love to be such a disposition, it must not be "given its law" by the feelings it involves, and it must not depend on pathological support, or indeed on any motive other than that of the loving itself. This point is so important to the Clerk because thinking of love and experiencing it as affect – that is, being committed in theory and practice to a sentimental account of love in the technical sense – is more than an intellectual mistake; it reinforces the weak-willed moral sentimentality that cannot stand up under the kind of pressures Grisilde or Abraham or Job faces. For those are pressures under which all of the affect that ordinarily accompanies love has been beaten out of you: if love depends on pathological support, in such a case it will die out, and so reveal the implicit conditions laid on it from the beginning.

The standards of moral stringency in this account are clearly very high, but as with the Ciceronian account of friendship on which it is partly based, the Clerk's point is that this is what we mean when we talk of giving and receiving love unconditionally. Beyond that, the Clerk also wants us to see that our ordinary attitude towards this ideal, and our ordinary ways of trying to pursue it, are fraught with ambivalence: we admire and desire it in a way that informs all of our experience and conduct of love, but we mostly do so in a sentimental mode that deprives love of its essence, and when faced with circumstances that reveal that essence, we tend to respond with suspicion that no one really loves that way, fear that we could never live up to that ideal, and horror at love's potential costs. In this ambivalence, we resemble the general form, if not the specific detail, of Walter's simultaneous attraction to and recoil from Grisildan virtue. In fact, if Grisilde allegorically figures the normative structure of what we want when we want to love and be loved – and if, in doing so, she embodies the monstrous excess of love's promise – then Walter allegorically figures the normal structure of our inhabitation of this desire, and in doing so embodies the monstrous privation of love's ordinary conduct. I will conclude this section by returning to Walter to suggest just how revelatory his pathology is of the normal case.

Walter's love for Grisilde, as we have seen, always involved a strong element of admiration for her moral beauty: in seeing her drive to autonomous unconditionality, he sees a figure both for what he wants in a love object and for his desire to have a coherent loving will himself. But no one is better situated than Walter to know the risks of embracing that desire, of opening oneself to the will of another who may harbor only suspicion and threat. So he tests Grisilde to make sure that her love for him knows no bounds, not simply as a way of establishing and confirming his power over her, but so that he can see that it is safe to live up to the demand she places on him and that he, in admiring her, places on himself. Here Walter reveals in himself a version of the sentimentality the tale has confirmed in its audience. For in looking for irrefutable signs of the inner fact in Grisilde that constitutes her love for him, he imagines love as a subjective state rather than a disposition of the will; and in torturing her to make her render forth the interiority he thinks is hidden from him, he imagines that he can know her love only by forcing her into a position of pure pathology, a passivity in which she will be flayed open for his sadistic gaze. But in wanting to base his love on things seen, Walter violates the demands of love in the very act of preparing to meet them, and so confirms his shameful inability to make himself whole. In the face of this failure, the love Grisilde continues to extend to him in his abject, corrupted state is only more shaming, further proof of his unworthiness. The depth of this shame provides further reason for the Clerk's interchangeable language of testing and tempting in describing Walter's actions: for the very features of Grisilde's love that make Walter desire her success in dealing with his tests also make that love unbearably revelatory of his own failures, and so something he wants to destroy as much as to confirm.

Here it will be helpful to recall the line of biblical association running through the *Clerk's Tale* to which we have so far paid the least direct attention: the association between Grisilde and Christ. Like Christ, Grisilde is the law of love made flesh; like Christ, her embodiment of love requires her to render herself up sacrificially to a fractured heart that cannot recognize its own desire, a heart that finds her love intolerably shaming and so rejects it; and again like Christ, her sacrifice functions to redeem that fractured heart, to call it back to the love it could not bear. Along this associational path, then, Walter's reaction to Grisilde – his impulse to crucify her, to destroy love's embodiment, and to doubt it in the absence of visual proof – appears not as the exceptional case but as the normal one, even among Christian subjects who, as the Good Friday liturgy serves to remind, continue in their hearts to respond to Christ's loving sacrifice by declaring "Crucify him!" If Walter's repeated testing of Grisilde's steadfastness and tempting her to forgo it represent his fear and shame in the face of the unbearable demands of unconditional love, then, we would seem to be little better off than he is – unless, that is, we are up to those demands in the way Grisilde is, which the Clerk, through scenes like the one in which she kisses her daughter goodbye, has taken pains to show us we are not. According to the Clerk's moral argument, then, there is something genuinely fearful, even terrible, about what love requires of us; and since we are no longer in the days of Abraham, Job, or the Apostles, since "this world is nat so strong . . . / As it hath been in olde tymes yoore" (IV.1139–40), it may even be impossible for us to live according to love's law. However we may condemn Walter's behavior, then, we are as divided as he is against our desire to love unconditionally. The very extremeness of his behavior, far from making him into an aberration from whom we can safely distinguish ourselves, functions allegorically to highlight the underlying structure of our ambivalence.

There is, however, more to our ambivalence – and for that matter more to Walter's – than the Clerk's moral argument can accommodate. For admiration and desire mixed with weakness, fear, and shame cannot fully explain the chill we feel in moments like that in which Grisilde announces to her daughter "now you will die *for my sake.*" The Clerk may want to cast this moment as an instance of Grisilde's heroic ability to unify her will in the face of the moral conflicts and sheer suffering entailed by her love for Walter, but he shows us a bit too much for such a reading to stick; there is something cold and self-regarding in Grisilde's way of putting the point, as though her drive to autonomy involved an impulse to wall herself off from others every bit as powerful as Walter's. Such a thought does not sort easily with the Clerk's central argument about Grisilde, since her love for Walter was supposed to be the very antithesis of narcissistic withdrawal. But, as we will see in the next section, the very moralism of that argument, however unrelenting its grip on the ambivalences that animate the experience and conduct of love, is itself an attempt to resolve a further set of conflicting intuitions

238

about love in which the Clerk remains entangled and for which he has no real solution, but which Chaucer uses the *Clerk's Tale* to stage and explore.

We can take our cue as to the general territory of the Clerk's entanglements from the tease with which the Host invites him to speak: " 'Ye ryde as coy and stille as dooth a mayde / Were newe spoused, sittynge at the bord' " (IV.2–3). As always, we need to take the Host's comments with a grain of salt: as Chaucer's mouthpiece for the "common sense" of bourgeois masculinity, Harry Bailey voices here a conventional association between clerical meditativeness and effeminacy, and does so out of an equally conventional anxiety concerning the conflicts between normative masculinity and the moral and intellectual demands he feels the Clerk is likely to make. But Harry is not entirely off-base in seeing in the Clerk a social diffidence with a sexual dimension – or, to read Harry's simile a bit more closely, a shyness and quiet withdrawal with respect to social and sexual visibility and possession, that still carries along with it an anticipatory desire. For in the *General Prologue* portrait of the Clerk, Chaucer the pilgrim notes a similar hesitancy concerning sensuality and sociality (cf. I.285–308). There, the Clerk who famously would gladly learn and teach is described as a man whose seriousness carries along with it, in his bookishness, his emaciated body and horse and his threadbare coat, and his reserved and fastidiously moral speech, an impulse to discipline bodily appetite and to allow himself to be socially available only in ways which, as far as possible, exclude the sensual, pointing beyond his bodily presence straight to the moral purpose he wishes to pursue.

If Grisilde's commitment to autonomy involves a certain cold withdrawal from others, then, the Canterbury pilgrims see the Clerk's moral seriousness as involving a similar impulse to withdraw from sensuality and sociality. And we should remember as well what I earlier referred to as the Clerk's rather too clerkly portrait of Grisilde's attractiveness: her beauty lies more in her virtue than in her appearance, that virtue consists partly in her having a heart free of sensual desire, and even Walter gazes on her with moral admiration rather than with "wantown lookyng of folye" (IV.236), a phrase which casts sexual attraction in suspiciously moralistic terms, as though a look of desire were automatically to be associated with the wanton-like prudential failures that characterize Walter's narcissized politics. The sexual thus begins to emerge as a particularly charged location for a broader anxiety that includes in its scope bodiliness, appetite, and the vulnerability of the Clerk's social presence to purposes not his own. Yet still Harry Bailey, in his usual way of stumbling as though by accident on an insight he does not know what to do with, describes the Clerk's attitude not as a stern rejection of sensuality and sociality but as coyness, a desire for availability that, for whatever reason, will not own up to itself. The Clerk wants that from which he withdraws; otherwise he could not be the glad learner and teacher Chaucer declares him to be.

To understand the Clerk's ambivalence concerning sociality and sensuality, and to see the connection between it and the coldness of Grisildan autonomy, we need to return to the centerpiece of the Clerk's representation of autonomous love, Grisilde's promise to unify her will with Walter's. We have already seen that a crucial feature of Grisilde's promise is her alteration of the terms Walter proposes for their marriage: her talk of a unity of wills replaces Walter's demand for an unflinching external obedience by shifting the focus from behavior to the disposition that supports it. Given that Walter's contractual demands are his way of imagining union with the Grisilde whose virtuous beauty so deeply compels him, with the only person he ever thought might free him from his narcissistic aversion to "tyme comynge," Grisilde's alteration of his terms might be read as a diagnosis and correction of them, as though to say "I know that you *think* you want instrumental control over me, but what you *really* want is for our wills to become one; I promise to fulfill your heart's deepest desire, not just the perverse desire you can bring yourself to voice." In this sense, Grisilde's embodiment of love's promise involves not only the ideal of two becoming one, but the further one of a lover who knows the best version of you, and who, in doing so, knows you better than you know yourself.

The Clerk's repeated emphasis on Grisilde's patience suggests how this initial correction can help us read her conduct throughout the tale. As Chaucer's Franklin argues, patience among friends and lovers involves a willingness to suspend both your reaction to being wronged and the connection you draw between a person's actions and their will:

> For in this world, certein, ther no wight is
> That he ne dooth or seith somtyme amys.
> Ire, siknesse, or constellacioun,
> Wyn, wo, or chaungynge of complexioun
> Causeth ful ofte to doon amys or speken.
> On every wrong a man may nat be wreken.
> (V.779–84)

You may have been wronged by your lover, and even have suffered terribly at their hands, but a patient response in such a situation involves thinking that in a certain sense *they* did not do it, and therefore are not appropriate targets of blame. Anger, sickness, wine, and other factors outside a person's will can often cause them to act or speak badly, and to the extent that you attribute their behavior to such a cause, you decline to hold them responsible for it: "it was the wine talking," as we say. Or, in the absence of such a causal explanation, you might think that they simply acted "amiss": they made a mistake, that's all, and in that sense their behavior was not really definitive of their will. Along this line of thinking, Grisilde's patience consists in a refusal to take Walter's behavior as action expressive of him. If love's promise involves Grisilde's knowing Walter better than he knows himself, that knowledge involves the patience of waiting for the causal sources of his misbehavior to pass, or of waiting for him to stop making mistakes and mistaking himself. As before, it does not matter here that Walter's behavior is more extreme than most of what people do out of drunkenness or basic fallibility. Nothing in the definition of patience tells you when to be patient and when not to be, and the point of Grisilde's exemplarity is that she shows a patience without limits, and *that* is what unconditional love requires.

Here again we are on the verge of a sentimental truism – for how many times have we heard that to love someone we must love the best version of them, and take the rest as detritus, the product of a hard time or the necessary imperfection that is always part of being human? And again the Clerk's central purpose is to show what would be involved in taking this truism seriously. For Grisilde must patiently wait for the "real" Walter to show himself in the absence of any indication that there is a better version of him; everything he does points the other way, towards the idea that this senseless brutality is all there is to him, that he is, as it were, pure detritus. This is a consequence of the Clerk's insistence on love being unconditional. Like Job's love for God, Grisilde's love for Walter is supported only by her faith that he does in fact love her and will so reveal himself; and, as Paul puts it, such faith is "hope in things unseen," not a rational appraisal of the available evidence.[18] But then, if Walter must show every sign of being unloving for Grisilde's patient love to confront the extremes that reveal its essential features, and if one of those features is that it refuses to count an unloving act as expressive of Walter's will, then patient love must involve a willingness not to count anything the beloved does as expressive of their will. And that is just what Grisilde does. She looks past everything about Walter that expresses the will he recognizes as his own – past his demand for a world of others conceived as his instruments, past his way of imagining a perfect external obedience as the proper expression of love, past his vampiric desire for knowledge of her will and his belief that he can make her will known to him only by her suffering, past his apparent willingness to murder his own children in the service of such knowledge – straight to the half-forgotten love that his sadistic narcissism perversely expresses, a love she has no reason to believe is there, except that she loves him.

This account of Grisilde's activity in unifying herself with Walter responds to the associations the Clerk draws between Grisilde and Job and between love and faith, and the contrasts he makes between a Grisildan heart that does not wait on reasons and a Walterish one that requires visible proof. But this is not the only account of loving union the Clerk imbeds in the tale. For the Walter Grisilde works to unify herself with is mostly not the better version of him to which she looks in her initial promise. After Walter is seized by his strange passion to tempt Grisilde, she no longer offers correction to whatever twisted thing he brings himself to say or do; she conforms herself to the pathological Walter expressed in his demands on her rather than the Walter she claimed to know in promising her love; becoming one with Walter does not involve looking past his failures of self-knowledge to the loving heart beneath, but taking those very failures as definitive of him, fixing him in his own perverse self-reifications. What is more, the Clerk's formulation of what Grisilde does changes from talk of her willing what Walter wills to that of her "conformynge hire to that the markys lyked" (IV.546). But the Clerk has made it absolutely clear that Walter's will, like anyone else's, is not definitively characterized by what *pleases* him: to think that it is is to miss the difference between willing something and being moved by a desire, and thus to miss the difference between Grisilde's strength of will and Walter's pathological weakness. In conforming herself to Walter's pleasure, then, Grisilde would seem to pursue a radically different version of loving union than the one she initially proposed and that informs the moral argument of the tale. Rather than suspending his perverse behavior and looking straight to the half-forgotten love that constitutes the only unfragmented will Walter could hope to have, she suspends the question of Walter's will entirely, looking instead to devote her love to the pathological pleasures that dominate him.

While there is nothing immediately erotic about what Grisilde does in offering herself up to Walter's perversity, this reformulation of what a loving union entails can help us understand the Clerk's aversion to the erotic and the broader ambivalence concerning sociality that that aversion expresses. For there was always something a bit chaste about the wall-like constancy of Grisilde's unconditional love as the Clerk mainly conceived it. Becoming one with Walter's pure potential for autonomy may have involved a lot of patient bearing up under the ugliness of his moral failures, but in constantly refusing to identify him with those failures, Grisilde was also closing herself off from that ugliness, never taking it as the object of her attachment; and in constantly refusing to identify herself with her pain, she was constantly closing herself off from Walter, never allowing him to see what he was doing to her. She was, as it were, keeping both Walter and herself clothed in the celestial raiment of her faith in him, covering the obscene nakedness of his compulsion by desire and of her suffering love for him; and in doing so, she was dictating the terms of her availability to him, pointing beyond their embodiment in ideology and desire to the moral aim that that embodiment both expresses and obscures. That kind of love is one for which an erotics is impossible; or, to put the point the other way, it is a love that tries to keep the possibility of an erotics at bay. But as Grisilde conforms herself to what pleases Walter, she foregoes her chaste withdrawal and opens herself to the possibility of an erotics, loving Walter in his shamed, naked failure to be the pure autonomous agent he wants to be; she attaches herself to the fleshy ugliness of his pathology rather than divorcing it from him and from her. And in doing so, she bares herself in her fleshy ugliness as well. For she is still on this account working to unify herself around this union, and forcibly excising everything about her that competes with it. Only now what she constitutes herself around is the embodiment of her promise in *this* man, and *this* history between them; and in doing that, she constitutes herself around Walter as a perverse love object, and constitutes herself as a lover of the perverse.

Throughout this chapter I have been arguing that the sense of scandal the *Clerk's Tale* generates is both an expression of and an attempt to handle what is disturbing about the ideal of unconditional love, however valued that ideal may be. Now we are in a position to see that what is disturbing about love in the tale cannot be restricted either to the politics in which it is imbedded or the monstrous sacrifices it may demand; it extends to the ontology of love itself. It is a necessary part of love's promise that it must be unconditional and autonomous. Yet as we have seen, unconditional autonomous love involves the erasure of the character that individuates the love object; it attaches itself only to the love object's pure abstract potential for autonomous love in his or her own right, a potential that is the same in everyone. And such love seems chaste, withdrawn from both the lover's and the beloved's embodiment in history, ideology, and desire. At the same time, then, it is a necessary part of love's promise that we love and be loved in terms of the specific characters we manage to have; but that also means embracing the interpellation of both ourselves and those we love into the ideological norms that historically organize character and desire. The ontology of love, then, is pitched on the Boethian antinomy we have been exploring throughout this book. That is why the scandal of the tale is both everywhere and nowhere in particular. For while there is scandal aplenty in the story the Clerk tells us, the core of that scandal does not lie in any local aberrations, however awful they may be. Nothing in the historical production and enactment of love stands at its source; but everything in love's histories is caught up in it. Scandal's energy in the tale derives from the unresolvable antinomy of love's promise, an antinomy we both fascinatedly stage for ourselves and seek to repress by projecting it on to a phantasmatic scene which we cannot quite convince ourselves is the scene of other people's traumas and perversions.

By staging and exploring love's antinomy, the *Clerk's Tale* provides further support for the idea that, even in poems that make philosophical arguments, what makes Chaucer's poetry philosophical are not the arguments themselves, but rather the relationship between those arguments and the unresolvable problems that motivate them. And, as I have also been arguing throughout this book, something similar can be said about Chaucer's use of character to explore complex psychological structures. Let me conclude this chapter and this book with some final comments along these lines concerning Walter and the Clerk.

In the analysis I have been pursuing of Walter's strange passion to test and tempt Grisilde, the first step was to explore the inner logic of Walter's tyrannical desire, a desire which, however self-defeating, provides Walter with the terms of his own preferred self-understanding. The second step was to connect that self-understanding with the muted, bent love and admiration he feels for Grisilde, and so to understand his testing and tempting as his abject way of trying to love her, and his shamed recoil from the unbearable demands unconditional love places on him. But if the ultimate source of scandal in the tale is not just our tragic inability to live up to the moral demands of love but an antinomy in love itself; and since Walter is the tale's embodiment of the perversity within the normal case of loving; then the energy of Walter's testing and tempting must ultimately derive from that antinomy as well. The resting place for an account of Walter's character thus lies in the way he exemplifies a philosophical problem rather than in some supposedly self-explanatory fact of his psychology; and, as I have been arguing throughout this book, that is what makes Chaucer's interest in character philosophical, and rather closer to allegory than we have usually supposed.

I argued earlier that Grisilde's will to the unconditional holds out the possibility of a fulfillment of Walter's autonomy; but given the depersonalizing trajectory of unconditional love, we can now see that in the very act of doing so it also entails an erasure of Walter's authority over his own identity. In waiting patiently for Walter to show his true self, Grisilde refuses to count Walter's own preferred self-understanding as expressive of him; what is more, her love sets aside everything about his character that distinguishes him as the particular person he is, attaching itself only to his pure abstract potential for autonomous love. In resisting Grisilde's love, then, Walter not only resists the loss of his authority over himself, he resists the loss of everything in him that is distinctively *him*, everything that goes beyond his characterization by a general human capacity. And this aspect of unconditional love also confirms Walter in his suspicion: for Grisilde's very success in the face of his tests, her ability to look past the particularity of his character to his potential as a lover, only seems to confirm that whatever she loves, she does not love *him*. She may love his abstract moral potential, but *he* seems to make so little impression on her; she hardly seems to care what he does; it is almost as though he were not there, doing all these terrible things to her. In this respect, Walter's torture of Grisilde can be read as an attempt to wring some kind of response out of her that shows that she cares about him and what he does, that she acknowledges him in his particularity, as though by doing so he could establish that what she loves is not an abstract capacity but *him*. Here, too, the terms in which Walter imagines confirming her love for him can only assure its failure: for the only way Walter is prepared to see that Grisilde cares about him and what he does would be for her to show that she no longer remains steadfast in the patient unconditionality that constitutes her love. But this is not only because Walter is a tyrant and a sadist, although that is a fair enough characterization of him; it is because his tyranny and sadism are his perverse expressions of a right but impossible feeling that for Grisilde truly to love him, her love must be unconditional, and yet at the same time it must pick him out as the particular person he is.

If Walter's tortures of Grisilde can thus be read as an attempt to break through her chaste withdrawal, there is yet another sense in which what Walter wants is to preserve that very chastity. For what I earlier referred to, in perhaps rather too clerkish a fashion, as love's obscenity – its dependency on perversion, its baring of an ugliness that is essential to desire and attachment – can afford us one further glimpse into what fuels Walter's behavior. Walter's simultaneous attempts to confirm Grisilde's unconditional love for him and tempt her to betray him are ways of trying to keep love's obscenity hidden, to preserve Grisilde as the site of an idealization that, even if it perpetually confirms him in his moral abjection, at least holds out the promise of an unpolluted ideal in relation to which he can understand his failures. According to Walter's logic, if Grisilde succeeds in living up to her promise of unconditionality, then she looks past his ugliness, thus confirming love's freedom from pathology; if she fails, then she confirms that she never really loved him. Either way, he never has to look at a love that involves devotion to his pathological pleasures, and so never has to look at those pleasures as the naked revelation of his character. This helps add further sense to a peculiar detail I have already discussed, namely the Clerk's description of Grisilde as "ay sad and constant as a wal" (IV.1047). Earlier in this chapter I followed one prevailing critical view in reading this phrase as a way of putting what taunts Walter in Grisilde's constancy, that in the face of his tyrannical desires her obedience to him looks as though it must harbor a hidden resistance.[19] That reading is true to much of the conceptual architecture of the tale and Walter's place in it; but as it turns out the Clerk uses this phrase to describe not Walter's fixation in tyrannical paranoia but rather his *release* from it.[20] It is only when he sees her wall-like constancy that he takes pity on her "wyfly stedfastnesse" (IV.1050) and calls a halt to his tests, declaring " 'this is ynogh, Grisilde myn' " (IV.1051). His tests are thus sufficient to allow him to address Grisilde with words of love only when her interiority appears blocked off from him by her constancy, when her idealized unconditionality removes the threat of his seeing her pathological attachment revealed, of seeing that what she loves in him is the very perversion that makes him want to stamp her love out.

It is clear why the Clerk would be as uncomfortable with the revelation of Grisilde's perverse attachment as Walter is; for on this second account, instead of love being the site of autonomy's embodiment, love's own embodiment appears as the site of its pathological nature. We can read in the Clerk's skinny asceticism and antieroticism another way Chaucer figures such discomfort, and thus as a link between the Clerk and the figure he uses to represent the condition he pitches his tale's moral argument against. But saying that does not diminish the force of the Clerk's moral argument in the tale; I think we should rather say that, under the pressure of imagining love's promise embodied, the Clerk has done even more to elaborate the depth of our conflicting intuitions about love than his moral argument can accommodate. On the one hand, we must understand love to be an unconditional and autonomous disposition of the will in order to distinguish it from the half-measures that usually go by its name, but that ultimately sink back as Walter does into a morass of fractured desire, in which love's true aim gets refigured as fearful egoism and the narcissistic wish to reduce the love object to an instrument. On the other hand, the very perfection of patient autonomous love involves a self-enclosure of its own, a way of chastely sealing yourself off from the love object and your own desire for it; and in order to recapture the love object in all its fleshy specificity we must readmit pathology to the scene. For in Grisilde's love of Walter's ugliness, just as much as in her unconditionality, the Clerk captures intuitions concerning love without which it becomes unrecognizable: that we love not just, as Plato would have it, the good in our beloved, but this particular person; that we love them not just in spite of, but because of, their embodiment in the desires, habits, history, and ideology that constitute their character. The philosophical achievement of the *Clerk's Tale*, like that of the *Canterbury Tales* as a whole, lies in its refusal of easy conceptual and moral solutions to these conflicts, its constant return to the rough ground of our daily engagements with them, and its steady attention to what makes those conflicts matter.

Notes

1 Eustache Deschamps, Thomas Hoccleve, and Thomas Usk offered early characterizations of Chaucer as a philosophical poet: see Deschamps, "Ballade adresée à Geoffrey Chaucer," in *Oeuvres complètes*, II. 138, Hoccleve, *Regement of Princes*, 76; Usk, *Testament of Love*, III.iv. 559–60. Kathryn L. Lynch discusses Chaucer's early reputation in this respect in *Chaucer's Philosophical Visions*, 5–9. Chaucer's reputation as a love poet was, and continues to be, even more ubiquitous.

2 By "practical reason" I mean simply reason as it pertains to action. This formulation is meant to be neutral with respect to the different understandings of practical reason developed in medieval and modern philosophy.

3 Carolyn Dinshaw, *Getting Medieval* and "Chaucer's Queer Touches." Other important contributions to a queer reading of Chaucer, and of medieval culture more broadly, include Bruce Holsinger, *Music, Body, and Desire in Medieval Culture*, especially 175–87 and 259–92; Glenn Burger and Steven F. Kruger, eds., *Queering the Middle Ages*; and Burger, *Chaucer's Queer Nation*.

4 Recent psychoanalytic work that has been particularly important to this project includes Leo Bersani, *Freudian Body*; Slavoj Žižek, *Metastases of Enjoyment* and *Plague of Fantasies*; and L. O. Aranye Fradenburg, *Sacrifice Your Love*. Such work comes from what we might call the speculative rather than diagnostic and therapeutic wing of psychoanalysis. Bersani is particularly helpful in discussing the tension in psychoanalysis between an impulse to radical speculation concerning the ontology of sexuality and the kind of theory conducive to diagnosis and therapy and associated with professional knowledge.

5 Peter Brown, *Body and Society* and "Bodies and Minds."

6 My understanding of Chaucer's moral seriousness, and of its relation to a philosophical poetry for which issues of poetic form are essential, has been shaped by the work of Anne Middleton, including "*Physician's Tale* and Love's Martyrs," "Idea of Public Poetry in the Reign of Richard II," "Chaucer's 'New Men' and the Good of Literature," and "War by other Means." Equally important to this book has been Middleton's work on the literary-philosophical project of Chaucer's great contemporary Langland, including "Narration and the Invention of Experience" and "William Langland's 'Kynde Name.'" I agree with Middleton that, precisely because the subsequent English literary tradition stems more directly from Chaucer and so has deeply shaped our reception of his work, in order to recover what Chaucer thought he was doing it can be helpful to think of him as being rather closer in his main concerns to Langland than we have tended to believe.

7 All citations from Chaucer's works are from the *Riverside Chaucer*, and will be given in the body of the text by reference to fragment and line numbers.

8 For some very different accounts of what this tradition meant for Chaucer, see Charles Muscatine, *Chaucer and the French Tradition*; Donald R. Howard, *Chaucer*, especially 134–42; James I. Wimsatt, *Chaucer and his French Contemporaries*; and Lee Patterson, *Chaucer and the Subject of History*, especially 49–61 and 296–304.

9 For the *De Secretis* and the commentary tradition that grew around it, see Helen Rodnite Lemay, *Women's Secrets*. For the application of coverture to marriage, see William Blackstone, *Commentaries on the Laws of England*, I: 430. Although Blackstone is writing considerably later than Chaucer, he is explaining what he takes to be a long-standing doctrine. Elizabeth Fowler cites several instances of its application in the fourteenth and fifteenth centuries, and argues for its relevance to Langland, in "Civil Death and the Maiden."

10 Perhaps the single greatest contribution to our sense of the nuances, limits, and contradictions in this ideology has been made by Caroline Walker Bynum, in *Jesus as Mother*, *Holy Feast and Holy Fast*, and *Fragmentation and Redemption*. Other excellent studies include Joan Cadden, *Meanings of Sex Difference in the Middle Ages*, Thomas Laqueur, *Making Sex*, especially 25–62; Danielle Jacquart and Claude Thomasset, *Sexuality and Medicine in the Middle Ages*; James A. Brundage, *Law, Sex, and Christian Society in Medieval Europe*; Ruth Mazo Karras, *Common Women*; R. Howard Bloch, *Medieval Misogyny and the Invention of Western Romantic Love*; Michael Camille, *Medieval Art of Love*; Fradenburg, *Sacrifice Your Love*; Fradenburg and Carla Freccero, eds, *Premodern Sexualities*; and Karma Lochrie, Peggy McCracken, and James A. Schultz, eds, *Constructing Medieval Sexuality*.

11 Besides those Chaucerian studies already cited, critical works that focus on the instabilities and opacities of this ideology include Caroline Dinshaw, *Chaucer's Sexual Poetics*; H. Marshall Leicester, Jr., *Disenchanted Self*; Elaine Tuttle Hansen, *Chaucer and the Fictions of Gender*; and Susan Crane, *Gender and Romance in Chaucer's* Canterbury Tales.

12 The best discussion of this scene in Boethian terms is V. A. Kolve, *Chaucer and the Imagery of Narrative*, 86–105.

13 Augustine's account of the "perversion of the will," derived from his argument for the insubstantiality of evil and directed against any account of evil as having its source in desire or the body as such, can be found throughout his writings. Two particularly acute discussions are in *Confessions*, 7.12–16 and *City of God*, 12.1–8.

14 The touchstone for the moralizing reading of Chaucer remains D. W. Robertson, *Preface to Chaucer*.

15 Of course, gender and sexuality are not the only topics on the table in this kind of work. There is also an extensive body of work on the discourses of normality and deviancy circulating around such phenomena as race, ethnicity, class, madness, disease, and criminality. While these discourses overlap with and inform each other, for historical reasons which I will soon suggest, gender and sexuality remain the most important territories for a study of medieval normativity.

16 Besides the three volumes of Foucault's *History of Sexuality*, work that has particularly informed my thinking on the normalization of gender and sexuality includes Judith Butler, *Gender Trouble*, *Bodies that Matter*, and *Psychic Life of Power*; Eve Kosofsky Sedgwick, *Epistemology of the Closet*; Lauren Berlant, *Queen of America Goes to Washington City*, and with Michael Warner, "Sex in Public"; and Warner, *Trouble with Normal*. A historical and theoretical caveat is in order here. Particularly in work

with strong allegiances to Canguilhem and Foucault, normativity is sometimes understood as a distinctively modern phenomenon, related to the rise of statistics and its ideological uses in the social sciences and by the nation-state. No doubt normativity does have such a function in modern western societies. But, as Michael Warner points out, such a function "rests . . . on a confusion between statistical norms and evaluative norms" (*Trouble with Normal,* 56); and statistical normativity lacks the resources to explain evaluative normativity. This book will focus on evaluative norms in both their moral and ideological aspects. The ideal of sexual renunciation for the medieval Christian subject, for instance, could hardly have been a statistical norm, and predated by some centuries the kind of normativity Canguilhem and Foucault discuss. Yet it was normative in both of the senses in which I use the term, in that it had both a moral authority for and an ideological power over those who lived in its shadow. Further, even the idea that normativity can in some instances be related to what most people do or think need not invoke the modern science of statistics. When Carolyn Dinshaw discusses queerness as "a relation to a norm" characterized by a "lack of fit" (*Getting Medieval,* 39), she depends on a notion of normativity that involves both majoritarian prejudice and moral and ideological evaluation. But this does not imply the specific classificatory practices, disciplinary apparatuses, and state ideologies Canguilhem and Foucault discuss.

17 The normativity in question here is *practical* normativity, the kind of concern to philosophical ethics and the theory of action. Recent philosophical works that have informed this project include Bernard Williams, *Ethics and the Limits of Philosophy* and *Shame and Necessity*; Harry Frankfurt, *Importance of What We Care About* and *Necessity, Volition, and Love*; Thomas Nagel, *View from Nowhere* and *Equality and Partiality*; and Christine Korsgaard, *Sources of Normativity* and *Creating the Kingdom of Ends*. I am also indebted to discussions on these topics with Jay Schleusener and Candace Vogler.

18 For Butler's formulation of the problem, see *Psychic Life of Power,* 10–18; for Williams's, see *Limits of Philosophy,* 132–73.

19 The other possibility is that she could take my comment as a joke; that is, she could read it as my way of acknowledging that I allowed ideology to speak for me and as me. Whether or not I could offer such a comment as a joke, and whether or not she could take it that way, would depend on the tenor of our relationship – among other things, on the amount of mutual trust we could rely on. In any case, the very possibility of a joke of this kind, like the possibility of the hurtfulness of such a comment, depends on a sense of Julia's question as asking for reasons for action.

20 The ease of such a conflation provides one reason why it can seem that invoking the irreducibility of agency involves a wish to preserve the liberal-bourgeois subject.

21 A lack of clarity concerning the distinction between explanations of action that appeal to causes and those that appeal to reasons is behind some of the confusions of interest to Wittgenstein in the *Philosophical Investigations*. For a classic philosophical discussion of the distinction in a Wittgensteinian vein, see Anscombe, *Intention*, especially 9–25. The other main tradition for thinking about this distinction is Kantian: see chapter three of Kant's *Groundwork of the Metaphysic of Morals*, and Korsgaard's discussions of Kant's "two standpoints" in *Kingdom of Ends,* 173–76, 200–09, and 370–78.

22 Sedgwick and Frank discuss the way Foucault's critique of the repressive hypothesis has been misread in terms that keep in place a simplistic hegemonic – subversive binary, in "Shame in the Cybernetic Fold." On Foucault's interest in ethics, see Arnold Davidson, "Archaeology, Genealogy, Ethics" and "Ethics as Ascetics"; Ian Hacking, "Self-Improvement"; and James Bernauer and Michael Mahon, "Ethics of Michel Foucault."

23 Foucault's most explicit statement of the importance of Nietzsche is "Nietzsche, Genealogy, History," in Foucault, *Language, Counter-Memory, Practice.*

24 Nietzsche, *Beyond Good and Evil*, section 188.

25 Ibid., section 224.

26 Nietzsche, *Genealogy of Morals*, section 18.

27 Augustine, *Confessions*, 10.30. I have followed Peter Brown's translation, *Body and Society*, 407.

28 Brown, "Bodies and Minds," 481.

29 Paul, Romans 2:14.

30 Paul, I Corinthians 7:9.

31 These commitments continued to be part of the dominant theological tradition into the later Middle Ages and beyond. For Aquinas's articulation of them, which remains central to modern Catholic doctrine, see for instance *Summa Contra Gentiles*, chapters 122–26.

32 This is one of the main reasons Foucault gives for the normalization of sexuality in nineteenth-century Europe. See *History of Sexuality*, 115–50.

33 Augustine discusses human life as a kind of living death throughout Books 12 to 14 of *City of God.*

34 Much of the work on medieval gender and sexuality cited above might be described in such a way, but the description would be particularly applicable to the works of Brown, Bynum and Bloch. Mark Jordan's *Invention of Sodomy in Christian Theology* also fits this characterization, as he notes in his introduction (2).

35 Most of the phenomena mentioned above are discussed in secondary sources already cited. For the eroticism of clerical and monastic friendship, see John Boswell, *Christianity, Social Tolerance, and Homosexuality*, especially 187–94 and 216–28. For the medieval French interest in erotic subjectivity, see Michael Zink, *Invention of Literary Subjectivity.* For the invention of western romantic love, besides Bloch see C. S. Lewis, *Allegory of Love.* For the importance of the rediscovery of Aristotle for late medieval intellectual culture, see *Cambridge History of Later Medieval Philosophy*; particularly relevant are the essays on philosophy of mind, theory of action, and ethics.

36 Foucault, *Use of Pleasure*, 8.

37 Such a claim runs counter to impulses in a number of critical quarters. The "medieval" tends to function in our intellectual culture as an all-purpose contrast to a sense of our own modernity, which is taken to have its roots in a decisive historical break supposed to have taken place in the Renaissance, or perhaps with the Enlightenment and the rise of industrialized capitalism in the eighteenth century. This tendency to mark the medieval as radical other, where it does not lead to an outright dismissal of the Middle Ages as unworthy of serious critical engagement, makes it look as though the available inter-pretive options are a cold respect for medieval alterity, antiquarian enthusiasm for its obscurity, and anachronistic disregard for its cultural specificity. For discussions of the way this tendency appears in both reactionary and radical critics – and arguments that it thoughtlessly replicates Renaissance ideology – see Lee Patterson, "On the Margin," and David Aers, "Whisper in the Ear of Early Modernists."

38 For the pedantic eagle, see *House of Fame*, 499–1090; for the wicker cage of tidings, see *House of Fame*, 1916–2158.

39 Patterson, *Subject of History*, 165–230.

40 The humanist or New Critical tradition celebrated such a figure in works such as E. Talbot Donaldson's *Speaking of Chaucer*; Howard and many others belong squarely in this tradition. Many critics continue to share a sense that, if such a view can no longer

be upheld, it does characterize Chaucer's view of himself: see for instance Hansen's *Fictions of Gender.*

41 On this see also Fradenburg, *Sacrifice Your Love,* 79–80.

42 Patterson, *Subject of History,* 167. Patterson himself is hardly an advocate of the genial view of Chaucer.

43 This is more or less the position taken by both Patterson in *Subject of History* and David Wallace in *Chaucerian Polity.* See especially Patterson's account of Boethius and Chaucer's relation to the *Consolation of Philosophy,* in *Subject of History,* 75–78 and 152–53, and Wallace's account of Petrarchan philosophical idealism and its links to tyranny in *Chaucerian Polity,* 261–98. I think both Patterson and Wallace are substantially right about many of Chaucer's underlying commitments. But, as I will argue most extensively in chapter three below, many of those commitments are themselves philosophical and Boethian.

44 Maurice Keen, *English Society in the Later Middle Ages.* Besides the work of Patterson, Middleton, Wallace, and Keen, for what follows I also draw on Paul Strohm, *Social Chaucer,* especially 1–23; Howard's *Chaucer;* and Derek Pearsall, *Life of Geoffrey Chaucer.*

45 Historically, the hero of such a view of philosophy is Socrates, or, for those who take the dialogue form as philosophically significant, Plato. The figure most associated with such a view in modern philosophy is Wittgenstein, whose major work, the *Philosophical Investigations,* relentlessly probes the impulse to offer bogus clarity in the form of theory, and insistently returns to what he calls the "rough ground" of the competing intuitions that such theory must repress. My sense of Wittgenstein has been shaped by the work of Stanley Cavell, especially *Claim of Reason.* Cavell's work on Shakespeare in *Disowning Knowledge* has also shaped my sense of how to read literature's philosophical engagements.

1 NATURALISM AND ITS DISCONTENTS IN THE *MILLER'S TALE*

1 As early as 1948 Paul Beichner noted the importance of the scene's baring of "the natural" for an understanding of the functions Alisoun and Absolon play in the tale: see "Characterization in the *Miller's Tale.*" Charles Muscatine, in an account that was to set the terms for almost all subsequent discussion of the tale, placed the scene in relation to a more fully elaborated sense of the tale's literary and conceptual naturalism and its "quiting" of the *Knight's Tale:* see *Chaucer and the French Tradition,* 222–30. By the 1970s the terms of Muscatine's account had become quite widely accepted, and critics could make such offhand remarks as Alfred E. David's that Absolon's punishment is to "discover reality by kissing his lady's ass" with confidence that they were invoking a widely held sense of the Miller's conceptual commitments; see *Strumpet Muse,* 98. V. A. Kolve has offered perhaps the richest account of the scene's and the tale's naturalism in *Imagery of Narrative,* 158–216, especially 193–97. Even the patristic critical tradition, with its concern for a moralizing interpretation that would seem to have little in common with Muscatinian humanism, shares a basic sense of the scene's function and conceptual structure: see for instance D. W. Robertson's claim that Absolon's kiss cures a misguided love that is essentially the same in Absolon, Nicholas, Palamon, and Arcite by showing the true nature of that love's object, in *Preface to Chaucer,* 469.

2 The phrase "the real nature of what he sought" is Kolve's: see *Imagery of Narrative,* 197.

3 Kolve's phrase is in *Imagery of Narrative*, 158; Muscatine's is in *Chaucer and the French Tradition*, 224.

4 For various formulations of these questions, see Elaine Tuttle Hansen, *Fictions of Gender*, 223–36; H. Marshall Leicester, Jr., "Newer Currents in Psychoanalytic Criticism," 486–90; Karma Lochrie, *Covert Operations*, 164–76; and Glenn Burger, *Chaucer's Queer Nation*, 1–36, especially 28–36. I have cast the questions in a way meant to be neutral with respect to the rather different formulations of them, and the quite different senses of their import, in each of these critics. My purpose in doing so is to suggest the very broad way attention to questions of gender and desire problematizes the Miller's naturalism; my own sense of exactly how those problems should be formulated will emerge over the course of the chapter.

5 The best recent work on the identificatory lability of desire suggests that it would be a mistake to look down on naturalism as mere false consciousness, and that this mistake is closely related to a critical reliance on the gesture of exposure. See for instance Sedgwick, *Epistemology of the Closet*, especially 41; Sedgwick and Frank, "Shame in the Cybernetic Fold," 496–522; and Leo Bersani, *Homos*, especially 57. In the critical discussion of the *Miller's Tale*, Leicester's and Burger's accounts do the most to explore the ways gender and sexuality lend themselves to an impulse to exposure that misreads, or at least under-reads, the phenomena it means to describe.

6 The phrase is Muscatine's, in *Chaucer and the French Tradition*, 223.

7 For articulations of the conceptual structure of the Miller's naturalism, see especially the discussions by Muscatine, David, and Kolve cited above.

8 Leicester, "Gender and Desire," 489. While I am deeply indebted to Leicester's often brilliant reading of the tale, the different places he and I give to the idea of the world as a plaything of one's projects can help to clarify what distinguishes my argument from a psychoanalytic one. Leicester uses the phrase in discussing "the sort of pleasure that psychoanalysis conceives as stemming from a time before the self and the world were perceived as different, when the world was the plaything of one's projects, underwritten by the complete yet undemanding love of a mother who also was not differentiated from the self" (489). For Leicester, this sort of pleasure in an adult such as the Miller involves a boundary-destroying *jouissance* that looks forward to a world of desire "beyond the phallus" (489) and backwards to the infant's seamless connection to its mother; as such, it is the sign of the Miller's attachment to desires and identifications that are inappropriate to the Oedipalized identity in which his official views of gender and desire participate. As my citation of Leicester's line in my layout of the Miller's naturalism is meant to suggest, my own sense is that, however disturbing to Oedipalized masculinity the idea of the world as plaything may be, the Miller is pretty up-front in his commitment to it, and it functions as a central pillar of his official views of gender and desire rather than a challenge to them. As I will argue, the basic disturbance to those views comes from the necessity of living in a world that is *not* such a plaything, especially when the context for that necessity is one in which we are brought flesh-up against another who is not a mere plaything. Relying on the explanatory value of a psychoanalytic narrative of sexual development, even a post-Freudian one, such as that of Hélène Cixous, which attends to the value of non-Oedipalized pleasure, obscures the structure of the Miller's investment in and anxieties about normative masculinity. In what follows I will discuss those investments and anxieties as they emerge from the intersection of the Miller's naturalist theory of action and identity with a set of conventional views of gender difference that were widespread in the Middle Ages and familiar to Chaucer.

9 Kolve, *Imagery of Narrative*, 185.

10 The distinction between practical and speculative reason is a commonplace of medieval thought, inherited from classical philosophy, and particularly Aristotle. For the paradigmatic medieval articulation of the distinction, see Thomas Aquinas, *Summa Theologiae*, I–II.90–94.

11 For Palamon's envy of the animals, see I.1303–33.

12 The descriptive density of the tale, and its purpose in supporting a naturalistic view, is particularly central to the accounts of Muscatine and Kolve.

13 For an account of the importance of the term *hende* in the tale, as meaning clever, skillful, handy, and ready-to-hand, see Donaldson, *Speaking of Chaucer*, 13–29, especially 17–19.

14 This one remaining function for reason to play on a naturalistic view – the function of allowing the human creature a sense of gratitude and the capacity to articulate it – helps account for Kolve's sense of the tale's sweetness and childlike innocence.

15 Muscatine, *Chaucer and the French Tradition*, 224.

16 Kolve, *Imagery of Narrative*, 160.

17 For a fuller discussion of the problems normative naturalism has in cashing out its own claims to normativity, see Korsgaard, *Sources of Normativity*, especially 29–30, 145–46, and 160–61.

18 What follows is an attempt to imagine a tale which really would be, as Kolve says of the *Miller's Tale*, "a counter-vision of human experience" to the Knight's.

19 Kolve's account of the tropological function of animals and children in the tale is in this sense particularly apt: they figure the condition of something like human action, minus the burden of the normative problem in its adult form, to which, among other things, our notions of accountability and responsibility belong. (See Kolve, *Imagery of Narrative*, 167, 215.)

20 The discussions of Hansen and Lochrie have done the most to bring out the antifeminism that coincides with the Miller's attitude of erotic generosity, and that was for many years naturalized in the appreciative rhetoric of male critics of the tale. As I argue later in this chapter, however, I do not think such antifeminism constitutes the Miller's totalized view of women or of masculine desire for women; it is rather intertwined with a nonobjectifying view of and desire for women as subjects and agents that is no less deeply the Miller's, even if he marginalizes it and lacks the terms to articulate it.

21 I owe the example of the magic refrigerator, as well as the prompting to clarify why this attitude in its application to a sexual partner finally is not a form of rational generosity, to Richard Strier.

22 Muscatine, *Chaucer and the French Tradition*, 230.

23 This is a familiar duplicity in naturalistic discourse, which often makes out "the natural" to be a justifying category while having no recourse to explain the existence of what it takes to be unjustified actions or desires other than their natural existence as perversions.

24 I am adapting a phrase from Eve Sedgwick, and pursuing a line of thinking about secrecy, interiority, prohibition, and knowledge suggested by Sedgwick and Michel Foucault; see Sedgwick, *Epistemology of the Closet*, and Foucault, *History of Sexuality*. My understanding of the issues for which "the closet" has become such a commanding trope – particularly my sense of what it means to be caught in the grip of a reifying picture of interiority or subjectivity, together with the thought that "epistemology" quite precisely fails to capture what is fundamentally at issue in our relations to our inner lives – also owes a great deal to Wittgenstein's *Philosophical Investigations* and to Stanley Cavell's *Claim of Reason*. My use of the trope of the closet in this premodern context does not imply that I take the Miller's situation to be simply a version of the problems Foucault and Sedgwick

discuss concerning the interiority of erotic life in the nineteenth and twentieth centuries. The thought of a secret interior space in the *Miller's Tale* is part of a very different set of cultural practices and authoritative discourses in which sex and sexuality play different roles than they do in modern western culture. In particular, while I will argue that homoerotic desire is at issue here, it is not at issue in the same way as it is in the cases Foucault and Sedgwick discuss: it is not linked to the existence of, or worries over the existence of, a distinct type of human creature (or what Foucault calls a "species-being") known as "the homosexual." But neither is homoerotic desire in the *Miller's Tale* simply an instance of that other, medieval category, "the sodomitical." The resistance of homoeroticism to categorization in terms of a clear and distinct kind of sexuality or a desire for a particular kind of act is rather what marks it as queer, and more than that, as a sign that the "normal" desires expressed in the tale cannot firmly be distinguished from the queer. Homoeroticism in the *Miller's Tale* – and, as I will argue in chapter four below, in the basic structures of courtly or romance masculinity – thus provides an instance of what Carolyn Dinshaw calls the "inextricability and even, at times, [the] indistinguishability" of the normative and the deviant in Chaucer's poetry and in medieval culture more broadly (*Getting Medieval*, 13; see especially her discussion of Chaucer at 113–42, in which she argues that "perversion inheres in the normative sexuality" represented in the opening lines of the *General Prologue* and elsewhere in the *Tales* [126]). More pointedly, such homoeroticism is an instance of what Glenn Burger calls "the queer torsions produced by the production of hegemonic masculinities in the *Tales*," torsions which underscore the "dangerous proximity with the proper" of such queerness (*Chaucer's Queer Nation*, 121–22).

25 Muscatine and Kolve capture this aspect of the representation of Alisoun in referring to her respectively as a "delectable little animal" (*Chaucer and the French Tradition*, 230) and as "the object of all desires" (*Imagery of Narrative*, 162). Despite the differences among the accounts of Hansen, Leicester, Lochrie, and Burger, each is concerned, as I am here, to register both this function of the figure of Alisoun and its incoherence.

26 Many critics have recognized Alisoun's function as the embodiment of the Miller's ideal. Muscatine refers to her as "the one precious illusion in the poem" (*Chaucer and the French Tradition*, 229); Kolve says that "the way in which [Alisoun] moves... decisively establishes [the tale's] underlying ethos" (*Imagery of Narrative*, 162); and Patterson calls her "the norm by which we are invited to understand her world" and the tale's "presiding spirit" (*Subject of History*, 286). Patterson further registers the fact that this ought to be a surprise given the tale's presiding gender ideology – "however ungraspable, she remained an object" – and that this surprise is related to the limitations internal to the tale's naturalistic views.

27 Critics who have read the scene as one of anal penetration or sodomy include Dolores Warwick Frese, "Homoerotic Underside"; David Williams, "Radical Therapy in the Miller's Tale"; Hansen, *Fictions of Gender*, 232–36; and Lochrie, *Covert Operations*, 174. Frese helpfully connects the moment to Edward II's reputed predilection for sodomy and Higden's story of his being "sleyne with a hoote broche putte thro the secret place posterialle" ("Homoerotic Underside," 147.) While Kolve does not explicitly claim that the scene involves anal penetration, he describes Absolon's colter as "aimed at this other orifice," and compares it to "images in which persons shoot with bow and arrow at a bared bum, or attack such a target with spear or pole" (*Imagery of Narrative*, 192). Winthrop Wetherbee also notes the scene's "strong hint of sexual violence" in *Canterbury Tales*, 59.

28 In what follows I am indebted to Burger's discussion in *Chaucer's Queer Nation*, 23–36. My argument in this chapter might be taken as a way of bringing out the philosophical

stakes in Burger's claim that this scene and the tale as a whole give expression both to a hegemonic sadistic heteromasculinity and to a group of less easily categorizable desires which, with respect to that hegemony, appear as masochistic, shameful, and queer. I am, however, less confident than Burger that masochism and shame, or more broadly a Foucauldian appeal to "bodies and pleasures," provides a site of liberatory potential opposed to a sadism that is more closely tied to hegemonic norms. That is partly because on the account I offer, sadism itself cannot finally be understood in terms of those norms, and partly because, while as Burger argues masochism and shame can open up the hegemonic subject to disavowed possibilities of identification and desire, they can also remain as deeply implicated in hegemonic norms as a sadistic wish for control. Where I am in complete agreement with Burger is in seeing the masochistic, shameful, and queer as internal features of all sexuality rather than as classificatory categories that pick out the essential difference between distinct groups of people.

29 Hansen has done the most to bring out this feature of the scene, and my sense of it and its import for understanding the tale as a whole owes much to her discussion.

30 Both Kolve (*Imagery of Narrative*, 188) and Leicester ("Gender and Desire," 484) note this.

31 This, I take it, is the thought behind Muscatine's claim that "the ethic of the poem" is one of "assault" (*Chaucer and the French Tradition*, 227), and Kolve's that fabliau "admits no goals beyond self-gratification, revenge, or social laughter" (*Imagery of Narrative*, 160).

32 I do not mean to suggest that a full and satisfying account of altruism could be given in these terms; just that, given the thought that there is a clean distinction to be made between a concern for oneself and a concern for others, altruism will easily appear as motivated only by a concern for others. The best account of altruism I know argues that it cannot be understood in these terms: see Thomas Nagel, *Possibility of Altruism*. Much classical and medieval discussion of friendship makes it clear that, at least in the case of such intimate relations with others, there is no clean split of the kind to be made: see for instance Cicero's *De Amicitia* for a discussion which would have been familiar to Chaucer, and which I will take up in chapter four below.

33 The depth of the Miller's inability in this respect is responsible, I think, for what Leicester describes as the "[extraordinary] amount of slandering against John in the criticism" ("Gender and Desire," 484): the Miller's lack of focus makes it hard even to notice that John is a problem, so we have mostly just taken the Miller's characterizations of him at face value.

34 John Ganim notes the pun on "touching" here, as well as the further thought implied by the line's "thingifying" language that what John and Nicholas are imagined as touching is in the first place Alisoun's body, in *Chaucerian Theatricality*, 118.

35 The point is noted by Leicester, "Gender and Desire," 485, 494.

36 There could be some such thrill in looking at the sheep, but it would be parasitic on the thrill of looking at a human; it would involve imagining the sheep as looking back at you, or enjoying the proximity of the sheep to the capacity to do so, and finding excitement in that capacity being as it were narrowly averted. A scopophilic eroticism directed straight at animals would be a hyperbolic version of the eroticism directed towards the figure of Alisoun in the text, expressing a naturalism turned even more squarely away from the human conditions that give rise to it than the Miller's is.

37 In this context, another bit of Alisoun's portrait – the Miller's enthusiastically self-promoting claim that "In al this world, to seken up and doun, / Ther nys no man so wys that koude thenche / So gay a popelote [i.e., "little doll"] or swich a wenche" (I. 3252–54) – reads like a claim to having out-Pygmalioned Pygmalion.

38 I do not mean to imply that homoeroticism itself is necessarily narcissistic. The issue here is how a particular form of homoeroticism gets produced by a more broadly narcissized eroticism.

39 Leicester, "Gender and Desire," 486.

40 As Leicester argues, a reading of psychoanalytic thinking about castration anxiety, in particular in its Lacanian formulations, should also examine the tropological value of castration. An emphasis on castration as trope in turn suggests that psychoanalytic thinking about castration anxiety might be less a matter of a technical analysis that stands or falls with a specific theory of sexual development than it is sometimes taken to be.

41 The thought goes back at least as far as Ovid, who represents Narcissus as in recoil from Echo's love.

42 Patterson notes the Miller's surprising sympathy towards John and the problem of reconciling it with his more obvious hostility towards the character (*Subject of History*, 270–73).

2 NORMATIVE LONGING IN THE *KNIGHT'S TALE*

1 On the Knight's social and ethical nostalgia and its relation to his sense of moral incoherence, see Patterson, *Subject of History*, 165–230.

2 Critics who have emphasized the aestheticizing objectification of Emily and her availability to voyeuristic masculine desire include David Aers, *Chaucer*, 77–80; Angela Jane Weisl, *Conquering the Reign of Femeny*, 54–61; and Laura L. Howes, *Chaucer's Gardens*, 87–94. In linking the aesthetic and erotic formalism of this portrait to a fantasy of autonomy, I argue that, even for the Knight, such objectification is problematic from the start. For a psychoanalytic account of Emily's objectification that helpfully resists a too easy recognition of the phenomenon, see Fradenburg's discussion of Emily as "a captivating image of freedom" who is nevertheless "always already subdued," in *Sacrifice Your Love*, 164. Leicester provides a helpful discussion of the tendencies in the *Knight's Tale* that run counter to the objectification of the feminine, in *Disenchanted Self*, especially 232–36 and 267–94. My understanding of Chaucer's critical interest in the relation between aesthetic and erotic formalism in courtly literature has also been significantly shaped by Patterson, *Subject of History*, especially 52–54.

3 Kolve emphasizes the point and stresses Emily's function as a figure for autonomy in *Imagery of Narrative*, 86–90.

4 The most substantial accounts of the Knight's Thesean ethos and its limitations are in Kolve, *Imagery of Narrative*, 85–157; Patterson, *Subject of History*, 165–230; Wallace, *Chaucerian Polity*, 104–24; and Fradenburg, *Sacrifice Your Love*, 155–75. Kolve, Patterson, and Wallace locate the troubles that plague the Knight in ideology conceived of as a discrete cultural phenomenon, pertaining either to the pre-Christian world represented in the text (Kolve) or the sociopolitical world inhabited by the Knight (Patterson and Wallace). While I agree that the Knight's ideology is problematic, and that it is related to what is problematic in his culture, my argument here and in this book as a whole is that such ideology is a product not only of the sociopolitical world but of the ontology of agency itself. In this turn to the ontological sources of ideology my account resembles Fradenburg's, although we provide different accounts of what the ontological problem finally is.

5 Kolve, Patterson, and Wallace in one way or another suggest that the critique of the Knight entails an accusation of rationalism. For Patterson this includes an association of

rationalism with a kind of social and aesthetic narcissism, and for Wallace it includes an association of rationalism with a kind of political narcissism. While I think the accusation of rationalism is hasty, I think Patterson and Wallace are right that a species of narcissism is at issue here.

6 I borrow the language of reflective endorsement from Korsgaard, *Sources of Normativity*. As Korsgaard suggests, the notion that reflective endorsability defines the conditions of decisive action has its roots in Aristotelian ethics.

7 Here too Chaucer and the Knight are developing essentially Aristotelian ideas. See Aristotle's comments on the nature of a good character throughout the *Nicomachean Ethics*, especially II.1–III.5, and his ongoing distinction between his claim that virtue involves a rational principle and the Socratic, rationalist claim that virtue consists in knowing the good (as for instance in VI.13.)

8 See Patterson, *Subject of History*, 165–230 for a fuller discussion of the contrasts between Athenianness and Thebanness in the tale, and 47–83 for a broader discussion of Chaucer's interest in the trope of "Thebanness."

9 Theseus could thus be read as a type – although, in significant ways, a flawed one – of Aristotelian *megalopsychia*; see *Nicomachean Ethics*, IV.3.

10 A number of critics have found Theseus's violent anger and what some suppose to be his despotic tendencies to be the dark side of his noble designs. The view traces back to Elizabeth Salter, *Knight's Tale and Clerk's Tale*, 9–37; more recent examples include David Aers, *Chaucer, Langland, and the Creative Imagination*, 174–95 and Leicester, *Disenchanted Self*, 223 *et passim*. Fradenburg helpfully resists the separation of Thesean nobility and violence into different "sides," however closely related: see *Sacrifice Your Love*, 159–60ff.

11 For discussions of the links among identification, desire, and the constitution of the will, see Frankfurt, *Importance of What We Care About*, especially 58–68 and 159–76.

12 This is one of the crucial differences between classical and medieval moral psychology and the psychology we have inherited from the empiricist tradition, according to which desires, emotions, passions, and the like are distinct psychic states which reason can only approve or disapprove of.

13 The view goes back at least to Muscatine, *Chaucer and the French Tradition*, and is shared by such critics as Kolve and Patterson, even if they find the contrast more problematic than did Muscatine.

14 The most extensive discussion is in Kolve, *Imagery of Narrative*, 136–49; see also Salter, *Knight's Tale and Clerk's Tale*, 34–36; Aers, *Creative Imagination*, 188–95; Patterson, *Subject of History*, 202–03; Leicester, *Disenchanted Self*, 359–71.

15 See Crane, *Gender and Romance*, 79–80 and Wallace, *Chaucerian Polity*, 105–06 and 110–14.

16 See Crane, *Gender and Romance*, 20–23. For a more optimistic reading of Theseus's internalization of feminine pity, see Jill Mann, *Geoffrey Chaucer*, 173, 176, 179–81.

17 For a discussion of the way such a normative ground differs from those usually associated with autonomy, see Harry Frankfurt, *Necessity, Volition, and Love*, 129–41.

3   AGENCY AND DIALECTIC IN THE *CONSOLATION OF PHILOSOPHY*

1 While Kolve, Patterson, and Fradenburg discuss the *Consolation* in relation to the *Canterbury Tales*, only Kolve does so at any length. Dinshaw, Aers, Leicester, Hansen, Strohm, Crane, Wallace, and Burger mention it only in passing.

2 For the first of these views, see Robertson, *Preface to Chaucer*, 472–74. For the second, see Patterson, *Subject of History*, 73–78. For the moderate view, see Donaldson, *Speaking of Chaucer*, 84–101.

3 Wetherbee, *Platonism and Poetry*, especially 74–82.

4 Seth Lerer, *Boethius and Dialogue*.

5 The literature on Platonic dialectic is enormous, and of course has a history of disagreements of its own. For some helpful studies of Platonic dialectic, see Gregory Vlastos, "Socratic Elenchus"; G. R. F. Ferrari, *Listening to the Cicadas*; and Michael Frede, "Literary Form of the *Sophist.*"

6 Daniel Westberg, *Right Practical Reason*, chapter 7, "The Distinctiveness of Thomist Psychology" (95–115), discusses Aquinas's place in medieval moral psychological work generally, and underscores how different his view is from the paradigmatic empiricist one advanced by Hume. Chapter 8, "Stages in Human Action" (119–35), gives an account of how Thomas's moral psychology derives from his analysis of action. I also owe a great deal of my understanding of these matters to conversations with Candace Vogler, and to her discussions of Thomistic ethics and psychology in *Reasonably Vicious*.

7 The ultimate source is Aristotle's argument concerning *eudaimonia* in *Nicomachean Ethics*, especially I.1–12.

8 The idea that agents pursue ends under the aspect of some good, as well as the stronger one that there is something that constitutes the good as such, has its source in the opening of Aristotle's *Nicomachean Ethics*. For Aquinas's discussion of the first, narrower claim, see *Summa Theologiae*, I–II. qu. 8. Even that claim seems counter-intuitive from the perspective of modern empiricist and postempiricist philosophical psychology; see for instance the objections raised by Bernard Williams to Aristotle's version of the argument, in *Ethics and the Limits of Philosophy*, 58. Candace Vogler offers an excellent discussion of the argument in its Thomistic elaboration in *Reasonably Vicious*; see especially 26–52 and 53–73.

9 This is not to discount the importance of Stoicism to Boethius, although more crucial to my purposes are Boethius's commitments to a Platonist metaphysics and an Aristotelian theory of action. For an account of Boethius's Stoicism, see Marcia Colish, *Stoic Tradition*, II: 280–90. My point above is that too thin a reading of the happiness argument produces a hyperbolic version of Stoicism that verges on nonsense. More generally, the idea of Boethius as a Stoic depends on taking Philosophy's lessons on Fortune and the transitoriness of earthly goods as recommending a withdrawal from passionate attachments and the self-understandings such attachments encourage. As I will argue later in this chapter, while the *Consolation* does express the value of such a withdrawal, it also expresses the impoverished notion of selfhood such a goal entails. Boethius should thus in my view be understood not as a Stoic *per se*, but rather as a philosopher who takes the measure both of Stoicism's appeal and of its limitations.

10 Anthony Kenny offers a criticism of Aristotle's argument quite like the one I imagine above, in "Happiness."

11 *Felicitas* and *beatitudo* are the two terms in the *Consolation* routinely translated as "happiness." The second becomes in effect a technical term that analytically replaces the more colloquial first.

12 For Augustine's discussion of perversion of the will, see for instance *City of God*, 12.6–8.

13 All citations from the *Consolation* are from Boethius, *The Theological Tractates and the Consolation of Philosophy*. Translations are from *The Consolation of Philosophy*, trans. Richard Green. Since Green's translation is somewhat free, I have provided my own

translations at times when the precise sense of the original is particularly important to my argument.

14 This is one point at which a Boethian, and for that matter Augustinian, psychology yields the kind of complexities we tend to associate with psychoanalysis. See for instance Žižek's Augustinian definition of the fetish as "a 'regressive' shift of focus towards a 'lower' and partial element which conceals (and at the same time designates) the true point of reference," in *Plague of Fantasies*, 124.

15 In returning to the constellation of topics informing chapter one above, I am suggesting how the critical procedures of that chapter respond to the main intellectual traditions to which we have always thought Chaucer belongs. I am also offering further support for my claim in that chapter that "naturalism" does not stand for some distinct conceptual or moral error, but is rather something deep and in a sense inescapable.

16 Peter Brown's discussion, throughout *Body and Society*, of the long Christian investment in the trope of world rejection is relevant here; like Brown, I think of this investment as considerably more than a sign of moralistic crabbiness or dualistic self-hatred. The above account is meant in part to suggest the philosophical weight that such a trope could bear in the Middle Ages.

17 Freud, "Mourning and Melancholia," in *Standard Edition*.

18 On Chaucer's interest in this territory, see Lee Patterson, "Writing Amorous Wrongs"; Louise O. Fradenburg, " 'Voice Memorial' "; and, more obliquely but as a result more elaborately, Fradenburg, *Sacrifice Your Love*.

19 The point is stressed by Lerer, *Boethius*, 134–54.

20 D. P. Simpson, *Cassell's Latin Dictionary*.

21 This argument is in V.pr. 4–6.

22 This is Donald Davidson's formulation of what he calls "the myth of the subjective." On Davidson's account, this is a founding myth of empiricist psychology; to the extent that this is so, it suggests why premodern psychology is so difficult for us to get a handle on. See Davidson, "Myth of the Subjective," in *Subjective, Intersubjective, Objective*, 39–52.

23 Again, a shift away from empiricist psychology allows for the recovery of psychological structures that can seem to us to require psychoanalytic articulation; I have lifted the italicized phrase from Žižek's account of the structure of fantasy, in *Plague of Fantasies*, 119.

24 Kant's argument to this effect is in the *Groundwork*; the works already cited by Korsgaard and Nagel offer contemporary versions of such an argument.

25 See Williams, *Shame and Necessity*, 158–59; other relevant discussions by Williams include *Limits of Philosophy*, 174–202 and *Moral Luck*, 1–19.

26 On this point, besides the work of Williams see Frankfurt, *Importance of What We Care About*, 80–94 and *Necessity, Volition, and Love*, 155–80.

27 My articulation of an antinomy at the heart of agency is an attempt to hold in place what I find valuable in both the Kantian and the neo-Aristotelian strains of thought I have been citing. I hope it is clear that I mean to align these strains of thought, albeit roughly, with what I began by describing as the Boethian and Thesean strains of thought in the *Knight's Tale*; although I also hope it is clear that on the account I am proposing neither Boethius nor Theseus can simply be identified with the strain of thought to which they give dominant expression. My account of the antinomy is perhaps closest to that of Nagel in *View from Nowhere*, 110–37.

28 Bersani, *Freudian Body*, 41.

29 Lee Patterson, "Chaucer's Pardoner on the Couch."

30 Patterson's essay gives extensive citation to antipsychoanalytic literature, which I will not reproduce here. It should be noted that the critiques Patterson invokes have not

gone without a response. For one salient example that focuses, as I do not, on the question of Freud's relation to clinical evidence, see David Sachs, "In Fairness to Freud." For another example that focuses both on questions of evidence and on the tension between the professionalizing goals of psychoanalysis, which tend towards the kind of reductiveness Patterson critiques, and the philosophical goal of understanding the complexity of human desire, see Jonathan Lear, *Open Minded*, especially 16–32.

31 The citation is from Patterson, "Pardoner on the Couch," 651. The above characterization of Patterson's argument summarizes his key points on 639–56.

32 For Foucault's discussion of "scientia sexualis" see *History of Sexuality*, I: 53–73.

33 Bersani, *Freudian Body*, 3. Lear's *Open Minded*, cited above, also contributes to an understanding of this tension.

34 For the game of fort/da see *Beyond the Pleasure Principle*, 13–17. For mourning and melancholia, see "Mourning and Melancholia," in *Standard Edition*; for the denaturalizing of the relation between sexual instinct and sexual aim, see *Three Essays on the Theory of Sexuality*, especially "Essay One: The Sexual Aberrations," 1–38. Arnold Davidson offers a clear formulation of the latter argument in "How to do the History of Psychoanalysis." That argument has been immensely productive for a queer theory that has rejected the normalizing force of the core principles of psychoanalysis as articulated by Patterson.

35 In developing the idea of a "constitutive masochism" I am responding, although in a somewhat different vein, to a proposal made by Jean Laplanche and Leo Bersani, to the effect that masochism is constitutive of sexuality (see Laplanche, *Life and Death in Psychoanalysis*, especially 87–97; Bersani, *Freudian Body*, especially 29–47). For Laplanche and Bersani, the constitutive nature of masochism can be traced back to the infant's susceptibility to being violently but pleasurably overwhelmed by stimuli it lacks the ego structures necessary to organize and resist. On this account, all of adult sexuality, not just some presumably marginal "perversion," is structured around the urge masochistically to repeat such pleasurable self-shattering. Masochism in its paradigmatic form emerges as "a kind of melodramatic version of the constitution of sexuality itself," whose marginality consists in "its isolating, even its making visible, the ontological grounds of the sexual" (Bersani, *Freudian Body*, 41). This account of the sources of pain's pleasurability is suggestive and powerful, not least because of its difference from what is often expected of psychoanalysis: its "primal scene," as it were, is independent of family romance, and while it might be thought of as "pre-Oedipal," it can also be understood as simply indifferent to Oedipal theory. The account of constitutive masochism I am offering differs from Laplanche and Bersani's in that it does not appeal to a developmental narrative of any kind, and does not focus on sexuality, even on a capacious definition of that famously elusive term.

36 Patterson, "Chaucer's Pardoner on the Couch," 680.

37 My hesitation concerning the charge that psychoanalysis "reduces everything to sex" stems from my sense that one of the great contributions of psychoanalysis has been its challenge to the separation of sexuality into a distinct sphere of human activity and desire: reduction, after all, depends on the idea that something of one distinct kind is being explained in terms of something else of another distinct kind.

38 I am not claiming that causal analysis, psychoanalytic or otherwise, is misguided. I am simply claiming that it does not tell us everything, and that we need to know some of what it does not tell us.

39 See Galloway, "Chaucer's Former Age." I agree with Galloway that the poem suggests that "redemption from a history that has shaped and generated one's historical vision, even one's diction, remains far to seek" (547).

40 Susan Stewart, *On Longing*, 23.
41 As Galloway argues, this is true even of "The Former Age."
42 For Boethius's treatment of the Golden Age, see 2m5; for Boethius's nostalgic meta-physics, see 2m8, and especially the stretch of argument from III.pr. 10–IV.pr. 6. My discussion here follows Plato's use of philosophical myth in the *Timaeus*, the ultimate source for Boethius's metaphysics.
43 V.pr. 4–6. Augustine's doctrine of the unspeakability of the divine (*De Doctrina Christiana*, I) flows from similar commitments.

4 SADOMASOCHISM AND UTOPIA IN THE *ROMAN DE LA ROSE*

1 I must however repeat the caveat that what is most interesting and powerful in psycho-analysis goes well beyond the production of a conceptual apparatus.
2 Besides the discussions of the *Canterbury Tales* cited elsewhere in this book, and the discussions of courtly love and of the *Roman de la Rose* cited throughout this chapter, my understanding of Chaucer's interest in such an eroticism is indebted to David Aers, *Community, Gender, and Individual Identity*, 117–52.
3 The primal scene of psychoanalytic discussion of courtly love is Jacques Lacan, *Ethics of Psychoanalysis*, especially "Courtly love as anamorphosis" (139–54). The French critic who has done the most to elaborate Lacanian notions while remaining attentive to courtly love as a historical phenomenon is Jean-Charles Huchet, in *L'Amour discourtois* and *Littérature médié-vale et psychanalyse*. See also Bloch, *Medieval Misogyny*, 113–64; Slavoj Žižek, *Metastases of Enjoyment*, 89–112; Sarah Kay, *Subjectivity in Troubadour Poetry* and *Courtly Contradictions*; Fradenburg, *Sacrifice Your Love*; and Jeffrey J. Cohen, *Medieval Identity Machines*, 78–115.
4 Lewis, *Allegory of Love*, 2–3.
5 Gilles Deleuze and Leopold von Sacher-Masoch, *Masochism*, 278–79.
6 This is my reformulation of Patterson's point, discussed in the previous chapter, concerning the need to be more rather than less theoretical.
7 See the works cited above by Lewis, Muscatine, Howard, Patterson, Dinshaw, Fradenburg, Huchet, Bloch, Žižek, Kay, and Cohen.
8 Many accounts of the *Rose* invoke what I am calling sadistic structures of male repre-sentation and desire, that is, erotic structures that depend on actual or imaginary violence to the feminine love object. For versions of the thought in strikingly different critics whose contrasting accounts of the *Rose* indicate how widespread the idea is, see David F. Hult, *Self-Fulfilling Prophecies*, 244; Leslie Cahoon, "Raping the Rose"; Kathryn Gravdal, *Ravishing Maidens*, 71; Sarah Kay, *Romance of the Rose*, 45–47; Douglas Kelly, *Internal Difference and Meanings in the* Roman de la Rose, 4, 9, and 39. Heather Arden has provided a useful guide to this and other critical issues in *The Roman de la Rose: An Annotated Bibliography*.
9 Guillaume de Lorris and Jean de Meun, *Le Roman de la Rose*, ed. Félix Lecoy; all citations are from this edition and are given by line numbers in the body of the text. Translations are from Guillaume de Lorris and Jean de Meun, *The Romance of the Rose*, trans. Charles Dahlberg and are cited by page number in the body of the text. I have at times revised Dahlberg where some aspect of the original seemed to me lost in transla-tion; these revisions are noted in the text.
10 For the texts surrounding Christine de Pizan's critique of the *Rose* and medieval responses to it, see *Le Débat sur le Roman de la Rose*, ed. Eric Hicks and "*La Querelle de la rose*," trans. Joseph L. Baird and John R. Kane.

11 For Huchet as well, narcissism becomes the site in the *Rose* at which the perverse and the normal come to be indistinguishable; see *Littérature médiévale et psychanalyse*, 157–92.

12 This implication of the "plucking" trope for male erotic satisfaction is noted by Hult, *Self-Fulfilling Prophecies*, 244.

13 In linking sadism and masochism here I am resisting what I find to be a somewhat exaggerated tendency to uncouple them which follows in the wake of Gilles Deleuze's *Coldness and Cruelty*. Deleuze took an important step beyond the oversimplified pairing of sadism and masochism expressed in the ideas that masochism is just a case of an originary sadism that then gets directed on the self, and that, since a masochist wants pain and a sadist wants to inflict it, they are a complementary pair, the masochist in effect wanting a sadist and vice versa. But, keeping in mind Deleuze's analysis of the importance of contract to masochism, I think it can be profitable to return to the idea that there is a link between sadism and masochism, especially when they are understood not just demographically, as distinct pathological conditions afflicting a certain subset of the population, but as indices of fundamental structures of sexuality, at least as sexuality has been organized in the West since the Middle Ages. As I indicated in the previous chapter, here I am following out some ideas of Leo Bersani's in *The Freudian Body*, although with an analytical trajectory less attached to psychoanalytic concepts than his is.

14 Both Huchet (*Littérature médiévale et psychanalyse*, 157–92) and Hult (*Self-Fulfilling Prophecies*, 300) also argue that narcissism in the *Rose* cannot be understood through a strong contrast between the normal and the perverse. Much critical discussion, by contrast, has understood narcissism in the *Rose* as an avoidable pathology, and on that basis has debated the question of whether the dreamer succeeds in avoiding it. Marta Powell Harley provides a useful survey of earlier critical arguments that the dreamer is redeemed from narcissism while arguing that finally he is not; see "Narcissus, Hermaphroditus, and Attis." Sarah Kay offers more nuanced versions of the redemptive reading than those Harley critiques; see *Subjectivity in Troubadour Poetry*, 174–79 and *Romance of the Rose*, 78–83.

15 While I do not want here to invoke some putatively fixed psychoanalytic theory, the attempt to guard against psychoanalytic misreading of a medieval interest in narcissism can lead to exaggeration in the other direction. So Michael Camille, whose writings on medieval sexuality are among the most sensitive and searching we have, writes that in the Middle Ages "the sin of Narcissus was not falling in love with himself, as in our modern Freudian notion of narcissism, but with an image" (*Medieval Art of Love*, 45). The problem with this formulation lies in its separation of the idea of falling in love with oneself from that of falling in love with an image. What Narcissus does in the *Rose*, and even for that matter in Ovid, is to fall in love with an image of himself. That is presumably what Camille means; but then a psychoanalytic understanding of narcissism also involves foregrounding the function of the imaginary here. The danger in worrying over anachronism is often that the contrasts between the medieval and the modern on which such worries depend lose their purchase on both ends of the historical spectrum.

16 Here I am extending some thoughts of Patterson, *Subject of History*, 296–304.

17 For the classic example of imagining "courtly love" as formalizable within a set of rules, see Andreas Capellanus, *Art of Courtly Love*.

18 Critical works that emphasize these difficulties include those already cited by Kay, Hult, and Kelly. Also see Michael Murrin's argument that allegory in general is best understood as "thinking in tropes" rather than a strict correspondence between literary representations and abstract ideas, and that the notion of "personification allegory" on which the latter view tends to rely is an eighteenth-century idea rather than a medieval

one, in *Veil of Allegory*. Maureen Quilligan also emphasizes allegory's excess of its apparent formal constraints in *Language of Allegory*.

19 Patterson makes this point in *Subject of History*, 296–99.

20 For a fuller discussion of the destabilizing effects of Bel Acueil's masculinity on the normative sexuality represented in the *Rose*, see Simon Gaunt, "Bel Acueil." Kay and Harley also note the homoeroticism implied by the gender of Bel Acueil, and Harley extends the point to a broader reading of Guillaume's poem. See Kay, *Romance of the Rose*, 46 and Harley, "Ovidian Lovers," 333–34.

21 Winthrop Wetherbee, "Theme of Imagination"; Kelly, *Medieval Imagination*; Kay, *Romance of the Rose*, 72–93.

22 *De Anima*, 427b27. I follow D. W. Hamlyn's translation in *Aristotle's De Anima*, although I follow a number of Aristotle scholars in emending Hamlyn's translation of *phantasma* from "image" to "appearance," or in other places "phantasm," for reasons I discuss above.

23 I focus this discussion on Aristotle rather than on late medieval discussions of philosophical psychology for two reasons. First, what I am after is a very general (though by no means universal) feature of premodern philosophical psychology, whose source is Aristotle. A discussion of late medieval theories would have to take a good deal of time to lay out the various competing ways of responding to Aristotle, which, while interesting in itself, would distract from the current discussion. Second, the critical literature on Aristotle is more advanced than that on medieval thinkers, particularly on the score of understanding the difference between his theory and a modern empiricist psychology for which "mental images" play a central explanatory role. Given the interest throughout this book in the difficulty of resisting empiricism's spell, that difference seems especially important to preserve. I am indebted here to many discussions with Jay Schleusener, to conversations with Candace Vogler and Christine Korsgaard, and to three subtle discussions of the place of *phantasia* in Aristotelian psychology: Malcolm Schofield, "Aristotle on the Imagination"; Dorothea Frede, "Cognitive Role of *Phantasia* in Aristotle"; and Martha Craven Nussbaum, *Aristotle's De Motu Animalium*, 221–69.

24 *De Anima*, 428b10–17.

25 The essays cited above make this argument in some detail and in different ways. For capsule formulations of the point, see Schofield, "Aristotle on the Imagination," 259; Frede, "Cognitive Role," 287; and Nussbaum, *De Motu Animalium*, 268.

26 *De Anima*, 431a14–17.

27 Ibid., 433b28.

28 For an account of the importance of medieval psychological theory, and of its interest in *phantasia* in particular, to Chaucer's poetics, see Kolve, *Imagery of Narrative*, 9–84.

29 The idea that *phantasia* constitutes incoherent structures of thought and desire that at once imbed ideological fantasies and gesture towards something else they cannot figure is my way of putting an insight of Wetherbee's in "Theme of Imagination." As Wetherbee argues, imagination or "ingenium," which is derived from Aristotelian *phantasia*, is shaped both by the imperfections and self-deceptions that beset human cognition and desire, and by the way those very imperfections are ways of reaching for higher truths. This conception of imagination is part of what gives medieval allegory its "capacity to communicate complex and ambiguous experience" ("Theme of Imagination," 45). Wetherbee further argues that this interest in psychological complexity finds one of its greatest refinements in the allegorical engagement with the narcissistic structures of *fin'amors*; see "Theme of Imagination," 50–61. Here, as in *Platonism*

and Poetry, Wetherbee has done much to shape my sense of the intellectual and psychological richness with which medieval poetry engages philosophical topics, as well as the importance of those topics for understanding poetic representations of sexuality and love.

30 The earth: "la terre . . . velt avoir novele robe . . . l'erbe et les flors blanches et perses / et de maintes colors diverses, / c'est la robe que je devise" (59–65). The birds: "Li oisel . . . sont en may por le tens serin / si lié qu'il mostrent en chantant / qu'en lor cuers a de joie tant / qu'il lor estuet chanter par force" (67–73). The human mimesis of natural eroticism: "lors estuet joines genz entendre / a estre gais et amoreus / por le tens bel et doucereus" (78–80).

31 Muscatine (in *French Tradition*, 11–97) provides a version of this contrast, although I have inflected it to also accommodate Fleming's view of the contrast in *Reason and the Lover*.

32 For a confession of boredom with Reason, see Kay, *Romance of the Rose*, 31. Fleming's *Reason and the Lover* provides the best example of a moralistic reading of Reason's discourse.

33 There is an obvious parallel here to Reason's discussion of language, 6913–7154. That discussion is prompted by the dreamer's objection to Reason's use of the word "coilles": "testicles are not well thought of in the mouth of a courteous girl," "coilles . . . / ne sunt pas bien renomees / en bouche a cortaise pucele" (6899–901). Reason diagnoses the dreamer's combination of prudishness and pornographic titillation, expressed in the *double entendre* of his objection, as the product of his fetishistic overinvestment in an arbitrary sign.

34 See Cicero, *De Senectute, De Amicitia, De Divinatione*, 130. For Cicero, as for much of the tradition that follows him, friendship was considered a relation between men, since one of its grounding assumptions was an equality which was held to be impossible between a man and a woman. In the Middle Ages, this view came to be challenged, for instance by Aquinas, for whom friendship was essential to marital relations: see *Summa Contra Gentiles*, III.123.4–6. The idea of marital friendship was widespread by the thirteenth century; in arguing that the companionate marriage was a medieval rather than seventeenth-century invention, Patterson provides a helpful summary of some key primary and secondary sources on the topic in *Subject of History*, 344–49. My argument above is that the *Rose* radicalizes this development. For Jean de Meun, it is not just that friendship provides a model for idealized marital relations, but that erotic relations generally speaking are built out of the dialectical interplay between narcissized desire and a desire for friendship which narcissized erotic relations both depend on and repress. Marital friendship is thus the site of a fundamental incoherence in the norms that structure hegemonic gender and sexuality in the later Middle Ages. For an argument that comes to a similar conclusion along different paths, and that provides a further account of the historical conditions under which marital friendship came to matter in late medieval England, see Burger's *Chaucer's Queer Nation*, especially 37–77 and 78–118.

35 Friendship is thus also a candidate for that mysterious "greater good" the dreamer earlier claimed to be dispensable in favor of erotic repletion.

36 This is Augustine's reformulation of the Ciceronian phrase "ut efficiat paene unum ex duobus" (*De Amicitia*, 188). See Augustine, *Confessions*, IV.6: "nam ego sensi animam meam et animam illius unam fuisse animam in duobus corporibus."

37 The account I am pursuing thus agrees with Fleming's articulation of the ultimate values Reason endorses, without taking this position as licensing a moralistic judgment of the

dreamer's "folly." I have translated the Old French "charite" with the Latin "caritas" from which it derives to preserve the sense that it is a technical term in an analytics of desire, and to avoid the association with moral sentimentalism now carried by the English term "charity."

38 The ideal of marital love thus emerges as a rather uneasy compromise: while it helps to tame some of hegemonic masculinity's worst tendencies, it also reinforces preferential bonds and social structures that resist the ultimate aims of Christian moral perfectionism. Homoeroticism, sadistic narcissism, and other phenomena that settled society would readily label as "perverse" are thus not the only perversions that the *Rose* reveals to be already inside the "normal." While marriage may be modeled on *caritas*, the relation between Christ and Church, and other Christian ideals, it supports and is supported by a "turning away" from a perfected Christian community. In discussing Margery Kempe's desire to wear white as a married woman, Carolyn Dinshaw makes a similar argument: "Margery's clothes function as a signal of this unlivable difficulty of contradictory imperatives ... [Margery] allows us to recognize not only the unlivable logic of that scale of perfection ... but even more generally the perversion within the normative: Margery's white clothes point to the disjunction in an orthodox Christianity that establishes marriage as a sacrament yet always maintains its taint, maintains that it is a perversion from the ultimately perfect perfection" (*Getting Medieval*, 148–49).

39 *De Anima*, 432a1–2.

40 It might be tempting here to gloss one French analysis of desire's impossibility with another, the Lacanian dictum that "there is no sexual relation." Of course Lacan took a great interest in courtly love, and there must be some story to tell about the relationship between his thought and his inheritance of the erotic and philosophical traditions to which the *Rose* belongs. It may also be the case that Lacan can help in an analysis of the ways the *Rose* and other medieval texts imagine and handle the utopian impasse of love. Fradenburg's work is exemplary in this regard: see especially her discussion of *caritas* in *Sacrifice Your Love*, 176–98. My goal here, however, is to preserve a sense of the specific paths the *Rose* takes in to and out from love's self-divisions. Without an account of these paths, we will be too likely to think that this impasse was only brought to light by psychoanalysis or some other modern intellectual project, and too likely as well to move towards a critique of medieval forms of self-understanding which does not appreciate the sophistication of that self-understanding at its best.

41 On this score see especially lines 7957–8091; pp. 149–51 in Dahlberg's translation.

42 Such a view animates Muscatine's *Chaucer and the French Tradition* and Patterson's *Subject of History* among others.

43 As Stanley Cavell has argued, Shakespeare explores a similar structure of desire in *Othello*; see Cavell, *Disowning Knowledge*, 125–42.

5 SUFFERING LOVE IN THE *WIFE OF BATH'S PROLOGUE* AND *TALE*

1 This is Patterson's argument in *Subject of History*, 280–321. For one of the best early accounts of the Wife of Bath in terms of realistic effects and lifelike character, see Muscatine, *Chaucer and the French Tradition*, 197–98 and 204–13.

2 Since this passage appears in the Ellesmere manuscript but not in the Hengwrt, there is some scholarly disagreement over whether it represents Chaucer's revisions to an earlier version of the text or a scribal addition. For a review of the dispute over the authority of

Hengwrt and an argument that the Hengwrt additions are Chaucer's, see Ralph Hanna III, "Hengwrt Manuscript." My own view is that, given the absence of a definitive empirical method for judging matters of textual authority, we ought to ask how a substantive interpretation of the Hengwrt passages inform and are informed by substantive interpretations of the tales in which they appear and of Chaucer's project in the *Canterbury Tales* as a whole. One purpose of this chapter is to offer an interpretive argument that this passage, at least, is either Chaucer's or written by someone so deeply in tune with Chaucer's project that it doesn't make any difference.

3 My account of this passage is indebted to Leicester's sense of it as embodying an anxiety over patriarchal violence towards women and commodification of female sexuality, along with a wish for noncommodified mutual love (*Disenchanted Self,* 101–06).

4 For some exemplary instances of this line of thinking, see Muscatine, *Chaucer and the French Tradition,* 204–13; Mary Carruthers, "Painting of Lions"; Aers, *Chaucer,* 68–70; and Leicester, *Disenchanted Self,* 65–158.

5 There is room for considerable disagreement within such a position. For the argument that the Wife is miming the operations of patriarchal discourse, see Dinshaw, *Sexual Poetics,* 113–31. For the argument that she strategically deploys antifeminist tropes for erotic purposes, see Patterson, *Subject of History,* 280–321. For a version of this position that, unlike Dinshaw's and Patterson's, leaves no room for the Wife's recuperation of autonomy, see Hansen, *Fictions of Gender,* 26–57.

6 This tendency is most pronounced in Hansen, who declares that "her fundamental status . . . [is that of] a person acted upon rather than acting" (*Fictions of Gender,* 30). Patterson notes some ambivalences in the Wife's identifications but finds that "try as she (and Chaucer) might, she remains confined within the prison-house of masculine language" (*Subject of History,* 313). Dinshaw's formulations are the most productively unresolved in this respect. On the one hand, she claims that the Wife "explicitly and affirmatively assumes the place that patriarchal discourse accords the feminine" (*Sexual Poetics,* 115), showing a "full embrace of her own commodification" (118). On the other hand, she claims that "[the Wife] herself remains elsewhere, with a body, a will, a desire beyond that which she is accorded by patriarchal discourse" (120). Dinshaw's preferred trope for figuring the Wife's alterity to patriarchal discourse is the Irigarayan one of "the persistence of matter" and of sexual pleasure (120). I think Dinshaw is right that patriarchal ideology does not determine all the contours of the Wife's conception of herself, although one thing this means is that she does *not* fully embrace her own commodification. And as I will argue, the Wife's identification with matter and pleasure do not afford a grounding for her alterity to ideology: they are rather central features of the persistence of ideology, and are in themselves sites of deep ambivalence for the Wife.

7 The idea goes back at least as far as Muscatine, *Chaucer and the French Tradition,* 204–13.

8 See Brundage, *Law, Sex, and Christian Society,* for a survey of the medieval Church's teachings about and attempted regulations of sexuality.

9 Patterson emphasizes this combination of titillating allure and dauntingness in *Subject of History,* 292.

10 As is so often the case, Muscatine stands behind the insights of more recent criticism: the binary commitments critics have found in the Wife of Bath's discourse are already laid out in Muscatine's claim that the Wife "represents practical experience as against received authority, female freedom as against male domination, and unblushing sensuality as against emotional austerity" (*Chaucer and the French Tradition,* 204).

11 Patterson, *Subject of History,* 282.

12 The title of Patterson's chapter on the Wife of Bath in *Subject of History* is "The Wife of Bath and the Triumph of the Subject," and one of its central claims is that the Wife's "invocation of the rights of the subject" (283) models Chaucer's own sense of the grounds of poetic identity. I am arguing in contrast that Chaucer's poetic project can best be understood as an investigation of what makes the *myth* of the subject incoherent yet so alluring. Since Patterson is concerned throughout *Subject of History* to offer a critique of that myth, his formulations in discussing the Wife of Bath suggest that he sees Chaucer as more deeply and directly implicated in that myth than I do.

13 See my discussion of *phantasia* in the previous chapter.

14 As the language of being "held captive by a picture" suggests, my understanding of this myth has been informed by the work of Ludwig Wittgenstein, especially the *Philosophical Investigations*. The phrase "the myth of the subject" is an adaptation of a phrase of Donald Davidson; see *Subjective, Intersubjective, Objective*, 39–52.

15 The idea that the Wife fully and directly identifies with her body has been shared not only by the critics involved in the feminist debates I have tracked, but by both sides of the older argument over whether the *Wife of Bath's Prologue* and *Tale* represent a humanistic Chaucerian appreciation of sexuality or a moralistic judgment of it. See for instance Muscatine, *Chaucer and the French Tradition*, 204–13 and Robertson, *Preface to Chaucer*, 317–31.

16 Dinshaw, *Sexual Poetics*, 125.

17 Patterson's case is a bit more complex on this score. On the one hand, his discussion frequently preserves a sense of the Wife's "characteristically ambivalent self-image" (*Subject of History*, 309). On the other hand, he claims that her contradictory self-presentation as devouring female and as loving wife involves a self-knowing rhetorical strategy in the service of her desire for love: "mastery is sought only that it may be abandoned" (313–14). For Patterson, then, there is finally a bedrock desire to which the Wife's ambivalence does not reach.

18 The view that the tale's conclusion expresses the Wife's wish to be young and beautiful and loved is the older one, dating back to George Lyman Kittredge, *Chaucer and his Poetry*, 191. The revisionist view that it expresses a masculine wish-fulfillment in which the Wife is complicit can be found in Patterson, *Subject of History*, 314 and Dinshaw, *Sexual Poetics*, 116–17. In locating the object of a wish as a subjective gratification, and in suspecting that there is finally some identifiable single wish that drives the narrative to its close, the wish-fulfillment reading in all of its forms replicates core features of the myth of the subject to which this *Prologue* and *Tale* give such powerful voice.

6   LOVE'S PROMISE: THE *CLERK'S TALE* AND THE
SCANDAL OF THE UNCONDITIONAL

1 See for instance Thomas R. Lounsbury, *Studies in Chaucer*, III: 340ff.; J. Burke Severs, *Literary Relationships*, especially 231–33; Salter, *Knight's Tale and Clerk's Tale*, 38–64; David, *Strumpet Muse*, 159–69; Donald Reiman, "The Real *Clerk's Tale*"; Mary J. Carruthers, "The Lady, the Swineherd, and Chaucer's Clerk"; Wetherbee, *Canterbury Tales*, 90–95; Dinshaw, *Sexual Poetics*, 132–55; Hansen, *Fictions of Gender*, 188–207; Wallace, *Chaucerian Polity*, 261–93; Nicholas Watson, "Christian Ideologies," 84–86. I owe a great deal to each of these discussions, particularly those of Salter, Dinshaw, and Wallace. As I indicate in the body of the chapter, my claim here is not that each of these critics makes scandal their central theme, but rather that for each of them the tale's main

events or characters or metaphorical structures embody a scandal or outrage to important moral or political values, and that the core interpretive questions surrounding the tale concern how we are to understand that scandal or outrage, and how Chaucer means us to understand it. Dinshaw puts the point in another way in arguing that the appeal of the story of Walter and Grisilde has always been its way of posing the problem of how their difficult, even repugnant relationship can be explained (*Sexual Poetics*, 132–33). My own sense of how to explain that repugnance and Chaucer's interest in it will emerge over the course of the chapter. But quite apart from the specifics of my account, I think there is something to be learned from the fact that such reaction to the tale persists across many differences of interpretation and critical methodology, and even across strong differences concerning what values are being violated, and by whom. Charlotte C. Morse offers a similar character-ization of the tale's critical history, along with a useful guide to it, in "Critical Approaches."

2 See for instance George Lyman Kittredge, "Chaucer's Discussion of Marriage"; James Sledd, "*Clerk's Tale*: Monsters and Critics"; Dolores Warwick Frese, "Chaucer's *Clerk's Tale*: Monsters and Critics Reconsidered." Kittredge offers a brilliantly unguarded formulation of the (often implicit) assumptions of such a view: "The Middle Ages delighted (as children still delight) in stories that exemplify a single human quality, like valor, or tyranny, or fortitude. In such cases, the settled rule (for which neither Chaucer nor the Clerk was responsible) was to show to what lengths that quality may conceivably go. Hence, in tales of this kind, there can be no question of conflict between duties" (436). Kittredge is right that the *Clerk's Tale* shows the lengths to which Grisilde's virtue requires her to go. He is also right that it is a child's perspective to believe that the perfect embodiment of a virtue can involve no question of a conflict of duties. But he is wrong to think of the Clerk, or Chaucer, or medieval people in general as having such a childish perspective. As I will argue later in this chapter, to identify such a perspective with a medieval understanding of the tale misses the point, not only of the tale but of the biblical models on which Grisildan heroism is based. In this I follow Linda Georgianna's "Grammar of Consent."

3 See the discussions already cited by Reiman, Carruthers, Dinshaw, Wallace, Georgianna, and Watson. For an overview of Chaucer's alterations of his sources, see Severs, *Literary Relationships*, especially 229–48. Both Carruthers and Dinshaw point out that repugnance is part of not only the modern reception of Chaucer's version of the story but also the medieval reception of the story in a number of its versions.

4 Besides the Clerk's formulations of Walter's conduct, think of the moralizing postures taken by public figures and the media during the Clinton–Lewinsky affair.

5 The *Riverside Chaucer* comes quite close to this in glossing the phrase as "the ill-fame of his bad reputation."

6 See the critics cited in notes 1 and 2 above.

7 In what follows I am indebted to a number of discussions that have helped to bring out the complexities in the tale's representations of gender, politics, and their intersection: see especially the studies cited above by Dinshaw, Hansen, Wallace, and Georgianna, as well as Jill Mann, *Geoffrey Chaucer*, 146–64; Lesley Johnson, "Reincarnations of Griselda"; and Sarah Stanbury, "Regimes of the Visual."

8 For Nature's view of reproduction as the means to individual self-replacement and species immortality, see *Roman de la Rose*, 15891–976. David Wallace traces the link between Walter's tyrannical polity and his fantasy of immortality to a Chaucerian critique of Petrarchan humanism in *Chaucerian Polity*, 261–98.

9 Or at least, that is a Walterish description of one's goal in pursuing such activities. Even absent-minded roaming about, however, will present you with situations in which you

must weigh the sacrifice of present pleasure against the prospect of some greater pleasure down the road. This suggests that Walter's leisured aristocratic activities are less pure expressions of wantonness than wishful attempts to inhabit such a condition.

10 This is my way of putting a point Stanbury makes, that the tale exhibits "a conflict between a desire to pin down and focus the wife's body, to focalize it within a domesticating and/or sexualizing gaze, and a desire or habit of using the iconic body as a sign of authority" ("Regimes of the Visual," 281). My argument here is that Walter occupies both sides of something like this conflict, and that in him the two sides, far from being segregated into distinct behaviors or states of affect, overlap in his attraction to Grisilde.

11 Muscatine, *Chaucer and the French Tradition*, 191.

12 One reading of the tale's use of Christian iconography holds that the presence of such iconography by itself shows that any recoil from Grisilde's actions involves historical, theological, and aesthetic mistakes (see the works by Sledd, Muscatine, and Frese cited above). My argument here is that a close reading of what the Clerk does with such iconography suggests that it reinforces such a response rather than obviating it, and that this is essential to the Clerk's religious and moral purposes.

13 For such representations in the visual arts see for instance "Jesus Descended from the Cross," anonymous Gospel book, twelfth century, Abbey Library, Nonantola, Modena; *Lamentation*, Giotto di Bondone, 1290s, fresco, Upper Church, San Francesco, Assisi; *Weeping on Christ Dead*, Giotto, 1303–05, Scrovegni Chapel, Padova. For some medieval English lyrics that treat Mary's grief, see *Medieval English Lyrics*, ed. Thomas G. Duncan: "Lullay, lullay, litel child" (115–17), "Jesu Cristes milde moder" (122–24), "Stond wel, moder, under rode" (124–26), "Why have ye no routhe on my child?" (126).

14 See IV.498–511, 645–67, 814–89.

15 Georgianna's discussion in "Grammar of Assent" is particularly apposite here. As I hope is clear from the above discussion, I see in Grisilde's apostolic purity and strength of will something that, however admirable, is considerably darker than what Georgianna sees there, as well as something against whose example we are divided by more than a pathological Walterity. But Georgianna's argument does much to rescue the tale's religiosity from a sentimental misreading.

16 See for instance Matthew 10:34–39.

17 Here I am indebted to Harry Frankfurt's discussions of love in *Necessity, Volition, and Love*; see especially 129–41 and 155–80. The view of love I am attributing to the Clerk is however significantly different from Frankfurt's.

18 Romans 8:24–25.

19 David Wallace provides the fullest articulation of this reading in *Chaucerian Polity*, 288–89.

20 Winthrop Wetherbee reads the line in this second sense in *Canterbury Tales*, 93. I owe my sense of the line's significance to Michelle Yacht.

Bibliography

Aers, David, *Chaucer*, Atlantic Highlands, NJ: Humanities Press International, 1986

    Chaucer, Langland, and the Creative Imagination, London: Routledge and Kegan Paul, 1980

    Community, Gender, and Individual Identity: English Writing 1360–1430, London and New York: Routledge, 1988, 117–52

    "A Whisper in the Ear of Early Modernists; or, Reflections on Literary Critics Writing the 'History of the Subject,' " in David Aers, ed., *Culture and History, 1350–1600: Essays on English Communities, Identities, and Writing*, Detroit: Wayne State University Press, 1992, 177–202

Anscombe, G. E. M., *Intention*, New York: Blackwell, 1957

Aquinas, Thomas, *Commentary on Aristotle's De Anima*, trans. Kenelm Foster and Silvester Humphries, Notre Dame: Dumb Ox Books, 1994

    Commentary on Aristotle's Nicomachean Ethics, trans. C. I. Litzinger, Notre Dame: Dumb Ox Books, 1993

    Summa Contra Gentiles, trans. Vernon Bourke, Notre Dame: University of Notre Dame Press, 1975

    Summa Theologiae, trans. Members of the Dominican Order, New York: McGraw-Hill and Blackfriars, 1963

Arden, Heather, *The Roman de la Rose: An Annotated Bibliography*, New York: Garland, 1993

Aristotle, *Aristotle's De Anima Books II, III*, trans. D. W. Hamlyn, Oxford: Clarendon Press, 1968

    Nicomachean Ethics, trans. W. D. Ross, in *The Basic Works of Aristotle*, ed. Richard McKeon, New York: Random House, 1941

Augustine, *On Christian Doctrine*, trans. D. W. Robertson, Indianapolis: Bobbs-Merrill, 1958

    The City of God, trans. Henry Bettenson, Harmondsworth: Penguin, 1984

    Confessions, ed. W. H. D. Rouse, Cambridge, MA: Harvard University Press, 1912

    Confessions, trans. R. S. Pine-Coffin, Harmondsworth: Penguin, 1961

Baird, Joseph L., and John R. Kane, *"La Querelle de la rose": Letters and Documents*, Chapel Hill: University of North Carolina Press, 1978

Bibliography

Beichner, Paul, "Characterization in the *Miller's Tale*," in *Chaucer Criticism*, vol. I, *The Canterbury Tales*, ed. Richard J. Schoeck and Jerome Taylor, Notre Dame: University of Notre Dame Press, 1960, 117–29

Berlant, Lauren, *The Queen of America Goes to Washington City: Essays on Sex and Citizenship*, Durham: Duke University Press, 1997

Berlant, Lauren, and Michael Warner, "Sex in Public," *Critical Inquiry* 24 (1998), 547–66

Bernauer, James, and Michael Mahon, "The Ethics of Michel Foucault," in *The Cambridge Companion to Foucault*, ed. Gary Gutting, Cambridge: Cambridge University Press, 1994, 141–58

Bersani, Leo, *The Freudian Body: Psychoanalysis and Art*, New York: Columbia University Press, 1986

Homos, Cambridge, MA: Harvard University Press, 1995

Blackstone, William, *Commentaries on the Laws of England: A Facsimile of the First Edition of 1765–1769*, Chicago: University of Chicago Press, 1979

Bloch, R. Howard, *Medieval Misogyny and the Invention of Western Romantic Love*, Chicago: University of Chicago Press, 1991

Boethius, *The Consolation of Philosophy*, trans. Richard Green, Indianapolis: Bobbs-Merrill, 1962

The Theological Tractates and the Consolation of Philosophy, Cambridge, MA: Harvard University Press, 1973

Boswell, John, *Christianity, Social Tolerance, and Homosexuality: Gay People in Western Europe from the Beginning of the Christian Era to the Fourteenth Century*, Chicago: University of Chicago Press, 1980

Brown, Peter, *The Body and Society: Men, Women, and Sexual Renunciation in Early Christianity*, New York: Columbia University Press, 1988

"Bodies and Minds: Sexuality and Renunciation in Early Christianity," in David M. Halperin, John J. Winkler, and Froma I. Zeitlin, eds, *Before Sexuality: The Construction of Erotic Experience in the Ancient Greek World*, Princeton: Princeton University Press, 1990

Brundage, James A., *Law, Sex, and Christian Society in Medieval Europe*, Chicago: University of Chicago Press, 1987

Burger, Glenn, *Chaucer's Queer Nation*, Minneapolis: University of Minnesota Press, 2003

Burger, Glenn, and Steven F. Kruger, eds, *Queering the Middle Ages*, Minneapolis: University of Minnesota Press, 2001

Butler, Judith, *Bodies that Matter: On the Discursive Limits of "Sex"*, New York: Routledge, 1993

Gender Trouble: Feminism and the Subversion of Identity, New York: Routledge, 1990

The Psychic Life of Power: Theories in Subjection, Stanford: Stanford University Press, 1997

Bynum, Caroline Walker, *Fragmentation and Redemption: Essays on Gender and the Human Body in Medieval Religion*, New York: Zone Books, 1992

Holy Feast and Holy Fast: The Religious Significance of Food to Medieval Women, Berkeley: University of California Press, 1987

Jesus as Mother: Studies in the Spirituality of the High Middle Ages, Berkeley: University of California Press, 1982

Cadden, Joan, *Meanings of Sex Difference in the Middle Ages: Medicine, Science, and Culture*, Cambridge: Cambridge University Press, 1993

Cahoon, Leslie, "Raping the Rose: Jean de Meun's Reading of Ovid's *Amores*," *Classical and Modern Literature* 6 (1986), 261–85

Camille, Michael, *The Medieval Art of Love: Objects and Subjects of Desire*, New York: Harry N. Abrams, 1998

Canguilhem, Georges, *The Normal and the Pathological*, trans. Carolyn R. Fawcett and Robert S. Cohen, New York: Zone Books, 1989

Capellanus, Andreas, *The Art of Courtly Love*, trans. John Jay Parry, New York: Columbia University Press, 1960

Carruthers, Mary, "The Lady, the Swineherd, and Chaucer's Clerk," *Chaucer Review* 17 (1982–83), 221–34

"The Wife of Bath and the Painting of Lions," *PMLA* 94 (1979), 209–22

Cavell, Stanley, *The Claim of Reason: Wittgenstein, Skepticism, Morality, and Tragedy*, Oxford: Oxford University Press, 1979

Disowning Knowledge in Six Plays of Shakespeare, Cambridge: Cambridge University Press, 1987

Chaucer, Geoffrey, *The Riverside Chaucer*, ed. Larry D. Benson, 3rd edn, Boston: Houghton Mifflin, 1987

Cicero, *De Senectute, De Amicitia, De Divinatione*, ed. and trans. W. A. Falconer, Cambridge, MA: Harvard University Press, 1923

Cohen, Jeffrey Jerome, *Medieval Identity Machines*, Minneapolis: University of Minnesota Press, 2003

Colish, Marcia, *The Stoic Tradition from Antiquity to the Early Middle Ages*, Leiden: E. J. Brill, 1985

Crane, Susan, *Gender and Romance in Chaucer's* Canterbury Tales, Princeton: Princeton University Press, 1994

David, Alfred E., *The Strumpet Muse: Art and Morals in Chaucer's Poetry*, Bloomington: Indiana University Press, 1976

Davidson, Arnold, "Archaeology, Genealogy, Ethics," in David Couzens Hoy, ed., *Foucault: A Critical Reader*, New York: Basil Blackwell, 1986, 221–33

"Ethics as Ascetics: Foucault, the History of Ethics and Ancient Thought," in *The Cambridge Companion to Foucault*, ed. Gary Gutting, Cambridge: Cambridge University Press, 1994, 115–40

"How to do the History of Psychoanalysis: A Reading of Freud's *Three Essays on the Theory of Sexuality*," *Critical Inquiry* 13 (1987), 252–77

Davidson, Donald, *Subjective, Intersubjective, Objective*, Oxford: Clarendon Press, 2001

Deleuze, Gilles, and Leopold von Sacher-Masoch, *Masochism*, trans. Jean McNeil, New York: Zone Books, 1989

Deschamps, Eustache, *Oeuvres complètes*, ed. Le Marquis de Quex de Saint-Hilaire, 11 vols., Paris: Firmin Didot, 1878–1903

Bibliography

Dinshaw, Carolyn, "Chaucer's Queer Touches/A Queer Touches Chaucer," *Exemplaria* 7 (1995), 76–92
    Chaucer's Sexual Poetics, Madison: University of Wisconsin Press, 1989
    Getting Medieval: Sexualities and Communities, Pre- and Postmodern, Durham: Duke University Press, 1999
Donaldson, E. Talbot, *Speaking of Chaucer*, New York: Norton, 1970
Duncan, Thomas G., ed., *Medieval English Lyrics*, Harmondsworth: Penguin, 1995
Ferrari, G. R. F., *Listening to the Cicadas: A Study of Plato's Phaedrus*, Cambridge: Cambridge University Press, 1987
Fleming, John, *Reason and the Lover*, Princeton: Princeton University Press, 1984
Foucault, Michel, *The History of Sexuality*, vol. I, *An Introduction*, trans. Robert Hurley, New York: Vintage, 1990
    The History of Sexuality, vol. II, *The Use of Pleasure*, trans. Robert Hurley, New York: Vintage, 1990
    The History of Sexuality, vol. III, *The Care of the Self*, trans. Robert Hurley, New York: Vintage, 1990
    Language, Counter-Memory, Practice: Selected Essays and Interviews, trans. Donald F. Bouchard and Sherry Simon, Ithaca: Cornell University Press, 1977
Fowler, Elizabeth, "Civil Death and the Maiden: Agency and the Conditions of Contract in *Piers Plowman*," *Speculum* 70 (1995), 760–92
Fradenburg, L. O. Aranye, *Sacrifice Your Love: Psychoanalysis, Historicism, Chaucer*, Minneapolis: University of Minnesota Press, 2002
    " 'Voice Memorial': Loss and Reparation in Chaucer's Poetry," *Exemplaria* 2 (1990), 169–202
Fradenburg, Louise, and Carla Freccero, eds, *Premodern Sexualities*, New York: Routledge, 1996
Frankfurt, Harry, *The Importance of What We Care About*, Cambridge: Cambridge University Press, 1988
    Necessity, Volition, and Love, Cambridge: Cambridge University Press, 1999
Frede, Dorothea, "The Cognitive Role of *Phantasia* in Aristotle," in Martha C. Nussbaum and Amélie Oksenberg Rorty, eds, *Essays on Aristotle's De Anima*, Oxford: Clarendon Press, 1992, 279–96
Frede, Michael, "The Literary Form of the *Sophist*," in Christopher Gill and Mary Margaret McCabe, eds, *Form and Argument in Late Plato*, Oxford: Clarendon Press, 1996, 135–51
Frese, Dolores Warwick, "Chaucer's *Clerk's Tale*: The Monsters and the Critics Reconsidered," *Chaucer Review* 8 (1973), 133–46
    "The Homoerotic Underside in Chaucer's *Miller's Tale* and *Reeve's Tale*," *Michigan Academician* 10 (1977), 144–50
Freud, Sigmund, *Beyond the Pleasure Principle*, trans. and ed. James Strachey, New York: Norton, 1961
    The Standard Edition of the Complete Psychological Works of Sigmund Freud, trans. and ed. James Strachey, London: Hogarth Press, 1955

Three Essays on the Theory of Sexuality, trans. and ed. James Strachey, New York: Basic Books, 1962

Galloway, Andrew, "Chaucer's Former Age and the Fourteenth-Century Anthropology of Craft: The Social Logic of a Premodernist Lyric," *ELH* 63 (1996), 535–54

Ganim, John, *Chaucerian Theatricality*, Princeton: Princeton University Press, 1990

Gaunt, Simon, "Bel Acueil and the Improper Allegory of the *Romance of the Rose*," *New Medieval Literatures* 2 (1998), 65–93

Georgianna, Linda, "The Clerk's Tale and the Grammar of Consent," *Speculum* 70 (1995), 793–821

Gravdal, Kathryn, *Ravishing Maidens: Writing Rape in Medieval French Literature and Law*, Philadelphia: University of Pennsylvania Press, 1991

Hacking, Ian, "Self-Improvement," in David Couzens Hoy, ed., *Foucault: A Critical Reader*, New York: Blackwell, 1986, 235–40

Hanna, Ralph, III, "The Hengwrt Manuscript and the Canon of the *Canterbury Tales*," *English Manuscript Studies 1100–1700* 1 (1989), 64–84

Hansen, Elaine Tuttle, *Chaucer and the Fictions of Gender*, Berkeley: University of California Press, 1992

Harley, Marta Powell, "Narcissus, Hermaphroditus, and Attis: Ovidian Lovers at the Fontaine d'Amors in Guillaume de Lorris's *Roman de la Rose*", *PMLA* 110 (1986), 324–37

Hicks, Eric, ed., *Le Débate sur le Roman de la Rose*, Paris: Champion, 1977

Hoccleve, Thomas, *The Regement of Princes*, ed. Frederick J. Furnivall, EETS ES 72, London: Early English Text Society, 1897

Holsinger, Bruce, *Music, Body, and Desire in Medieval Culture: Hildegard of Bingen to Chaucer*, Stanford: Stanford University Press, 2001

Howard, Donald R., *Chaucer: his Life, his Works, his World*, New York: Fawcett Columbine, 1987

Howes, Laura L., *Chaucer's Gardens and the Language of Convention*, Gainesville: University Press of Florida, 1997

Huchet, Jean-Charles, *L'Amour discourtois: La "Fin'Amors" chez les premiers troubadours*, Toulouse: Bibliothèque Historique Privat, 1987

Littérature médiévale et psychanalyse: pour une clinique littéraire, Paris: Presses Universitaires de France, 1990

Hult, David F., *Self-Fulfilling Prophecies: Readership and Authority in the First* Roman de la Rose, Cambridge: Cambridge University Press, 1986

Jacquart, Danielle and Claude Thomasset, *Sexuality and Medicine in the Middle Ages*, trans. Matthew Adamson, Princeton: Princeton University Press, 1988

Johnson, Lesley, "Reincarnations of Griselda: Contexts for the *Clerk's Tale*?," in Ruth Evans and Lesley Johnson, eds, *Feminist Readings in Middle English Literature: The Wife of Bath and All her Sect*, New York: Routledge, 1994, 195–220

Jordan, Mark, *The Invention of Sodomy in Christian Theology*, Chicago: University of Chicago Press, 1997

Bibliography

Kant, Immanuel, *Groundwork of the Metaphysic of Morals*, trans. H. J. Paton, New York: Harper, 1964

Karras, Ruth Mazo, *Common Women: Prostitution and Sexuality in Medieval England*, Oxford: Oxford University Press, 1996

Kay, Sarah, *Courtly Contradictions: The Emergence of the Literary Object in the Twelfth Century*, Stanford: Stanford University Press, 2001

    The Romance of the Rose, London: Grant and Cutler, 1995

    Subjectivity in Troubadour Poetry, Cambridge: Cambridge University Press, 1990

Keen, Maurice, *English Society in the Later Middle Ages, 1348–1500*, Harmondsworth: Penguin, 1990

Kelly, Douglas, *Internal Difference and Meanings in the* Roman de la Rose, Madison: University of Wisconsin Press, 1995

Kenny, Anthony, "Happiness," *Proceedings of the Aristotelian Society* 66 (1965–66), 93–102

Kittredge, George Lyman, *Chaucer and his Poetry*, Cambridge, MA: Harvard University Press, 1915, rpt. 1972

    "Chaucer's Discussion of Marriage," *Modern Philology* 9 (1911–12), 435–67

Kolve, V. A., *Chaucer and the Imagery of Narrative: The First Five Canterbury Tales*, Stanford: Stanford University Press, 1984

Korsgaard, Christine, *Creating the Kingdom of Ends*, Cambridge: Cambridge University Press, 1996

    The Sources of Normativity, Cambridge: Cambridge University Press, 1996

Kretzmann, Norman, Anthony Kenny, and Jan Pinborg, eds, *The Cambridge History of Later Medieval Philosophy*, Cambridge: Cambridge University Press, 1982

Lacan, Jacques, *The Ethics of Psychoanalysis: 1959–60*, ed. Jacques-Alain Miller, trans. Dennis Porter, New York: Norton, 1992

Laplanche, Jean, *Life and Death in Psychoanalysis*, trans. Jeffrey Mehlman, Baltimore: Johns Hopkins University Press, 1976

Laqueur, Thomas, *Making Sex: Body and Gender from the Greeks to Freud*, Cambridge, MA: Harvard University Press, 1990

Lear, Jonathan, *Open Minded: Working Out the Logic of the Soul*, Cambridge, MA: Harvard University Press, 1998

Leicester, H. Marshall, Jr., *The Disenchanted Self: Representing the Subject in the* Canterbury Tales, Berkeley: University of California Press, 1990

    "Newer Currents in Psychoanalytic Criticism, and the Difference 'It' Makes: Gender and Desire in the *Miller's Tale*," *ELH* 61 (1994), 473–99

Lemay, Helen Rodnite, *Women's Secrets: A Translation of Pseudo-Albertus Magnus's* De Secretis Mulierum *with Commentaries*, Albany: SUNY Press, 1992

Lerer, Seth, *Boethius and Dialogue: Literary Method in the* Consolation of Philosophy, Princeton: Princeton University Press, 1985

Lewis, C. S., *The Allegory of Love*, Oxford: Oxford University Press, 1936

Lochrie, Karma, *Covert Operations: The Medieval Uses of Secrecy*, Philadelphia: University of Pennsylvania Press, 1999

Lochrie, Karma, Peggy McCracken, and James A. Schultz, eds, *Constructing Medieval Sexuality*, Minneapolis: University of Minnesota Press, 1997

Lorris, Guillaume de, and Jean de Meun, *Le Roman de la Rose*, ed. Félix Lecoy, Paris: Champion, 1979–83

The Romance of the Rose, trans. Charles Dahlberg, Princeton: Princeton University Press, 1983

Lounsbury, Thomas R., *Studies in Chaucer*, New York: Harper, 1892

Lynch, Kathryn L., *Chaucer's Philosophical Visions*, Cambridge: D. S. Brewer, 2000

Mann, Jill, *Geoffrey Chaucer*, Atlantic Highlands, NJ: Humanities Press International, 1991

Middleton, Anne, "Chaucer's 'New Men' and the Good of Literature," in Edward Said, ed., *Literature and Society*, Baltimore: Johns Hopkins University Press, 1980, 15–56

"The Idea of Public Poetry in the Reign of Richard II," *Speculum* 53 (1978), 94–114

"Narration and the Invention of Experience: Episodic Form in *Piers Plowman*," in Larry D. Benson and Siegfried Wenzel, eds, *The Wisdom of Poetry: Essays in Early English Literature in Honor of Morton W. Bloomfield*, Kalamazoo: Medieval Institute Publications, 1982, 81–122

"The *Physician's Tale* and Love's Martyrs: 'Ensamples Mo than Ten' as a Method in the *Canterbury Tales*," *Chaucer Review* 8 (1973–74), 9–32

"War by other Means: Marriage and Chivalry in Chaucer," *Studies in the Age of Chaucer: Proceedings* 1 (1984), 119–33

"William Langland's 'Kynde Name': Authorial Signature and Social Identity in Late Fourteenth-Century England," in Lee Patterson, ed., *Literary Practice and Social Change in Britain, 1380–1530*, Berkeley: University of California Press, 1990, 15–82

Morse, Charlotte C., "Critical Approaches to the *Clerk's Tale*," in C. David Benson and Elizabeth Robertson, eds, *Chaucer's Religious Tales*, Cambridge: D. S. Brewer, 1990, 71–83

Murrin, Michael, *The Veil of Allegory*, Chicago: University of Chicago Press, 1969

Muscatine, Charles, *Chaucer and the French Tradition: A Study in Style and Meaning*, Berkeley: University of California Press, 1957

Nagel, Thomas, *Equality and Partiality*, Oxford: Oxford University Press, 1991

The Possibility of Altruism, Princeton: Princeton University Press, 1970

The View from Nowhere, Oxford: Oxford University Press, 1986

Nietzsche, Friedrich, *Beyond Good and Evil: Prelude to a Philosophy of the Future*, trans. Walter Kaufmann, New York: Vintage, 1989

On the Genealogy of Morals, trans. Walter Kaufmann, New York: Vintage, 1989

Nussbaum, Martha Craven, *Aristotle's* De Motu Animalium, Princeton: Princeton University Press, 1978

Patterson, Lee, *Chaucer and the Subject of History*, Madison: University of Wisconsin Press, 1991

"Chaucer's Pardoner on the Couch: Psyche and Clio in Medieval Literary Studies," *Speculum* 76 (2000), 638–80

"On the Margin: Postmodernism, Ironic History, and Medieval Studies," *Speculum* 65 (1990), 87–108

Bibliography

"Writing Amorous Wrongs: Chaucer and the Order of Complaint," in James M. Dean and Christian K. Zacher, eds, *The Idea of Medieval Literature: New Essays on Chaucer and Medieval Culture in Honor of Donald R. Howard*, Newark: University of Delaware Press, 1992, 55–71

Pearsall, Derek, *The Life of Geoffrey Chaucer: A Critical Biography*, Oxford: Blackwell, 1992

Plato, *Timaeus*, trans. Donald J. Zeyl, Indianapolis: Hackett, 2000

Quilligan, Maureen, *The Language of Allegory: Defining the Genre*, Ithaca: Cornell University Press, 1979

Reiman, Donald, "The Real *Clerk's Tale*; Or, Patient Griselda Exposed," *Texas Studies in Language and Literature* 5 (1963), 356–73

Robertson, D. W., *A Preface to Chaucer: Studies in Medieval Perspectives*, Princeton: Princeton University Press, 1962

Sachs, David, "In Fairness to Freud: A Critical Notice of *The Foundations of Psychoanalysis* by Adolf Grünbaum," in Jerome Neu, ed, *The Cambridge Companion to Freud*, Cambridge: Cambridge University Press, 1991, 309–38

Salter, Elizabeth, *Chaucer: The Knight's Tale and the Clerk's Tale*, London: Edward Arnold, 1962

Schofield, Malcolm, "Aristotle on the Imagination," in Martha C. Nussbaum and Amelie Oksenberg Rorty, eds, *Essays on Aristotle's De Anima*, Oxford: Oxford University Press, 1992, 249–78

Sedgwick, Eve Kosofsky, *Epistemology of the Closet*, Berkeley: University of California Press, 1990

Sedgwick, Eve Kosofsky, and Adam Frank, "Shame in the Cybernetic Fold," *Critical Inquiry* 21 (1995), 496–522

Severs, J. Burke, *The Literary Relationships of Chaucer's Clerk's Tale*, New Haven: Yale University Press, 1942

Simpson, D. P., *Cassell's Latin Dictionary*, New York: John Wiley, 1977

Sledd, James, "The *Clerk's Tale*: The Monsters and the Critics," *Modern Philology* 51 (1953–54), 73–82

Stanbury, Sarah, "Regimes of the Visual in Premodern England: Gaze, Body, and Chaucer's Clerk's Tale," *NLH* 28 (1997), 261–89

Stewart, Susan, *On Longing: Narratives of the Miniature, the Gigantic, the Souvenir, the Collection*, Durham: Duke University Press, 1993

Strohm, Paul, *Social Chaucer*, Cambridge, MA: Harvard University Press, 1989

Usk, Thomas, *The Testament of Love*, ed. R. Allen Shoaf, Kalamazoo: Medieval Institute Publications, 1998

Vlastos, Gregory, "The Socratic Elenchus," *Oxford Studies in Ancient Philosophy* 1 (1983), 27–58

Vogler, Candace, *Reasonably Vicious*, Cambridge, MA: Harvard University Press, 2002

Wallace, David, *Chaucerian Polity: Absolutist Lineages and Associational Forms in England and Italy*, Stanford: Stanford University Press, 1997

Warner, Michael, *The Trouble with Normal: Sex, Politics, and the Ethics of Queer Life*, New York: Free Press, 1999

Watson, Nicholas, "Christian Ideologies," in Peter Brown, ed., *A Companion to Chaucer*, Oxford: Blackwell, 2000, 75–89

Weisl, Angela Jane, *Conquering the Reign of Femeny: Gender and Genre in Chaucer's Romance*, Cambridge: D. S. Brewer, 1985

Westberg, Daniel, *Right Practical Reason: Aristotle, Action, and Prudence in Aquinas*, Oxford: Clarendon Press, 1994

Wetherbee, Winthrop, *Geoffrey Chaucer: The Canterbury Tales*, Cambridge: Cambridge University Press, 1989

    Platonism and Poetry in the Twelfth Century: The Literary Influence of the School of Chartres, Princeton: Princeton University Press, 1972

    "The Theme of Imagination in Medieval Poetry and the Allegorical Figure 'Genius'," *Medievalia et Humanistica* n.s. 7, ed. Paul Maurice Clogan, Cambridge: Cambridge University Press, 1976, 45–64

Williams, Bernard, *Ethics and the Limits of Philosophy*, Cambridge, MA: Harvard University Press, 1985

    Moral Luck, Cambridge: Cambridge University Press, 1991

    Shame and Necessity, Berkeley: University of California Press, 1993

Williams, David, "Radical Therapy in the Miller's Tale," *Chaucer Review* 15 (1981), 227–35

Wimsatt, James I., *Chaucer and his French Contemporaries: Natural Music in the Fourteenth Century*, Toronto: University of Toronto Press, 1991

Wittgenstein, Ludwig, *Philosophical Investigations*, trans. G. E. M. Anscombe, 3rd edn, New York: Macmillan, 1958

Zink, Michael, *The Invention of Literary Subjectivity*, trans. David Sices, Baltimore: Johns Hopkins University Press, 1999

Žižek, Slavoj, *The Metastases of Enjoyment: Six Essays on Women and Causality*, New York: Verso Books, 1994

    The Plague of Fantasies, New York: Verso Books, 1997

Index

Abraham 216, 229, 232, 234, 235, 236, 238
action, theories of 32, 33, 39, 57, 58, 59, 60, 62,
    69, 72, 77, 83, 84, 88, 93, 94, 96, 97, 99,
    101, 104, 107, 109, 113, 114, 115, 119, 121,
    132, 133, 135, 153, 162, 190, 241, 251, 252,
    254, 260
  and reflective endorsement 92, 94, 96,
    97, 99, 100, 102, 106, 107, 108, 109,
    132, 259
  see also normativity and reflective
    endorsement
  see also psychology, reflection
  see also Aristotle on action
Aers, David 252, 258, 259, 263, 268
agency 1, 3, 4, 5, 13, 14, 15, 17, 18, 20, 25, 33, 36,
    37, 56–69, 69, 71, 73, 78, 83, 87, 88, 89, 90,
    100, 101, 104, 105, 106, 113, 115, 116, 120,
    129, 130–144, 136, 146, 157, 160, 167, 178,
    182, 187, 190, 191, 192, 193, 194, 196, 204,
    213, 244, 251, 259, 260
  and normativity see normativity and agency
  and masochism 139, 152, 153, 156, 157,
    204–209
  antinomy of 33, 130–144, 187, 244, 261
  feminine 11, 12, 67, 72, 86, 107, 161, 179, 182,
    191, 197, 199, 255
  masculine 11, 67, 69, 72
  perspective of 16, 17, 18, 25, 136
Alain de Lille 2, 27
allegory 1, 4, 34, 107, 109, 140, 142, 153, 154, 156,
    162, 191, 192, 245, 264, 265
  see also Chaucer, Canterbury Tales, "Wife of
    Bath's Prologue and Tale," allegory in
  see also Roman de la Rose, allegory in
altruism 65, 66, 257
Andreas Capellanus 264
Anscombe, G.E.M. 251
antifeminism 13, 16, 32, 41, 52, 161, 193, 198,
    255, 268

  see also Chaucer, "Wife of Bath's Prologue
    and Tale," antifeminism in
  see also Roman de la Rose, misogyny
Aquinas, Thomas see Thomas Aquinas
Arden, Heather 263
Aristotle 3, 7, 24, 116, 153, 162, 176, 252, 255,
    259, 260, 265
  De Anima 265, 267
  Nicomachean Ethics 259, 260
  on action 260, 261
  on eudaimonia 116, 260
  on phantasia 162, 163, 265 see also fantasy,
    Phantasia
  on phantasma 153, 162, 265 see also fantasy,
    and phantasm
  on psychology 153, 162, 163
  on virtue 259
attachment 114–123, 246
Augustine 3, 9, 10, 21, 22, 23, 89, 103, 105, 117,
    136, 137, 138, 152, 176, 250, 252, 261
  and evil 250
  City of God 250, 252, 260
  Confessions 21, 23, 250, 252, 266
  De Doctrina Christiana 263
autonomy 1, 3, 4, 9, 10, 11, 12, 13, 14, 15, 16, 18,
    20, 22, 83, 84, 85, 89, 90, 91–101, 101–110,
    130, 132, 133, 134, 135, 136, 137, 138, 139,
    144, 146, 147, 148, 150, 152, 191, 196, 208,
    209, 220, 235, 236, 238, 239, 240, 243, 244,
    245, 246, 247, 258

Baird, Joseph L. 263
Beichner, Paul 253
Berlant, Lauren 250
Bernauer, James 251
Bersani, Leo 140, 141, 142, 249, 254, 261,
    262, 264
Bible 137, 235, 237, 270
  Matthew 10: 34–39, 271

Bible (cont.)
  Romans 2: 14, 252
  Romans 8: 24–25, 218, 271
  1 Corinthians 7: 9, 252
  the Fall 137
  the Passion 231
Blackstone, William 250
Bloch, R. Howard 250, 252, 263
Boccaccio, Giovanni 107
body 9, 60, 63, 73, 79, 100, 158, 213, 214, 233,
    239, 240
  virginal 24, 158, 195, 228
  female 24
Boethius 3, 10, 26, 27, 33, 38, 46, 50, 89, 110,
    111–151, 169, 171, 177, 187, 191, 244, 250,
    253, 260, 261, 263
  and Chaucer *see* Chaucer *and* Boethius
  Boethian dialectics 112, 113, 114, 117, 123,
      124–130, 144, 145, 146, 148, 152, 153, 156,
      163, 168, 176, 192
  and idealism 111
  and nostalgia 263
  and psychology 112, 113, 116, 117, 119, 120,
      121, 123, 129, 136, 138, 144, 156
  and Stoicism 116, 260
  Consolation of Philosophy 26, 30, 33, 46,
      50, 91, 110, 111–151, 177, 196, 201, 253,
      259, 260
    and *aporia* 112, 124–130, 131, 144, 145,
        176, 177
    and divinity 114, 115, 117, 122, 124, 125,
        126, 132, 133, 134, 137
    and evil 125, 127, 128, 130, 131
    and "the Good" 114–123
    and instrumentalization 118, 120, 122
    and judicial reform 130, 131, 132
    fantasy of mastery/possession 118, 120,
        121, 169
    happiness in 113, 114–123, 125, 126, 129,
        130, 131, 145, 260
    philosophy 33, 50, 114, 117, 118, 119, 120,
        123, 124–128, 129, 130–134, 144, 148,
        149, 169, 177, 260
    Prisoner, the 33, 119, 120, 123, 124–128,
        129, 130–134, 144, 169, 201
    trope of exile 119, 120, 136, 137
    trope of home/return 117, 119, 123, 137
    trope of imprisonment 132, 136,
        137, 138
Boswell, John 252
Brown, Peter 3, 22, 25, 152, 249, 252, 261
Brundage, James 250, 268
Burger, Glenn 61, 249, 254, 256, 257,
    259, 266

Butler, Judith 15, 250, 251
Bynum, Caroline Walker 250, 252

Cadden, Joan 250
Cahoon, Leslie 263
Camille, Michael 250, 264
Canguilhem, Georges 251
Carruthers, Mary 268, 269, 270
Cavell, Stanley 253, 255, 267
Chaucer, Geoffrey 1, 2, 3, 4, 5, 6, 7, 8, 9, 10, 11,
    13, 16, 21, 24, 26, 36, 37, 38, 39, 40, 45, 46,
    49, 50, 53, 56, 61, 63, 68, 82, 83, 101, 107,
    111, 112, 117, 123, 129, 140, 143, 144, 191,
    192, 194, 195, 196, 216, 219, 224, 239, 245,
    249, 250, 253, 256, 257, 258, 259, 261, 263,
    268, 269, 270
  and Boethius 10, 38, 50, 83, 84, 89, 91, 110,
      111, 112, 133, 144–151, 156, 196, 253, 261
  and the *Roman de la Rose* 6, 12, 71, 83, 113,
      140, 152, 153, 161, 163, 168, 178, 183, 184,
      186, 191
  as "love poet" 1, 2, 26, 68, 155, 249
  as "philosophical poet" 1, 2, 4, 5, 6, 12,
      26–35, 37, 38, 40, 45, 46, 47, 50, 51, 82,
      84, 101, 111, 123, 145, 148, 152, 153, 156,
      191, 201, 245, 249
  The Book of the Duchess 123, 145
  Canterbury Tales 1, 2, 4, 6, 9, 25, 26–35,
      38, 39, 50, 82, 110, 178, 183, 192, 256,
      259, 263
    manuscripts of 267–268
    "The General Prologue" 239, 256
      Harry Bailey (pilgrim) 239, 239, 240
      Chaucer (pilgrim) 239, 240
    "The Clerk's Tale" 2, 13, 35, 191, 214,
        216–248, 270, 271
      allegory in 236, 238
      and death 221, 222, 224, 225, 227, 231,
          232, 233, 234
      and freedom 222, 223, 226, 229,
          233, 247
      and God 230, 232, 234, 235, 242
      and instrumentalism 224, 225, 226,
          227, 240, 248
      and moral ambivalence 215, 218,
          219, 229, 230, 234, 238,
          240, 247
      and politics 220–229, 230, 234,
          240, 244
      and scandal 216, 217, 218, 219, 244, 245,
          269–270
      and subjection 216, 223
      Clerk, the (pilgrim) 35, 151, 215,
          216–248, 270, 271

Grisilde 11, 13, 35, 214, 215, 216–248, 270, 271
  love's promise in 220, 227, 229, 236, 240, 241, 247
  virtue in 219, 228, 229, 232, 239, 240
  Walter 13, 35, 214, 215, 216–248, 270, 271

the Franklin (pilgrim) 186, 234, 240
"The Knight's Tale" 2, 5, 7, 13, 26, 32, 37, 40, 42, 43, 44, 45, 82–110, 122, 145, 148, 178, 193, 253, 255, 261
  aestheticization in 84, 85, 86, 89, 90
  Arcite 5, 9, 10, 11, 26, 27, 28, 32, 42, 43, 84, 86, 89, 91, 92, 94, 97, 98, 99, 100, 101, 102, 103, 104, 105, 106, 107, 108, 109, 110, 123, 253
  Athenianness and Thebanness 101, 102, 107, 109, 259
  Boethianism in 9, 10
  Creon 92, 93, 109
  Diana 10, 102, 106
  Emily 5, 6, 7, 8, 9, 10, 11, 12, 13, 21, 26, 32, 42, 43, 84–91, 98, 99, 102, 104, 105, 107, 108, 109, 110, 258
  formalism in 32, 84–91, 101, 104, 105, 106, 140, 153, 258
  Hippolyta 107
  Knight, the (pilgrim) 5, 32, 37, 42, 45, 47, 48, 49, 56, 82–110, 132, 135, 140, 151, 153, 201, 258, 259
  Mars 93, 102, 106
  May, allegory of 88
  moral incoherence in 102, 258
  nostalgia in 82, 258
  Palamon 5,9, 10, 11, 32, 42, 43, 84, 86, 89, 91, 92, 94, 97, 98, 99, 100, 101, 102, 103, 104, 105, 106, 107, 108, 109, 110, 123, 253, 255
  "Prime Mover" 82, 88, 89, 90, 102, 104
  Theban Widows 91, 93, 94
  Thebes 92, 93
  Thesean Ethos 32, 91–101, 102, 103, 104, 107, 109, 132, 133, 135, 258, 261
  Theseus 10, 32, 40, 82, 88, 89, 90, 91–101, 102, 103, 104, 105, 106, 107, 108, 109, 148, 259, 261
  Venus 10, 106
"The Manciple's Tale" 184
"The Miller's Prologue and Tale" 2, 26, 31, 36–81, 82, 83, 85, 86, 91, 145, 148, 161, 178, 193, 254, 256, 257
  Absolon 36, 37, 38, 40, 41, 42, 44, 48, 56–69, 73, 75, 76, 77, 78, 79, 80, 253, 256

Alisoun 7, 11, 36, 37, 40, 41, 42, 44, 48, 52, 55, 57, 58, 59, 60, 62, 63, 64, 65, 66, 68, 69, 70, 71, 72, 73, 74, 75, 76, 79, 80, 85, 86, 87, 161, 253, 256, 257
  and "Knight's Tale" 37, 42, 44, 45, 91, 253, 255
  attitude towards women 41, 52, 58, 61, 63, 71, 73, 77, 86, 88, 129, 255
  confrontation with the Reeve 51, 53, 56, 64, 67
  "hende" 44, 255
  homoeroticism in 71, 72, 73, 77
  John 42, 43, 44, 48, 57, 59, 64, 65, 66, 67, 68, 69, 79, 80, 81, 257, 258
  Miller, the (pilgrim) 32, 36, 38, 39, 40, 41, 42, 43, 44, 45, 46, 47, 48, 49, 50, 51, 52, 53, 54, 55, 56, 57, 58, 59, 60, 61, 62, 63, 64, 65, 66, 67, 68, 69, 70, 71, 72, 73, 74, 75, 76, 77, 78, 79, 80, 81, 82, 83, 86, 87, 91, 92, 105, 129, 140, 151, 153, 161, 178, 202, 253, 254, 255, 256, 257, 258
  naturalism in 32, 36, 38, 39, 41, 45, 46, 47, 48, 49, 55, 56, 57, 59, 64, 65, 66, 67, 68, 74, 76, 77, 80, 82, 88, 201, 253, 254, 255, 256
  Nicholas 42, 44, 48, 57, 59, 60, 61, 62, 63, 64, 65, 67, 68, 69, 73, 74, 75, 76, 77, 79, 80, 253, 257
  nostalgia in 74, 82, 83
"The Nun's Priest's Tale" 28
The Pardoner (pilgrim) 143, 198
"The Physician's Tale" 184
"The Tale of Melibee" 145
"The Wife of Bath's Prologue and Tale" 2, 34, 191–215, 269
  allegory in 192, 194, 201, 211, 212, 213
  and the body 34, 198, 199, 202, 203, 204, 205, 206, 207, 208, 209, 210
  and patriarchy 195, 196, 208, 209, 211, 213
  antifeminism in 13, 196, 197, 198
  authority in 198, 199, 203
  commodification in 195, 200, 202, 208, 209
  death and resurrection in 209, 210–215
  ending of 210–215, 269
  "experience" 198, 199, 200, 204, 208
  "glossing" 198, 199, 200, 203, 205, 208
  instrumentalization in 200, 202, 204, 205, 206, 207, 208, 209, 210, 211, 213, 214

Chaucer, Geoffrey (cont.)
 Jankyn 193, 194, 195, 200, 203, 207, 208, 210, 211
 Loathly Lady 210, 211, 212, 213
 "maistrie" 203, 210
 Rapist Knight 210, 211, 212, 213
 trope of the curtain 212, 213
 trope of exchange 195, 200, 206, 207, 208, 210
 Wife of Bath, the/Alisoun (pilgrim) 7, 13, 34, 35, 151, 186, 191–215, 234, 267, 268, 269
 "The Former Age" 145–148
 House of Fame 27, 28, 145, 252
 "Lak of Stedfastnesse" 82, 145–148
 Troilus and Criseyde 1, 9, 26, 27
Christine de Pizan 263
Cicero 3, 174, 211, 266
 and friendship 153, 171–173, 213, 214, 232, 236
 De Amicitia 173, 257, 266
Cixous, Hélène 254
Cohen, Jeffrey Jerome 263
Colish, Marcia 260
"coverture" 7, 250
Crane, Susan 250, 259
Crews, Frederick 141

Dahlberg, Charles 157, 160, 263, 267
Dante Alighieri 2, 10, 27, 28, 145, 151, 155
David, Alfred E. 253, 254, 269
Davidson, Arnold 251, 262
Davidson, Donald 261, 269
Deleuze, Gilles 263, 264
De Secretis Mulierum 7, 250
Deschamps, Eustache 249
desire 3, 4, 5, 6, 8, 9, 12, 13, 14, 18, 23, 32, 33, 34, 35, 37, 38, 39, 40, 41, 42, 44, 46, 52, 55, 57, 58, 59, 60, 61, 62, 63, 64, 70, 71, 72, 73, 74, 75, 76, 79, 84, 87, 90, 91, 99, 100, 103, 105, 106, 108, 113, 114–123, 129, 130, 132, 133, 134, 135, 138, 139, 144, 145, 146, 149, 154, 158, 159, 161, 162, 163, 164, 166, 167, 168, 169–178, 179, 181, 182, 187, 188, 189, 190, 192, 193, 194, 196, 197, 200, 201, 205, 206, 207, 208, 209, 211, 213, 214, 217, 220, 222, 223, 227, 230, 235, 236, 237, 238, 240, 242, 243, 244, 246, 247, 248, 255, 256, 259, 266, 269
 and agency 75, 132, 188, 190
 and fantasy 162, 163
 and gender *see* gender and desire
 and intimacy 69, 71, 73, 74, 75, 186
 constitution of 2, 74
 courtly 154, 168

deadlock of 169–178, 183, 187, 189
erotic 24, 26, 38, 68, 70, 71, 98, 101, 161, 192, 197, 208
feminine 157, 179, 180, 182, 194, 195, 198, 203, 204, 212
homoerotic 72, 73, 256
identificatory lability of 254
masculine 5, 6, 41, 57, 62, 63, 71, 72, 73, 161, 182, 186, 255, 258, 263
"normal" 12, 87, 105, 256
object of 7, 32, 35, 37, 38, 39, 40, 41, 42, 43, 46, 47, 57, 62, 63, 67, 69, 70, 72, 73, 74, 76, 153, 156, 158, 161, 207, 208
ontology of 168, 176
sensual 228, 239
sexual 3, 32, 34, 74, 77, 143, 168
subject of 7, 34, 69, 176, 181, 182, 187, 188, 190
Dinshaw, Carolyn 2, 199, 204, 249, 250, 251, 256, 259, 263, 267, 268, 269, 270
Diogenes 146
disavowal 113, 232, 233
Donaldson, E. Talbot 252, 255, 260
Duncan, Thomas G. 271

Edward II 256
eroticism 1, 2, 22, 23, 24, 32, 33, 34, 35, 36, 37, 40, 41, 50, 51, 52, 53, 54, 55, 56, 57, 59, 60, 61, 63, 68, 70, 71, 72, 73, 74, 83, 84–91, 98, 101–110, 144, 145, 148, 152, 153, 156–169, 173, 175, 176, 178, 179, 180, 181, 184, 186, 187, 188, 189, 191, 193, 194, 195, 198, 203, 204–209, 213, 220, 228, 243, 244, 247, 257, 258, 263, 268
 for Erotic Subject, *see* subjectivity, erotic
 and courtly love 26, 153, 154, 155, 174
 and friendship 3, 24, 252, 266
 and masculinity 7, 74, 117, 157, 264
 and normativity *see* normativity and eroticism
 "erotic object" 24, 34, 52, 79, 129, 159, 174, 175, 185, 188, 193
 homoeroticism 161, 256, 258, 265, 267
  see also Chaucer, *Canterbury Tales*, "Miller's Prologue and Tale," homoeroticism in
 scopophilic 70, 71, 73, 85, 90, 257 *see also* voyeurism
estates theory 30, 30
ethics 19, 24, 36, 37, 38, 39, 45, 58, 83, 84–91, 94, 103, 104, 105, 146, 153, 252
 Aristotelian 259
 "philosophical ethics" 13, 14, 15, 18, 134, 136

fabliau 37, 45, 257
fantasy 154, 163, 192, 207, 208, 224, 228, 229
  Phantasia 138, 162, 163, 265, 269
  and *phantasm* 201, 207, 213, 227
femininity 7, 8, 11, 12, 61, 63, 67, 86, 88,
  90, 107, 108, 180, 194, 196, 198, 199,
  203, 212
  for femininity and agency, *see* agency,
    feminine
  aestheticization of 156 *see also* Chaucer,
    Canterbury Tales, "Knight's Tale,"
    aestheticization in
  and objectification 86, 89, 90, 153, 154, 156,
    158, 159, 161, 194, 207
  as site of passivity 5, 11, 12, 52, 67, 71, 161
  as site of self sacrifice 219, 229
  as site of victimization 182
  naturalized 5, 8
feminist theory 13, 38, 195, 196
Ferrari, G.R.F. 260
fetishism 33, 113, 118, 120, 135, 149, 150, 152, 159,
  170, 177
  see also psychoanalysis, fetishism
  "fetishistic reification" 118, 120, 149
Fleming, John 266
formalism 101
  aesthetic and erotic 84–91, 105, 258
  see also Chaucer, *Canterbury Tales*, "The
    Knight's Tale," formalism in
Foucault, Michel 19, 25, 141, 250, 251, 252, 255,
  256, 257, 262
see also historicism, Foucauldian
Fowler, Elizabeth 250
Fradenburg, L.O. Aranye 142, 249, 250, 253,
  258, 259, 261, 263, 267
Frank, Adam 251, 254
Frankfurt, Harry 251, 259, 261, 271
Frede, Dorothea 265
Frede, Michael 260
Frese, Dolores Warwick 256, 270, 271
Freud, Sigmund 123, 141, 142, 152, 262
  Mourning and Melancholia 123, 262
  Three Essays on the Theory of
    Sexuality 262
friendship 3, 17, 34, 173, 191, 201, 257, 266
  and eroticism *see* eroticism and friendship

Galloway, Andrew 146, 262, 263
Ganim, John 257
Gaunt, Simon 265
gender 1, 3, 6, 9, 38, 56–69, 70, 71, 73, 76, 83,
  105, 107, 108, 141, 143, 161, 197, 200, 219
  and desire 35, 36, 39, 50, 51, 57, 72, 153, 254
  and ideology 13, 71, 73, 161, 191, 194, 200

and sexuality 5, 6–9, 12, 13, 24, 32, 37, 38, 39,
  40, 47, 83, 141, 152, 153, 181, 191, 194,
  250, 252, 254
difference 11, 32, 107, 199
politics 216, 223, 230, 234
see also femininity, masculinity
Georgianna, Linda 270, 271
Giotto 271
"Golden Age," myth of *see* nostalgia, and the
  "Golden Age"
Gower, John 30, 145
Gravdal, Kathryn 263
Green, Richard 260
Grünbaum, Adolf 141
Guillaume de Lorris 2, 27, 155, 159, 161, 167,
  168, 170, 177, 178, 192, 263, 265
  for *Roman de la Rose see Roman de la Rose*
Guillaume de Machaut 2, 6, 10, 145, 155

Hacking, Ian 251
Hamlyn, D.W. 265
Hanna, Ralph, III 268
Hansen, Elaine Tuttle 250, 253, 254, 255, 256,
  257, 259, 268, 269, 270
happiness 196, 202, 203, 260 *see also* Boethius,
  happiness in
Harley, Marta Powell 264, 265
Hicks, Eric 263
Higden, Ralph 256
historicism 4, 12, 21, 155
  Foucauldian 13
  and "theory" 155, 155
Hoccleve, Thomas 249
Holsinger, Bruce 249
Howard, Donald R. 250, 252, 253, 263
Howes, Laura L. 258
Huchet, Jean-Charles 263, 264
Hult, David F. 263, 264
humanist criticism 252, 253, 269
Hume, David 260

identification 8, 12, 18, 32, 103, 104, 108, 142,
  199, 233, 243, 259
identity 3, 32, 33, 39, 40, 76, 78, 108, 109, 120,
  122, 123, 137, 141, 175, 177, 188, 201, 206,
  207, 214, 254
ideology 1, 12, 13, 15, 17, 18, 28, 35, 39, 51, 61, 71,
  73, 78, 84, 90, 133, 135, 136, 148, 149, 161,
  163, 181, 182, 183, 191, 192, 194, 196, 200,
  234, 243, 244, 251, 258, 268
  and gender *see* gender and ideology
  and normativity *see* normativity and
    ideology
  ontological sources of 196, 258

interiority 56, 62, 179, 192, 206, 224, 225, 226,
     237, 247, 255, 256
  of erotic life 256
  feminine 183, 199, 206
intimacy 67, 68, 69–81, 173, 175, 191, 192, 211,
     214, 224, 234
  and desire *see* desire and intimacy
  and love 68, 175
  utopian 186, 191, 204, 208, 209, 210, 213, 214

Jacquart, Danielle 250
Jean de Meun 2, 3, 10, 27, 50, 71, 145, 151,
     155, 161, 168, 169, 177, 178–190, 192, 211,
     263, 266
  for *Roman de la Rose see Roman de la Rose*
"Jesus Cristes milde moder" 271
"Jesus Descended from the Cross" 271
Job 216, 229, 232, 234, 235, 236, 238, 242
Johnson, Leslie 270
Jordan, Mark 252
justice 14, 15, 20, 30, 32, 46, 62, 95, 103, 108,
     122, 130, 145, 169, 182

Kane, John R. 263
Kant, Immanuel 134, 135, 251, 261
  Groundwork for a Metaphysics of Morals 261
Karras, Ruth Mazo 250
Kay, Sarah 263, 264, 265, 266
Keen, Maurice 253
Kelly, Douglas 263, 264, 265
Kempe, Margery 267
Kenny, Anthony 260
Kittredge, George Lyman 269, 270
Kolve, V.A. 37, 40, 41, 45, 62, 89, 250, 253, 254,
     255, 256, 257, 258, 259
Korsgaard, Christine 251, 255, 259, 261, 265
Kruger, Stephen 249

Lacan, Jacques 142, 152, 263, 267
Langland, William 2, 50, 145, 151, 249
Laplanche, Jean 142, 262
Laqueur, Thomas 250
Lear, Jonathan 262
Leicester, H. Marshall 41, 72, 250, 254, 256,
     257, 258, 259, 268
Lemay, Helen Rodmite 250
Lerer, Seth 112, 260, 261
Lewis, C.S. 153, 154, 155, 156, 160, 252, 263
Lochrie, Karma 250, 254, 255, 256
Lounsbury, Thomas R. 269
love 1, 3, 4, 24, 27, 35, 35, 37, 61, 62, 64, 66, 67,
     73, 98, 99, 101, 103, 104, 106, 107, 108, 122,
     123, 140, 154, 155, 159, 160, 165, 166, 167,
     170, 171, 174, 175, 177, 179, 180, 181, 184,

     185, 188, 189, 203, 208, 210, 212, 214, 215,
     216, 222, 225, 226, 227, 230, 232, 234,
     235, 236, 237, 238, 239, 252, 266, 267, 268,
     269, 271
  and intimacy *see* intimacy and love
  antinomy in 244–245
  caritas 153, 174, 175, 188
  courtly love 153, 155, 160, 168, 188, 264
     and masochism 153, 154, 158, 189
     and psychoanalysis 154, 263, 267
  ontology of 196, 215, 244
  romantic 34, 154, 155
  unconditional 216, 220, 234, 236, 237,
     238, 239
  see also Roman de la Rose, love as art; and
     love-object in
  see also Chaucer, as "love poet of";
     Canterbury Tales, "Clerk's Tale,"
     love's promise in
"Lullay, lullay, litel child" 271
Lynch, Kathryn L. 249

Mahon, Michael 251
Mann, Jill 259, 270
marriage 51, 52, 53, 191, 192, 197, 198, 200,
     201, 202, 203, 205, 206, 209, 215, 221,
     222, 223, 224, 225, 228, 229, 230, 240,
     266, 267
  "marital debt" 178, 197, 198, 200
  utopian 203, 204
Marian piety 8, 216, 231, 231, 232, 271
masculinity 5, 7, 8, 9, 10, 11, 12, 52, 59, 60,
     61, 62, 63, 67, 73, 90, 105, 108, 140, 153,
     154, 160, 161, 181, 182, 185, 194, 199,
     239, 268
  and agency *see* agency, masculine
  and eroticism 153, 154, 156, 161, 194
  and narcissism 10, 194, 208, 224, 226
  hegemonic 33, 140, 256, 257, 267
  "masculine gaze" 70
  normative 32, 34, 39, 50, 77, 239, 254
  Oedipalized 254
  "courtly or romance" 140, 191, 256
masochism 1, 33, 35, 113, 120, 139, 140, 141, 142,
     144, 152, 153, 154, 158, 159, 185, 188, 189,
     190, 208, 209, 214, 257, 262
  and narcissism 152, 188
  and sadism 34, 152, 159, 188, 190, 191, 264
  and sexuality 89, 153, 189, 262
  "constitutive masochism" 139, 152, 262
McCracken, Peggy 250
Middleton, Anne 249, 253
misrecognition 113, 143, 144, 148, 149,
     150, 229

moral psychology 3, 24, 113, 137, 138, 143, 152, 260, 265
 empiricist 113, 116, 162, 259, 260, 261, 265
  "myth of the subjective" 261
 medieval 259, 260, 265
Morse, Charlotte C. 270
Murrin, Michael 264
Muscatine, Charles 37, 40, 45, 52, 230, 250, 253, 254, 255, 256, 257, 259, 263, 266, 267, 268, 269, 271

Nagel, Thomas 134, 251, 257, 261
narcissism 1, 34, 71, 72, 73, 152, 172, 173, 188, 189, 190, 194, 201, 208, 213, 220–229, 230, 238, 240, 242, 248, 259, 264, 265, 266, 267
 and rationalism 258, 259
 and sadism 1, 152, 229
naturalism 35, 37, 38, 39, 40, 46, 47, 48, 49, 51, 54, 58, 60, 61, 68, 73, 77, 79, 84, 88, 100, 101, 254, 255, 257, 261
 and the "Miller's Tale" *see* Chaucer, the "Miller's Prologue and Tale," naturalism in
 normative 32, 39, 41, 46, 49, 57, 58, 64, 88, 255
New Criticism *see* humanist criticism
Nietzsche, Friedrich 19–21, 24, 252
normality 12, 13, 16, 30, 83, 122, 123, 157, 163, 177, 218, 219, 235, 236, 250, 256, 264
 and sexuality 157, 163
 and the perverse 245, 264, 267
normalization 39, 86, 141, 217
 of desire 86, 87
 of gender 13, 36, 86, 87, 250
 of sexuality 13, 22, 87, 250, 252
normativity 1, 22, 24, 25, 29, 31, 32, 33, 36, 39, 42, 47, 48, 57, 63, 82, 87, 89, 90, 91, 95, 97, 104, 105, 109, 110, 136, 140, 178–190, 255, 256
 and agency 25, 120
 and authority 88, 90, 94, 100, 102, 104, 105, 110, 131, 132, 133, 150
 and eroticism 4–12, 22, 39, 83
 and ideology 12–21, 24, 25, 29, 244
 and love 236
 and naturalism 32, 47, 48, 49, 60, 255
 and nostalgia 82, 83, 89, 103, 137, 138
 and reflective endorsement 109, 128, 259
 and sexuality 26, 32, 256
 and the will 12–21, 24, 120
 ethical 49, 83, 92
 evaluative 251
 heteronormativity 73, 77, 161
 medieval 250, 251

 modern theories of 251
 practical 32, 50, 251
 problem of 24, 25, 45, 48, 49, 55, 56, 68, 78, 86, 130, 255
nostalgia 82, 83, 137, 146, 148, 180, 181, 182
 and the "Golden Age" 82, 137, 145, 147, 148, 149, 179, 180, 181, 183
 and normativity, *see* normativity and nostalgia
 see also Chaucer, *Canterbury Tales*, "Miller's Prologue and Tale," nostalgia in and Chaucer, *Canterbury Tales*, "Knight's Tale," nostalgia in
Nussbaum, Martha 265

original sin 137
Ovid 107, 159, 167, 258
 Narcissus and Echo 7, 71, 159, 224, 258, 264
 Pygmalion 7, 71, 86

patriarchy 195, 196, 219, 228, 229
 patriarchal ideology 195, 196, 209
patristic criticism 253
Patterson, Lee 29, 30, 141, 142, 143, 199, 200, 201, 250, 252, 253, 256, 258, 259, 260, 261, 262, 263, 264, 265, 266, 267, 268, 269
Paul 3, 22, 23, 39, 152, 197, 206, 209, 213, 214, 215, 242
 for specific passages, see Bible
Pearl-poet, the 2, 50, 145
 Pearl 123
Pearsall, Derek 253
perversion 10, 12, 13, 54, 55, 56–69, 76, 77, 78, 86, 113, 117, 118, 120, 169, 187, 218, 219, 231, 232, 240, 242, 243, 244, 245, 246, 247, 267
Petrarch 2, 6, 155, 216
philosophical poetry 2, 36, 37, 45, 152, 249
 see also Chaucer as "philosophical poet"
philosophy 1, 4, 10, 37, 38, 39, 40, 42, 43, 45, 46, 50, 93, 111, 112, 113, 115, 126, 127, 128, 129, 130, 132, 134, 139, 144, 145, 148, 150, 151, 153, 156, 178, 192, 245, 248, 253
 see also philosophical poetry and ethics, "philosophical ethics"
 as therapy 123, 132, 201
Plato 50, 112, 248, 253
 and *aporia* 112
 Timaeus 263
Platonism 28, 46, 130, 137, 260
 Platonist dialectic 46, 112, 130, 260
pleasure 20, 22, 40, 48, 52, 54, 85, 148, 154, 166, 198, 199, 200, 205, 207, 208, 209, 211, 213, 214, 222, 223, 227, 243, 247, 262, 271

psychoanalysis 1, 2, 3, 4, 13, 33, 34, 38, 113,
    120, 123, 139, 141, 142, 143, 144, 152,
    155, 162, 168, 249, 258, 261, 262, 263,
    264, 267
    castration anxiety 72, 120, 141, 258
    fetishism 1 *see also* fetishism
    Lacanian 258, 267
    Oedipal Theory 4, 120, 139, 141, 142, 143,
        254, 262
    repression 1 *see also* repression
psychology 113, 120, 123, 135, 137, 138, 153, 156,
    179, 184, 193, 194, 218, 225, 245
    see also moral psychology, psychoanalysis,
        and Boethius and psychology
    for specific phenomena, see attachment,
        disavowal, fetishism, identification,
        misrecognition, narcissism,
        perversion, and repression
    pathology 194, 219, 236, 237, 242, 243, 244,
        247, 248
    reflection and the reflective drive 128, 129,
        130, 132, 133, 134, 136, 138, 146, 165, 166,
        168, 176, 194 *see also* action, theories of,
        and "reflective endorsement," Boethius
        and reflection, and normativity and
        "reflective endorsability"

queer theory 3, 13, 38, 262
queerness 2, 32, 251, 256, 257
Quilligan, Maureen 265

rationalism 91, 92, 96, 98, 106, 128, 129,
    258, 259
    and narcissism *see* narcissism and
        rationalism
reason 20, 41, 43, 44, 60, 67, 80, 92, 96, 99,
    100, 102, 105, 128, 255
    ethical 92
    instrumental 122
    "practical reason" 1, 3, 4, 32, 33, 34, 35, 36, 38,
        42, 44, 83, 91, 103, 104, 110, 113, 144,
        249, 255
    "speculative reason" 42, 44, 91, 255
Reiman, Donald 269, 270
repression 33, 113, 119, 120, 121, 122, 126, 134,
    152, 171, 175, 213, 221
Robertson, D.W. 148, 149, 250, 253,
    260, 269
Roman de la Rose 6, 7, 8, 12, 26, 27, 30, 33,
    34, 71, 83, 91, 113, 140, 144, 152, 191, 193,
    201, 227, 263, 266, 267
    and Chaucer, *see* Chaucer and the *Roman de
        la Rose*
    aestheticization in 159, 166, 176, 189

allegory in 157, 158, 160, 161, 163, 165, 166,
    167, 168, 171, 176, 178, 184, 184, 185,
    186, 192
Amis ("Friend") 157, 168, 176, 178–183
    and friendship 171–174, 175, 177
    and narcissism 159, 160, 161, 163, 167, 170,
        174, 175, 176, 177, 184, 187, 264
    and utopianism 153, 169–178, 180, 181, 182,
        183, 184, 186, 187, 188, 191
Bel Acueil ("Fair Welcoming") 160, 161, 265
dreamer/narrator, the 156–169, 169–178,
    178–183, 184, 185, 186, 187, 188, 266
Echo 167
fantasy in 162–164, 171, 181, 182, 184, 185,
    186, 187, 192
Faux Semblant 168, 183
Fountain of Love/Fountain of Narcissus
    159, 160
Garden of Love 159, 160, 165, 189
God of Love 188
Helen 185
Hibernia 180
instrumentalist fantasy 176, 179, 181
La Vielle 168, 178, 183, 192
love as art 159, 160, 161, 166, 189
love object in 153, 158, 159, 161, 167, 168, 173,
    176, 184, 185, 186, 187, 188, 189, 212
Male Bouche 171
misogyny in 156, 157, 161, 180
Narcissus 159, 166, 167, 168, 185, 264
Nature 221, 270
pathology in 156–169, 174, 176
Pygmalion 159, 184–187, 189, 212
Raison ("Reason") 168, 169–178, 187,
    188, 266
Rose, the 7, 157, 158, 159, 160, 161, 166, 170,
    176, 179, 182, 183, 184, 188, 189
self-enclosure in 159, 160, 165, 166, 168, 184
"trope of enclosure" 159, 163, 164, 170
"trope of plucking" 157, 158, 160, 161, 170,
    176, 179, 182, 187, 188, 189, 193
"trope of possession" 159, 160, 170, 171, 173,
    174, 177, 179, 180, 182, 187
Venus 186

sadism 1, 35, 152, 156, 158, 159, 177, 187, 188, 189,
    190, 193, 194, 216, 226, 227, 229, 234, 237,
    242, 246, 257, 263, 267
    and masochism *see* masochism and sadism
sadomasochism 156, 159, 167, 183, 191, 193
    and the constitution of sexuality 173,
        175, 189
    and utopian desire 191
Salter, Elizabeth 259, 269

Index

Schleusener, Jay 251, 265
Schofield, Malcolm 265
Schultz, James 250
Sedgwick, Eve Kosofsky 250, 251, 254, 255, 256
self 138, 140, 150, 172, 174, 175, 176, 188, 190,
    199, 200, 201, 203, 204, 206, 208, 209,
    210, 211, 213, 224, 242, 243, 245
  dissolution of 139, 177
  division of 138, 144
  ego 170, 172, 179, 211, 248
  enclosure of 213, 248 *see also Roman de la
    Rose*, self enclosure in
  estrangement from 132, 138
  violation of 140, 144, 190
Severs, J. Burke 269, 270
sex 1, 27, 36, 42, 52, 74, 122, 141, 159, 169, 180,
    184, 189, 190, 197, 198, 200, 202, 205
  and reproduction 221
  renunciation of 23, 32, 205, 206, 251
  sodomy or anal penetration 60, 61, 63, 71,
    73, 256
sexuality 1, 3, 4, 21, 25, 32, 33, 35, 52, 72, 73, 74,
    79, 84, 113, 129, 137, 139, 140, 141, 142, 143,
    144, 152, 164, 168, 174, 176, 177, 182, 184,
    189, 190, 191, 195, 197, 198, 200, 203, 239,
    240, 249, 256, 257, 262, 264, 266, 268
  and gender *see* gender and sexuality
  and masochism *see* masochism and sexuality
  and the Christian tradition 21–26, 152, 205,
    206, 209, 213, 214, 215
Shakespeare, William 253, 267
shame 59, 61, 124, 182, 183, 188, 189, 190, 218,
    237, 238, 244, 257
Simpson, D.P. 261
Sir Orfeo 123
Sledd, James 270, 271
Socrates 14, 37, 46, 253
Stanbury, Sarah 270, 271
Stewart, Susan 148, 263
Stoicism 260
  and Boethius *see* Boethius and Stoicism
"Stond wel, moder, under rode" 232, 271
Strier, Richard 255
Strohm, Paul 253, 259
subjectivity 5, 10, 12, 13, 15, 17, 18, 19, 24, 26, 29,
    31, 33, 34, 35, 60, 77, 78, 96, 100, 106, 123,
    129, 137, 142, 155, 163, 167, 170, 175, 177,
    184, 187, 188, 189, 190, 192, 194, 196, 206,
    207, 213, 214, 252, 255, 269
  Christian 22, 219, 238, 251
  feminine 11, 34, 35, 86, 191, 197, 255

liberal-bourgeois 15, 251
masculine 5, 34, 86, 107, 156, 178, 182, 185,
    186, 193
"myth of the subject" 192, 197–204, 209,
    213, 224
see also desire, subject of

Thomas Aquinas 113, 116, 252, 260, 266
  Summa Contra Gentiles 252, 266
  Summa Theologiae 255, 260
Thomasset, Claude 250
tyranny 20, 82, 146, 147, 154, 211, 214, 219, 245,
    246, 247, 253

Usk, Thomas 249
utopianism 34

violence 20, 98, 106, 140, 148, 157, 188, 189, 194,
    200, 207, 208, 212, 268
  sexual 157, 160, 179, 194, 207, 211, 256, 263
Vlastos, Gregory 260
Vogler, Candace 113, 251, 260, 265
Von Sacher-Masoch, Leopold 140, 153, 263
voyeurism 5, 6, 9, 11, 13, 153, 193, 194
  see also eroticism, scopophilic
  aestheticizing 84, 153

Wallace, David 253, 258, 259, 269, 270, 271
Warner, Michael 250, 251
Watson, Nicholas 269, 270
Weatherbee, Winthrop 112, 113, 256, 260, 265,
    266, 269, 271
Weisl, Angela Jane 258
Westberg, Daniel 113, 260
"Why have ye no routhe on my child?" 271
will 3, 9, 10, 12, 14, 15, 27, 35, 36, 53, 106, 107,
    108, 118, 135, 138, 146, 175, 180, 196, 203,
    210, 211, 224, 225, 226, 230, 232, 235, 236,
    237, 238, 240, 241, 242, 243, 245, 248
  antinomy of 150, 177
  constitution of 17, 92, 102, 139, 178, 183, 259
  unconditional 220
Williams, Bernard, 15, 134, 135, 251, 260, 261
Williams, David 256
Wimsatt, James I 250
Wittgenstein, Ludwig 251, 253, 255, 269

Yacht, Michelle 271

Zink, Michael 252
Žižek, Slavoj 142, 154, 155, 249, 261, 263

CAMBRIDGE STUDIES IN MEDIEVAL LITERATURE

1. Robin Kirkpatrick *Dante's Inferno: Difficulty and Dead Poetry*
2. Jeremy Tambling *Dante and Difference: Writing in the "Commedia"*
3. Simon Gaunt *Troubadours and Irony*
4. Wendy Scase *"Piers Plowman" and the New Anticlericalism*
5. Joseph Duggan *The "Cantar De Mio Cid": Poetic Creation in its Economic and Social Contexts*
6. Roderick Beaton *The Medieval Greek Romance*
7. Kathryn Kerby-Fulton *Reformist Apocalypticism and "Piers Plowman"*
8. Alison Morgan *Dante and the Medieval Other World*
9. Eckehard Simon (ed.) *The Theatre of Medieval Europe: New Research in Early Drama*
10. Mary Carruthers *The Book of Memory: A Study of Memory in Medieval Culture*
11. Rita Copeland *Rhetoric, Hermeneutics and Translation in the Middle Ages: Academic Traditions and Vernacular Texts*
12. Donald Maddox *The Arthurian Romances of Chrétien de Troyes: Once and Future Fictions*
13. Nicholas Watson *Richard Rolle and the Invention of Authority*
14. Steven F. Kruger *Dreaming in the Middle Ages*
15. Barbara Nolan *Chaucer and the Tradition of the "Roman Antique"*
16. Sylvia Huot *The "Romance of the Rose" and its Medieval Readers: Interpretations, Reception, Manuscript Transmission*
17. Carol M. Meale (ed.) *Women and Literature in Britain, 1150–1500*
18. Henry Ansgar Kelly *Ideas and Forms of Tragedy from Aristotle to the Middle Ages*
19. Martin Irvine *The Making of Textual Culture: Grammatica and Literary Theory, 350–1100*
20. Larry Scanlon *Narrative, Authority and Power: The Medieval Exemplum and the Chaucerian Tradition*
21. Erik Kooper *Medieval Dutch Literature in its European Context*
22. Steven Botterill *Dante and the Mystical Tradition: Bernard of Clairvaux in the "Commedia"*
23. Peter Biller and Anne Hudson (eds.) *Heresy and Literacy, 1000–1530*
24. Christopher Baswell *Virgil in Medieval England: Figuring the "Aeneid" from the Twelfth Century to Chaucer*
25. James Simpson *Sciences and Self in Medieval Poetry: Alan of Lille's "Anticlaudianus" and John Gower's "Confessio Amantis"*
26. Joyce Coleman *Public Reading and the Reading Public in Late Medieval England and France*
27. Suzanne Reynolds *Medieval Reading: Grammar, Rhetoric and the Classical Text*
28. Charlotte Brewer *Editing "Piers Plowman": the Evolution of the Text*
29. Walter Haug *Vernacular Literary Theory in the Middle Ages: The German Tradition in its European Context*

30. Sarah Spence *Texts and the Self in the Twelfth Century*
31. Edwin Craun *Lies, Slander and Obscenity in Medieval English Literature: Pastoral Rhetoric and the Deviant Speaker*
32. Patricia E. Grieve *"Floire and Blancheflor" and the European Romance*
33. Huw Pryce (ed.) *Literacy in Medieval Celtic Societies*
34. Mary Carruthers *The Craft of Thought: Meditation, Rhetoric, and the Making of Images, 400–1200*
35. Beate Schmolke-Hasselman *The Evolution of Arthurian Romance: The Verse Tradition from Chrétien to Froissart*
36. Siân Echard *Arthurian Narrative in the Latin Tradition*
37. Fiona Somerset *Clerical Discourse and Lay Audience in Late Medieval England*
38. Florence Percival *Chaucer's Legendary Good Woman*
39. Christopher Cannon *The Making of Chaucer's English: A Study of Words*
40. Rosalind Brown-Grant *Christine de Pizan and the Moral Defence of Women: Reading Beyond Gender*
41. Richard Newhauser *The Early History of Greed: the Sin of Avarice in Early Medieval Thought and Literature*
42. Margaret Clunies Ross *Old Icelandic Literature and Society*
43. Donald Maddox *Fictions of Identity in Medieval France*
44. Rita Copeland *Pedagogy, Intellectuals, and Dissent in the Later Middle Ages: Lollardy and Ideas of Learning*
45. Kantik Ghosh *The Wycliffite Heresy: Authority and the Interpretation of Texts*
46. Mary C. Erler *Women, Reading, and Piety in Late Medieval England*
47 D. H. Green *The Beginnings of Medieval Romance: Fact and Fiction 1150–1220*
48. J. A. Burrow *Gestures and Looks in Medieval Narrative*
49. Ardis Butterfield *Poetry and Music in Medieval France: From Jean Renart to Guillaume de Machaut*
50. Emily Steiner *Documentary Culture and the Making of Medieval English Literature*
51. William E. Burgwinkle *Sodomy, Masculinity, and Law in Medieval Literature*
52. Nick Havely *Dante and the Franciscans: Poverty and the Papacy in the "Commedia"*
53. Siegfried Wenzel *Latin Sermon Collections from Later Medieval England*
54. Ananya Jahanara Kabir and Deanne Williams (eds) *Postcolonial Approaches to the European Middle Ages: Translating Cultures*
55. Mark Miller *Philosophical Chaucer: Love, Sex, and Agency in the "Canterbury Tales"*